Mike's Multipurpose Polyrhythmic Utility Tooles

By Michael Tooles

Edition 1.0

Contents

Introduction 4
Binary Rhythms 5
Binary Rhythm Chart 6
Ternary Rhythm Chart 7
Natural Sticking Binary Accents 8-9
Natural Sticking Binary Rhythms 10-11
Quarter Notes 13
Quarter Note Binary Accents 14
Quarter Note Binary Broken Rhythm 15
8th Notes 16
8th Note Binary Alphabet and Accents 17-18
8th Accent Exercises 20-35
8th Note Binary Broken Rhythm Exercise 37-53
16th Notes 55
16th Notes Accents and Rhythms 56-57
16 Note Accent Exercises 58-89
16th Note Broken Rhythm Exercises 92-129
Ternary Rhythm Chart 131
Natural Sticking Ternary Accents 132
Natural Sticking Ternary Broken Rhythms 133
8th Note Triplet Accents and Rhythms 134-135
8th Note Triplet Accent Exercises 136-155
8th Note Triplet Rhythm Exercises 157-177
Adding Accents to Triplet Rhythms 178

Contents

32nd Notes 181
32nd Note Accents Exercises 184-199
32nd Note Broken Rhythms 201-217
6s- Sextuplets 218
6s- Sextuplet Accents 220-224
6s- Sextuplet Broken Rhythm Exercises 225-230
Playing Binary and Triplet Rhythms in the Same Measure 231-237
Expressing Binary Rhythms in Triplet Space 239-271
Expressing Ternary Rhythms in Binary Spaces 272-275
2:3 Polyrhythms 276-280
3:4 Polyrhythms Level One 281-297
5s- Fivelets- Quintuplet Rhythms 298-299
Quintuplet Accent 300-301
Quintuplet Broken Rhythms 302-303
7s- Septuplets 304-305
Septuplet Accents 306-312
Septuplet Broken Rhythms 313-320
A Few of the Many Uses 321-346
Swing Chart 338-339
Bass Tone Slap 344-346

Mike's Multipurpose Polyrhythmic Utility Tooles is a logical system of exercises for developing and understanding rhythm. It's not about any one style of music, but is meant to be used to develop rhythmic skills for playing all genres of music. This book should be used to accompany other books that focus on individual styles.

Mike's Multipurpose Polyrhythmic Utility Tooles is written specifically for non-sustaining percussion, but can be used for any instrument.

I originally developed this system to learn to play over different ostinato patterns on drum set, but quickly began to expand its uses to hand percussion and rudimental drumming. It has been a very effective tool for working with new drummers to develop basic skills, as well working with advanced musicians to add new ideas and strengthen established skills.

Playing through the exercises in this book has been very helpful in spotting problem areas and fixing them. For my drum set playing this process has removed physical barriers to creativity by allowing me to systematically anticipate and work through coordination issues, thus giving me the ability to play freely over various ostinato patterns in a relatively short period of time.

This book focuses mainly on binary and ternary rhythms, which could be considered Rudimental Rhythms or a Rhythmic Alphabet since the vast majority of rhythms we play are based on these building blocks. At the end of the book we briefly explore rhythms based on subdivisions of five and seven.

Binary Rhythms- Rhythms based on subdivisions of two.

If we were to divide a measure into two sections, two counts or beats, and only use whole beats we would have only four rhythmic possibilities in that measure. 1) Play both beats; 2) Play only the first beat; 3) Play only the second beat; 4) Play neither.

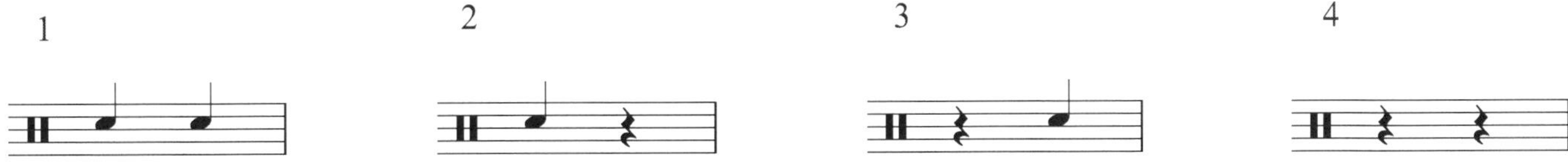

For each subdivision the choice is whether to make a sound or silence. Two choices, to make a sound, or not, in a given number of subdivisions has a limited number of possibilities. Two to the number of subdivisions gives you the number of rhythmic possibilities. 2^2 yields 4 possible rhythms. The four rhythms can be considered Binary Rudimental Rhythms or a Binary Rhythmic Alphabet. Just as letters are combined to create words, and words are used to create sentences that express thoughts, ideas and tell stories, these basic rhythms are combined to express rhythmic ideas, to create musical phrases, movements and entire compositions.

For our purposes we are going to use four subdivisions instead of two for our binary rhythmic alphabet. With four subdivisions you have sixteen rudimental rhythms. 2^4 yields 16 rudimental rhythms or a sixteen rhythm alphabet. These rhythms can be expressed over one measure of common time using quarter notes. Alternately, if we divide the beat in half we can play the same 16 rhythms in half the space, over two beats using eighth notes. If we were to divide the beat into four equal spaces or subdivisions (16th notes) the same sixteen rhythms would now exist in the space of one beat. Our binary rhythms can be expressed over one whole measure using quarter notes, over two beats using 8th notes, inside of one beat using 16th notes or in half of a beat using 32nd notes. The rhythms remain the same, the only thing that's changing is the size of the space we play them in.

Rhythms can be expressed as simple rhythms or as accented patterns.
I prefer working the accented patterns first because they force you to keep up with all of the subdivisions.

Rhythmic Build: to work up from playing no accents or subdivisions, to playing all.

Rhythmic Reduction: to work down from playing all subdivisions or accents, to playing none.

16 Binary Rhythms as 16th Note Accented Patterns.
Rhythmic Build.

16 Binary Rhythms as 16th Notes.
Rhythmic Reduction.

Ternary Rhythms- Rhythms based on subdivisions of three.
If we were to divide the beat into three equal subdivisions we would have eight possible rhythms. 2^3 yields an 8 rhythm alphabet. From playing all three subdivisions to playing none there are 8 rhythms that occur in one set of 3. I have also included Quarter Note Triplets, which occur over two beats, as part of the Ternary Rhythmic Alphabet for a total of 10 rhythms.

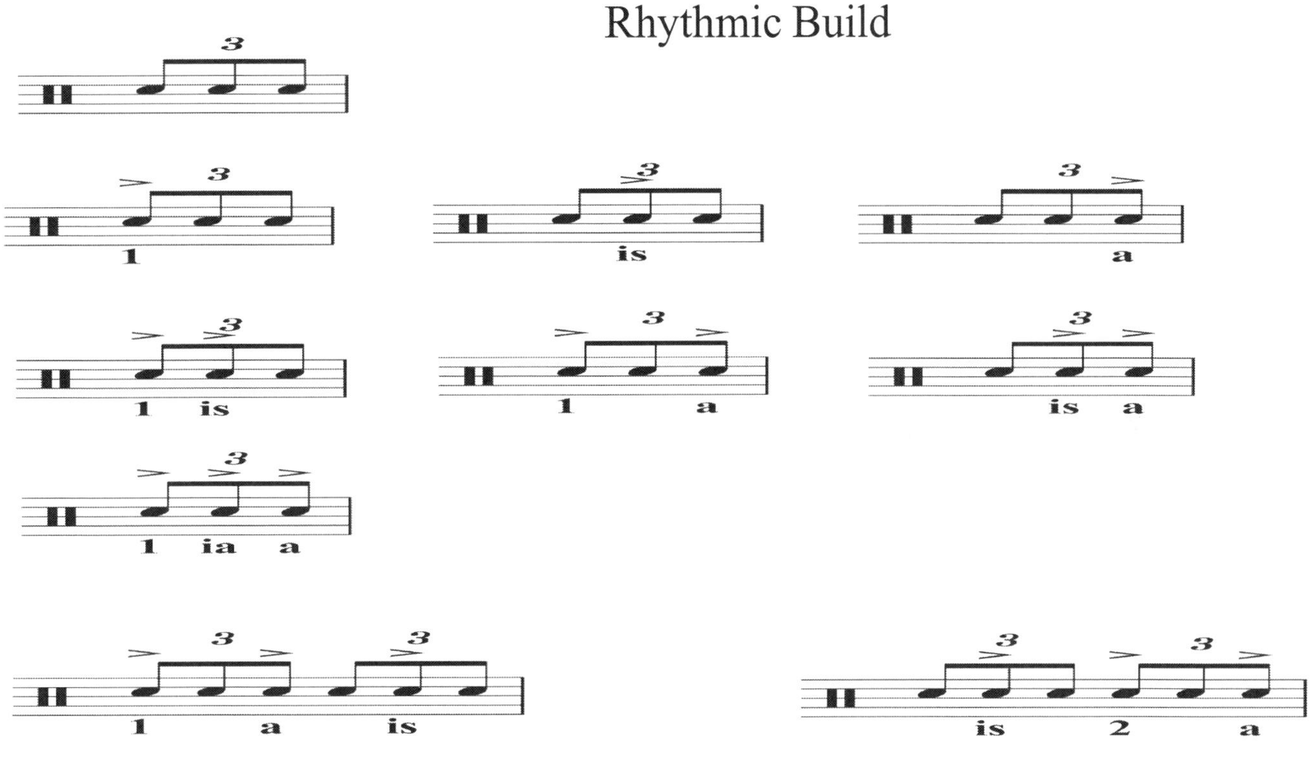

Ternary Rhythms as 8th Note Triplets
Rhythmic Reduction

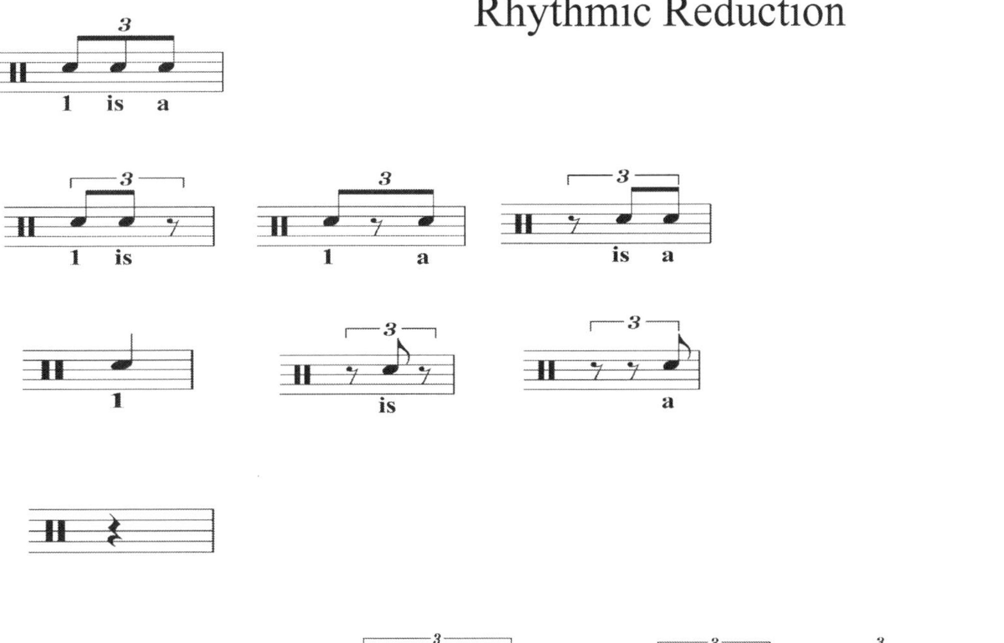

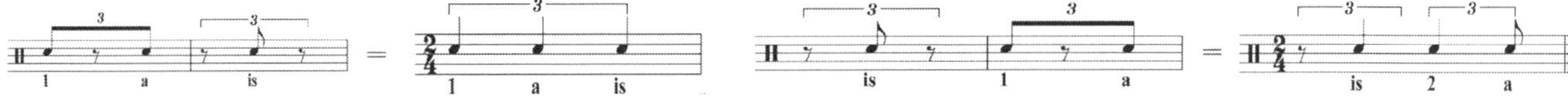

16 Accented Binary Rhythms Natural Sticking Right Hand Lead

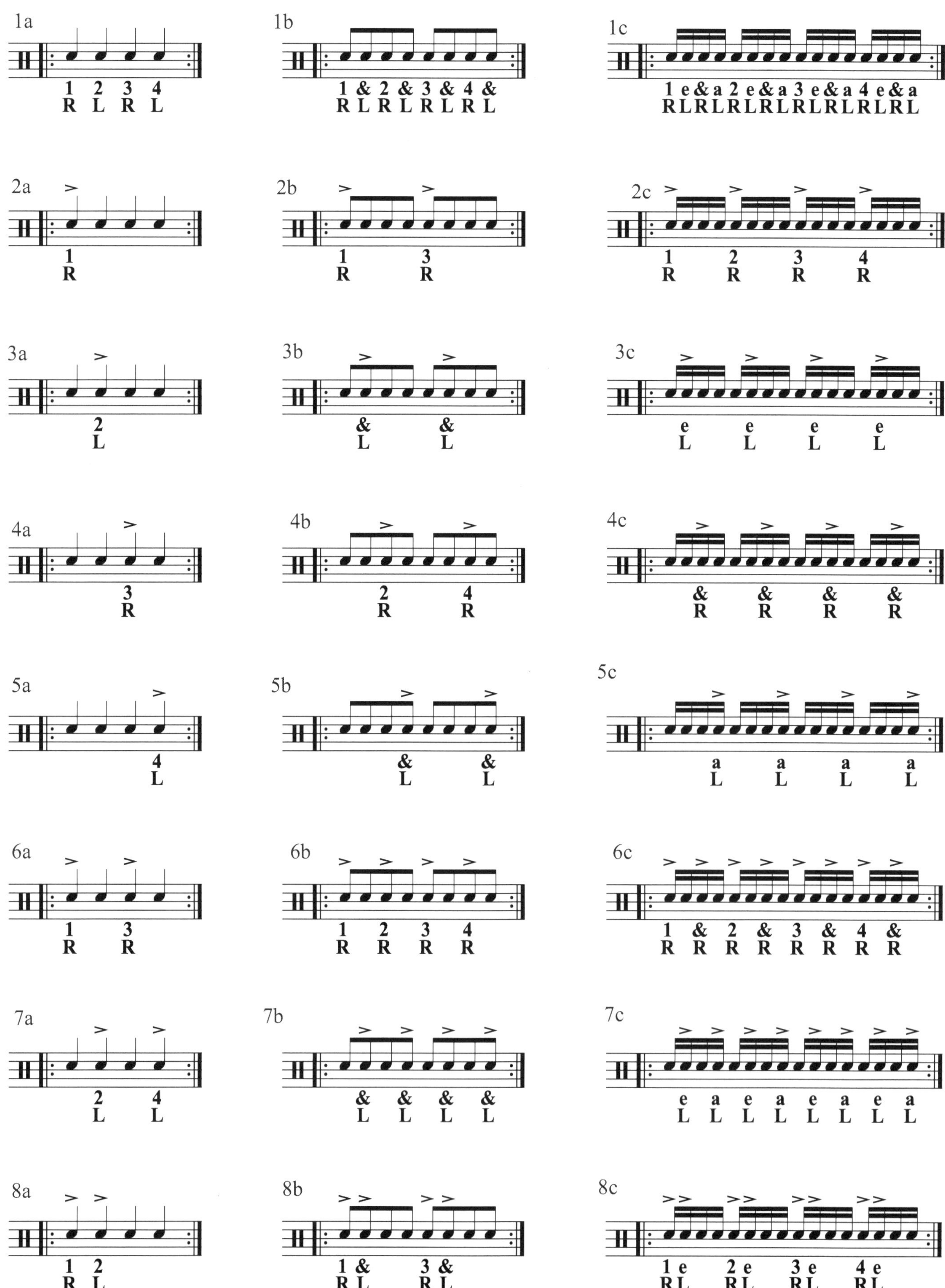

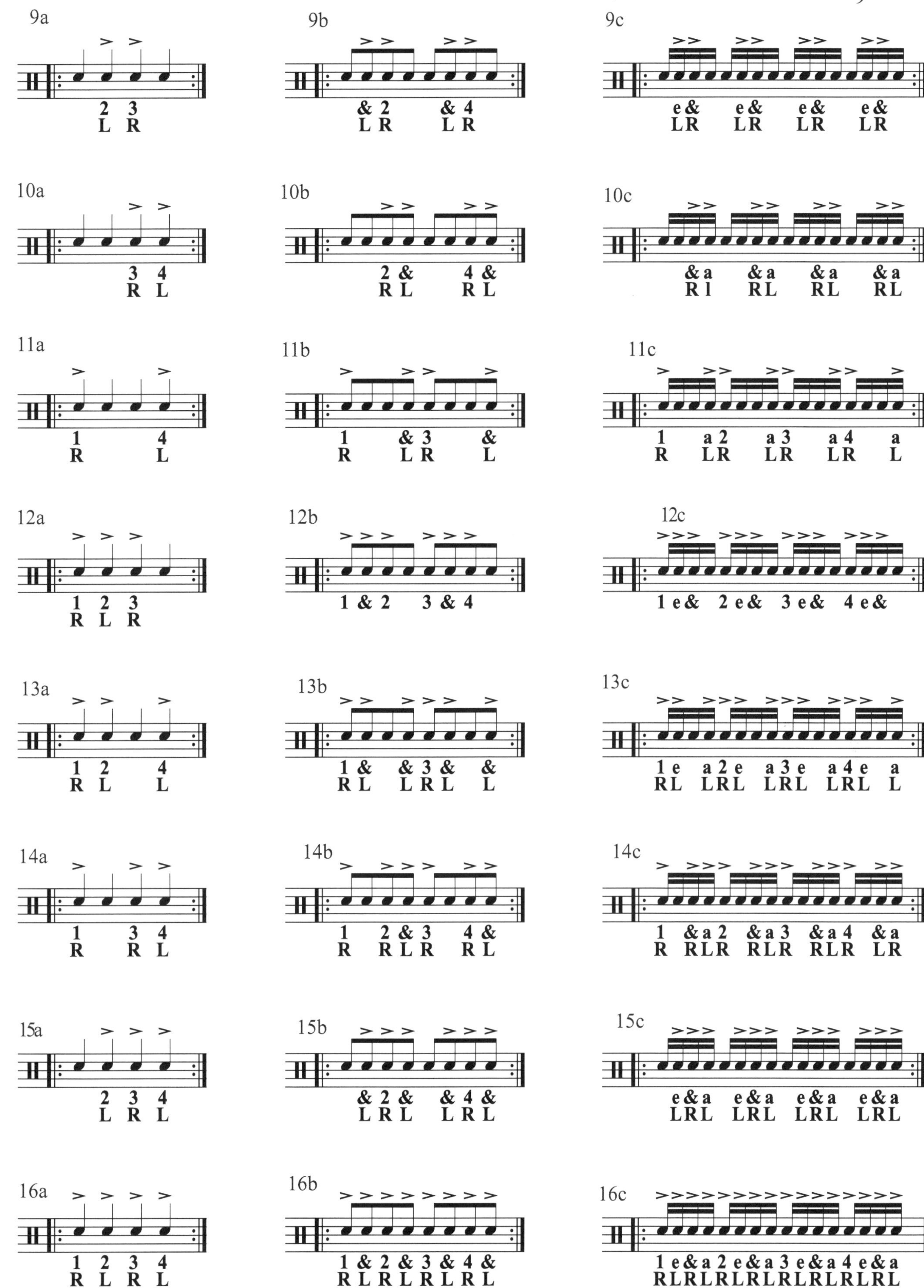
9a
2 3
L R
9b
& 2 & 4
L R L R
9c
e& e& e& e&
LR LR LR LR
10a
3 4
R L
10b
2 & 4 &
R L R L
10c
&a &a &a &a
R l RL RL RL
11a
1 4
R L
11b
1 & 3 &
R L R L
11c
1 a 2 a 3 a 4 a
R LR LR LR L
12a
1 2 3
R L R
12b
1 & 2 3 & 4
12c
1 e& 2 e& 3 e& 4 e&
13a
1 2 4
R L L
13b
1 & & 3 & &
R L L R L L
13c
1 e a 2 e a 3 e a 4 e a
RL LRL LRL LRL L
14a
1 3 4
R R L
14b
1 2 & 3 4 &
R R L R R L
14c
1 &a 2 &a 3 &a 4 &a
R RLR RLR RLR LR
15a
2 3 4
L R L
15b
& 2 & & 4 &
L R L L R L
15c
e&a e&a e&a e&a
LRL LRL LRL LRL
16a
1 2 3 4
R L R L
16b
1 & 2 & 3 & 4 &
R L R L R L R L
16c
1 e&a 2 e&a 3 e&a 4 e&a
RLRLRLRLRLRLRLRL

16 Binary Rhythms Natural Sticking Right Hand Lead

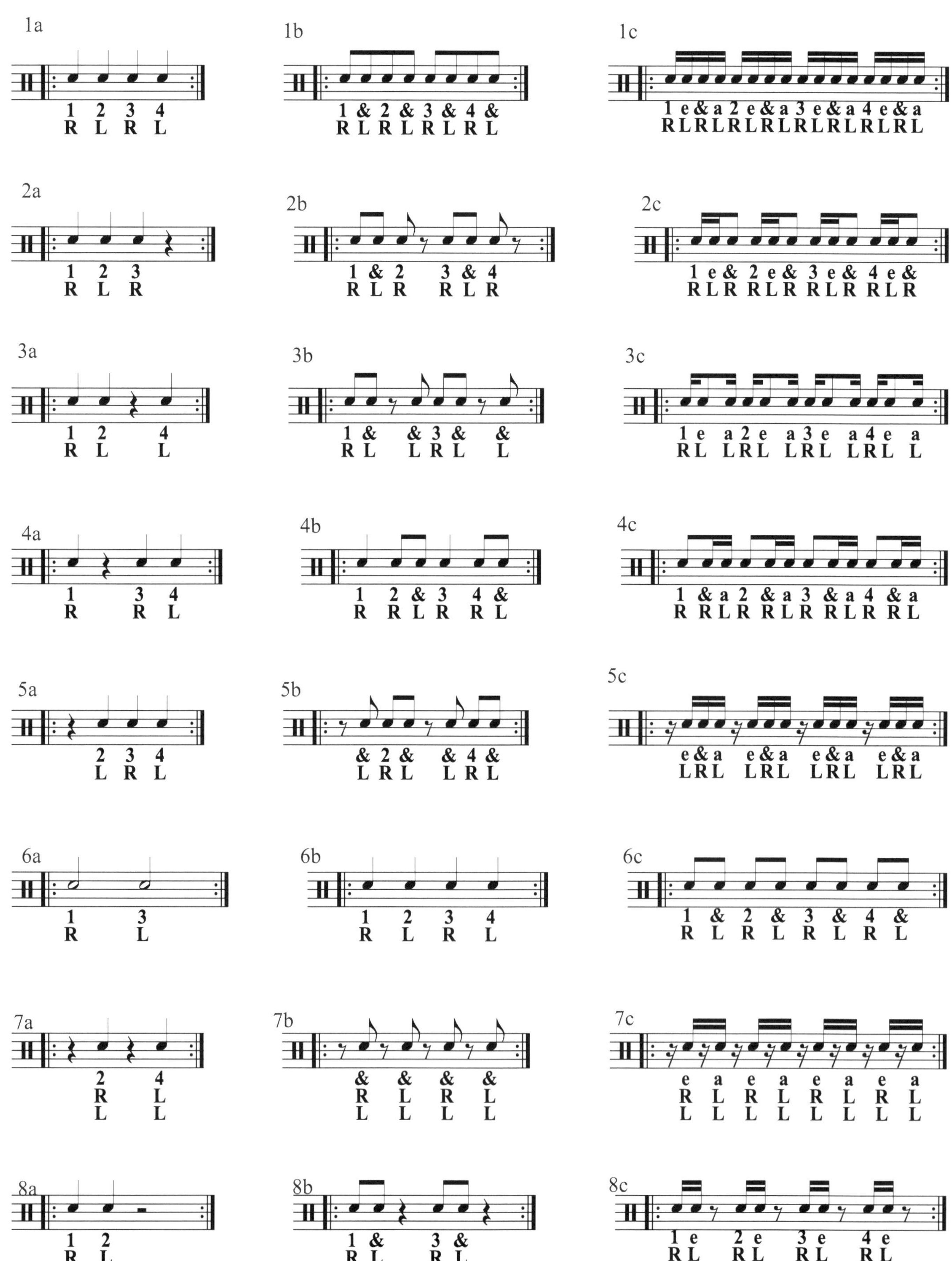

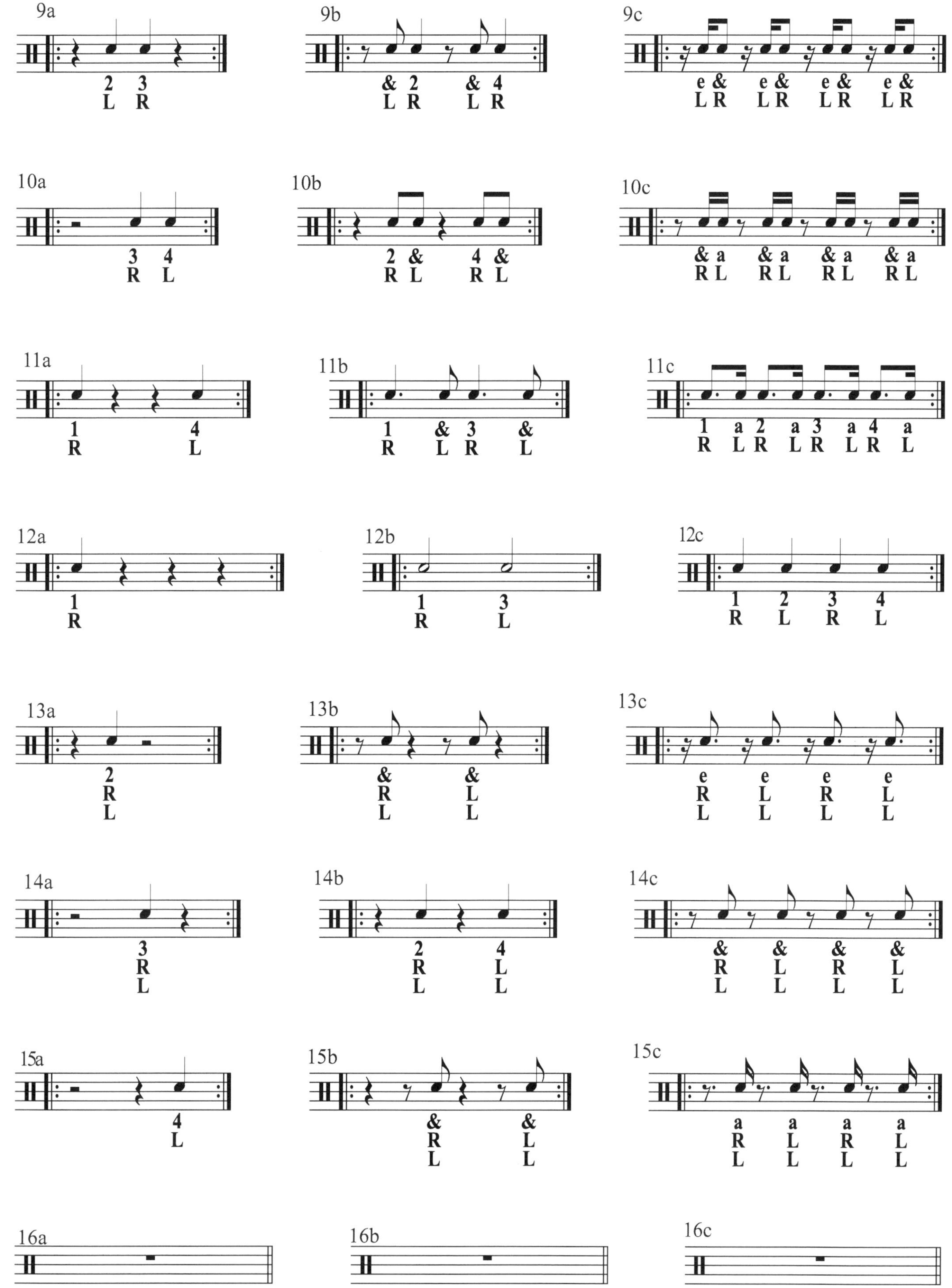
9a
2 3
L R
9b
& 2 & 4
L R L R
9c
e & e & e & e &
L R L R L R L R
10a
3 4
R L
10b
2 & 4 &
R L R L
10c
& a & a & a & a
R L R L R L R L
11a
1 4
R L
11b
1 & 3 &
R L R L
11c
1 a 2 a 3 a 4 a
R L R L R L R L
12a
1
R
12b
1 3
R L
12c
1 2 3 4
R L R L
13a
2
R
L
13b
& &
R L
L L
13c
e e e e
R L R L
L L L L
14a
3
R
L
14b
2 4
R L
L L
14c
& & & &
R L R L
L L L L
15a
4
L
15b
& &
R L
L L
15c
a a a a
R L R L
L L L L
16a
16b
16c

1
Whole Beat

Quarter Notes

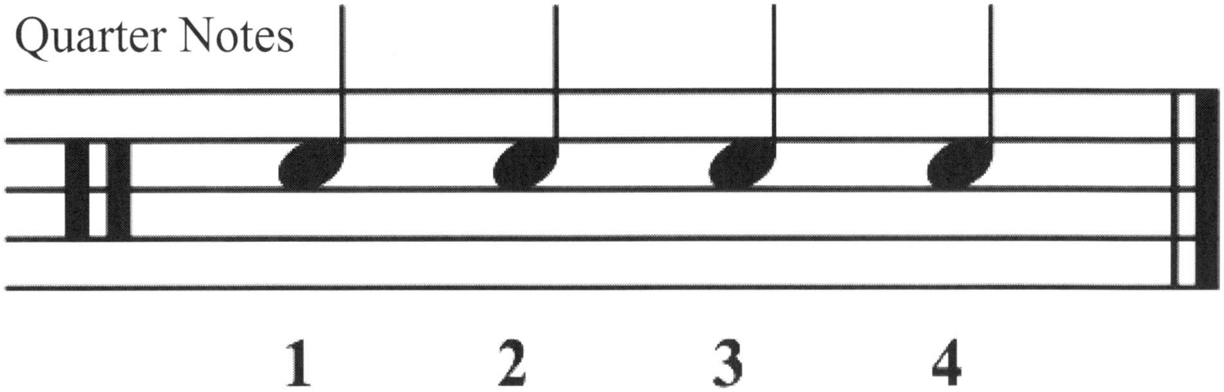

1 2 3 4

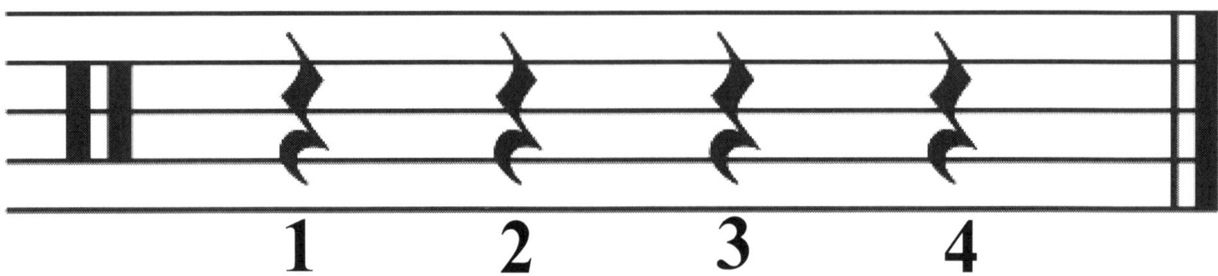

In 4|4, or common time (C), a measure of music contains four beats, or counts. I like to think of each beat as a section. In common time a quarter note sustains for one entire beat. With four quarter notes in a measure and using only quarter notes you have sixteen different rhythmic possibilities in one measure. The sixteen rhythms can be considered our Binary Rhythmic Alphabet and can be played as simple rhythms, or accented patterns.

$$2^4 = 16$$

Quarter Note Binary Rhythmic Alphabet Accented

Quarter Note Binary Rhythmic Alphabet

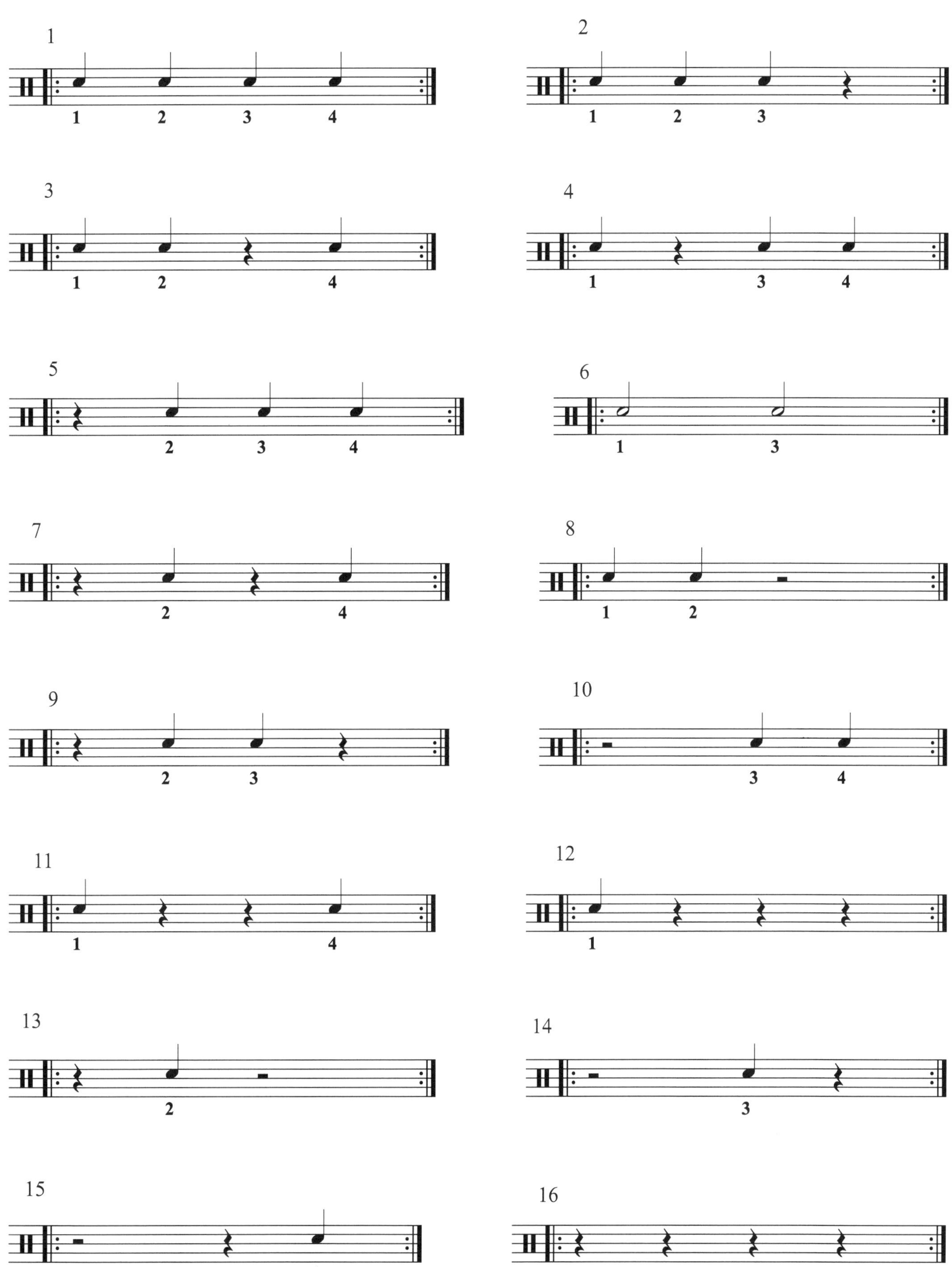

Subdivisions Per Beat

8th Notes

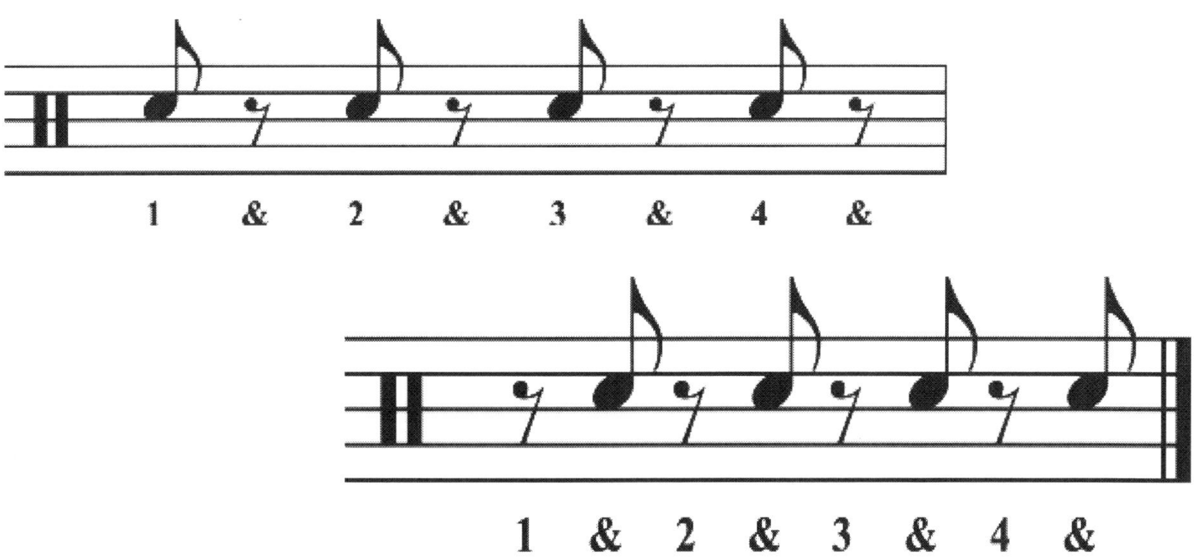

In 4|4 time the eighth note divides the beat into two equal subdivisions. Eighth notes sustain for half a beat in 4|4 time. With two beats of eighth notes you have four equal subdivisions. The binary rhythms we just did as quarter notes are now expressed in the space of two beats instead of four. They now fit in half of a measure of 4|4 time instead of one whole measure. They now occur twice in one measure. They are the exact same rhythms, but in a smaller space.

With the measure divided into 8ths we have 256 possible rhythms.

$$2^8 = 256$$

In the next section we explore all 256 as accented patterns and simple rhythms. We organize them using the rhythmic alphabet and work through them in a logical order.

* Make sure you come back and swing this section.See pages 338-339.

8th Note Binary Rhythmic Alphabet Accented

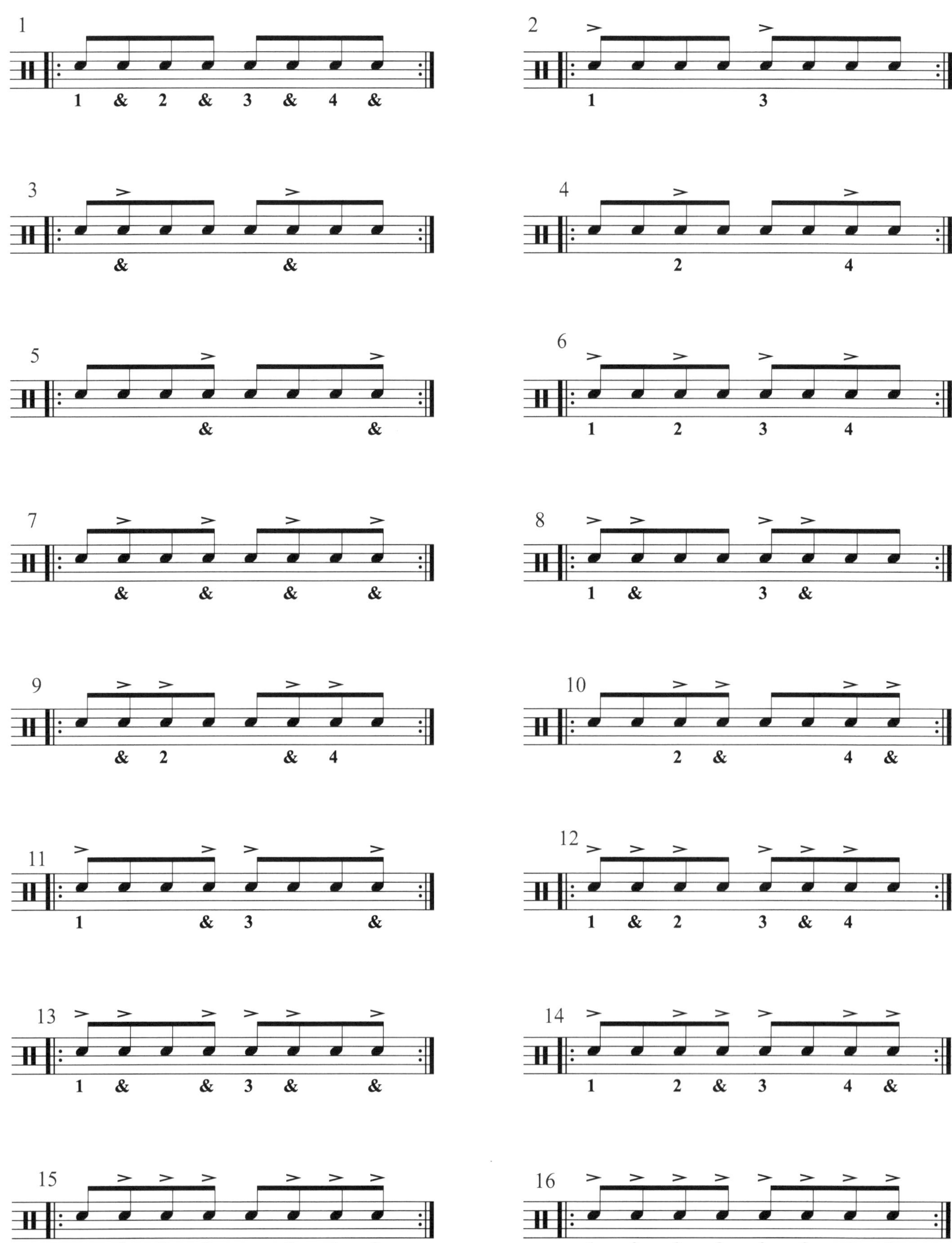

8th Note Binary Rhythmic Alphabet

8th Note Accents

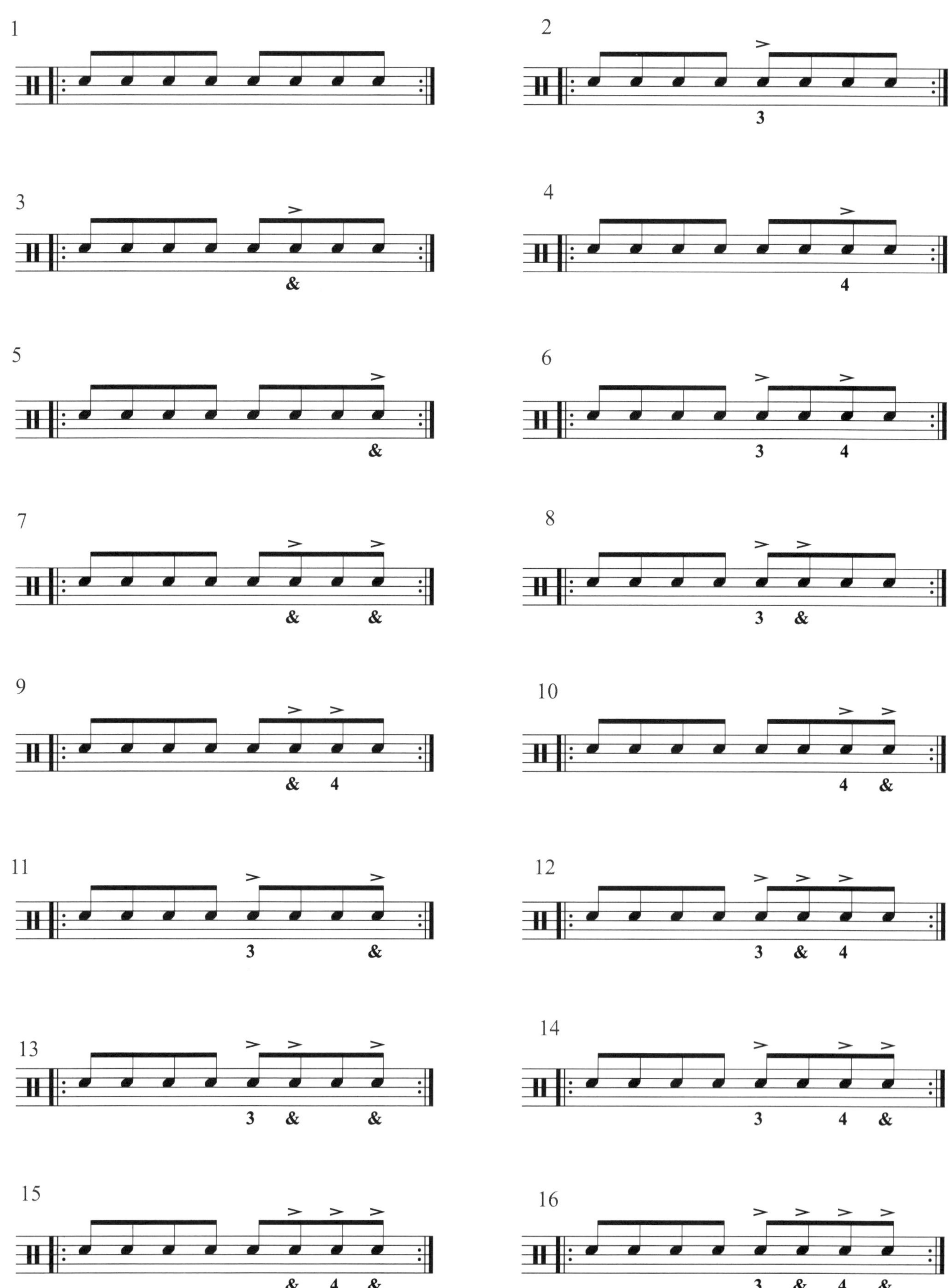

8th Note Accents

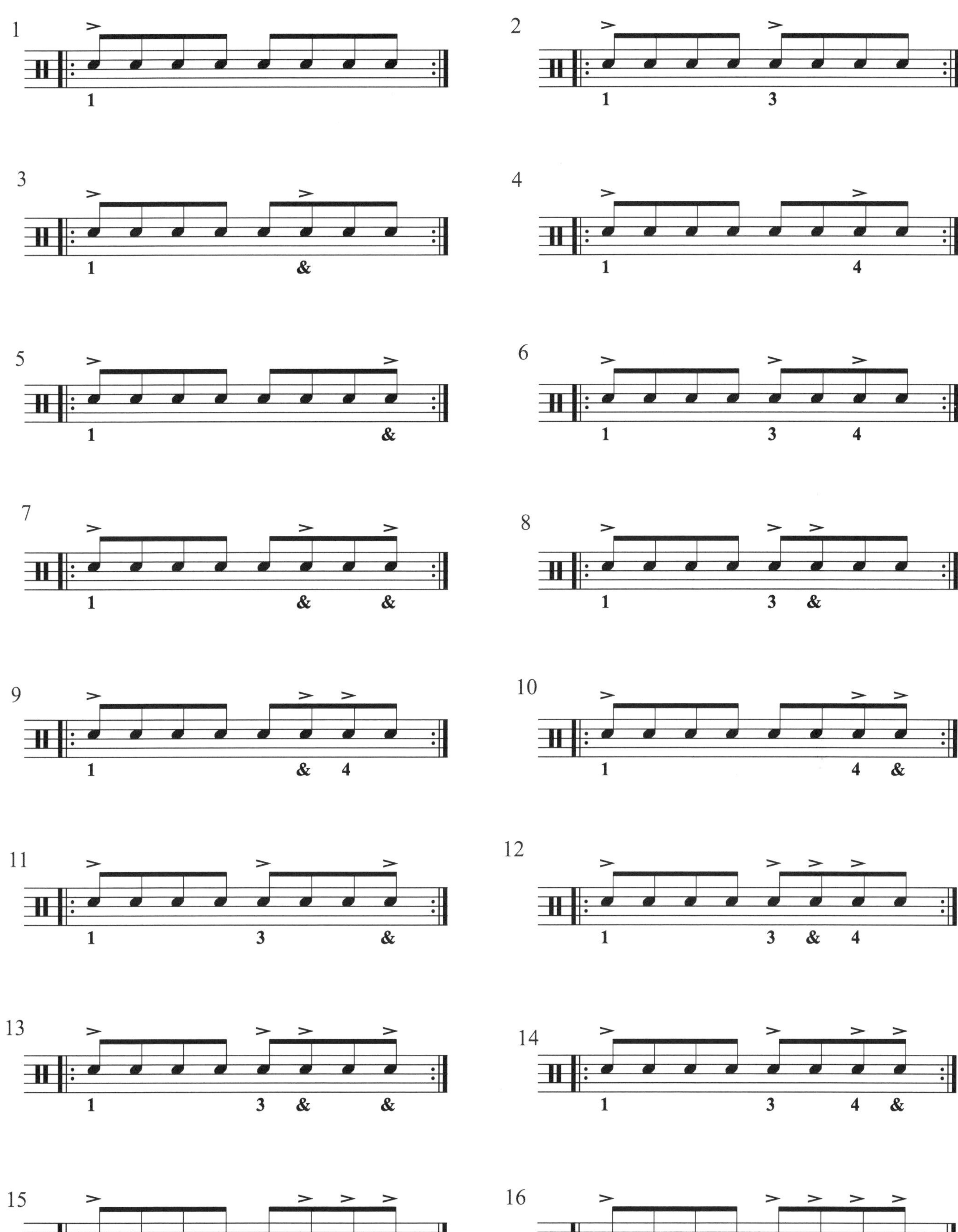

8th Note Accents

8th Note Accents

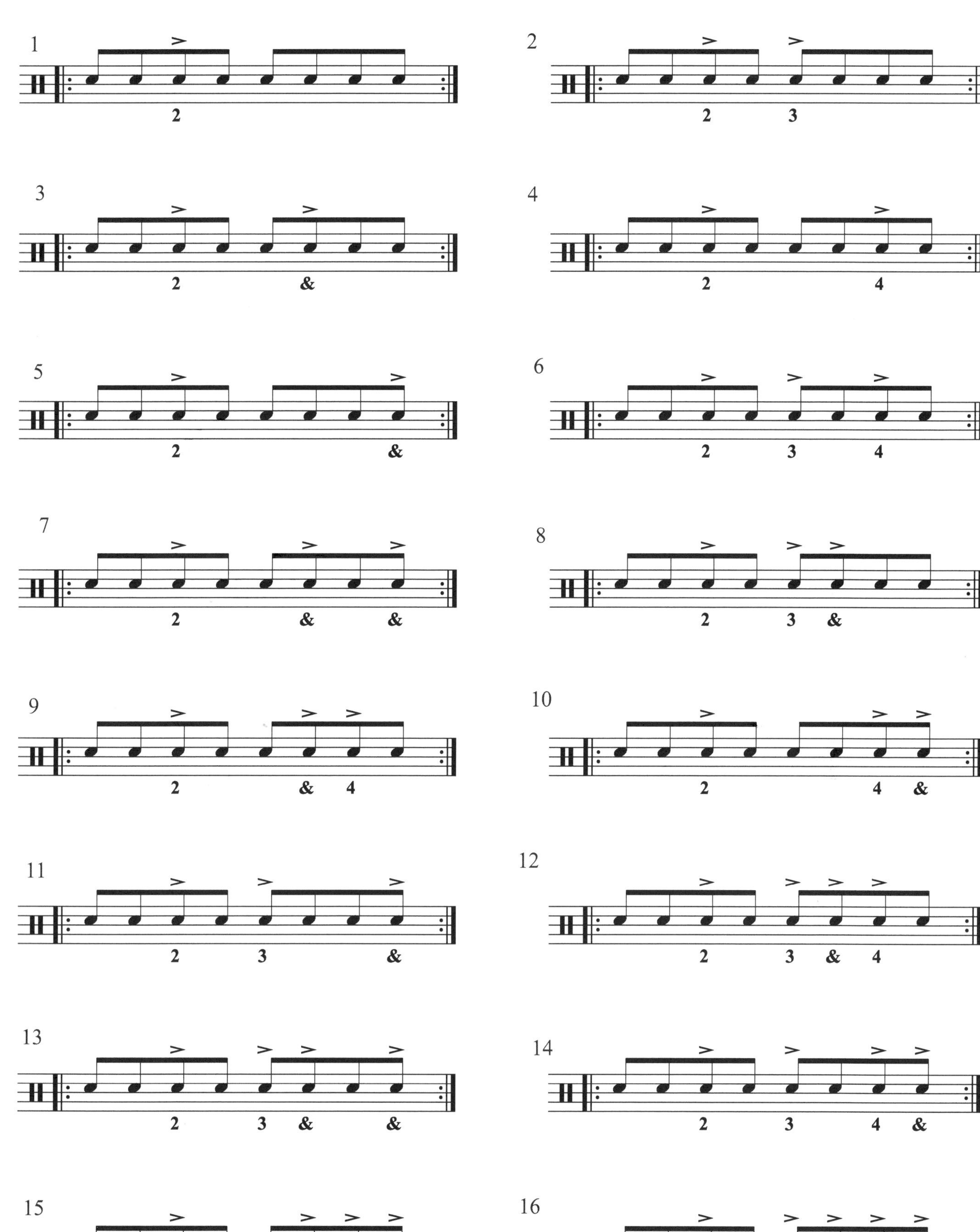

8th Note Accents

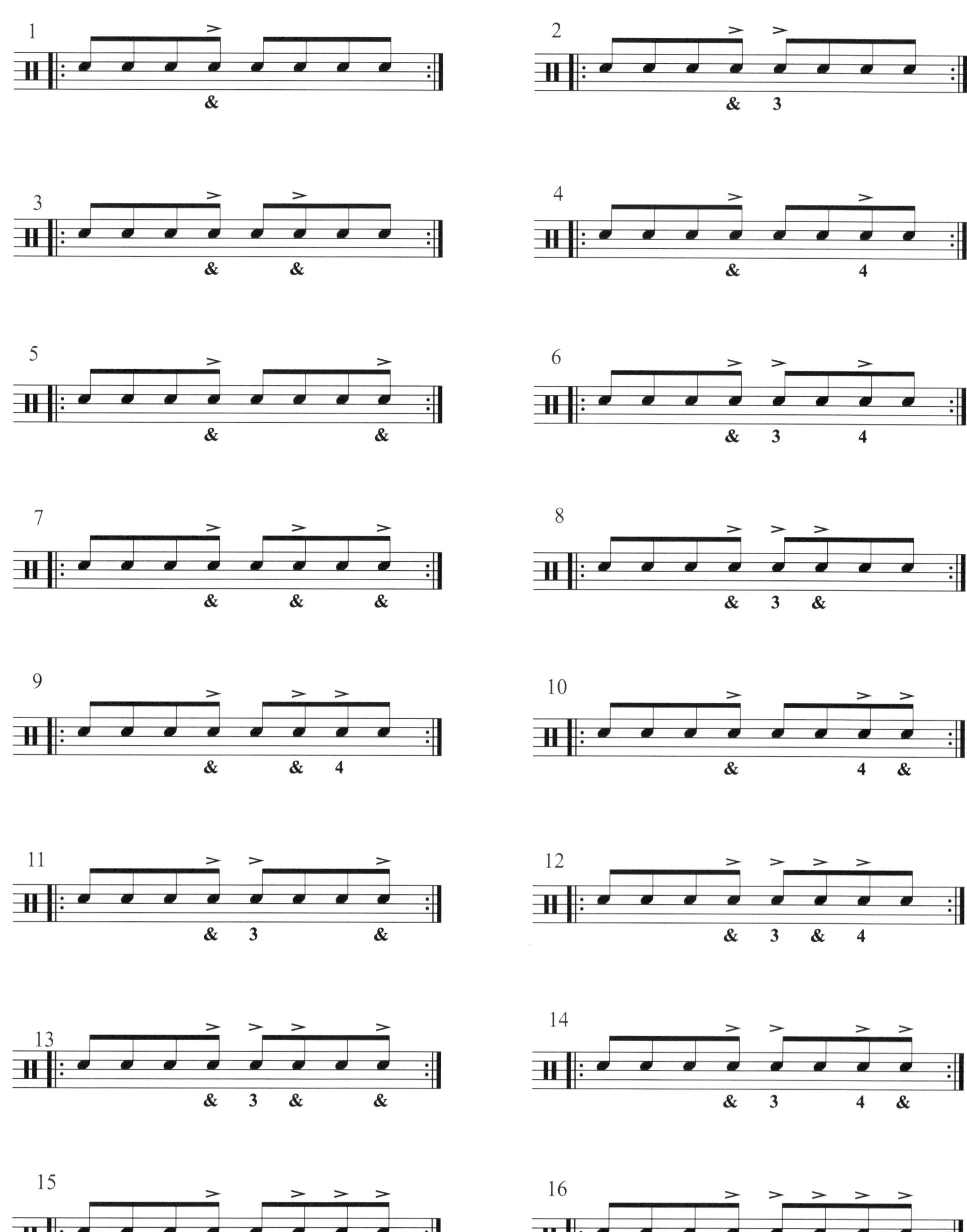

8th Note Accents

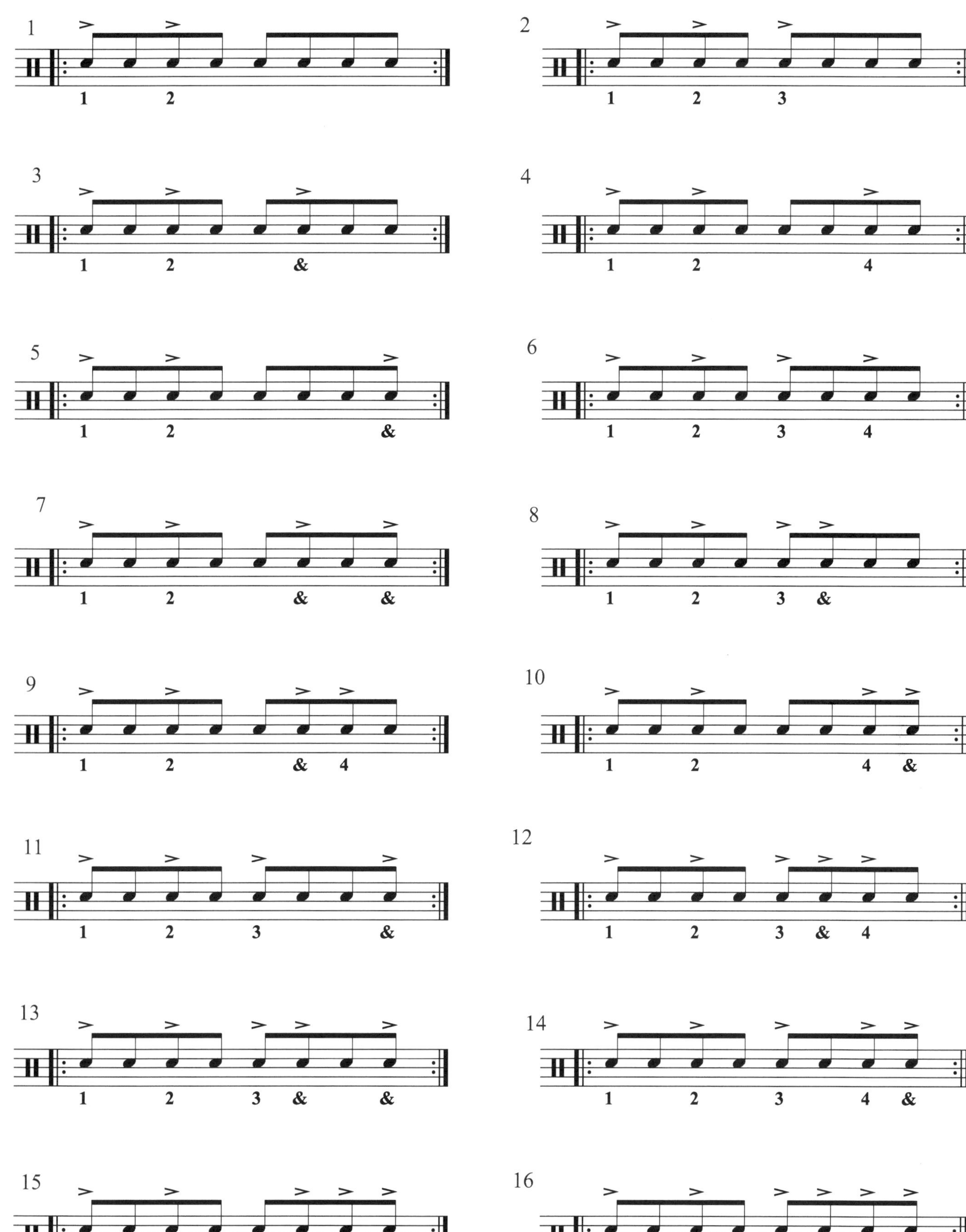

8th Note Accents

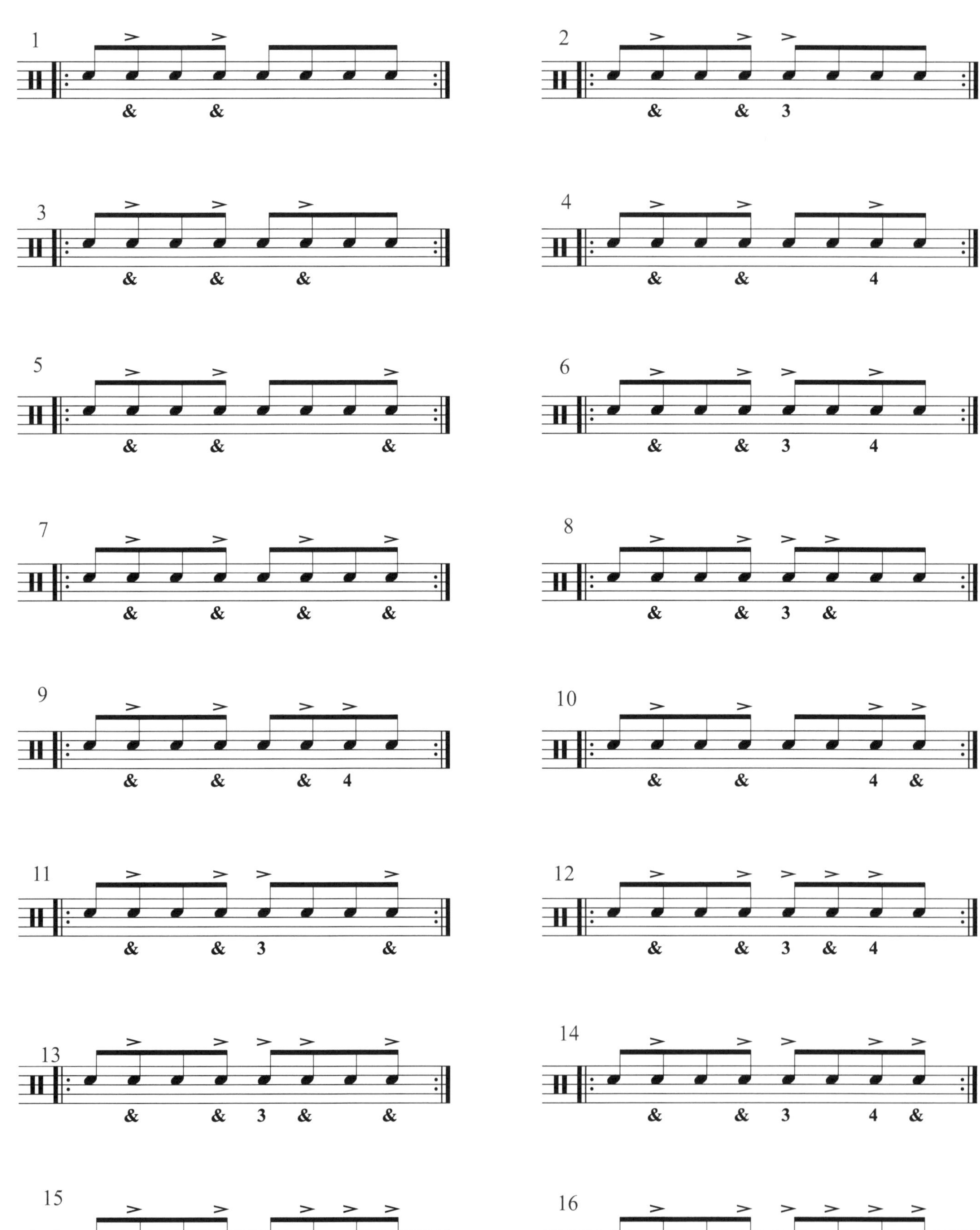

8th Note Accents

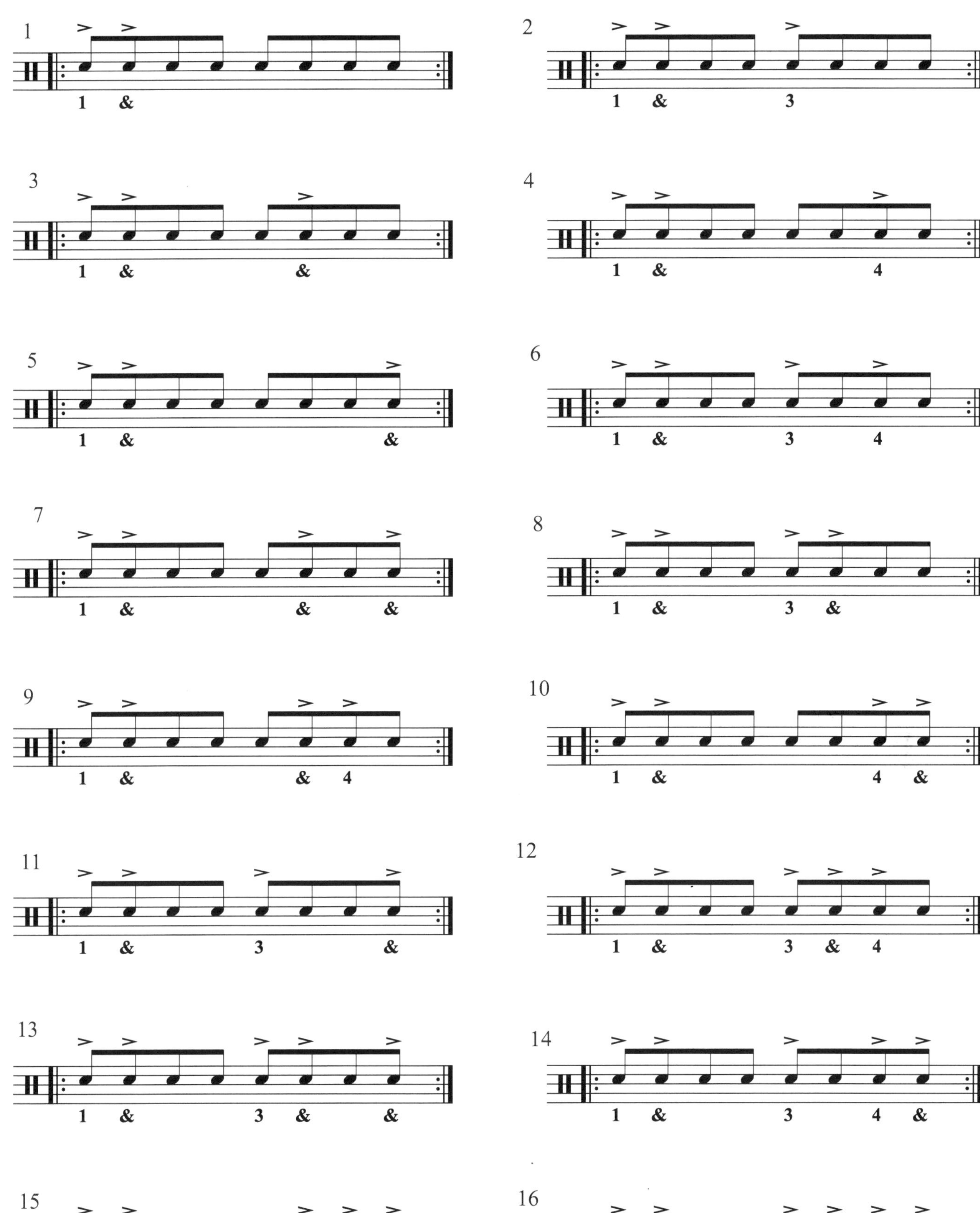

8th Note Accents

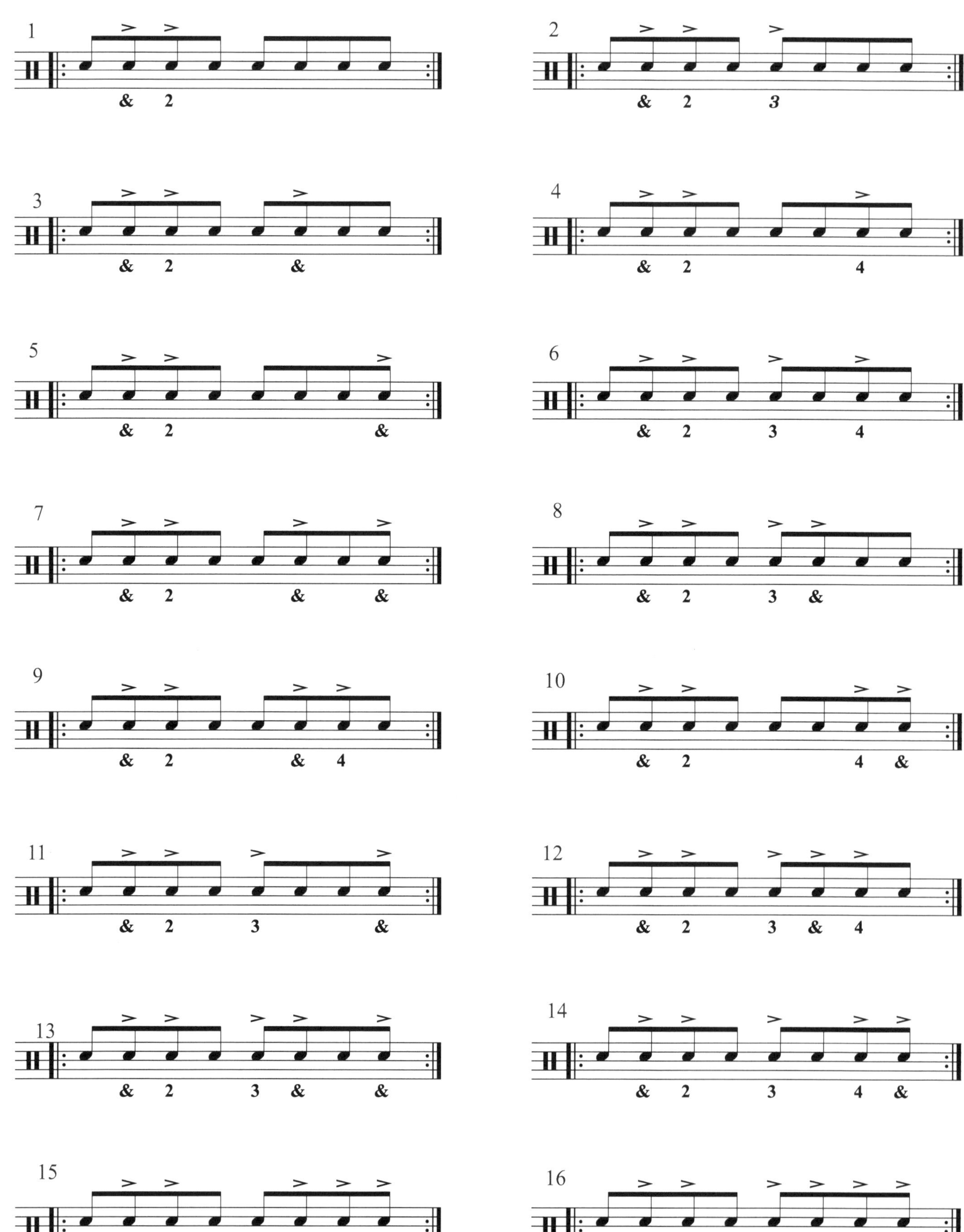

8th Note Accents

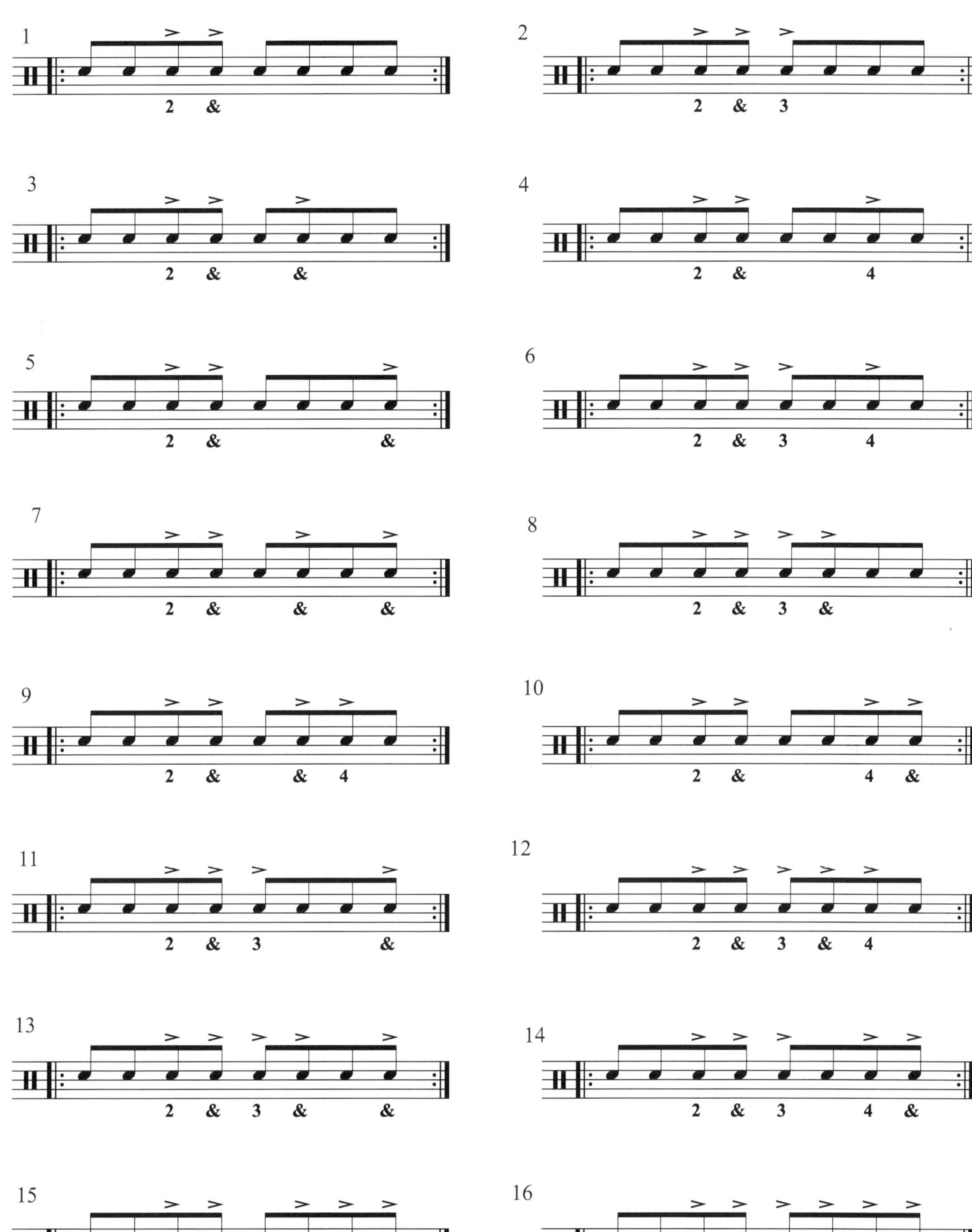

8th Note Accents

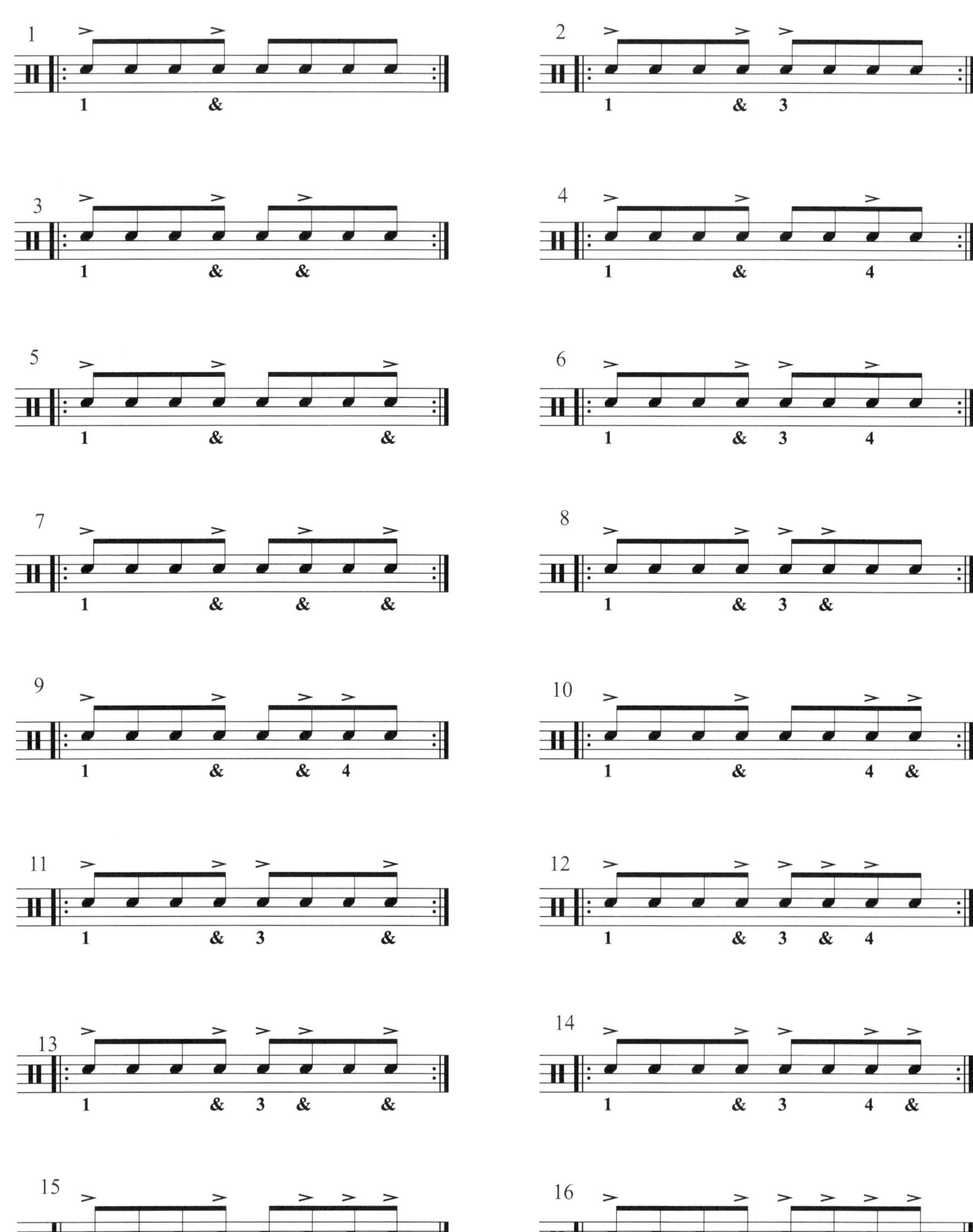

8th Note Accents

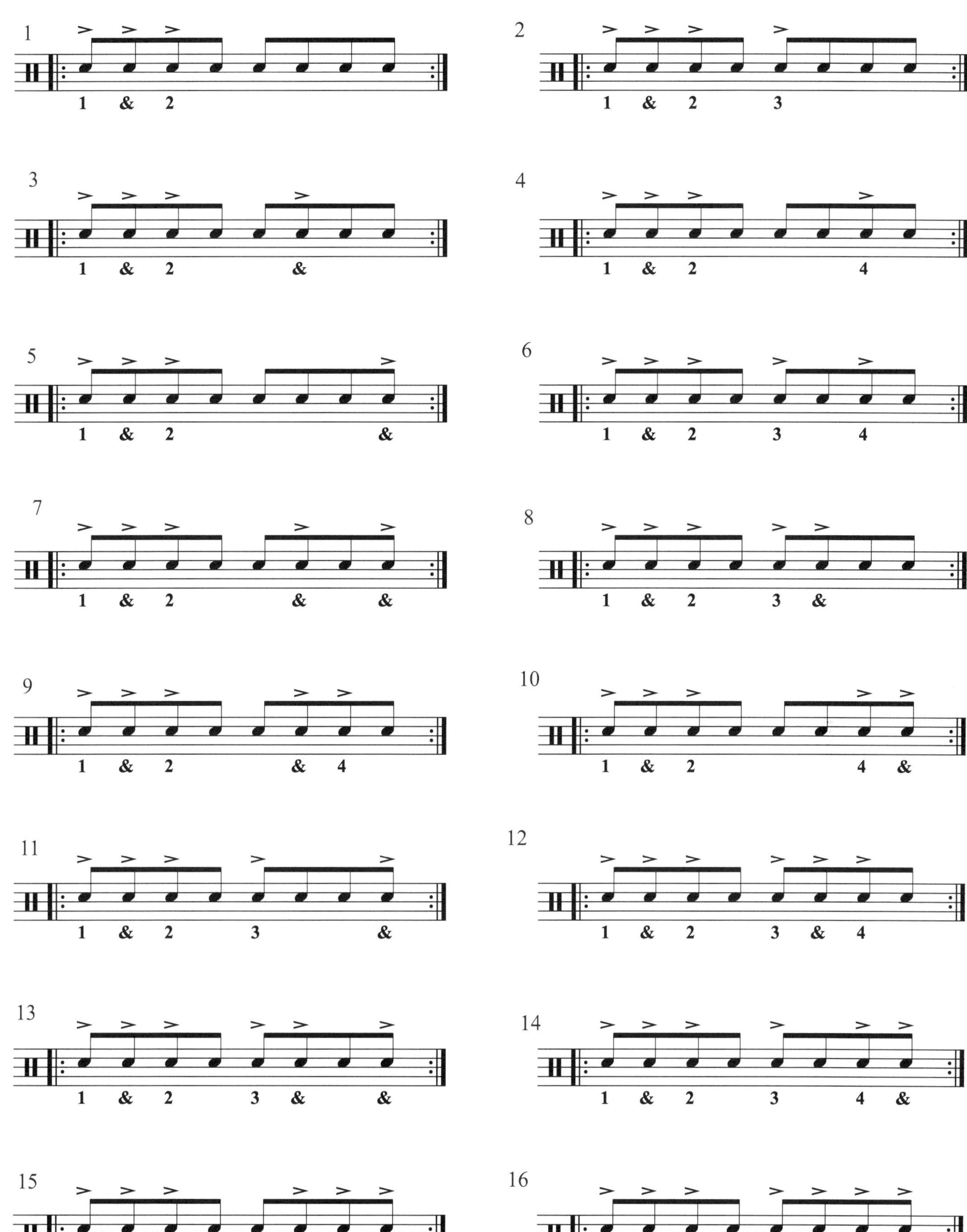

8th Note Accents

8th Note Accents

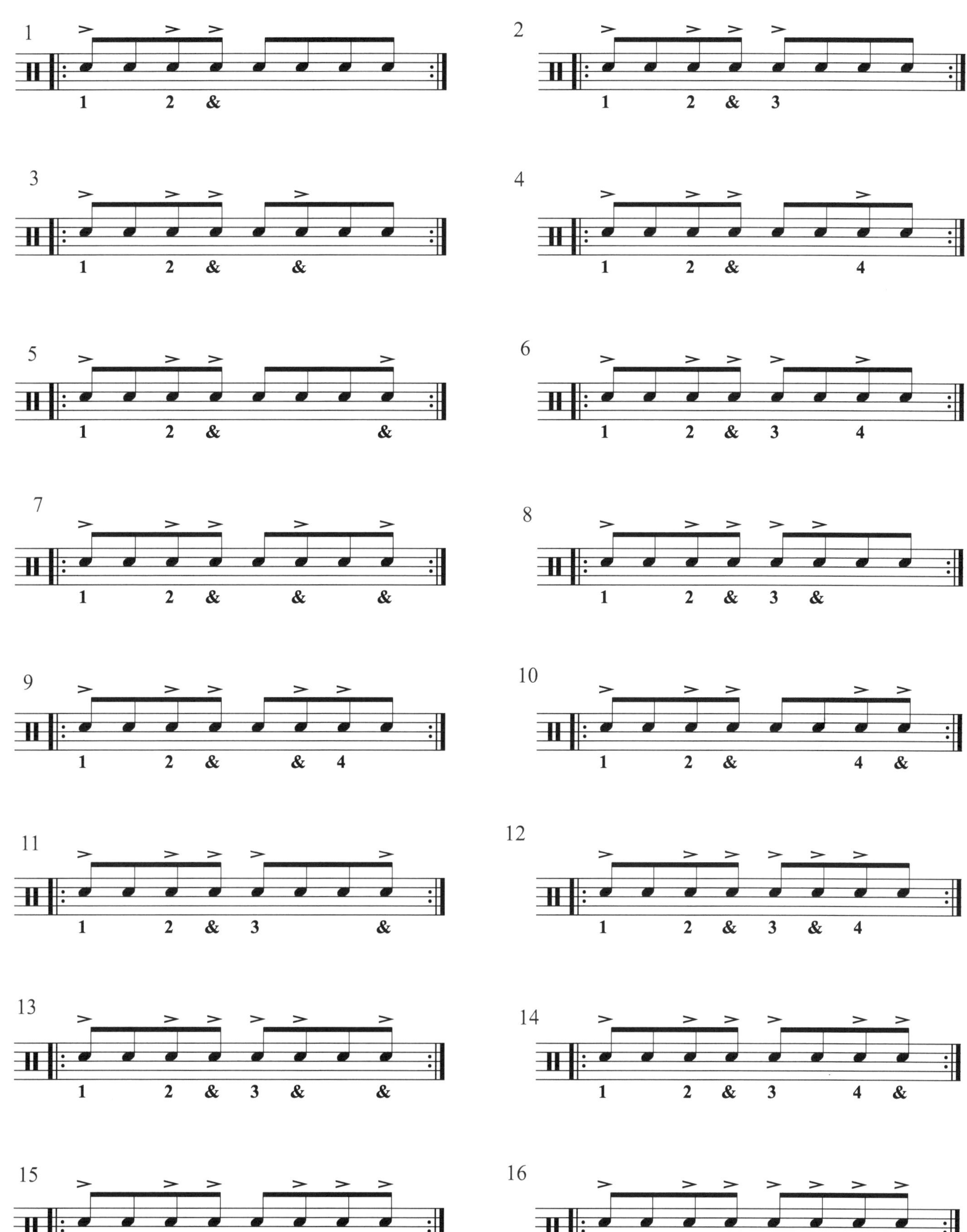

8th Note Accents

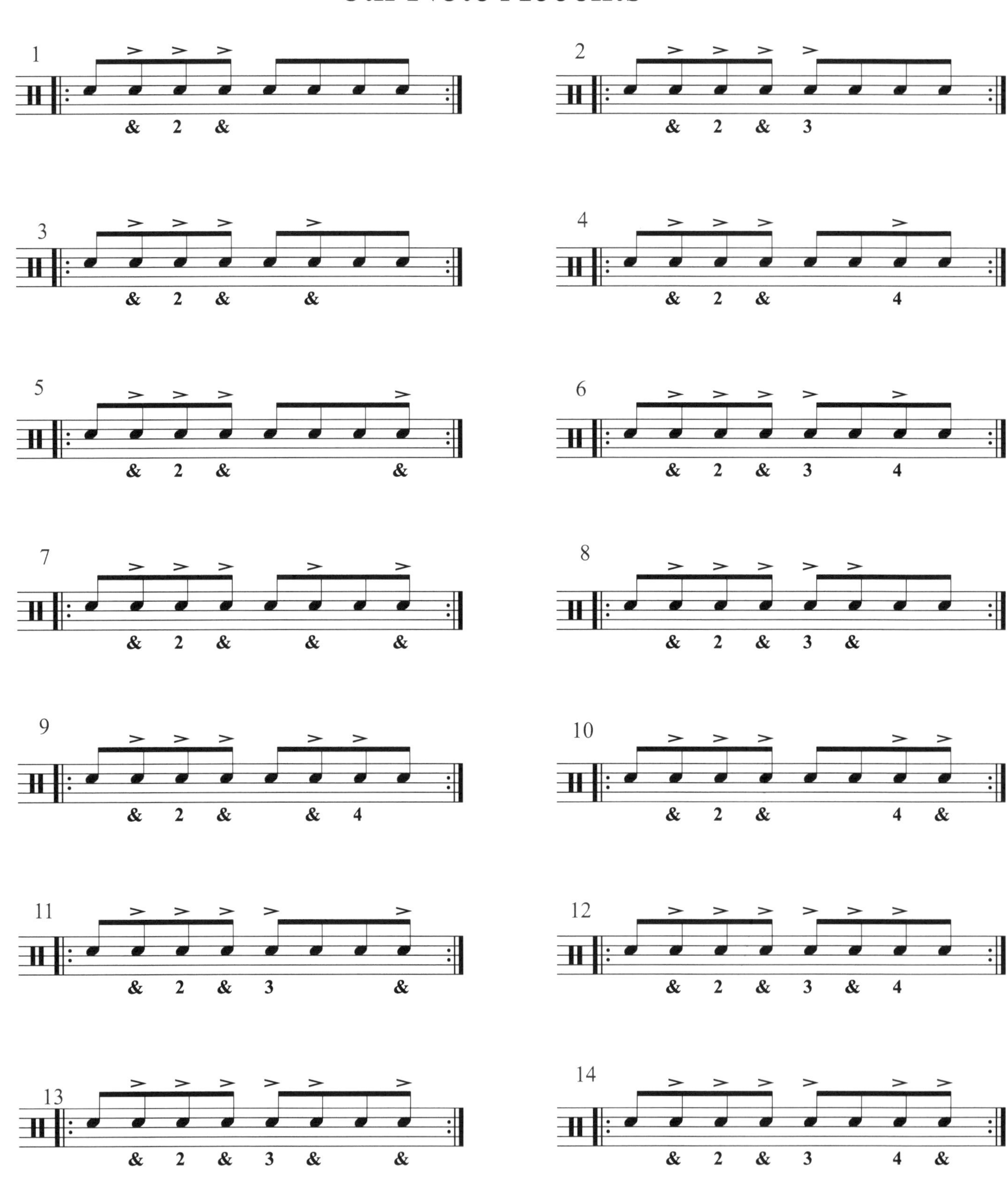

8th Note Accents

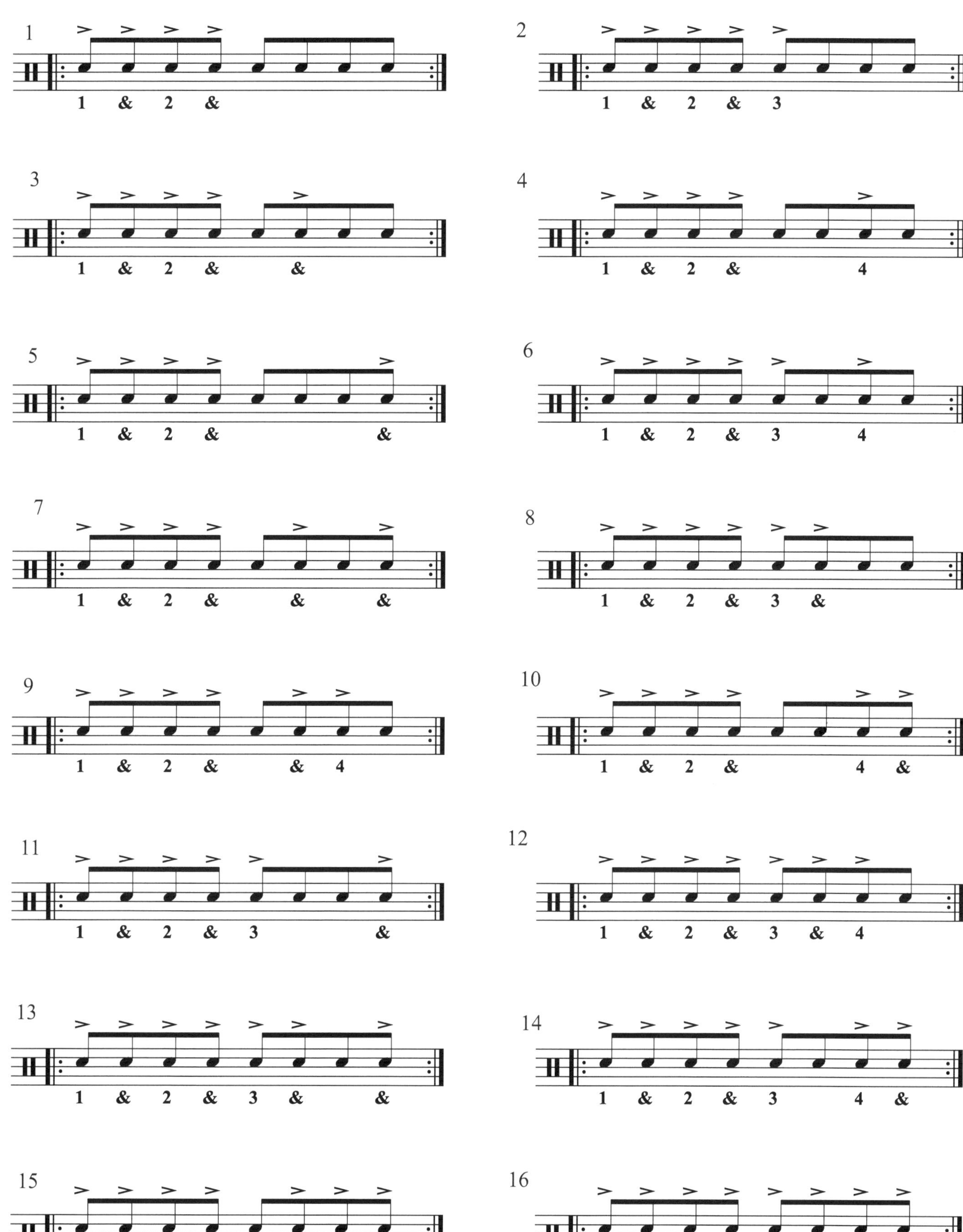

Subdivisions Per Beat

8th Note Rhythms.

1
1 & 2 & 3 & 4 &
2
1 & 2 3 & 4
3
1 & & 3 & &
4
1 2 & 3 4 &
5
& 2 & & 4 &
6
1 2 3 4
7
& & & &
8
1 & 3 &
9
& 2 & 4
10
2 & 4 &
11
1 & 3 &
12
1 3
13
& &
14
2 4
15
& &
16

8th Note Rhythms

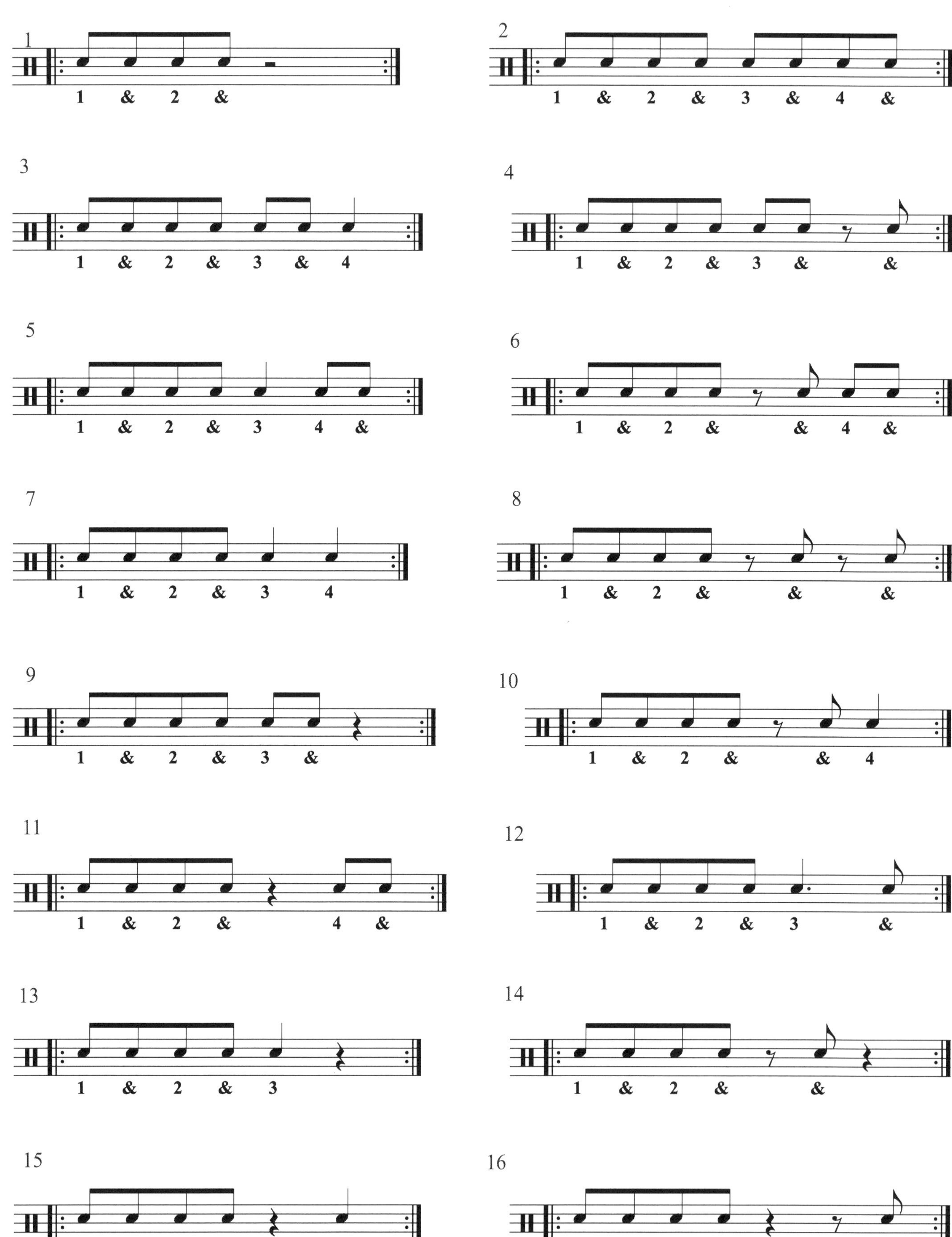

8th Note Rhythms

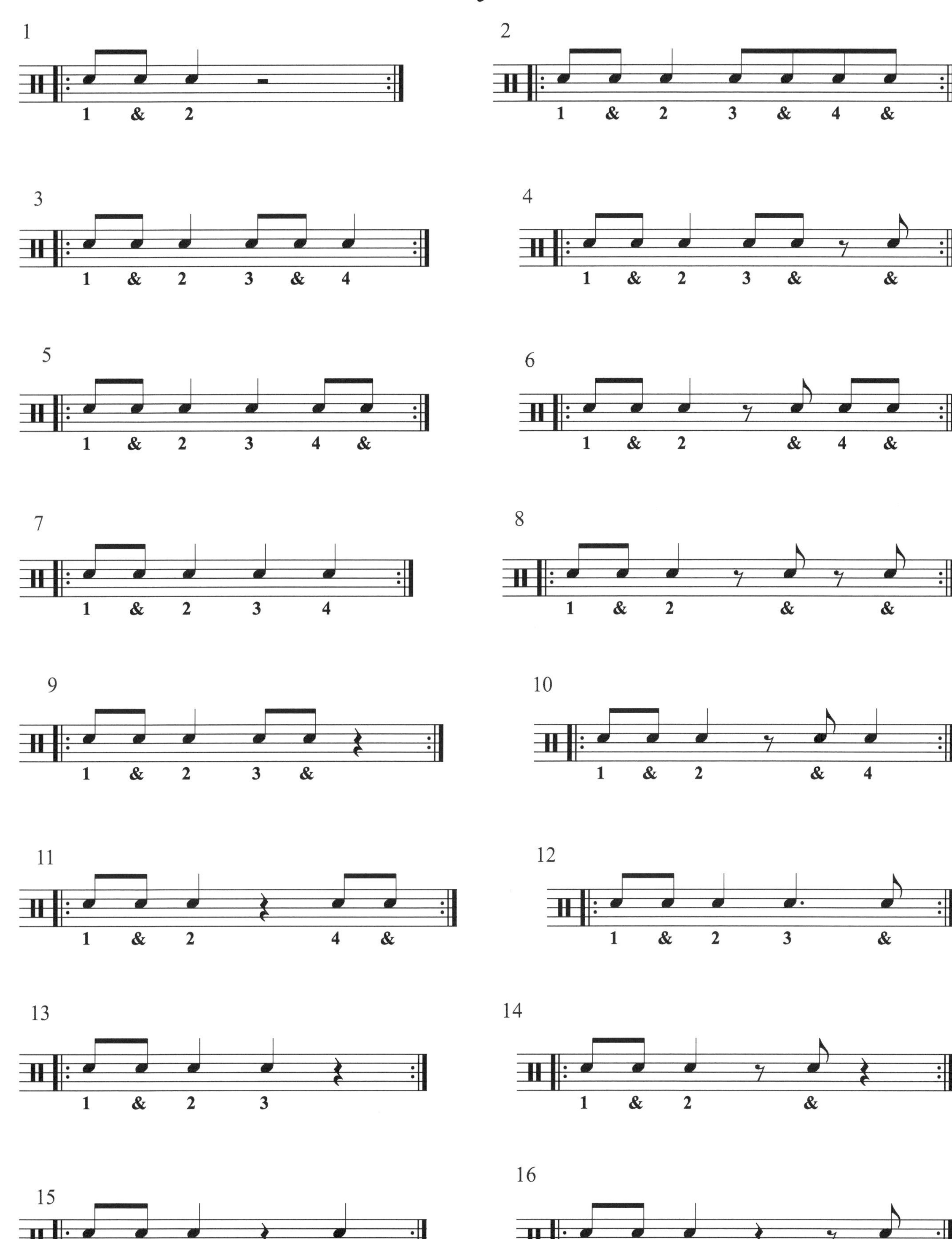

8th Note Rhythms

8th Note Rhythms

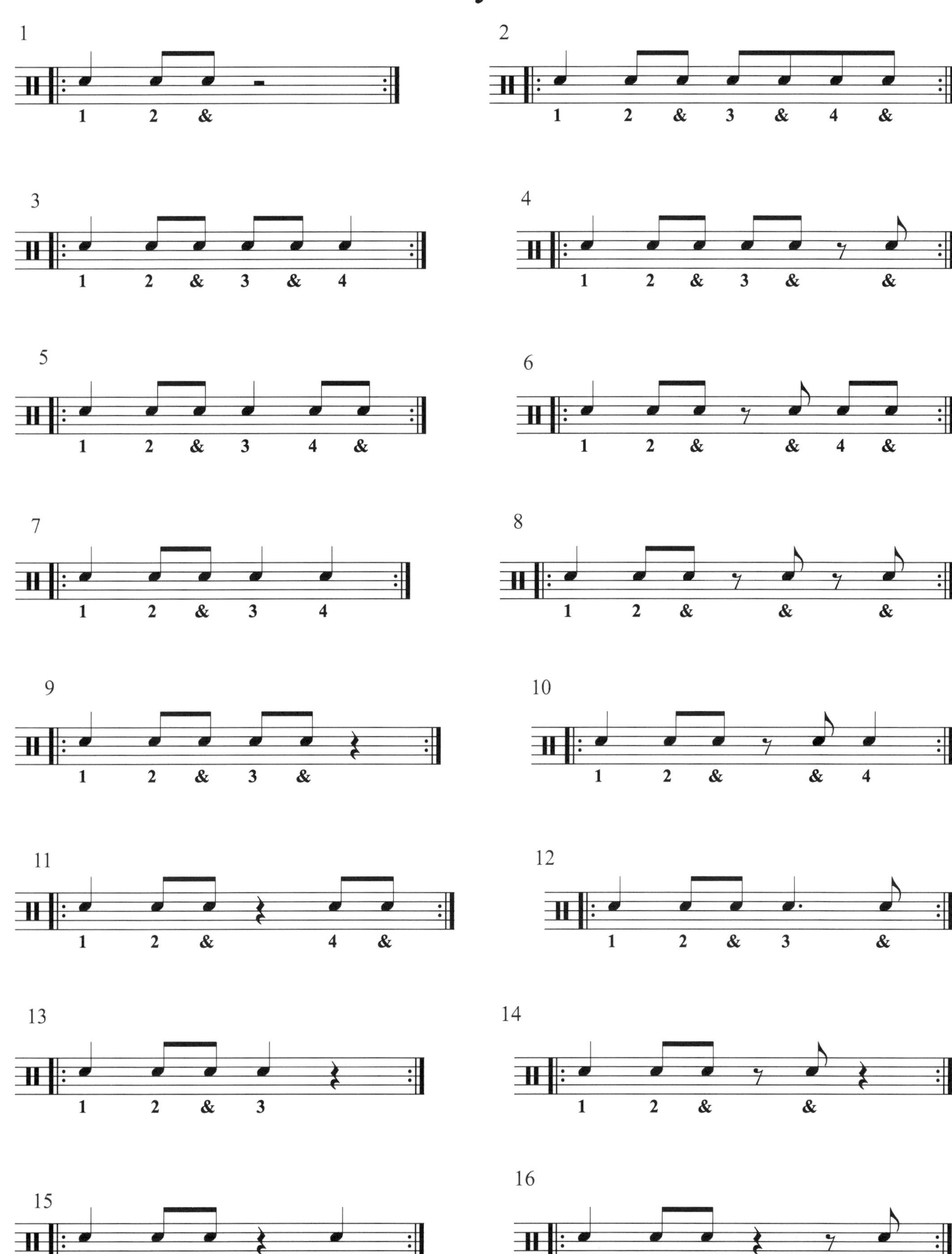

8th Note Rhythms

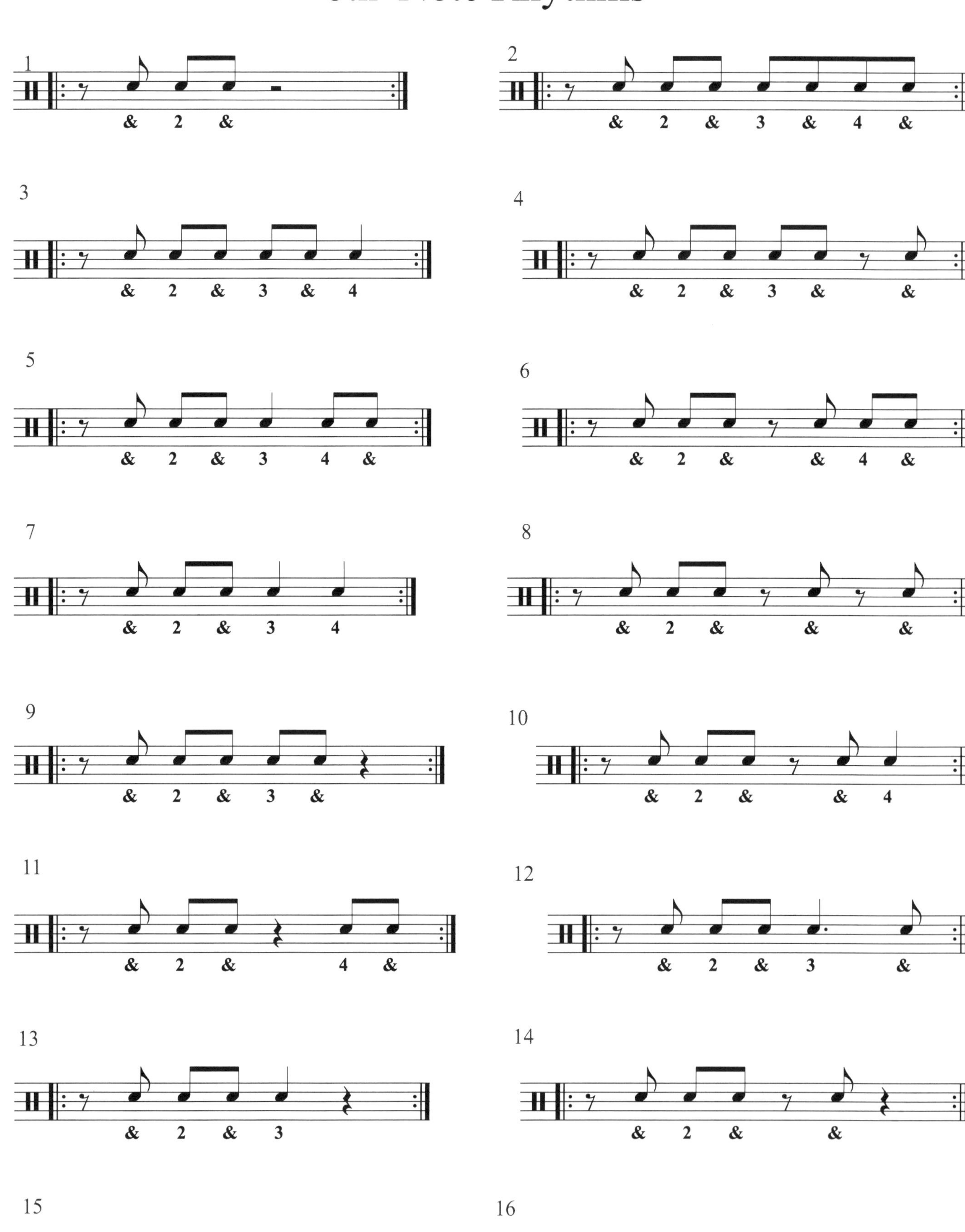

8th Note Rhythms

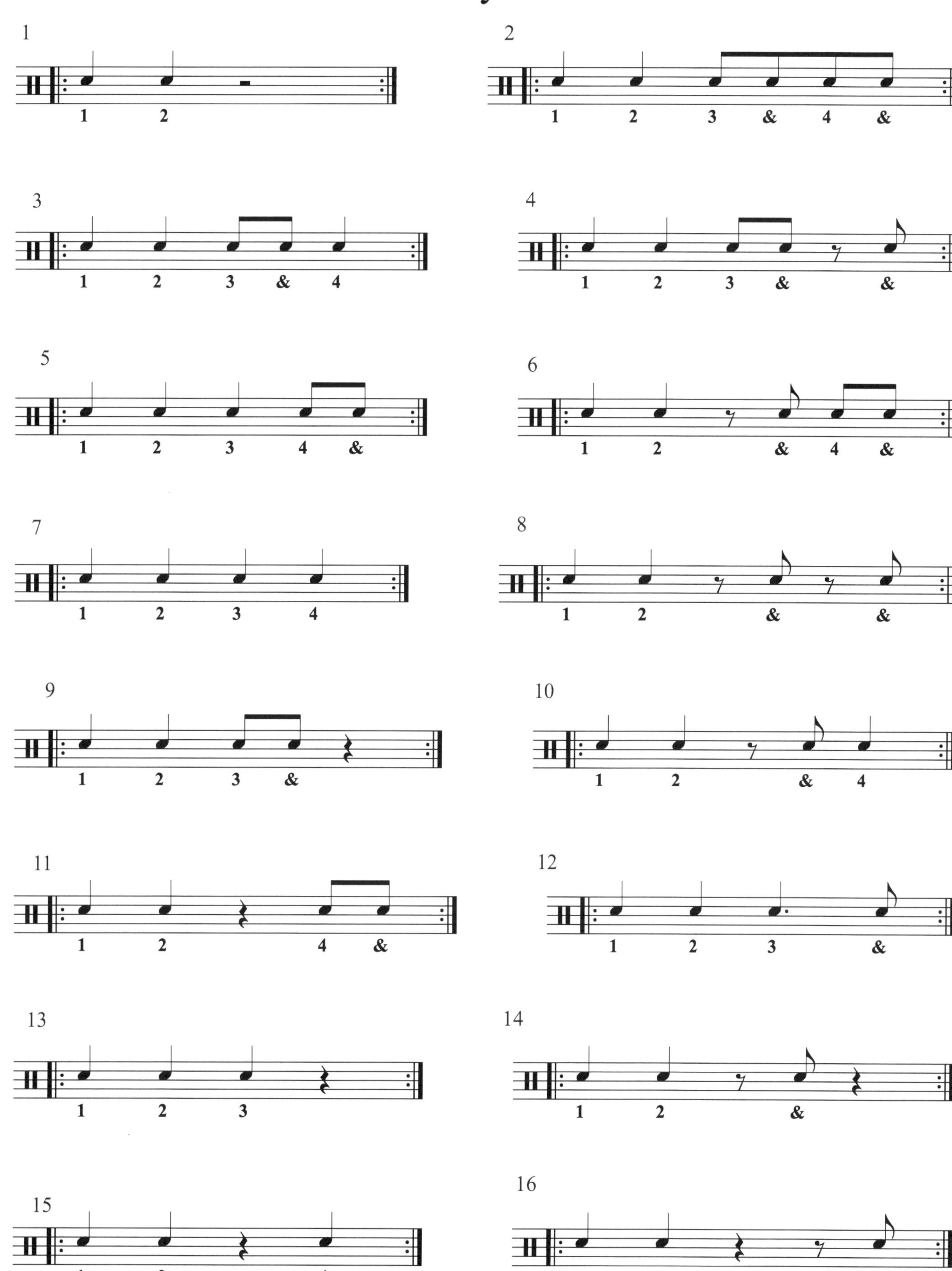

8th Note Rhythms

8th Note Rhythms

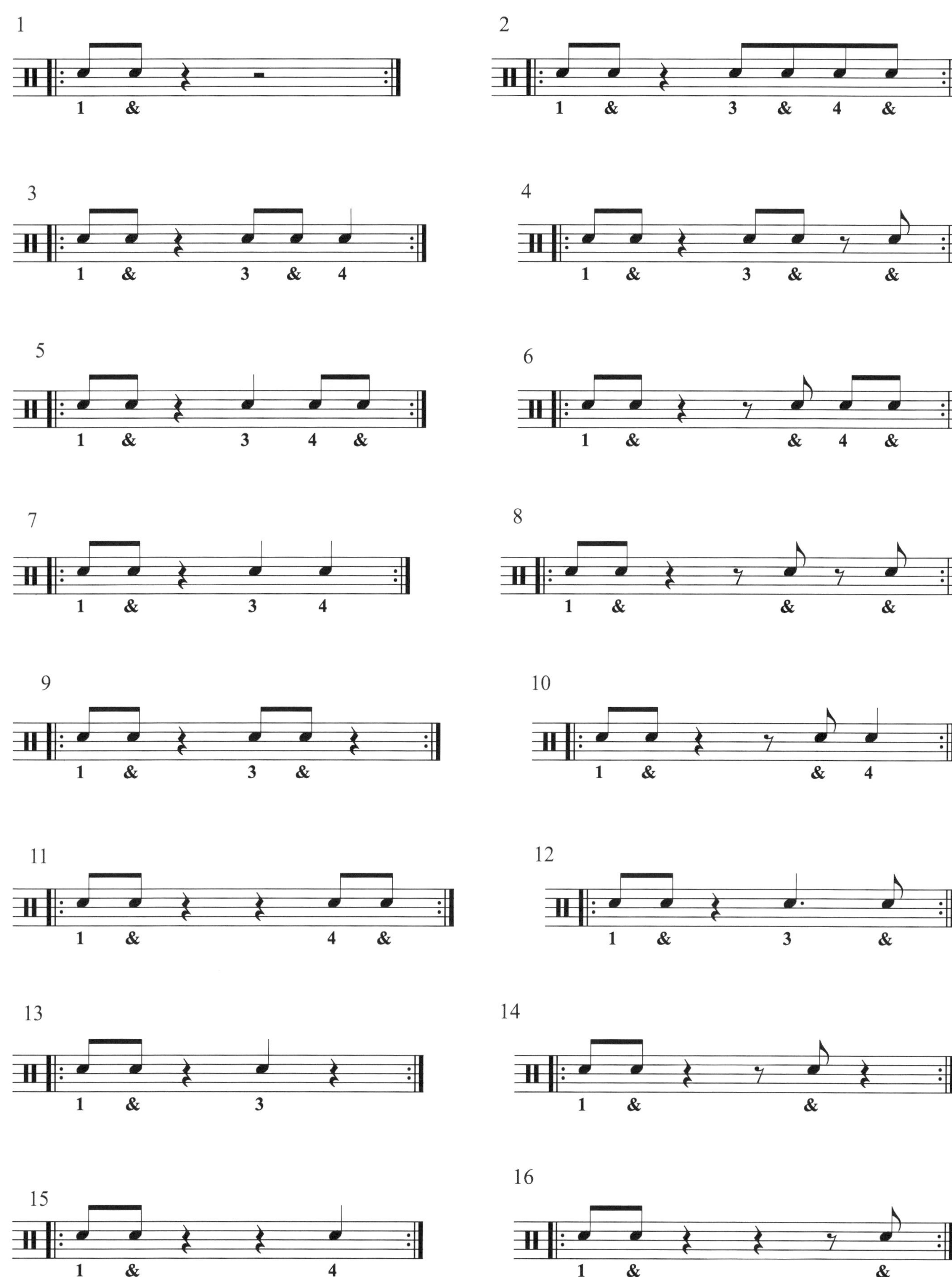

8th Note Rhythms

8th Note Rhythms

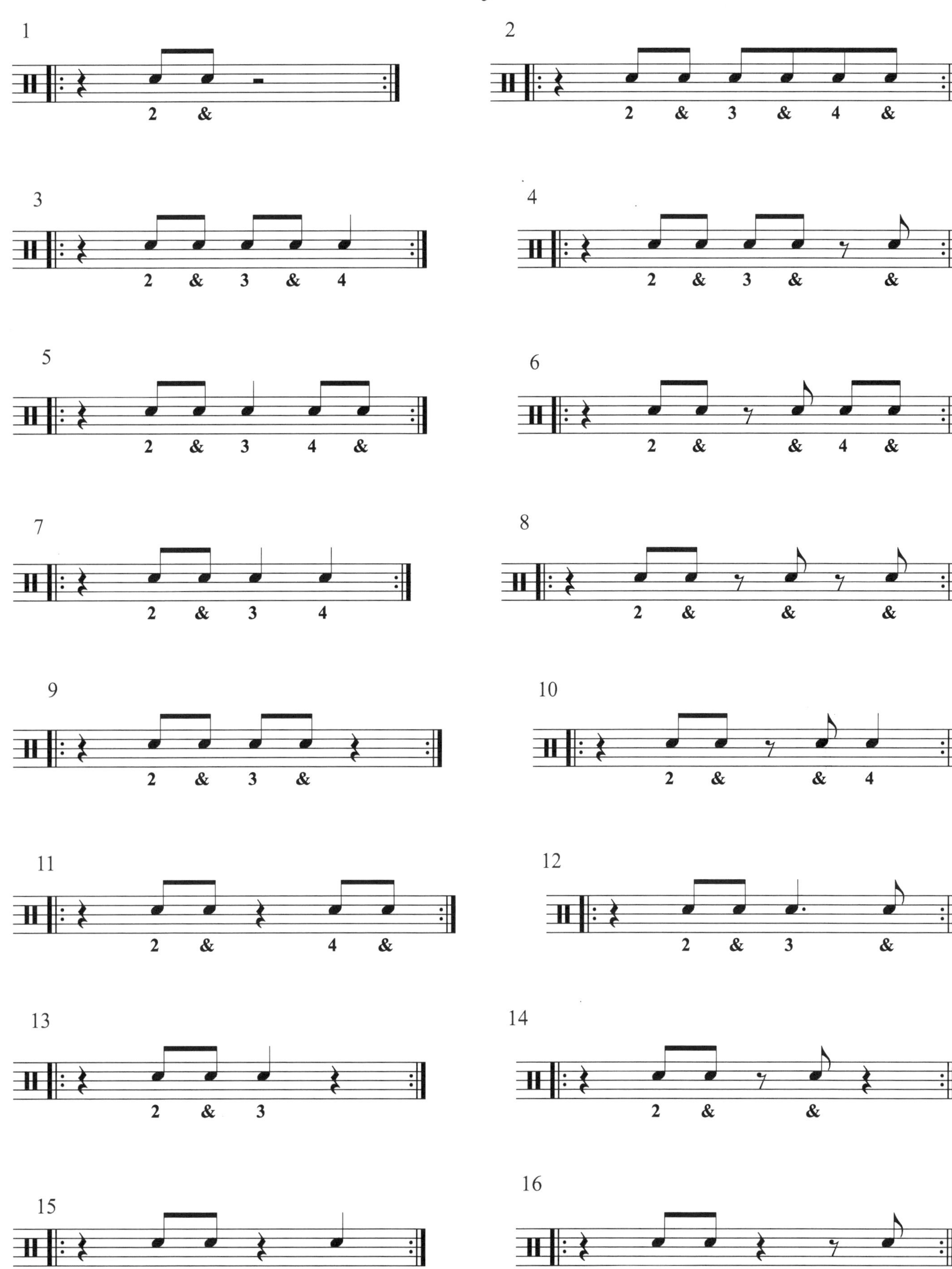

8th Note Rhythms

8th Note Rhythms

8th Note Rhythms

8th Note Rhythms

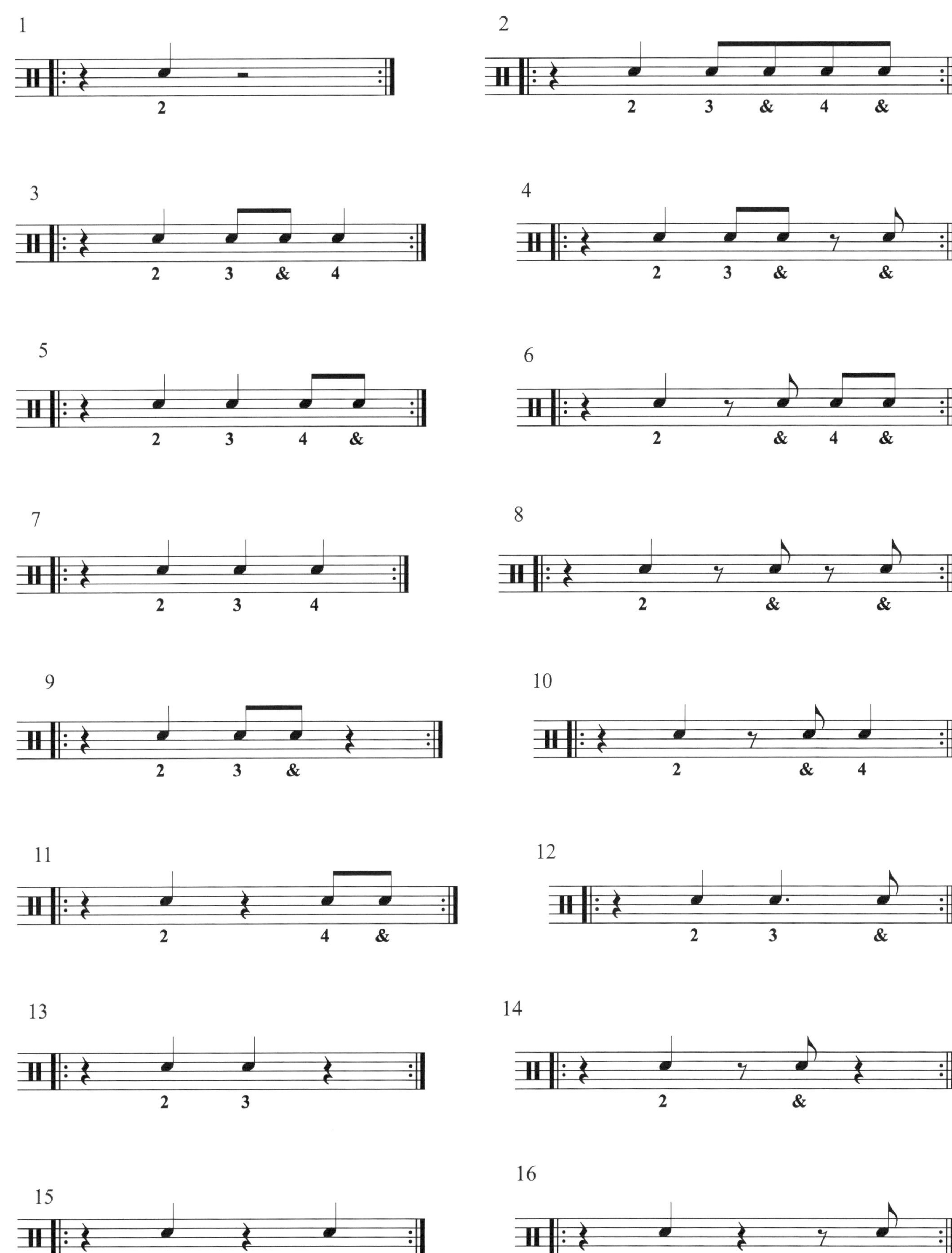

8th Note Rhythms

8th Note Rhythms

Subdivisions Per Beat

$2^4 = 16$ Binary Rhythms

$2^{16} = 65,356$

Rhythmic Possibilities In One Measure Of Common Time

1 e & a 2 e & a 3 e & a 4 e & a

In 4|4 time, 16th notes divide the beat into 4 equal subdivisions. With 4 equal subdivisions the 16 binary rhythms are now expressed within one beat.

With 16 subdivisions in one measure of 4|4 time there are 65,356 rhythmic possibilities. Needless to say we do not have all of them in this one book. We do explore all of AABB and ABAB combinations.

16th Note Accented Rhythmic Alphabet

16th Note Rhythms Rhythmic Alphabet

16th Note Accents

1

2

3

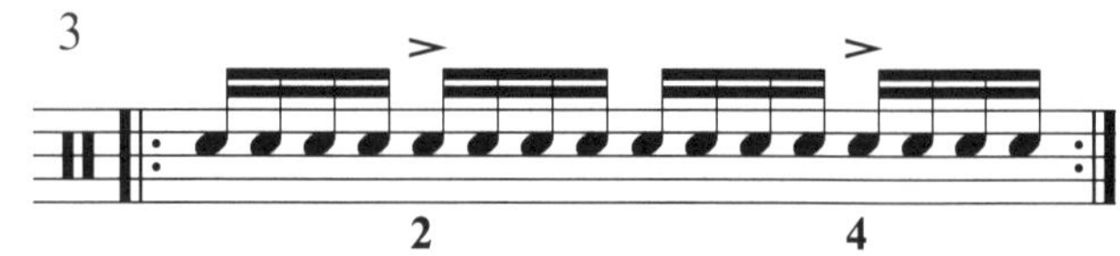

4

5

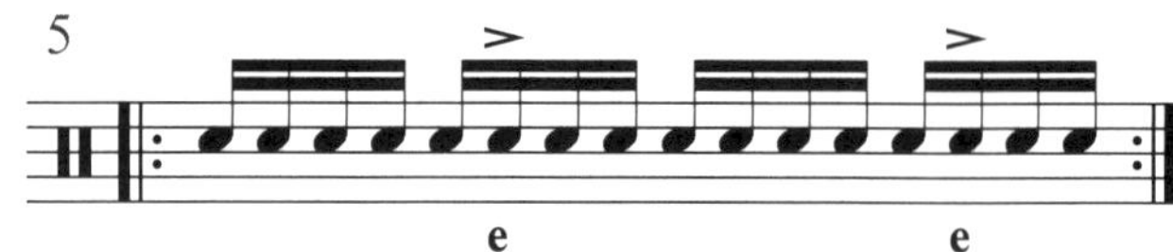

6

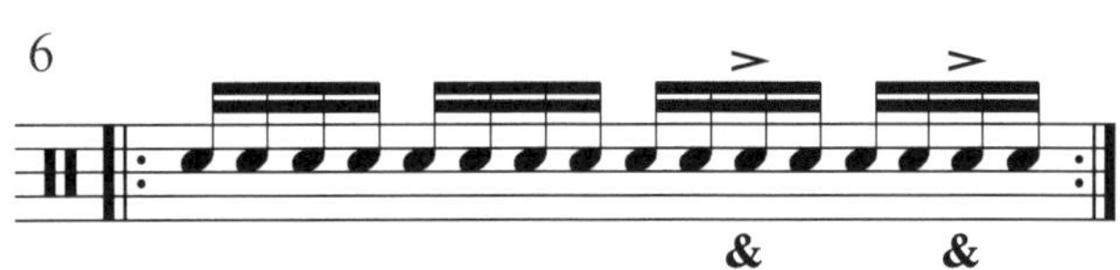

7

8

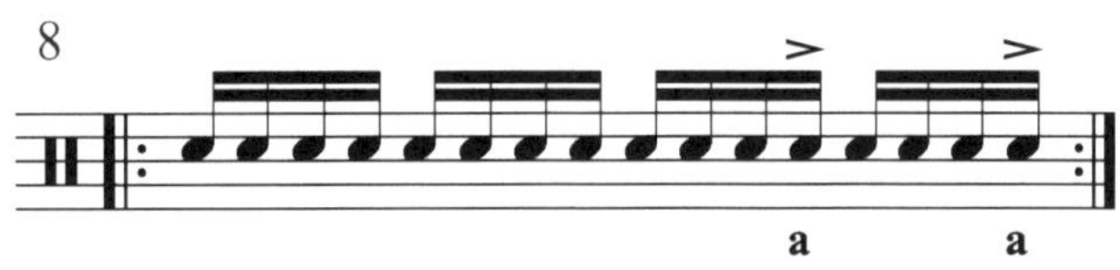

9

10

11

12

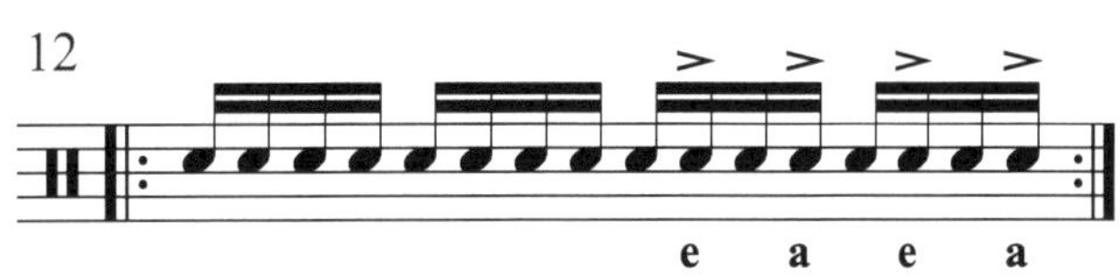

13

14

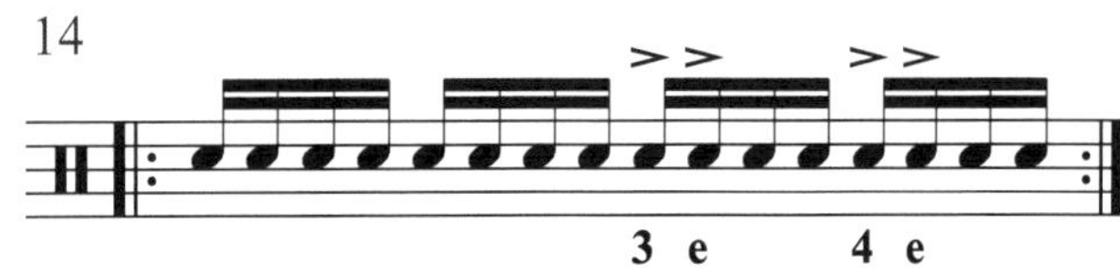

15

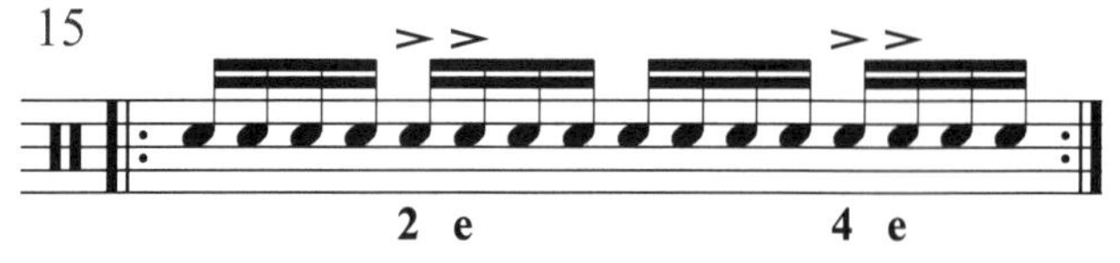

16th Note Accents

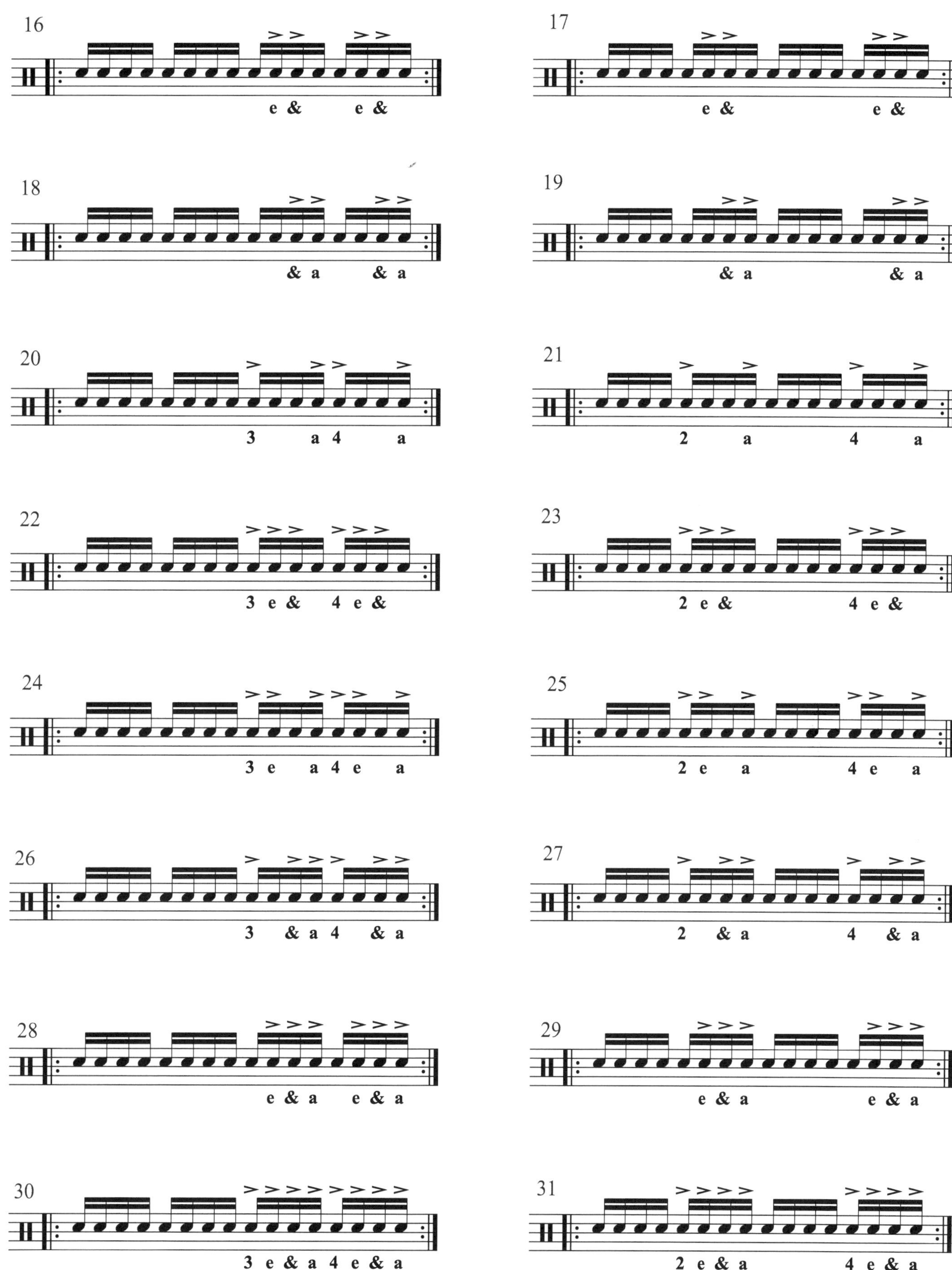

16th Note Accents

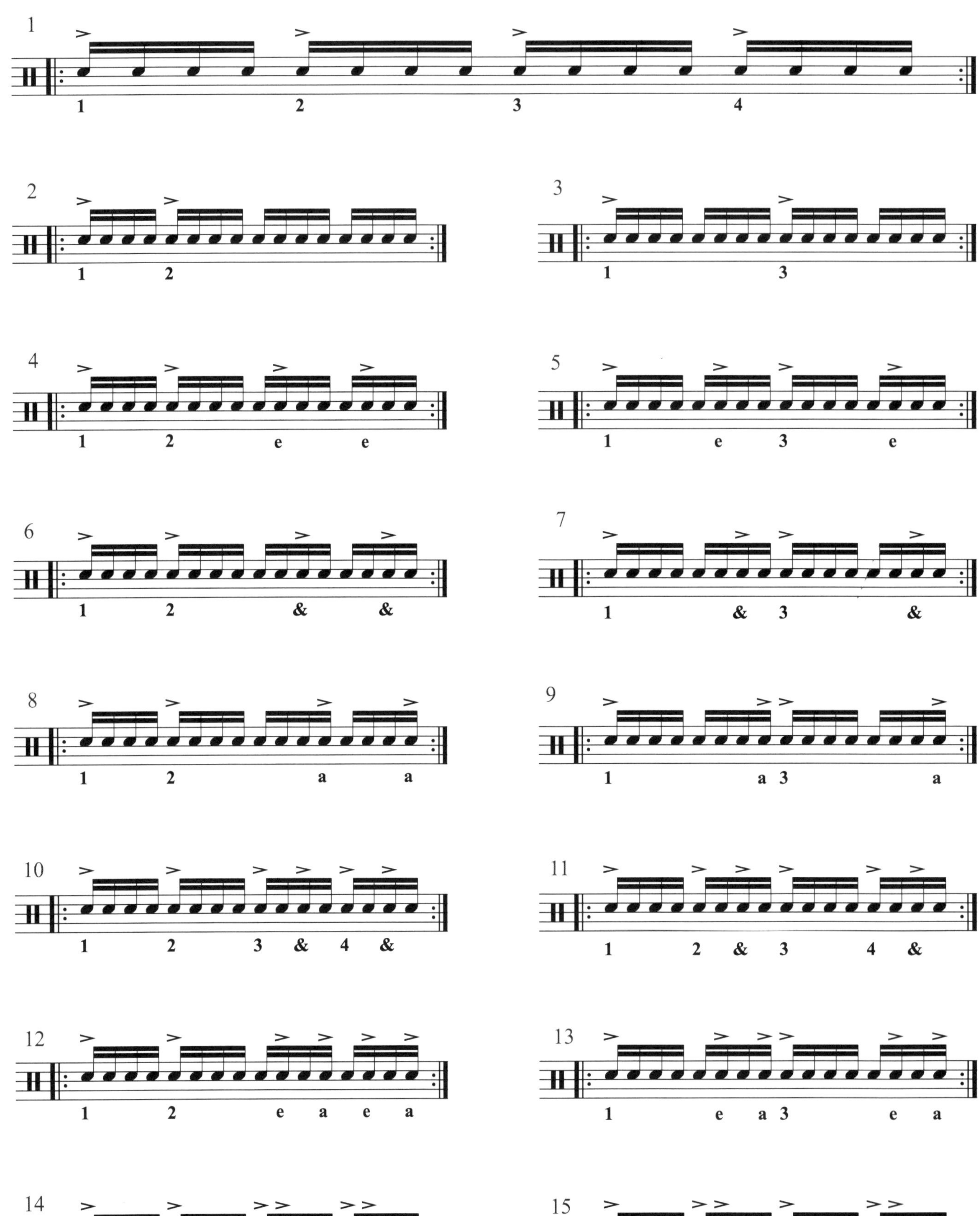

16th Note Accents

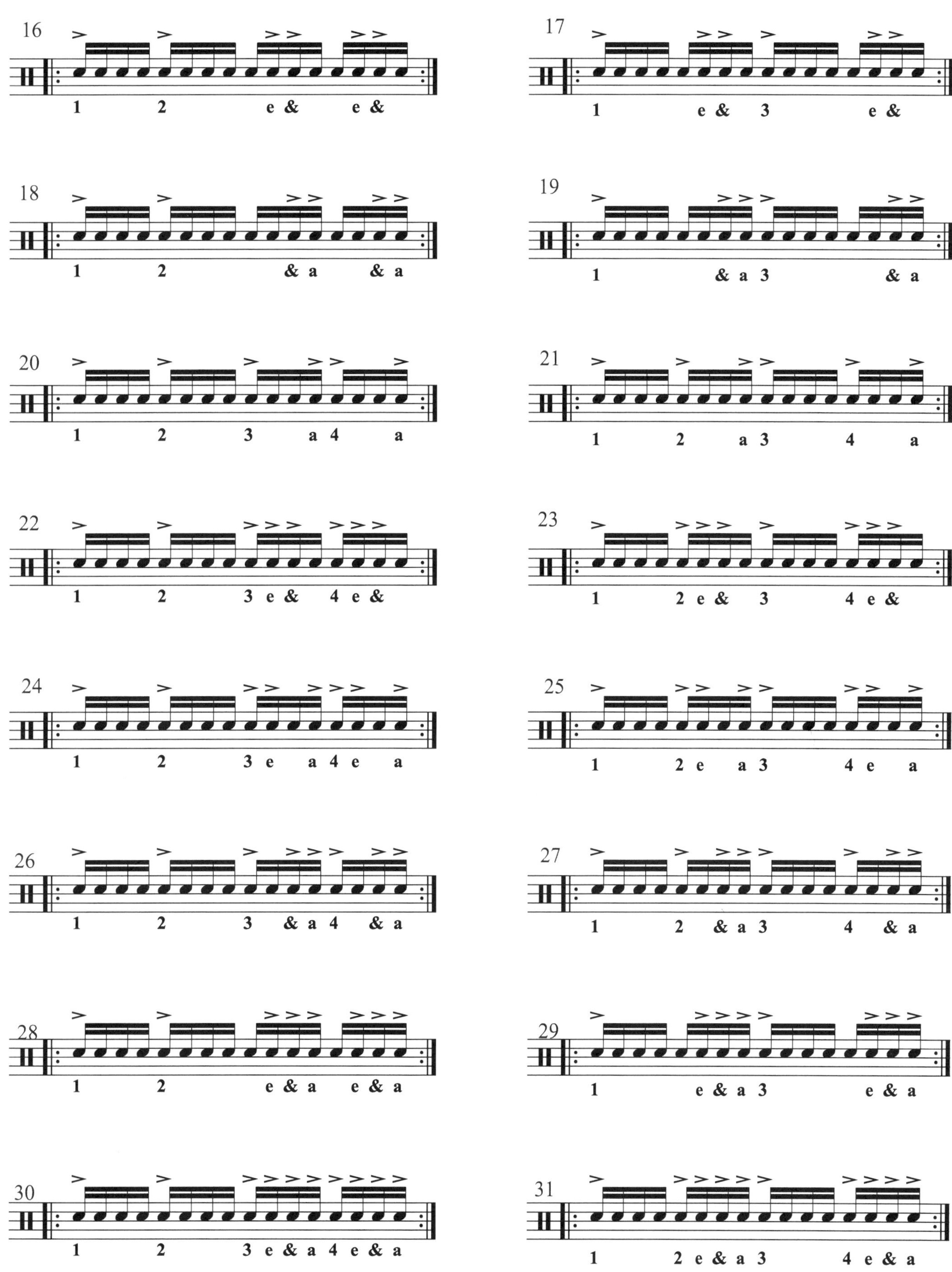

16th Note Accents

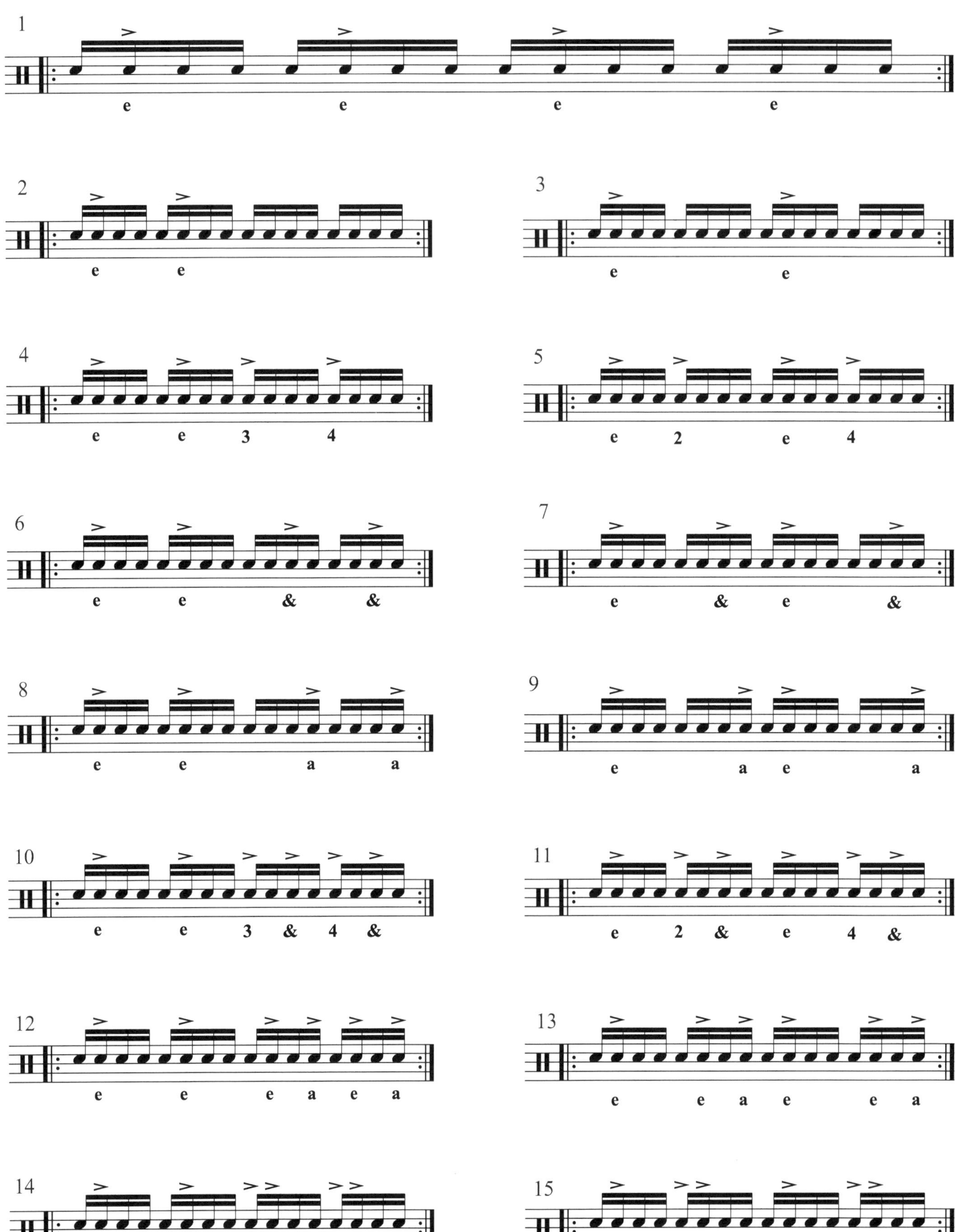

16th Note Accents

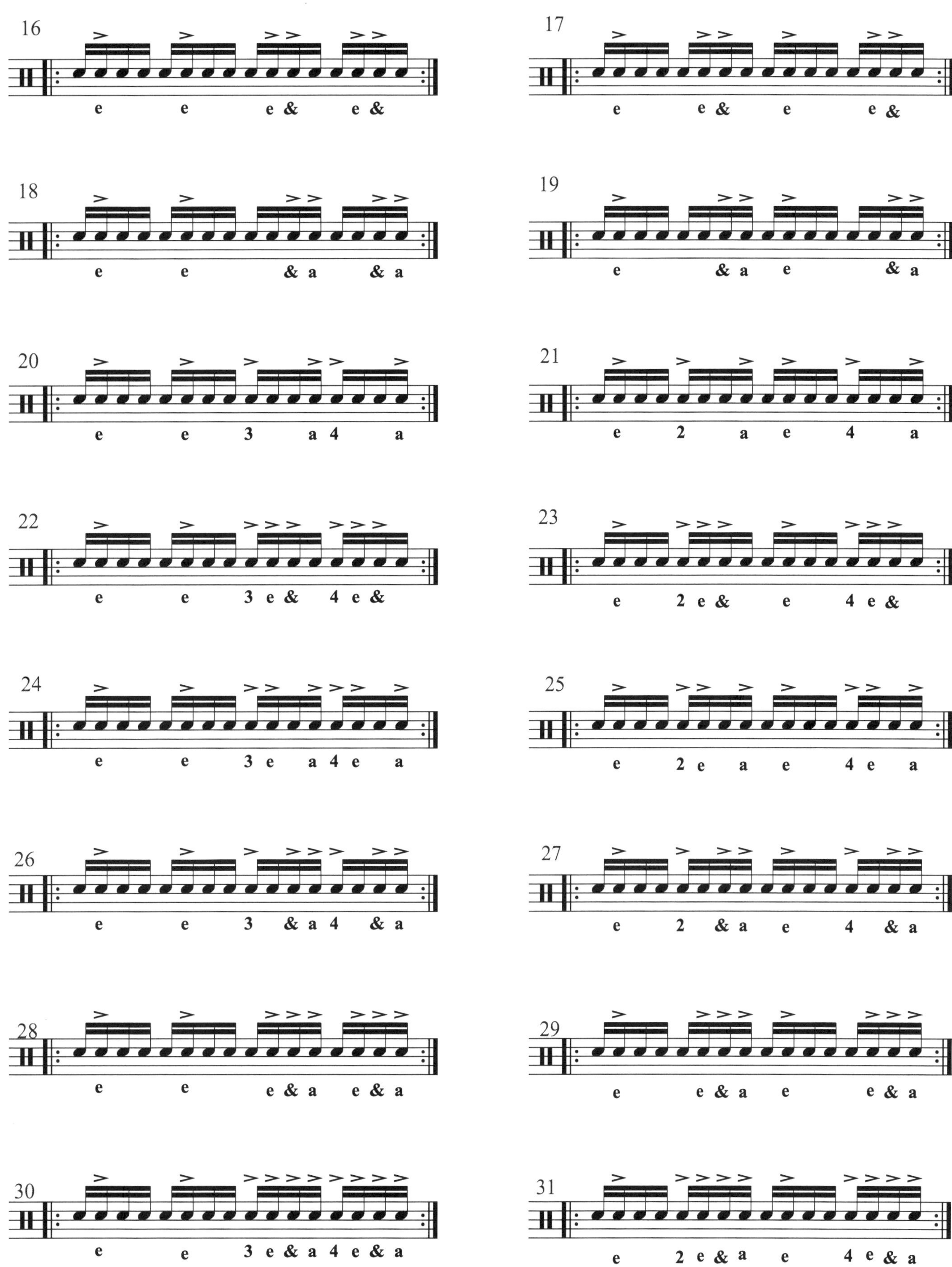

16th Note Accents

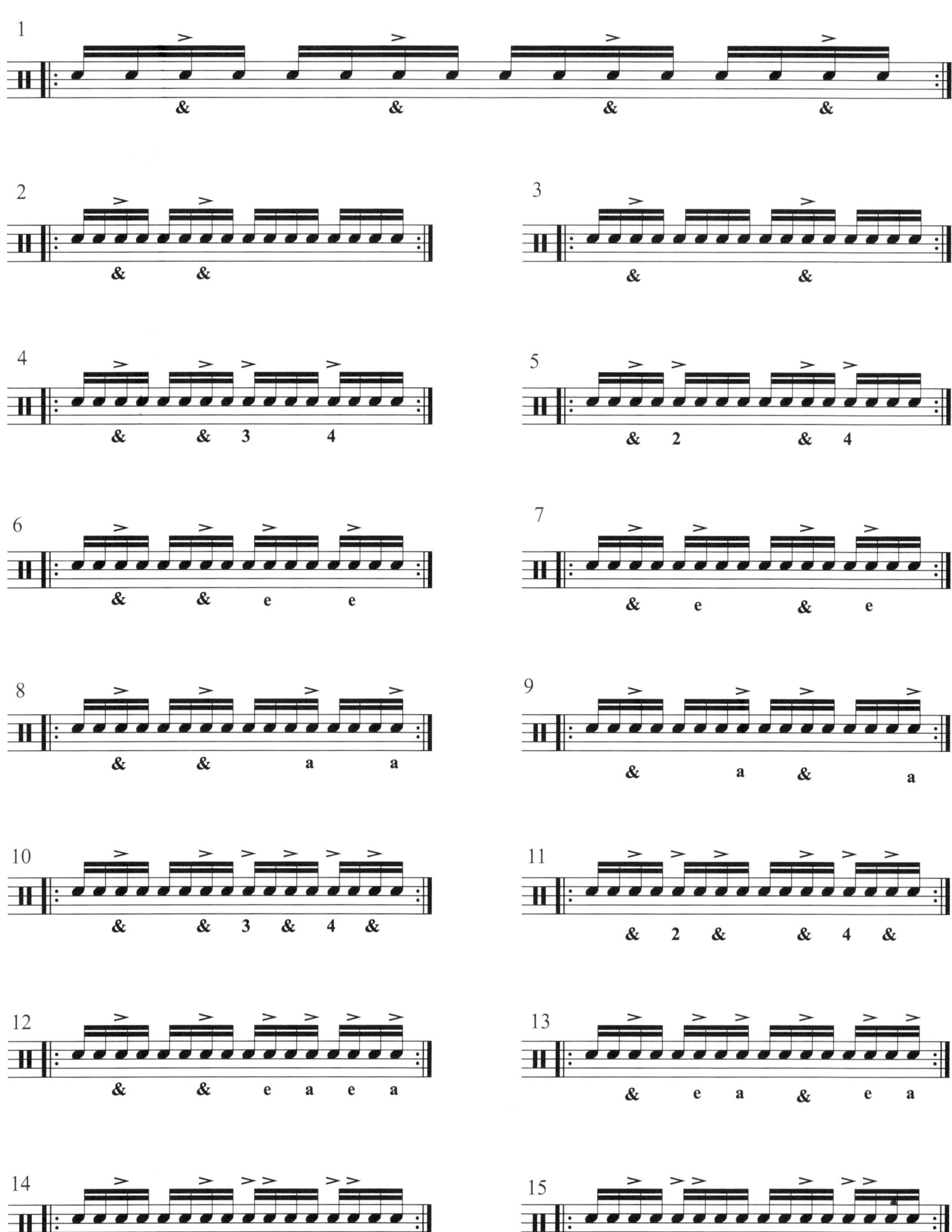

16th Note Accents

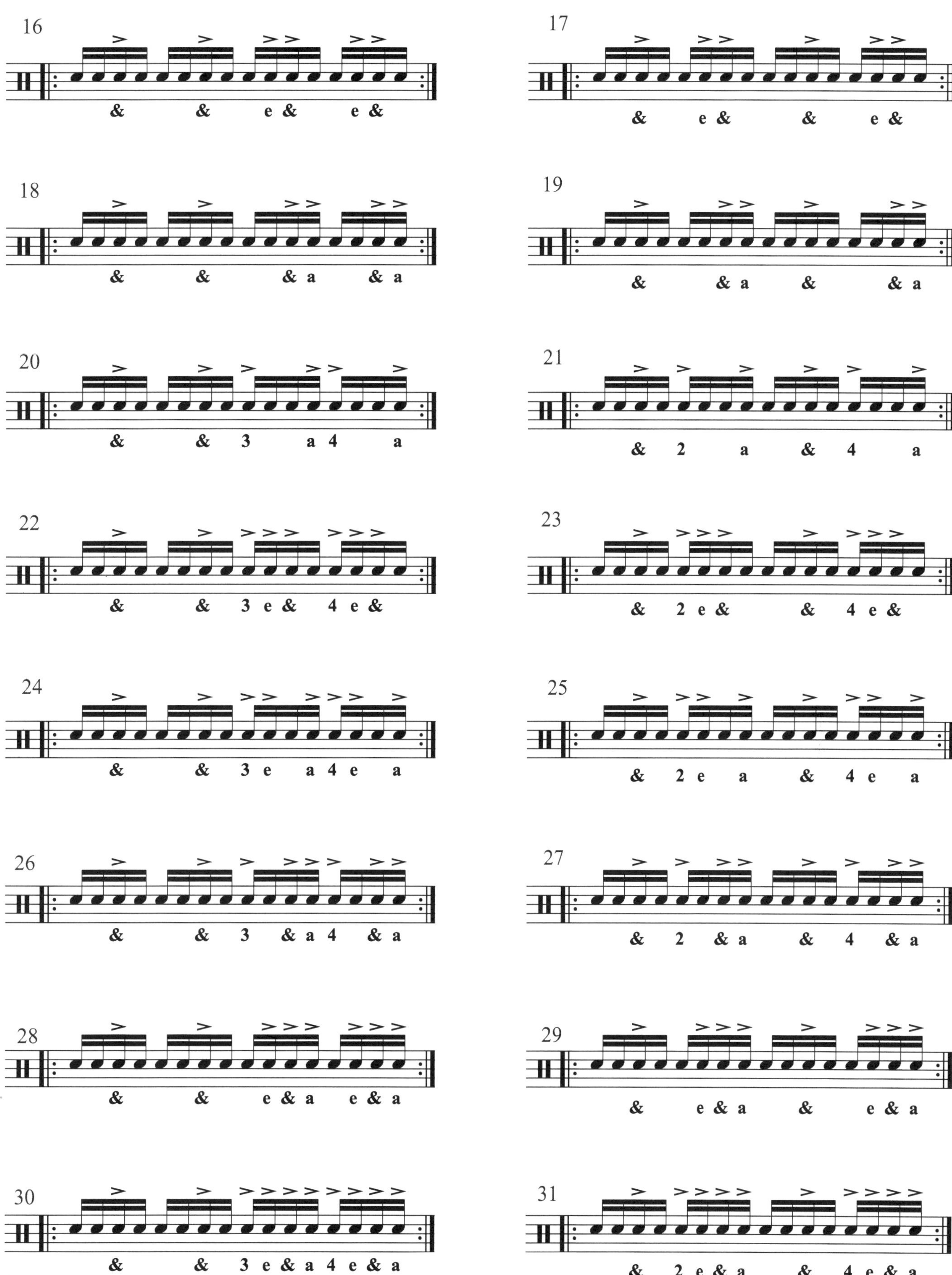

16th Note Accents

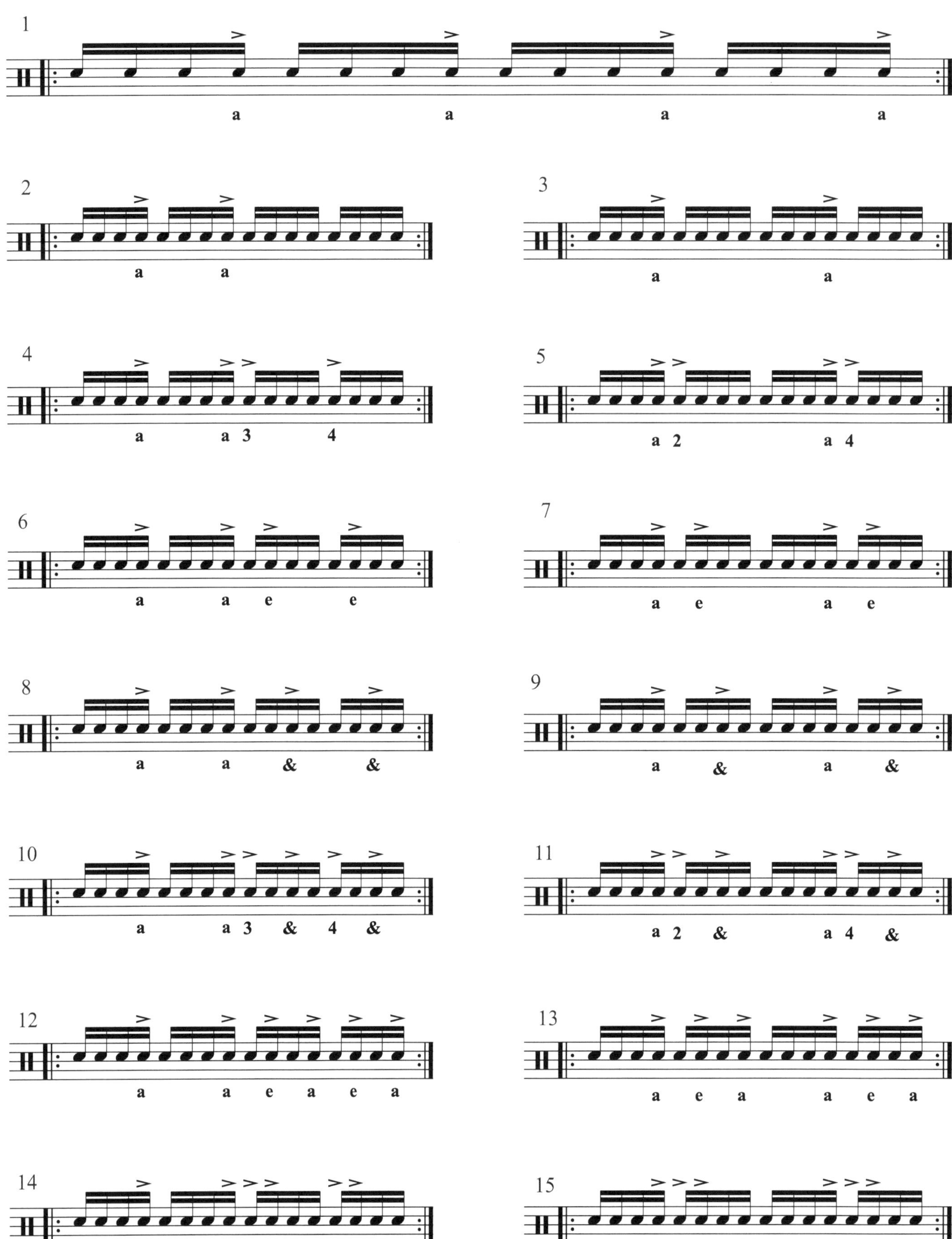

16th Note Accents

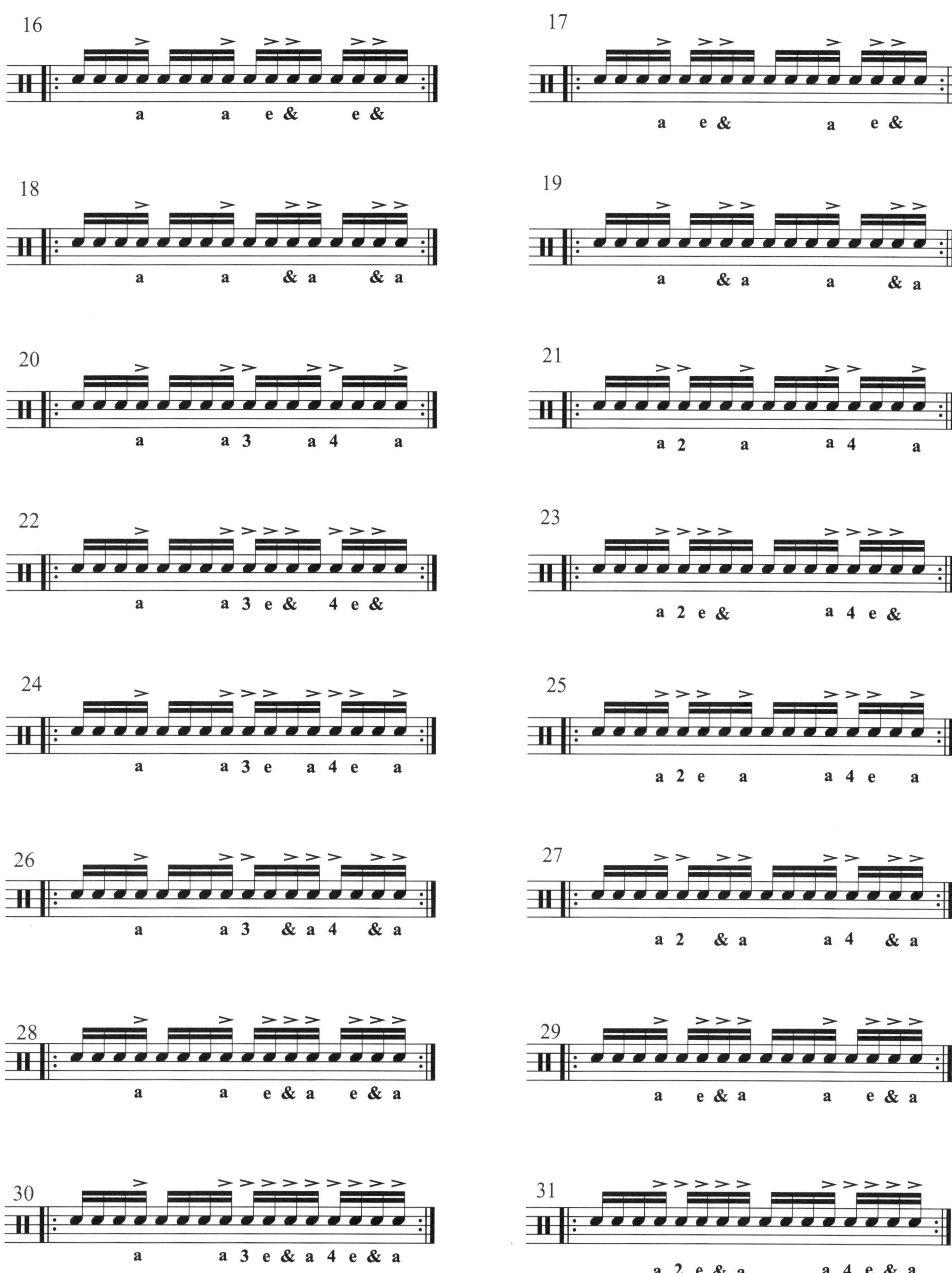

16th Note Accents

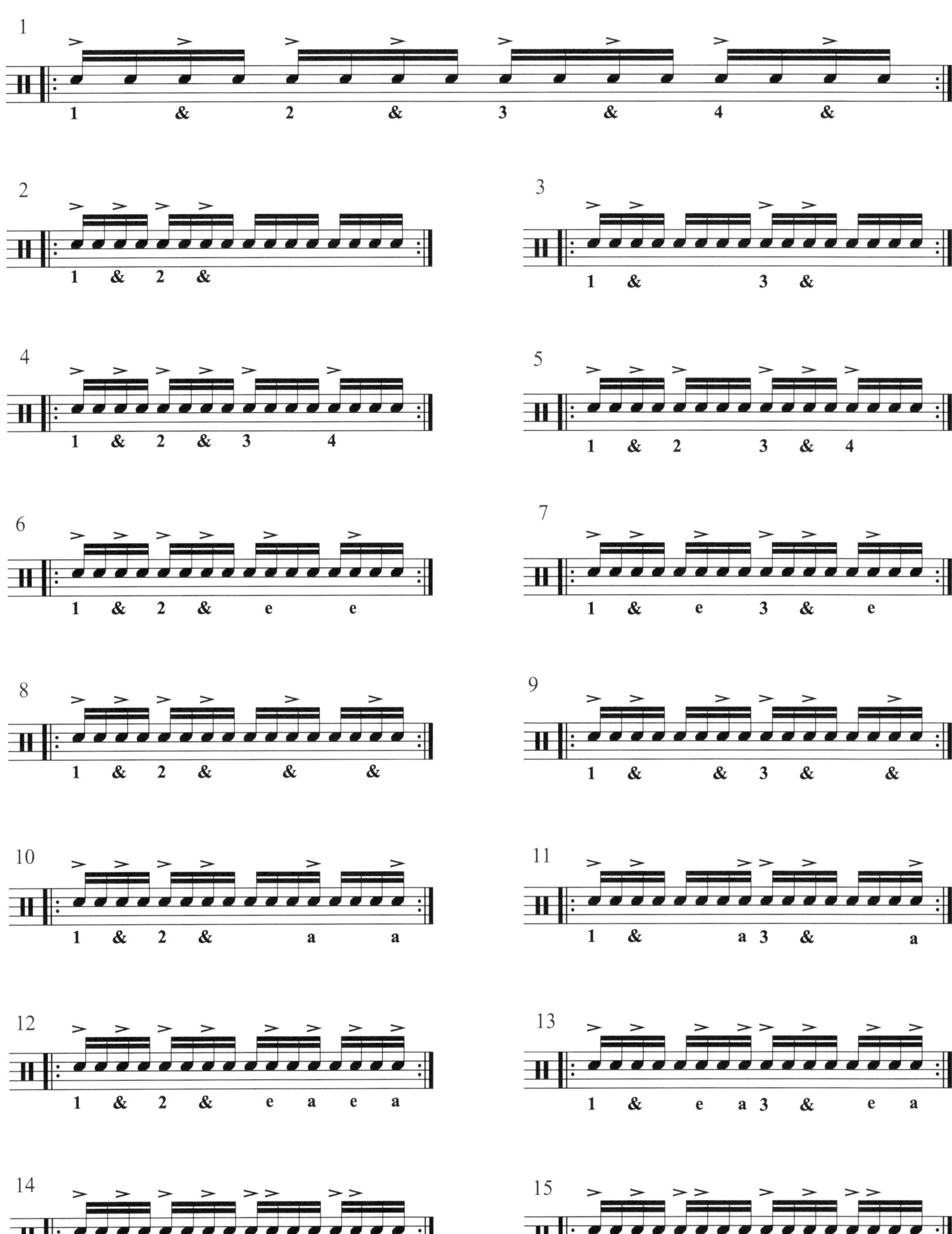

16th Note Accents

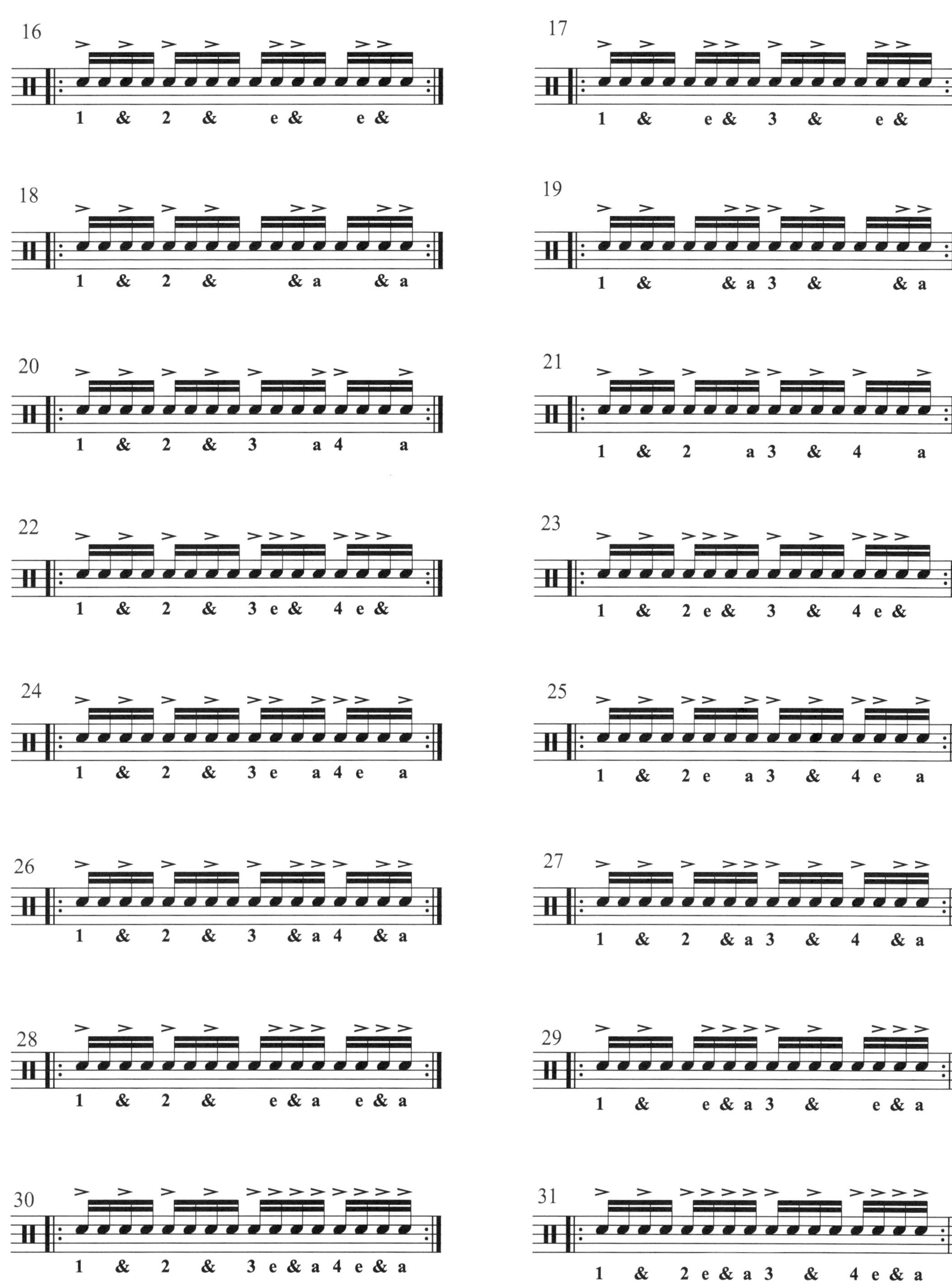

16th Note Accents

1

2

3

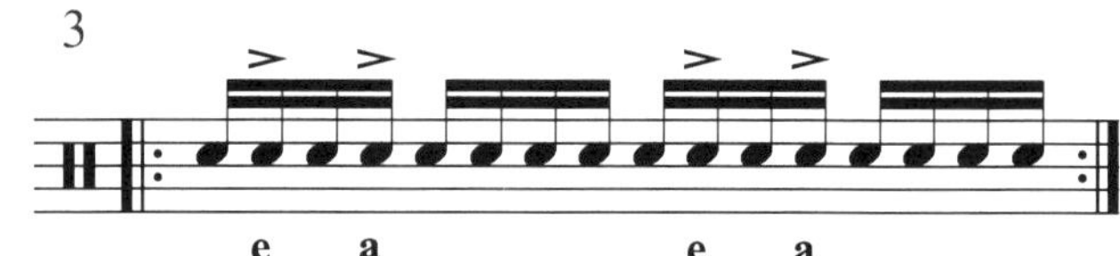

4

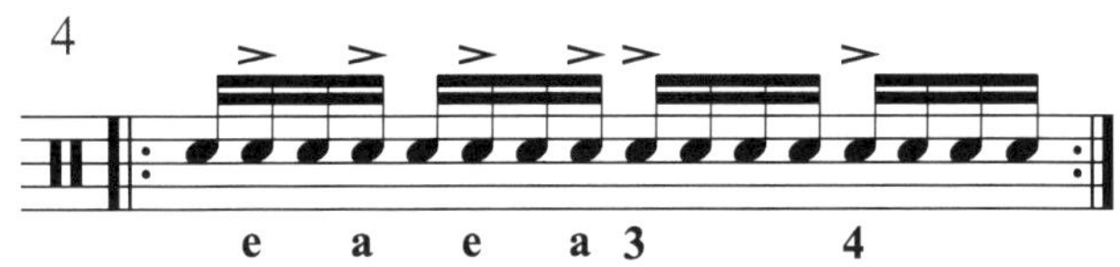

5

6

7

8

9

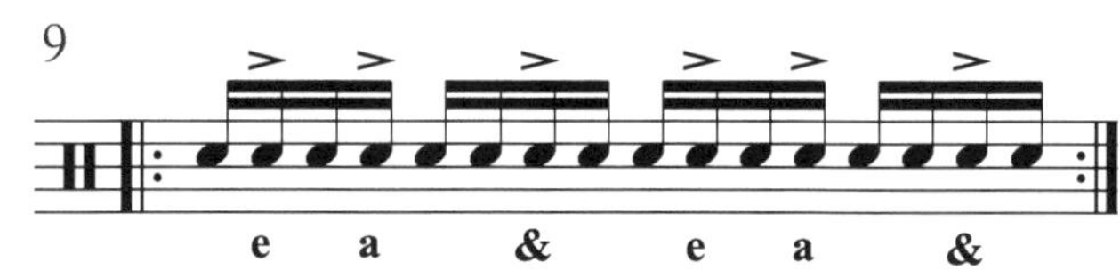

10

11

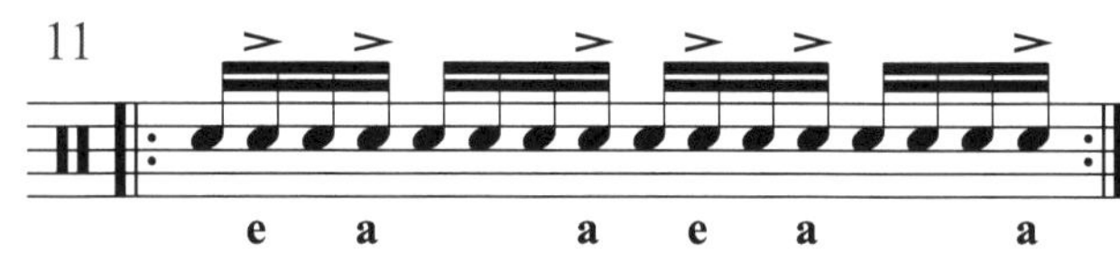

12

13

14

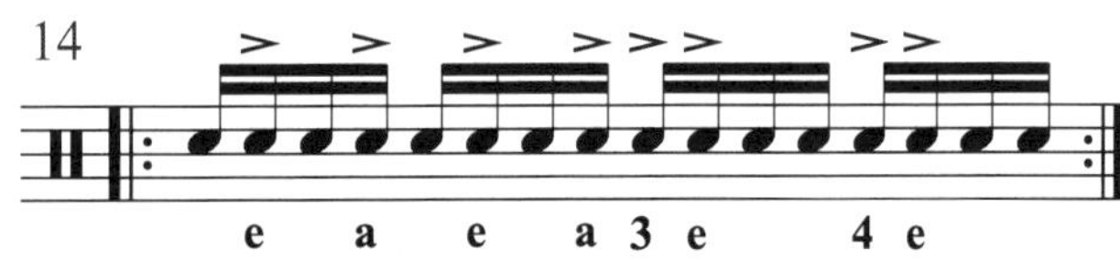

15

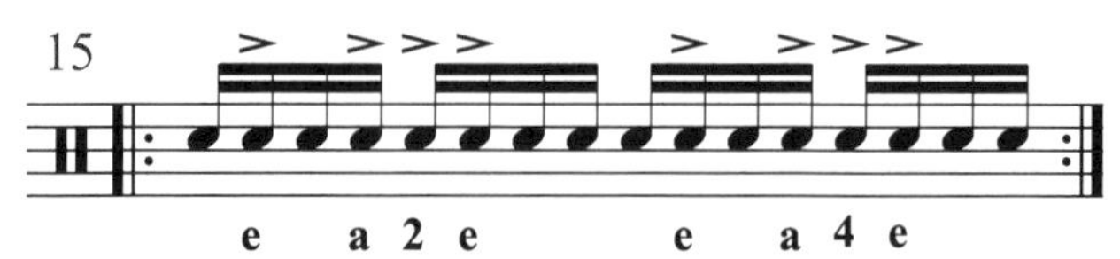

16th Note Accents

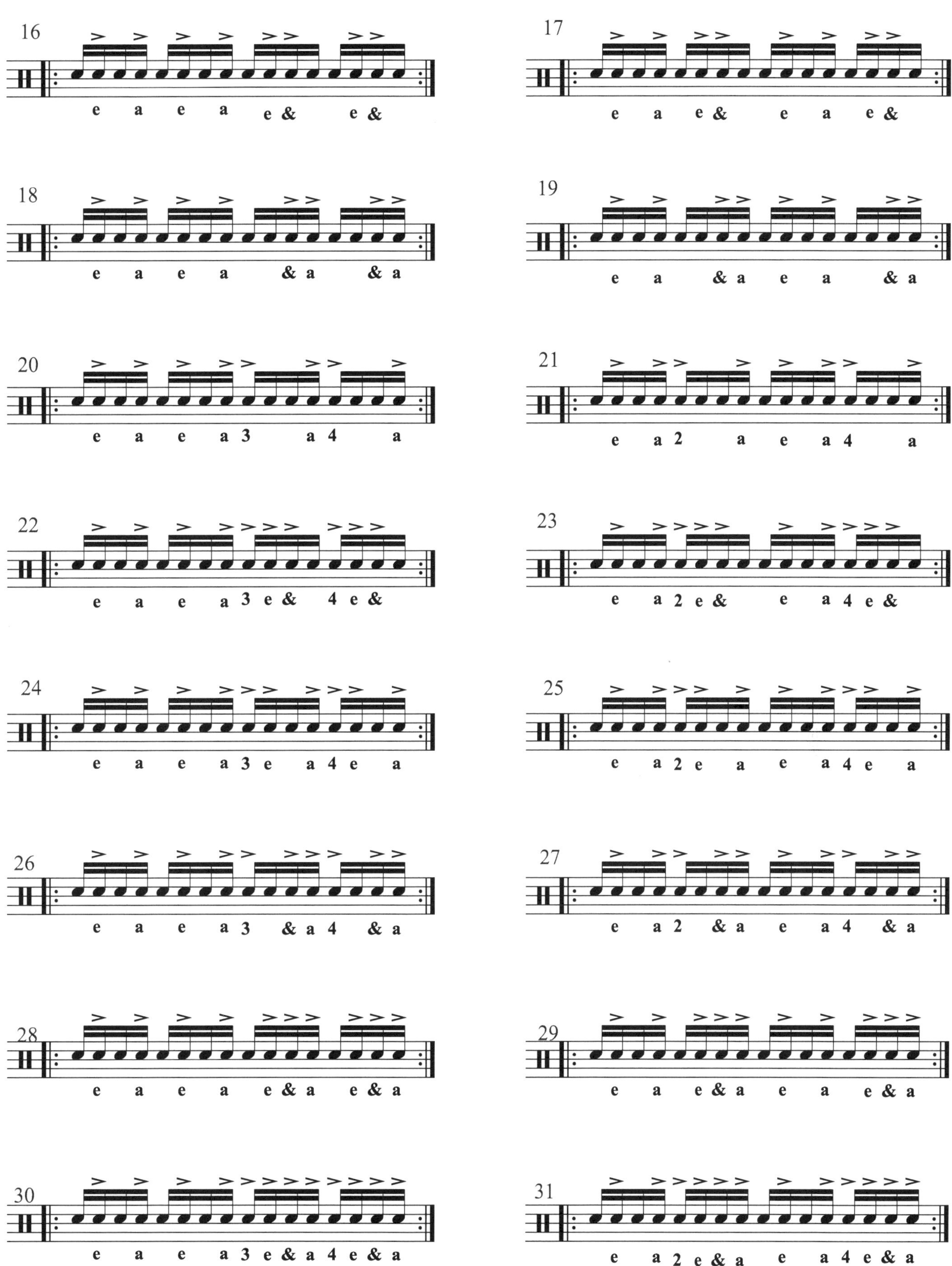

16th Note Accents

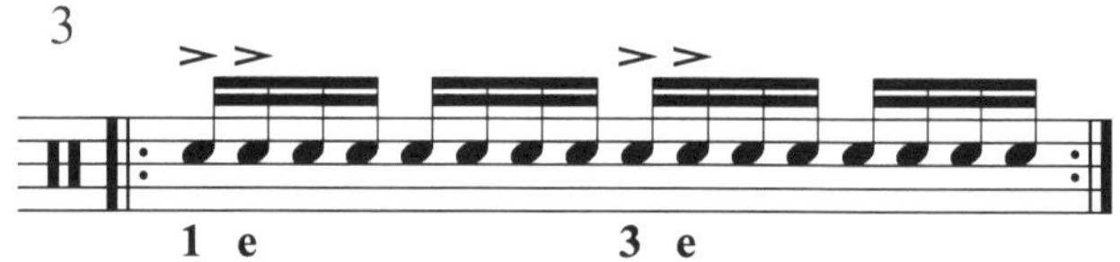

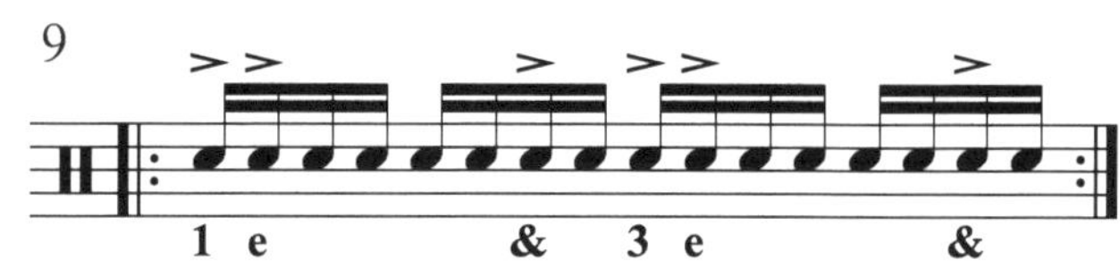

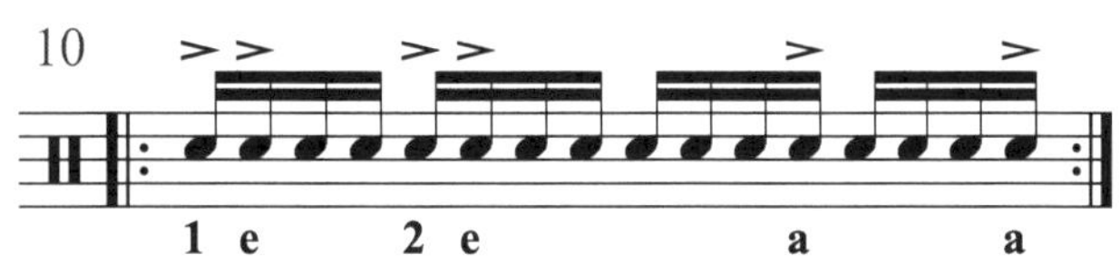

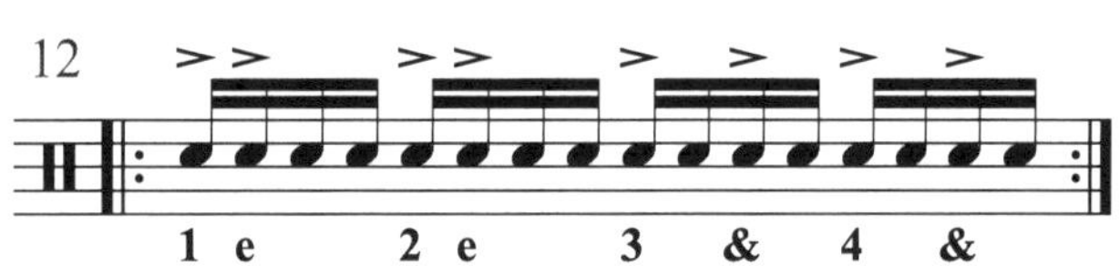

16th Note Accents

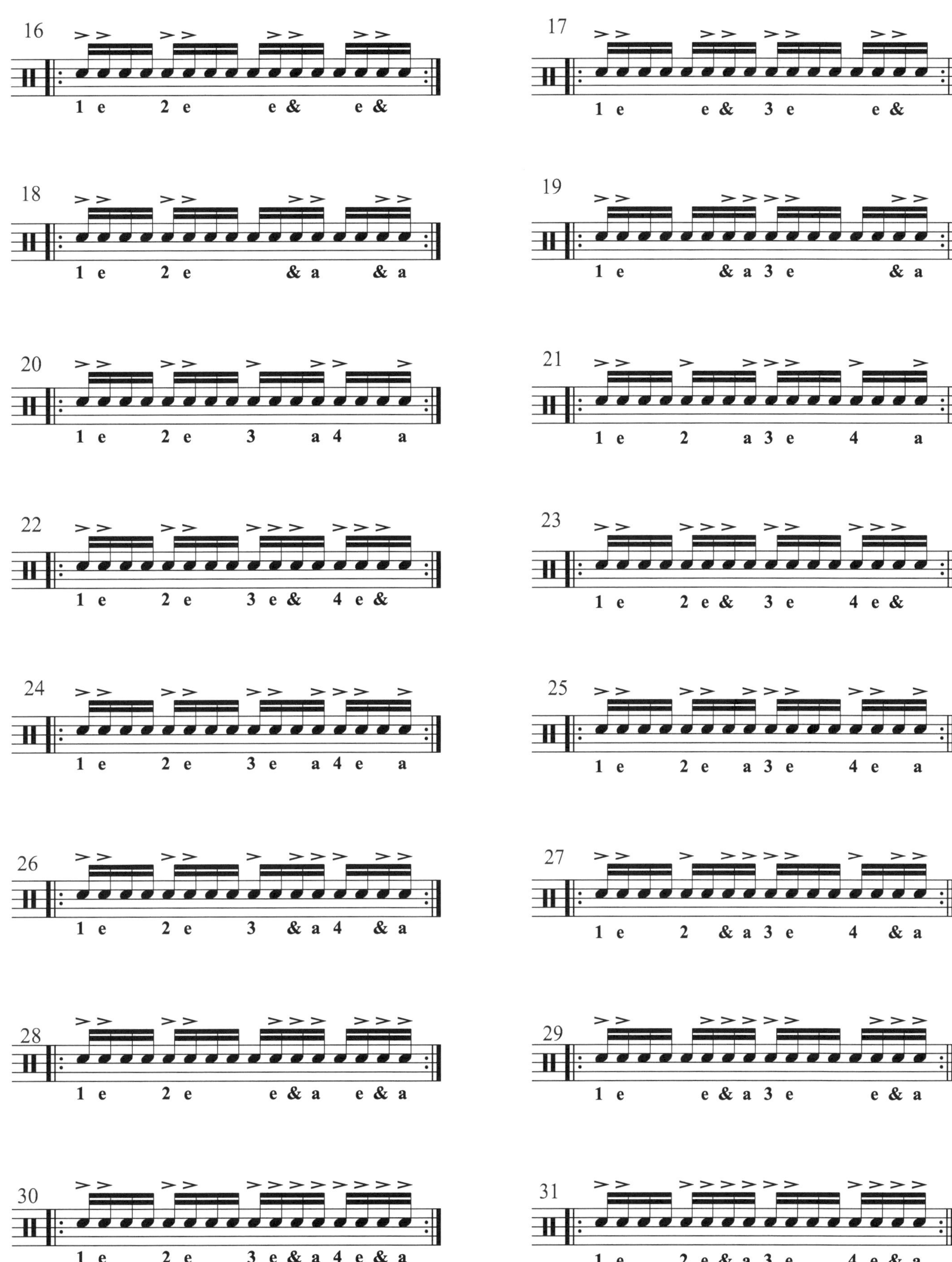

16th Note Accents

1

2

3

4

5

6

7

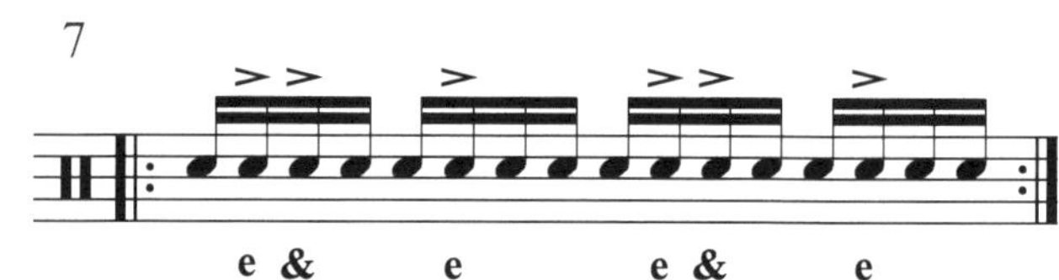

8

9

10

11

12

13

14

15

16th Note Accents

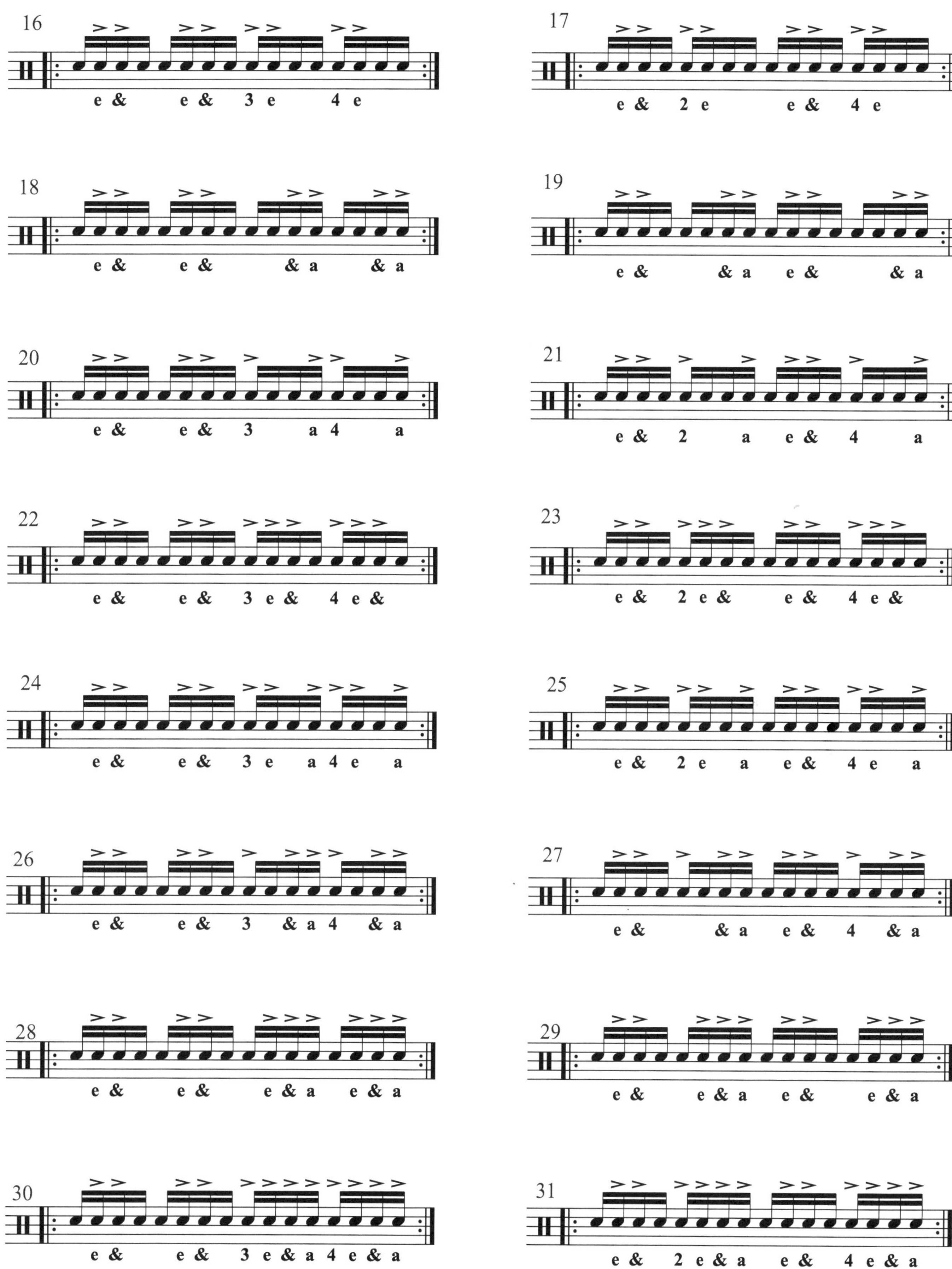

16th Note Accents

1

2

3

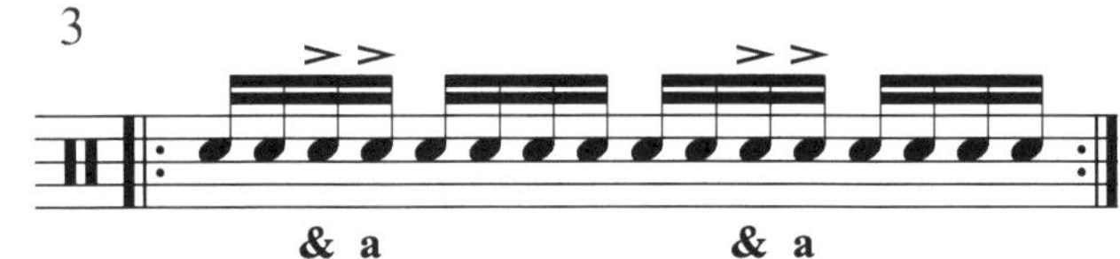

4

5

6

7

8

9

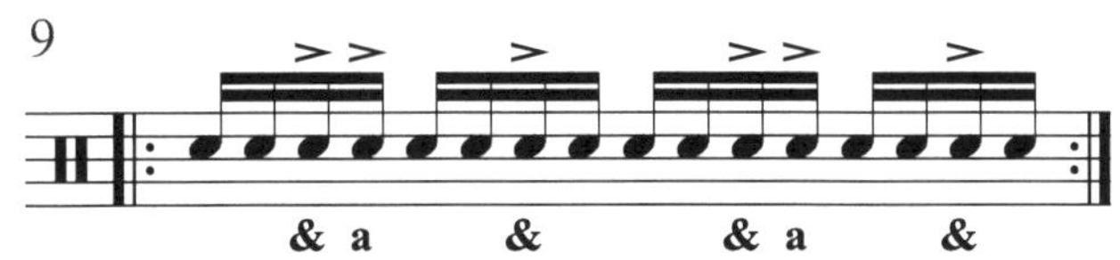

10

11

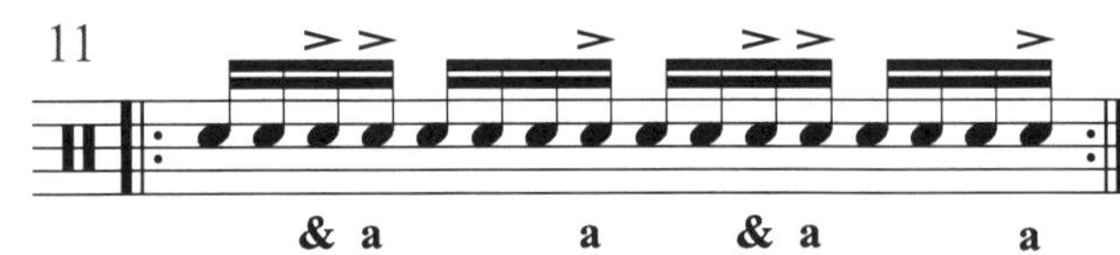

12

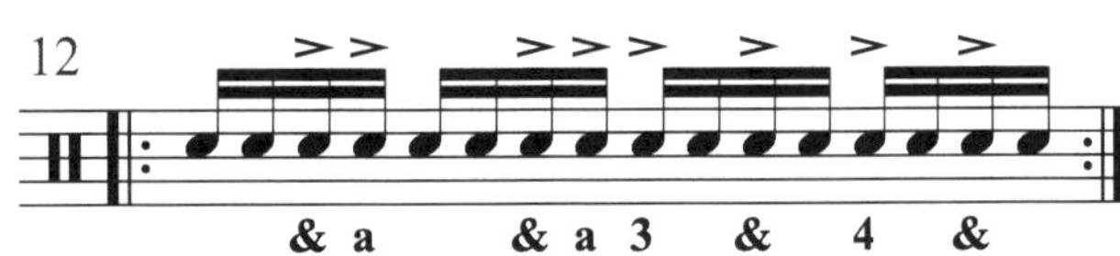

13

14

15

16th Note Accents

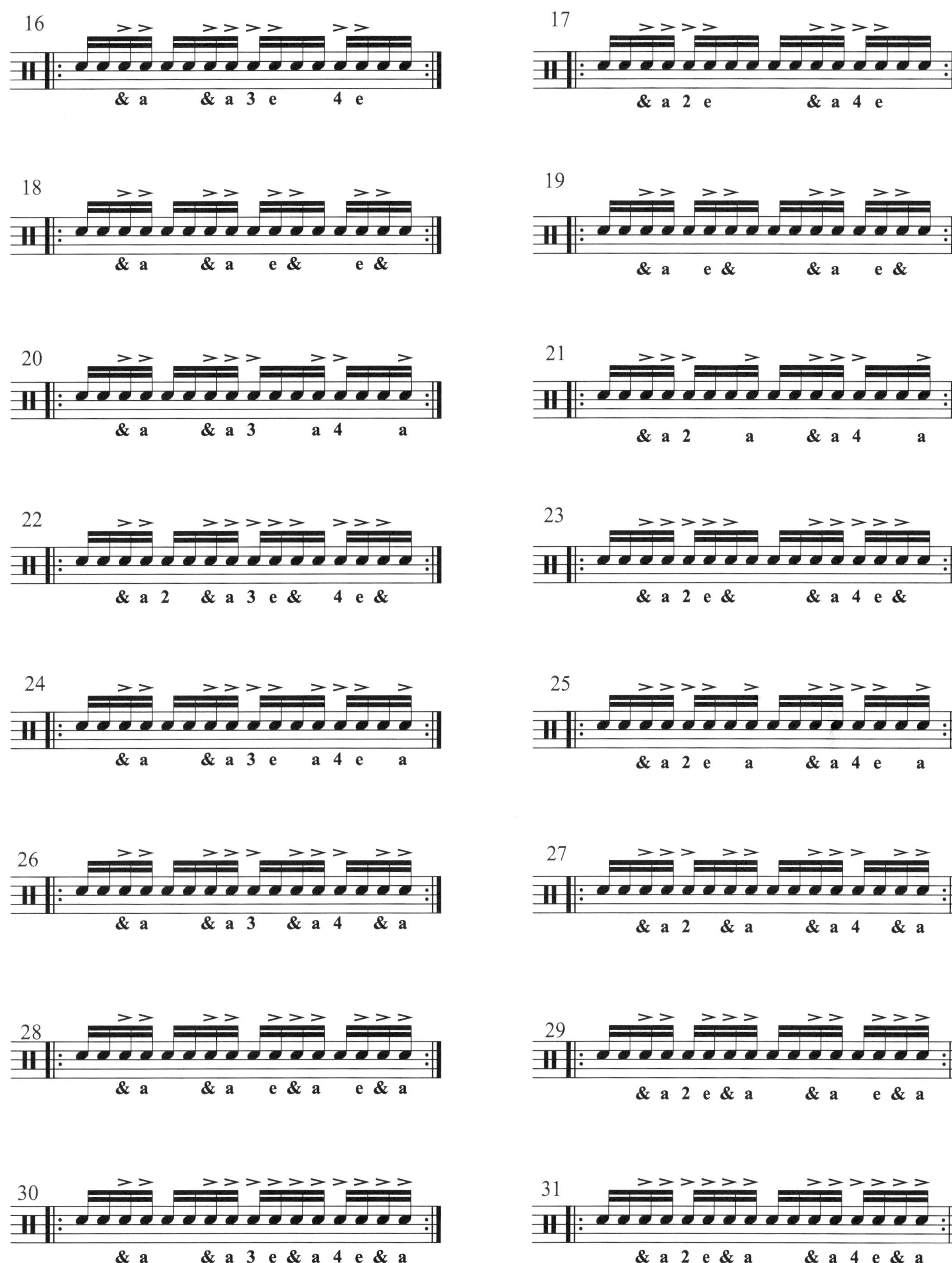

16th Note Accents

1

2

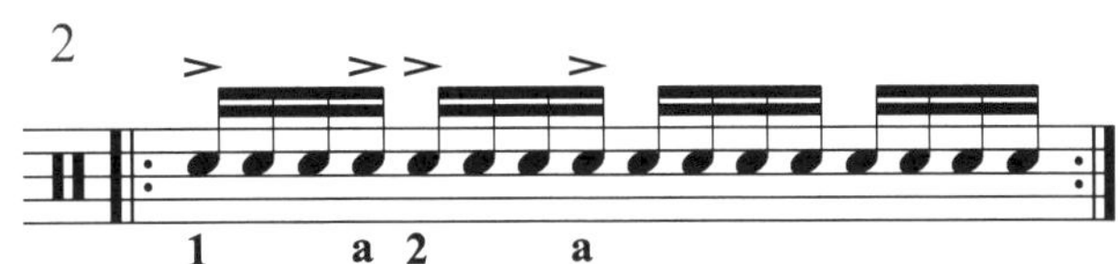

3

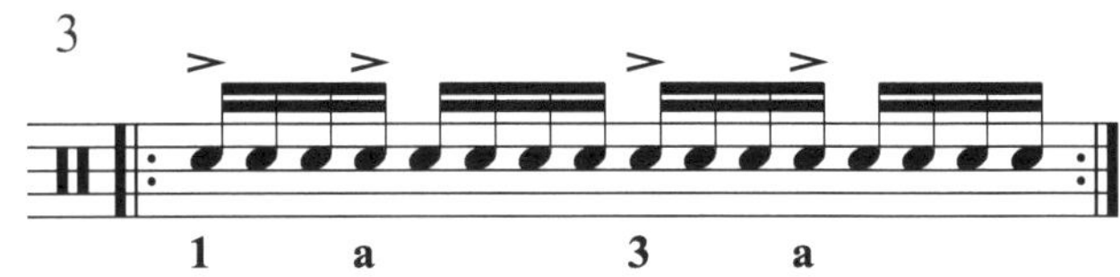

4

5

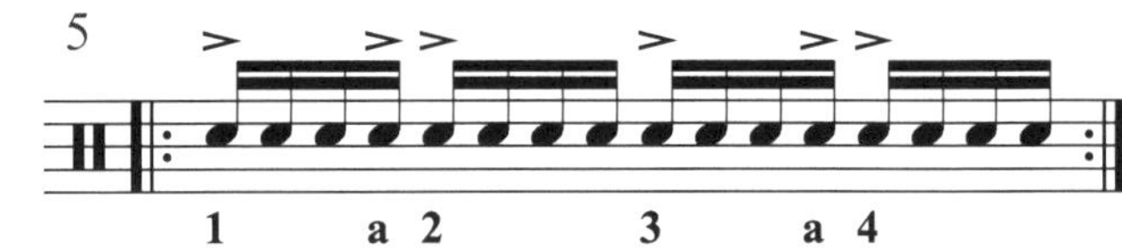

6

7

8

9

10

11

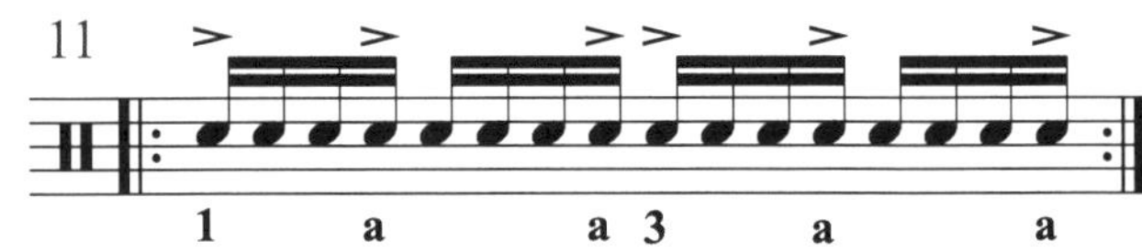

12

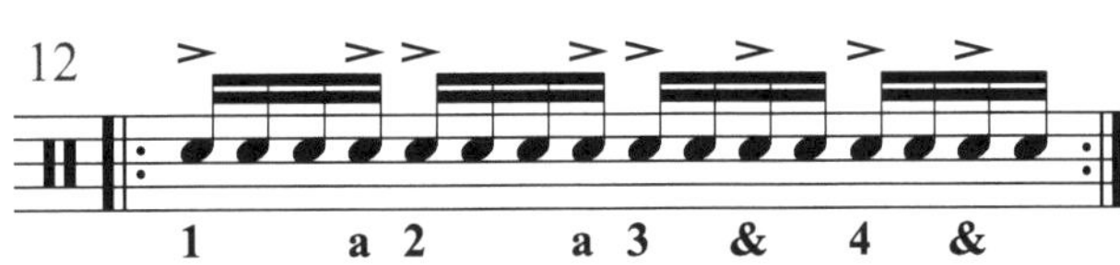

13

14

15

16th Note Accents

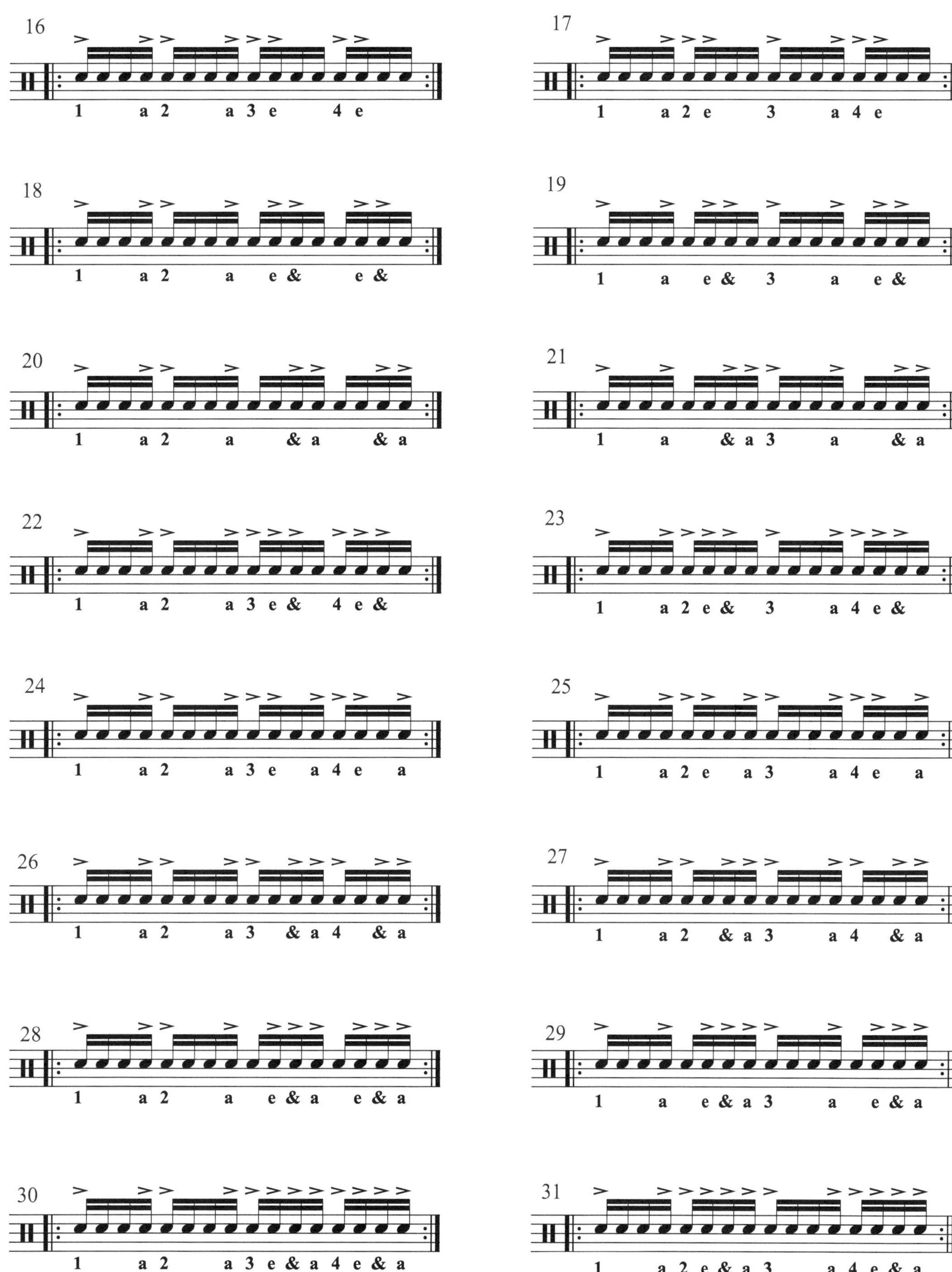

16th Note Accents

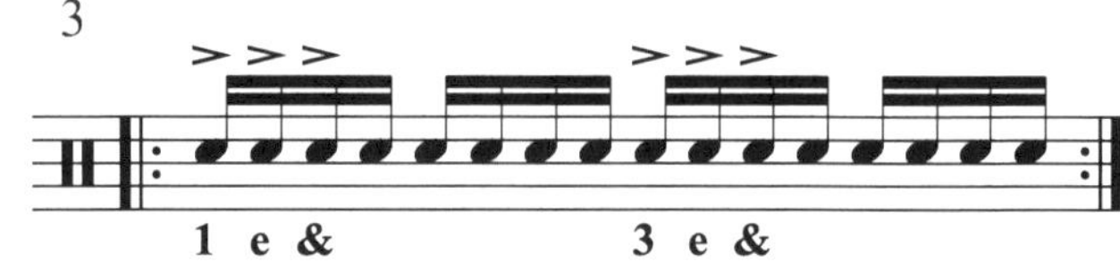

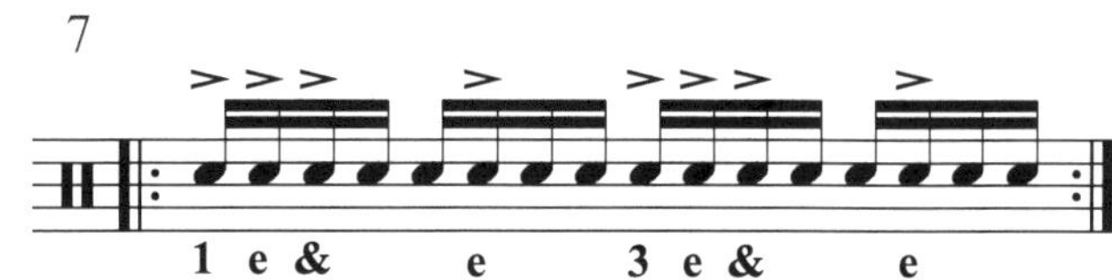

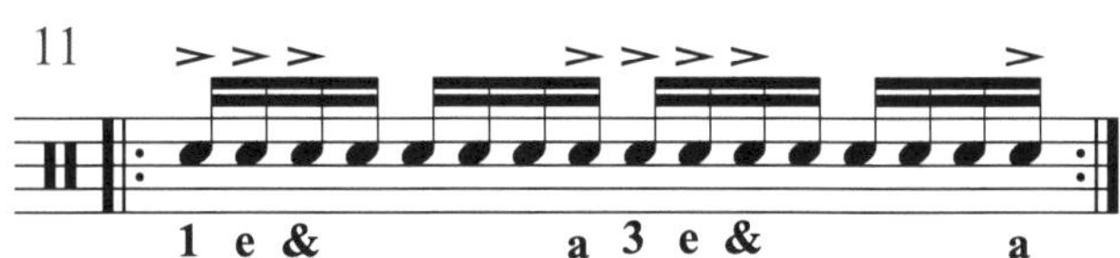

16th Note Accents

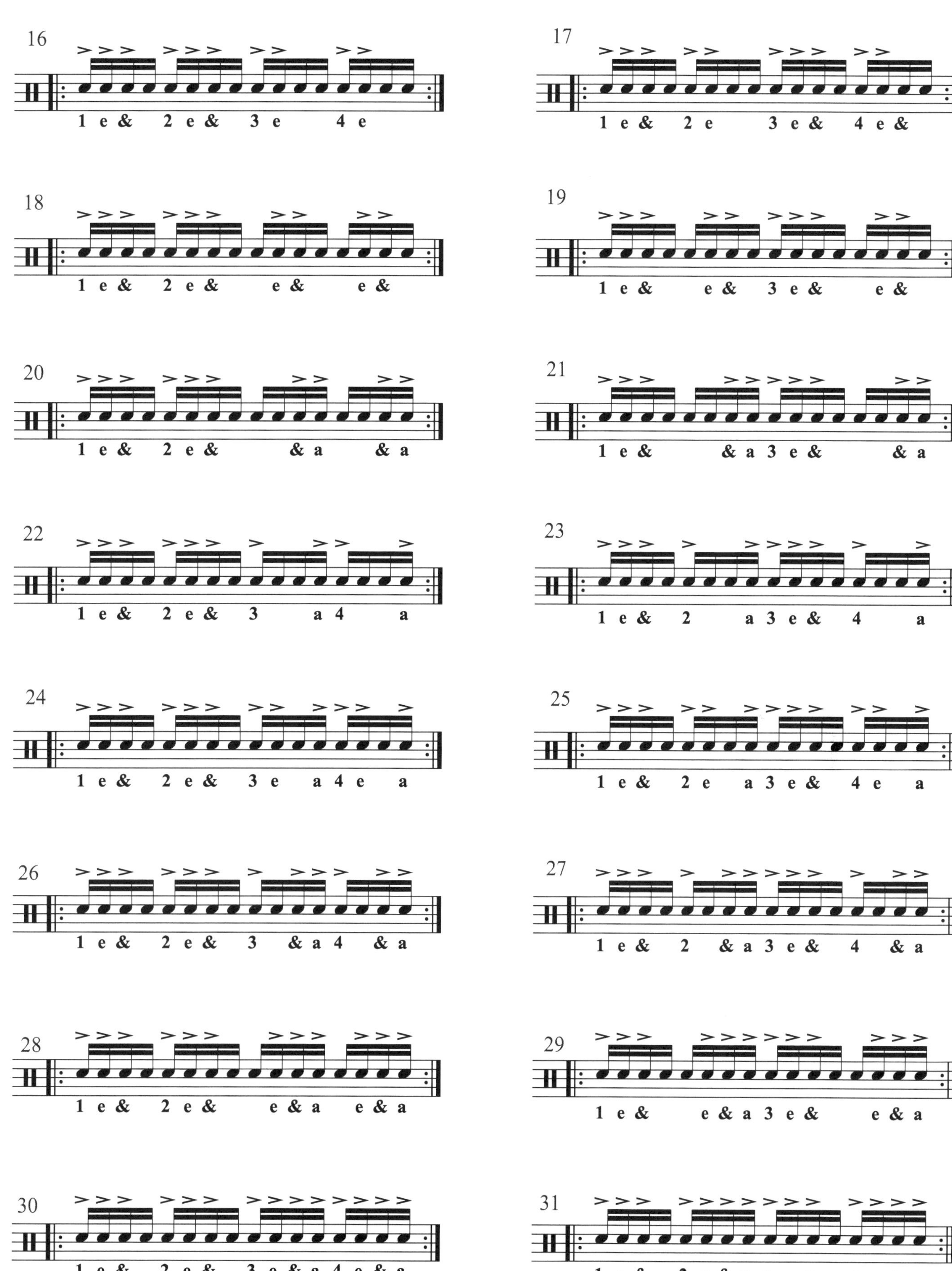

16th Note Accents

1

2

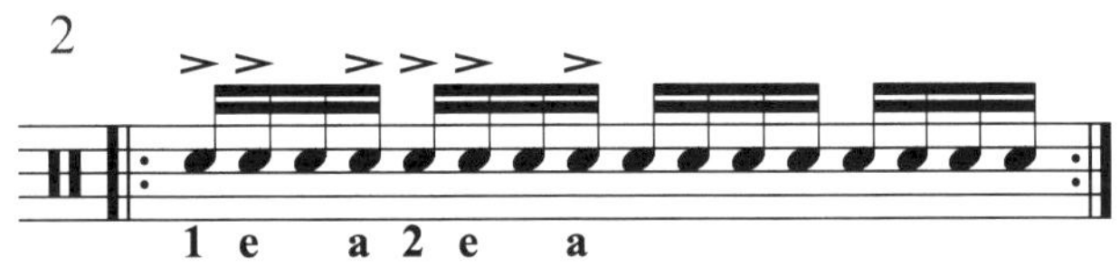

3

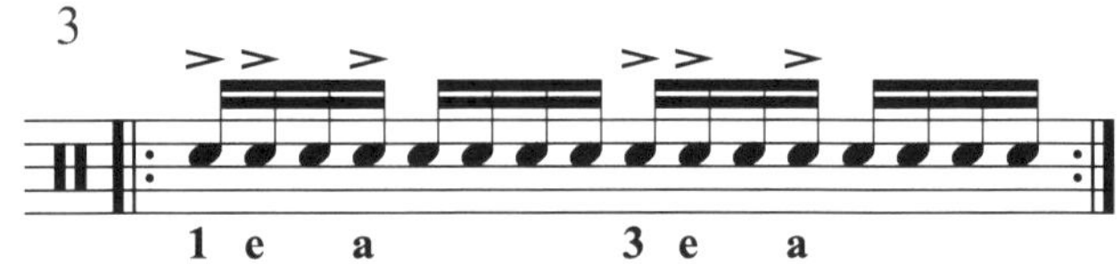

4

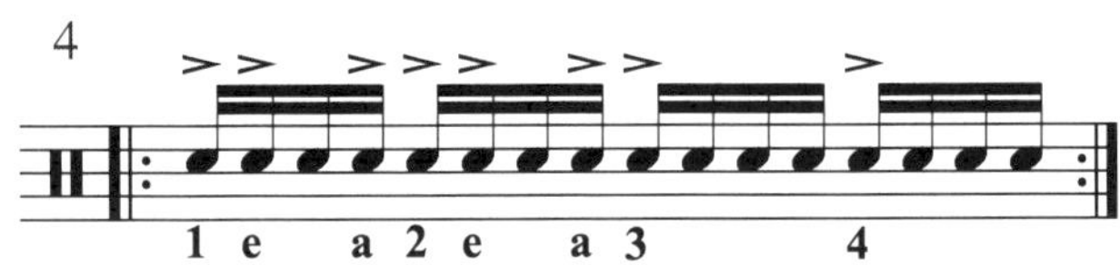

5

6

7

8

9

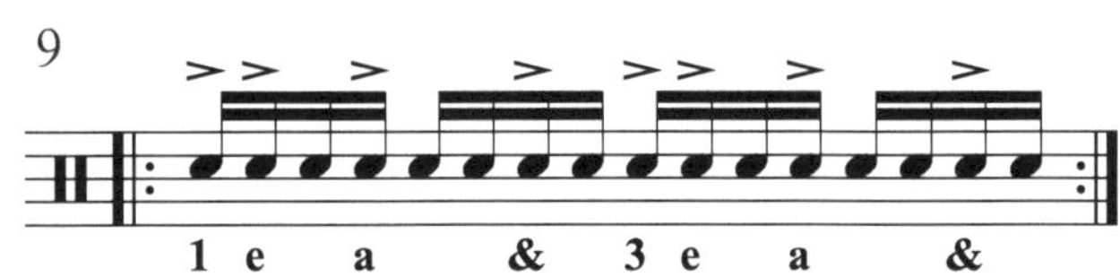

10

11

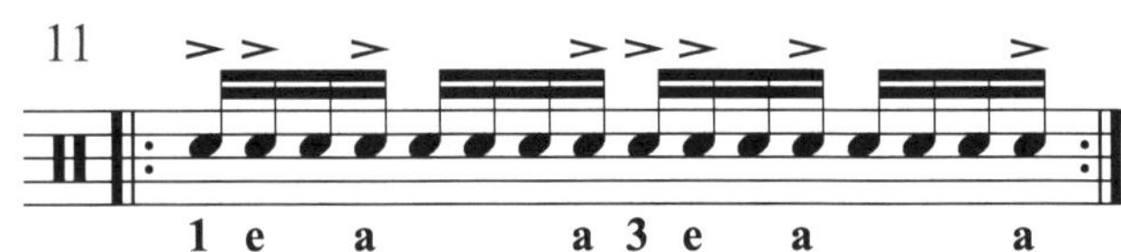

12

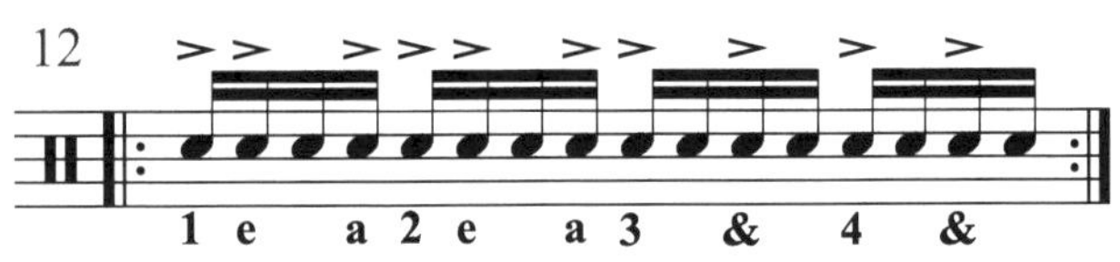

13

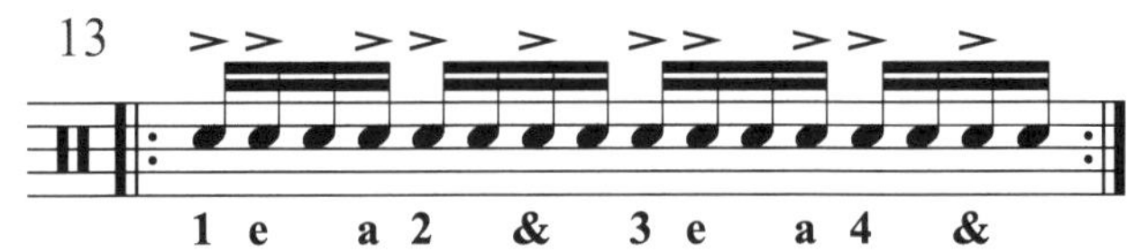

14

15

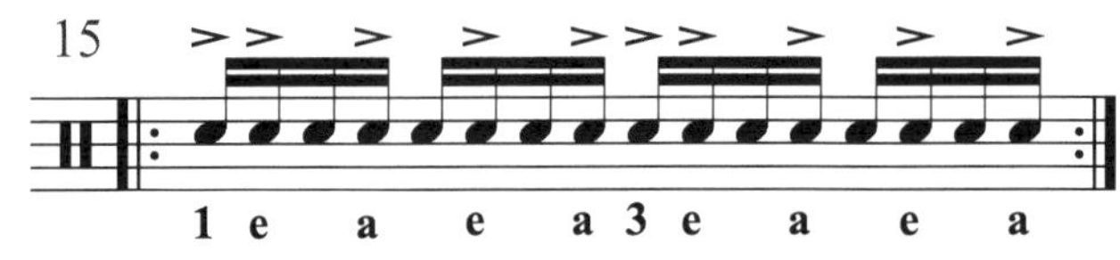

16th Note Accents

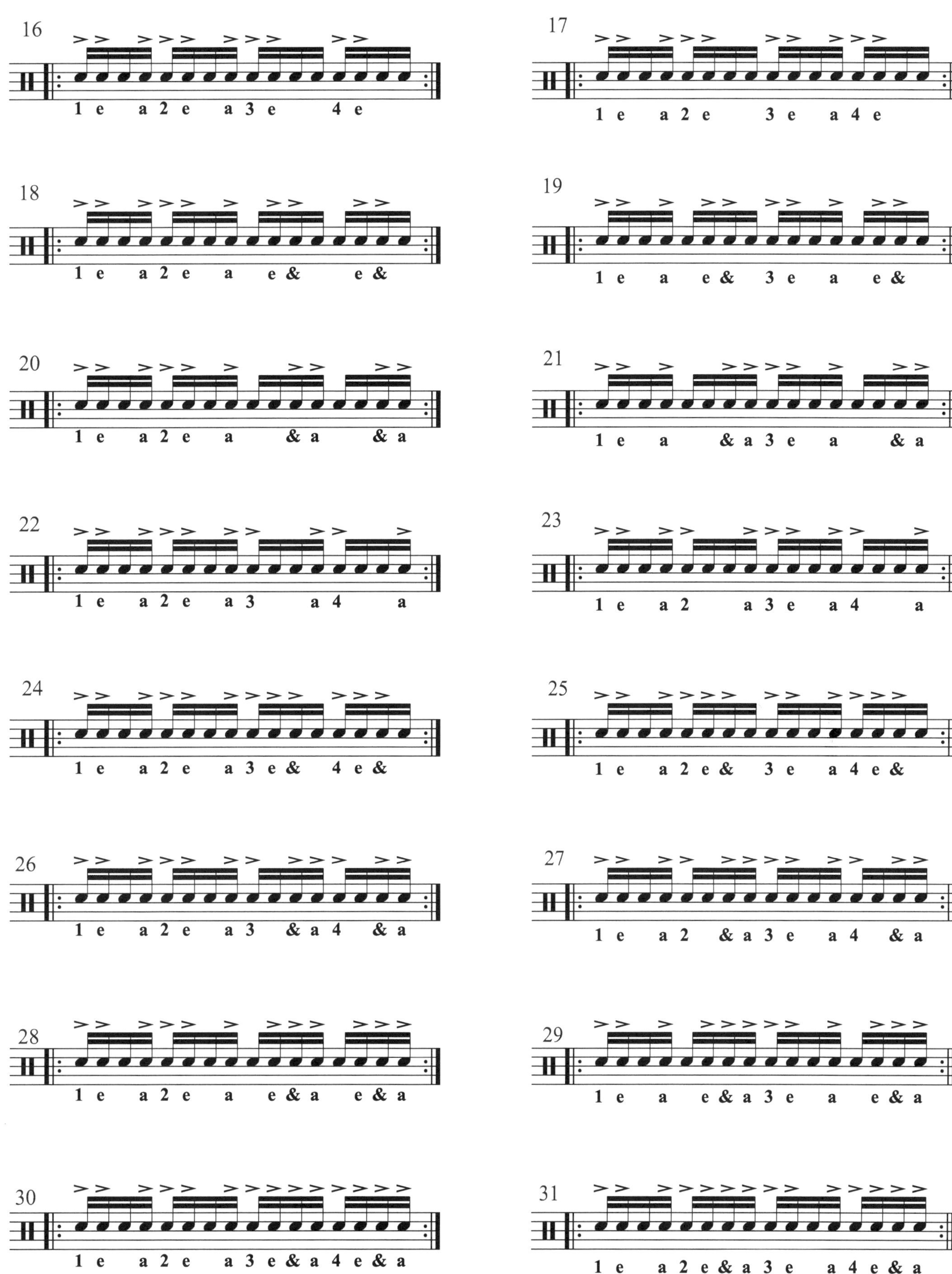

16th Note Accents

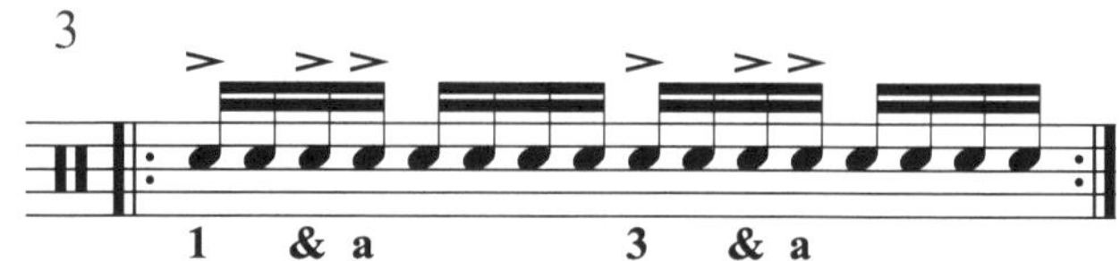

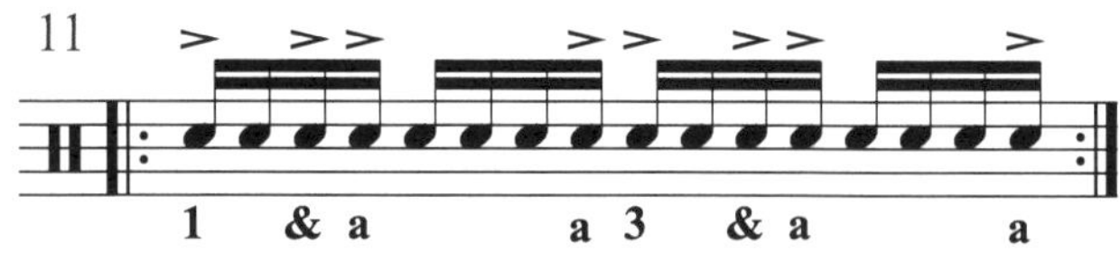

16th Note Accents

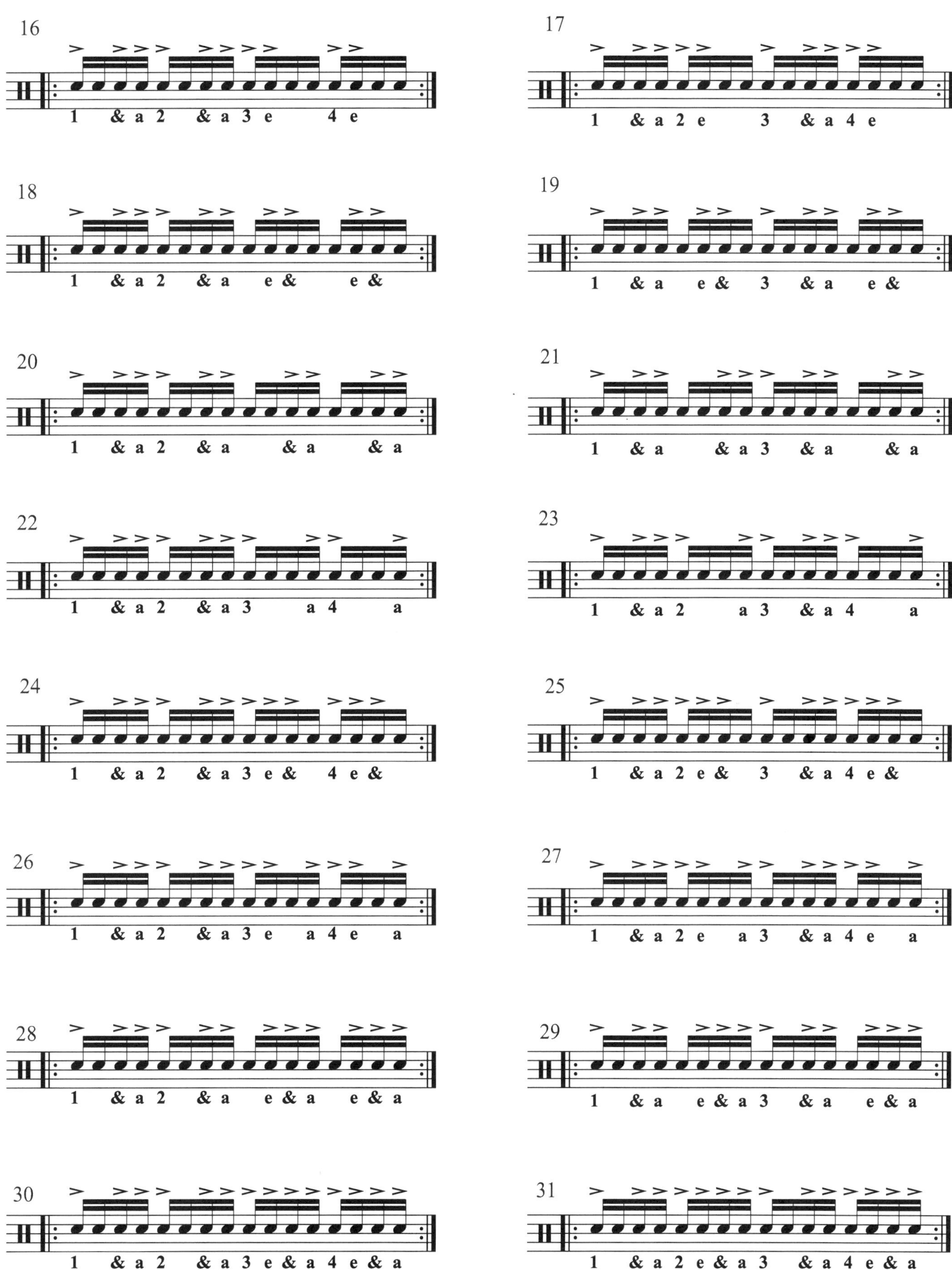

16th Note Accents

1

2

3

4

5

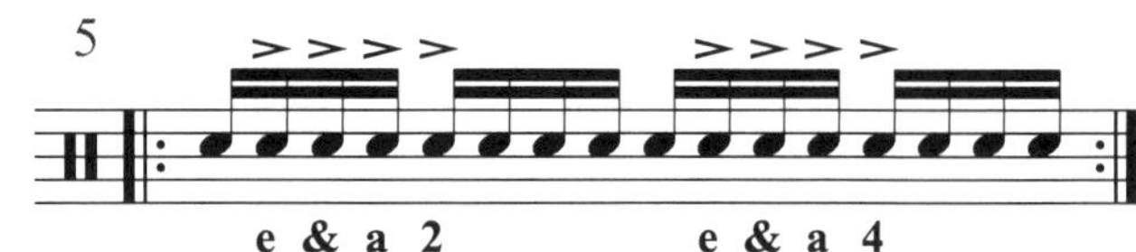

6

7

8

9

10

11

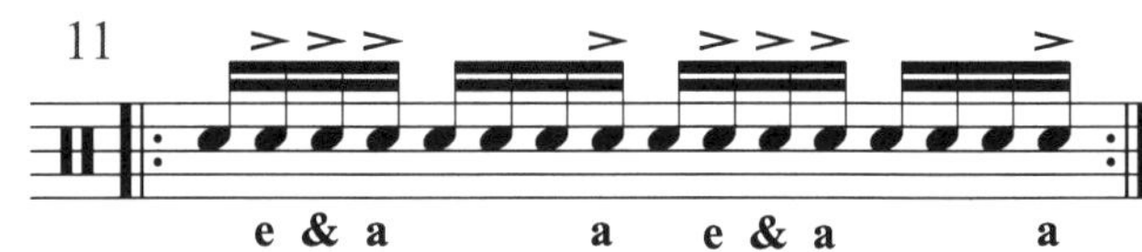

12

13

14

15

16th Note Accents

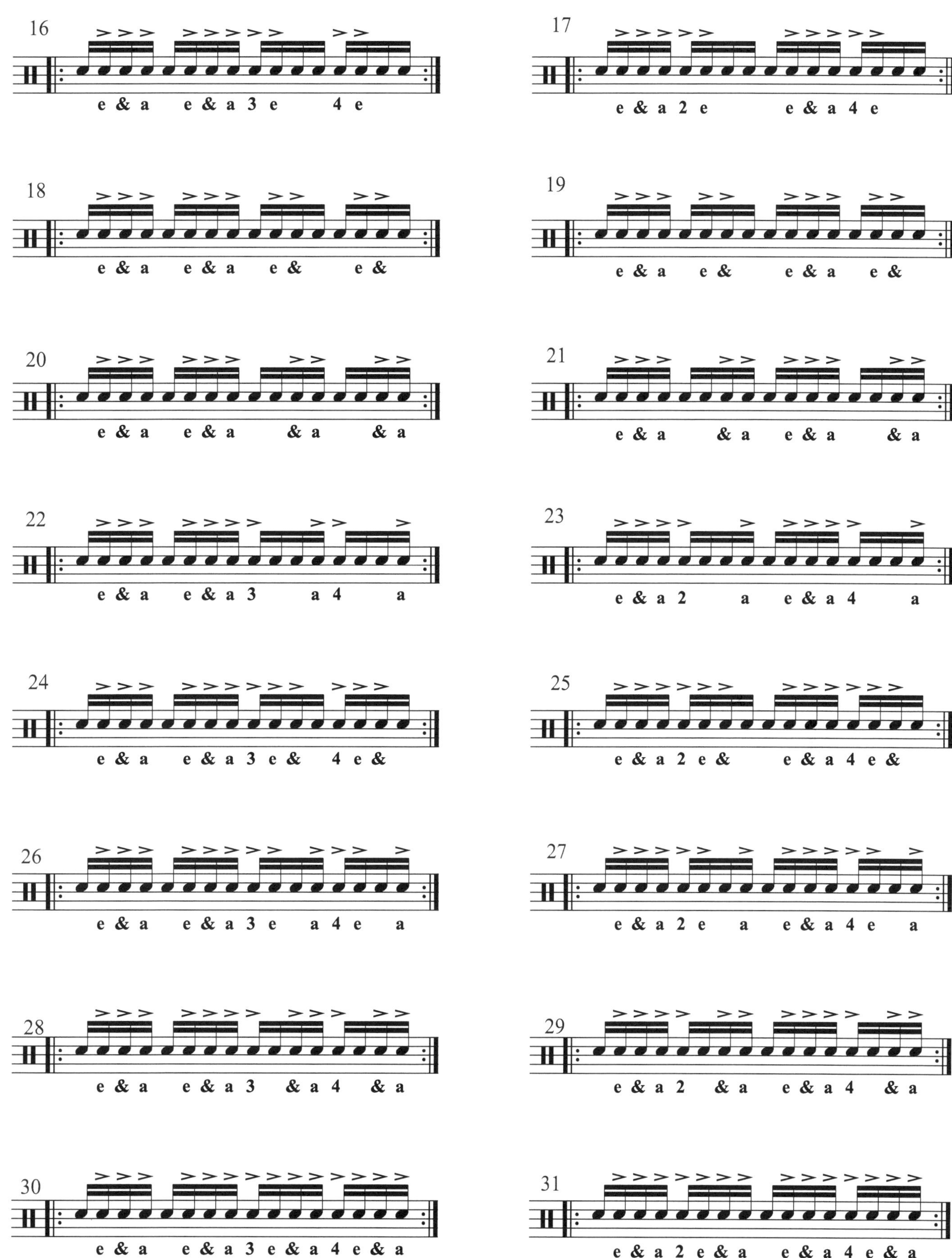

16th Note Accents

1

2

3

4

5

6

7

8

9

10

11

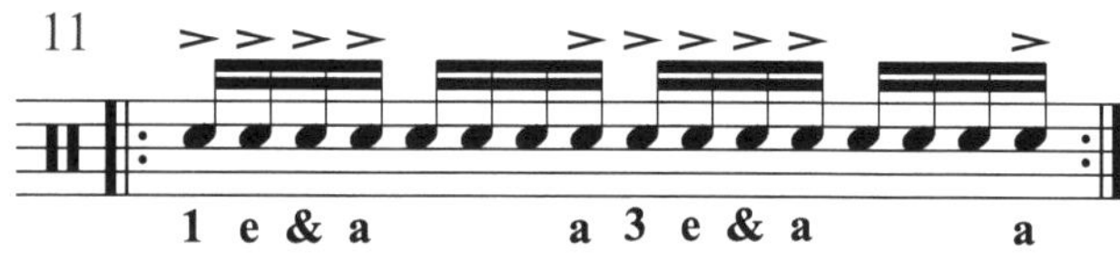

12

13

14

15

16th Note Accents

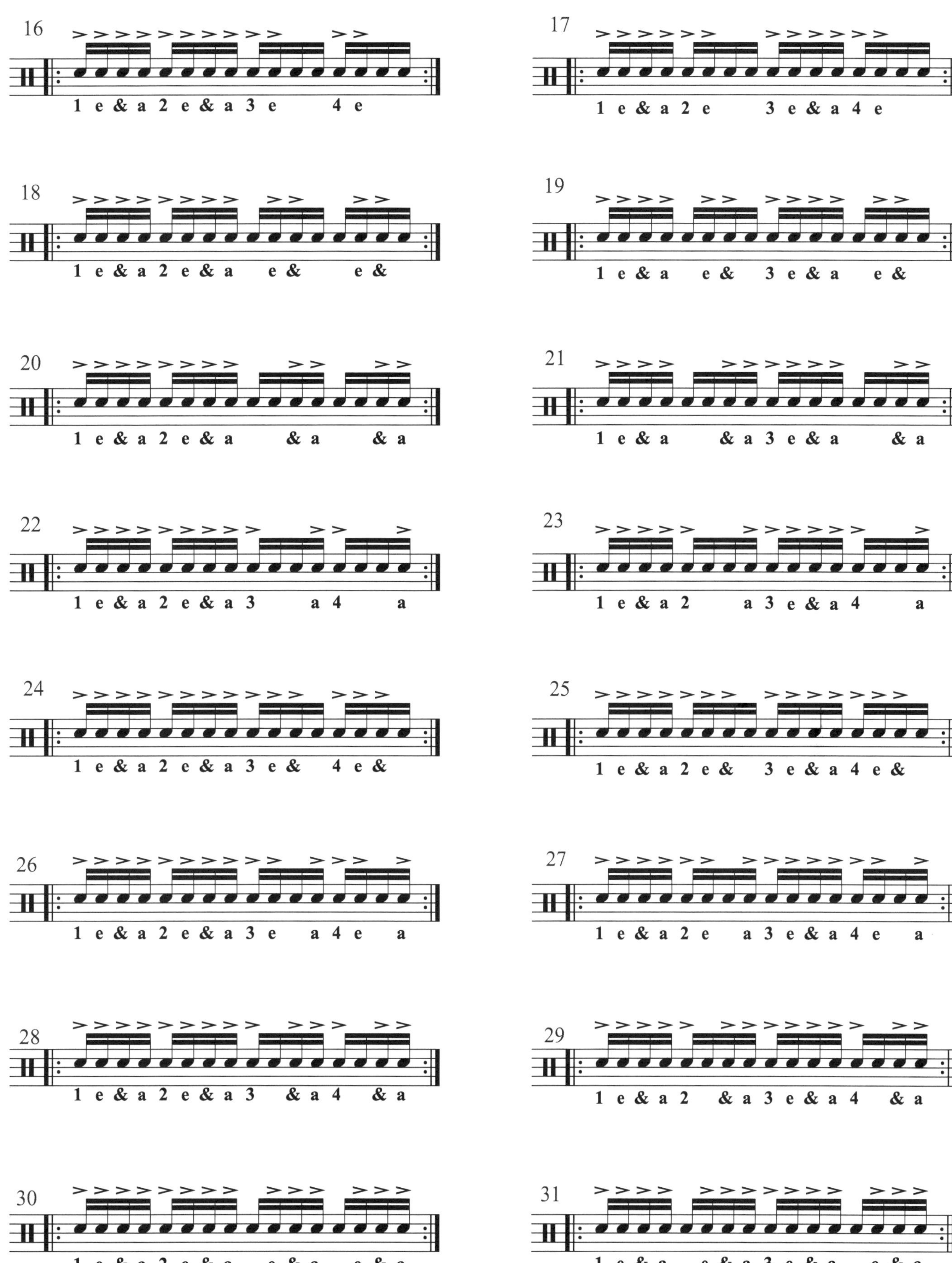

Subdivisions Per Beat

16th Note Rhythmic Alphabet

1
1 e & a 2 e & a 3 e & a 4 e & a
2
1 e & 2 e & 3 e & 4 e &
3
1 e a 2 e a 3 e a 4 e a
4
1 & a 2 & a 3 & a 4 & a
5
e & a e & a e & a e & a
6
1 e 2 e 3 e 4 e
7
e & e & e & e &
8
& a & a & a & a
9
1 a 2 a 3 a 4 a
10
1 & 2 & 3 & 4 &
11
e a e a e a e a
12
1 2 3 4
13
e e e e
14
& & & &
15
a a a a
16

16th Note Rhythms

1

2

3

4

5

6

7

8

9

10

11

12

13

14

15

16th Note Rhythms

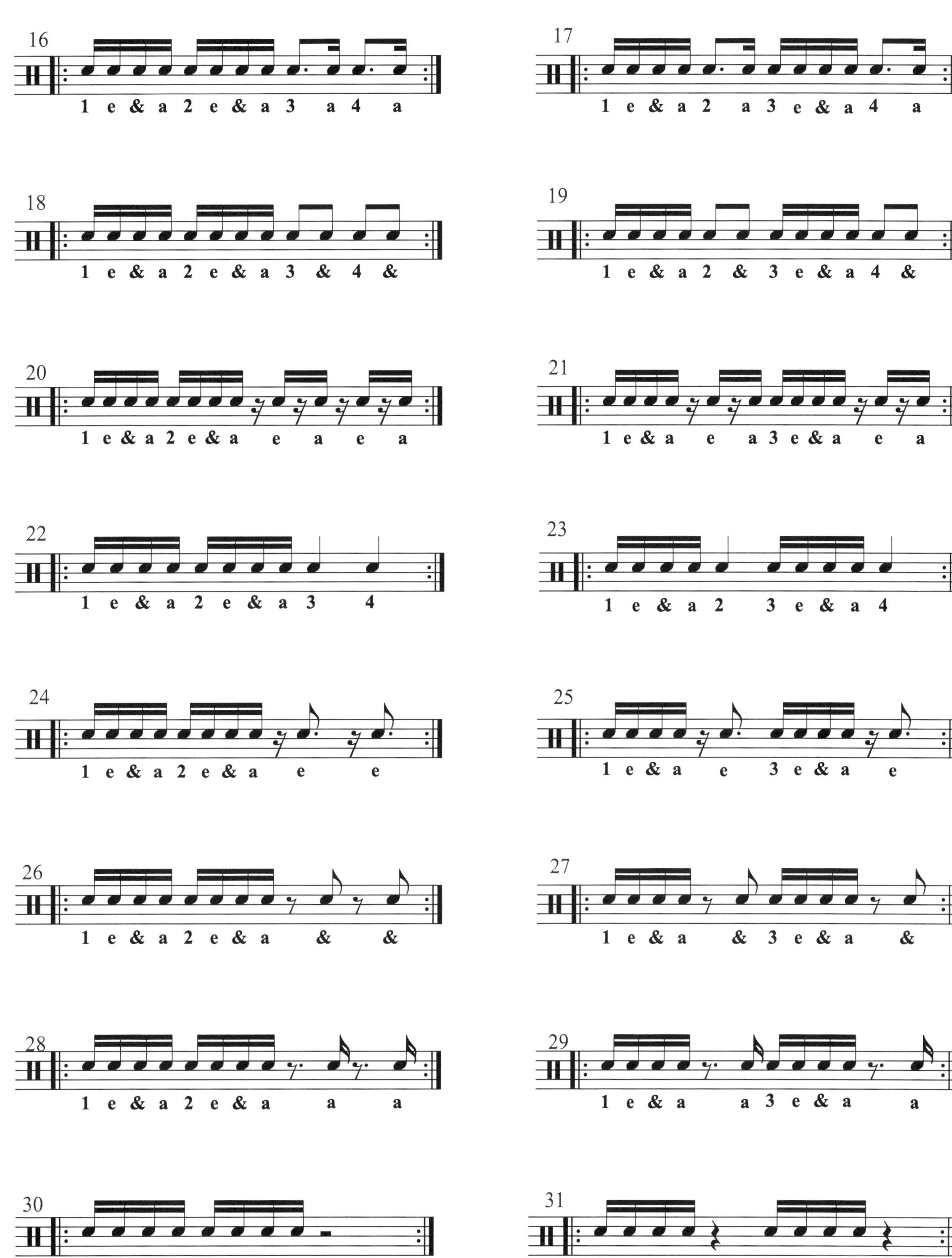

16th Note Rhythms

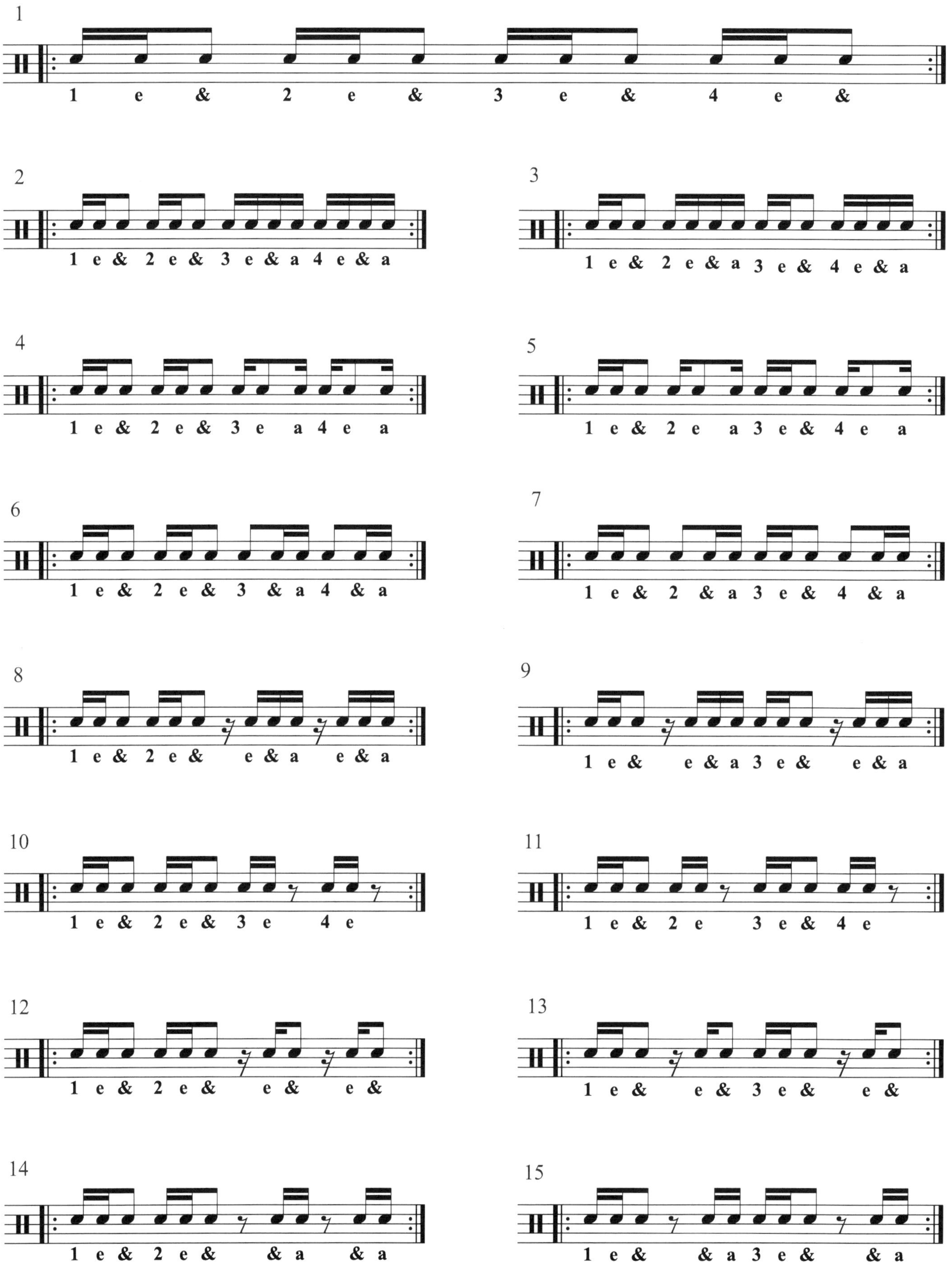

1

1 e & 2 e & 3 e & 4 e &

2

1 e & 2 e & 3 e & a 4 e & a

3

1 e & 2 e & a 3 e & 4 e & a

4

1 e & 2 e & 3 e a 4 e a

5

1 e & 2 e a 3 e & 4 e a

6

1 e & 2 e & 3 & a 4 & a

7

1 e & 2 & a 3 e & 4 & a

8

1 e & 2 e & e & a e & a

9

1 e & e & a 3 e & e & a

10

1 e & 2 e & 3 e 4 e

11

1 e & 2 e 3 e & 4 e

12

13

14

15

16th Note Rhythms

16th Note Rhythms

1

2

3

4

5

6

7

8

9

10

11

12

13

14

15

16th Note Rhythms

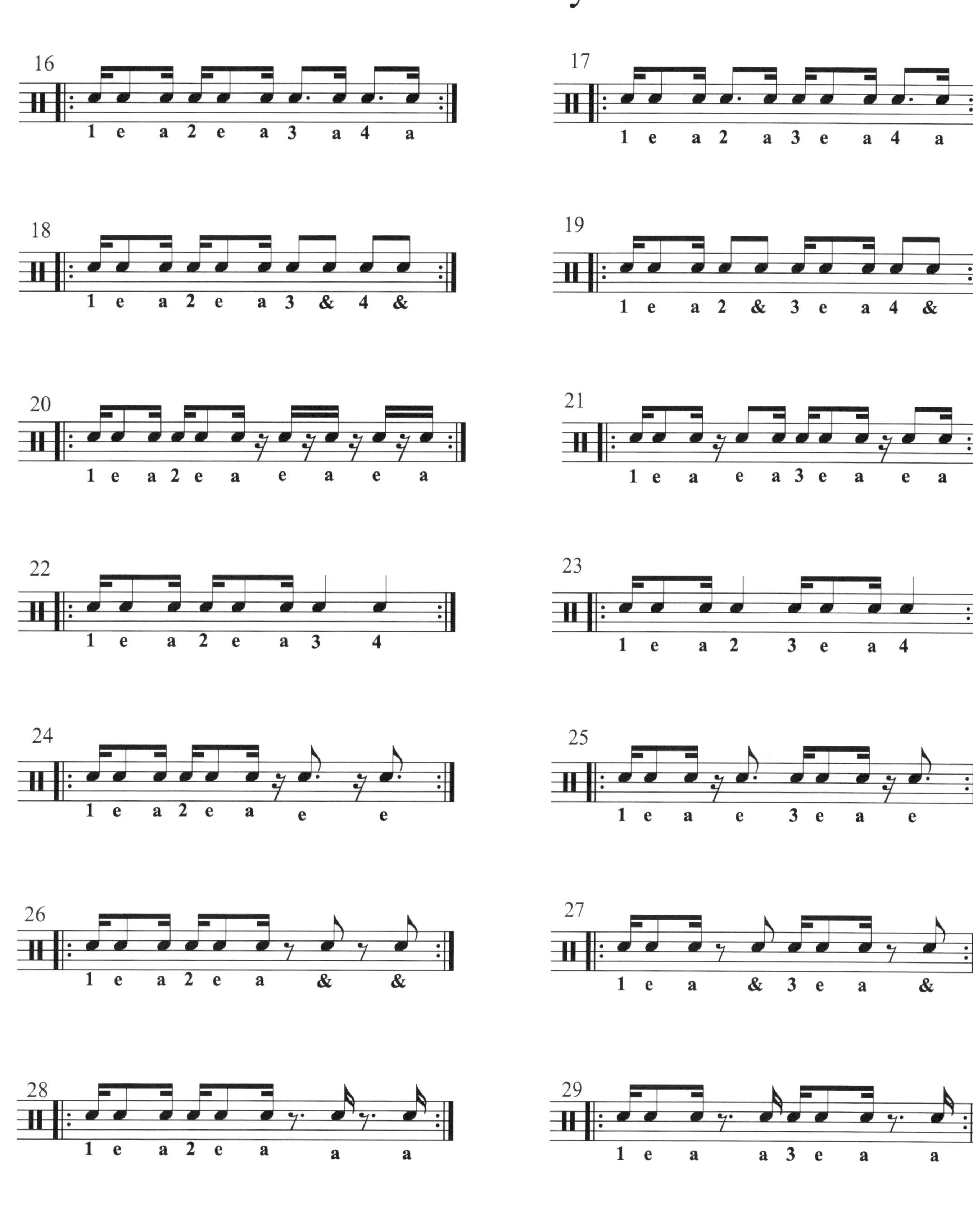

16th Note Rhythms

1

2

3

4

5

6

7

8

9

10

11

12

13

14

15

16th Note Rhythms

16th Note Rhythms

1

2

3

4

5

6

7

8

9

10

11

12

13

14

15

16th Note Rhythms

16th Note Rhythms

1

2

3

4

5

6

7

8

9

10

11

12

13

14

15

16th Note Rhythms

16th Note Rhythms

1

2

3

4

5

6

7

8

9

10

11

12

13

14

15

16th Note Rhythms

16th Note Rhythms

16th Note Rhythms

16th Note Rhythms

1

2

3

4

5

6

7

8

9

10

11

12

13

14

15

16th Note Rhythms

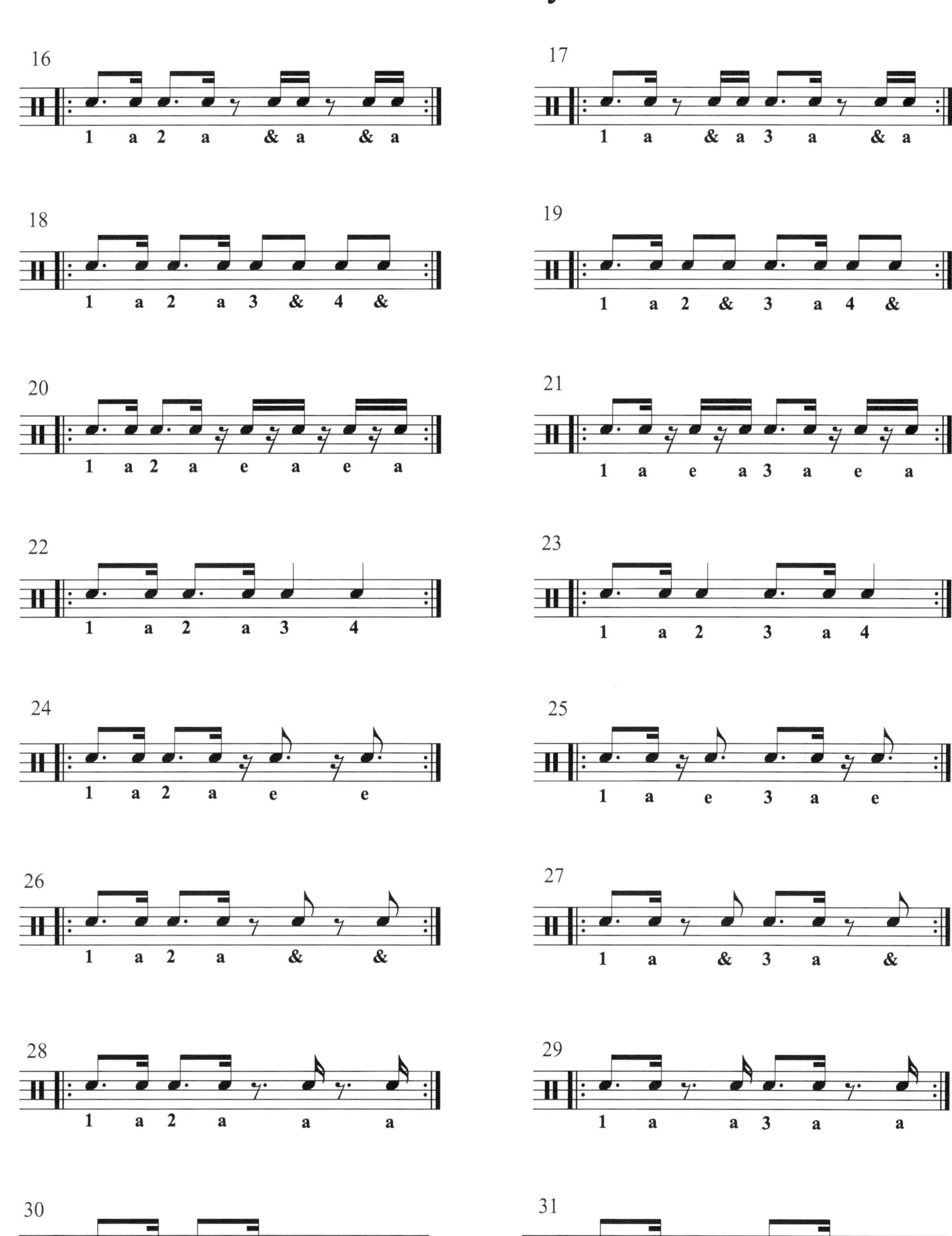

16th Note Rhythms

1

2

3

4

5

6

7

8

9

10

11

12

13

14

15

16th Note Rhythms

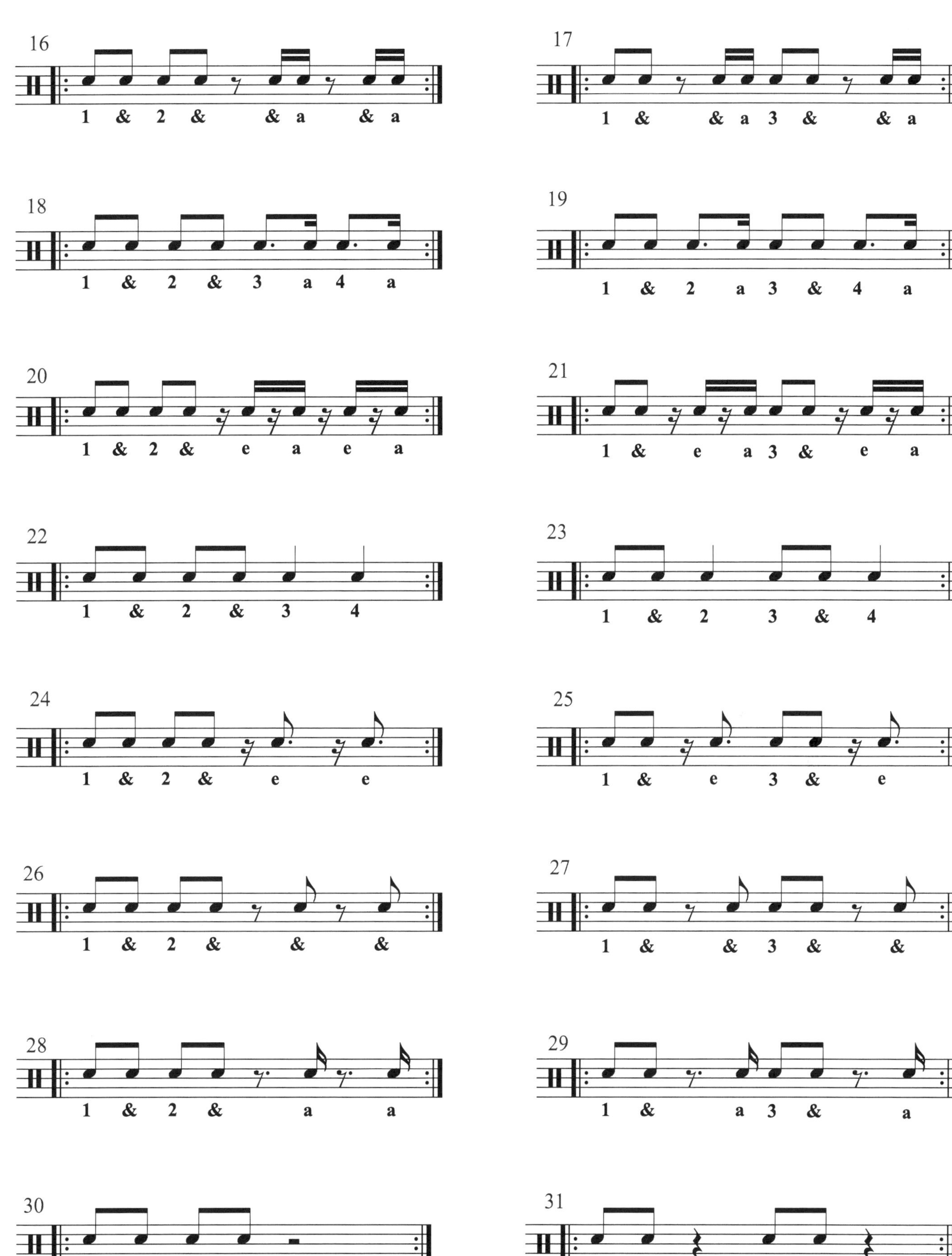

16th Note Rhythms

16th Note Rhythms

16th Note Rhythms

1

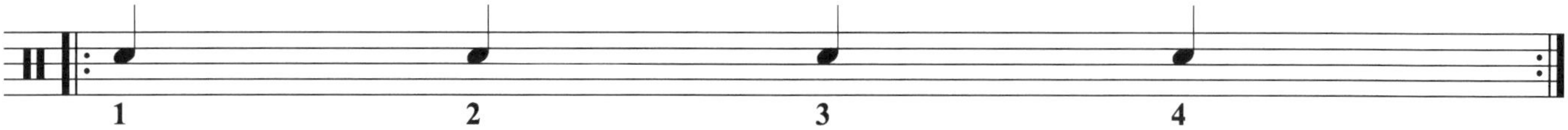
1 2 3 4

2

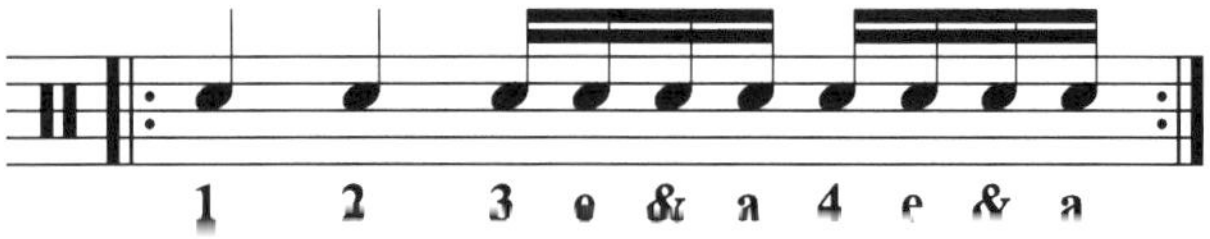
1 2 3 e & a 4 e & a

3

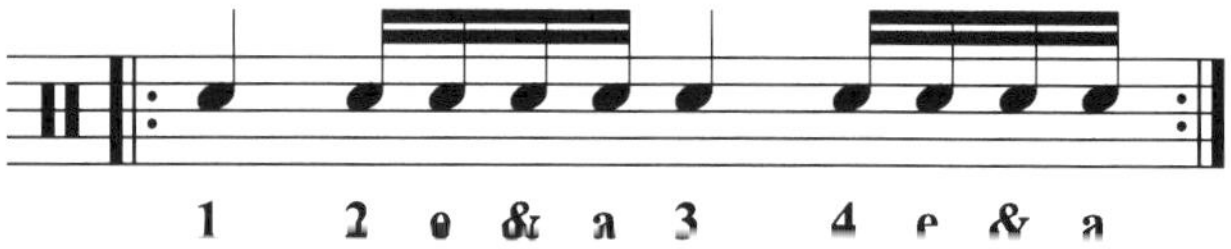
1 2 e & a 3 4 e & a

4

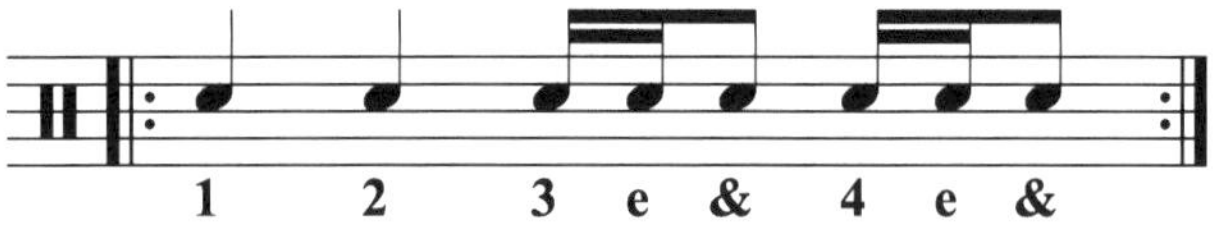
1 2 3 e & 4 e &

5

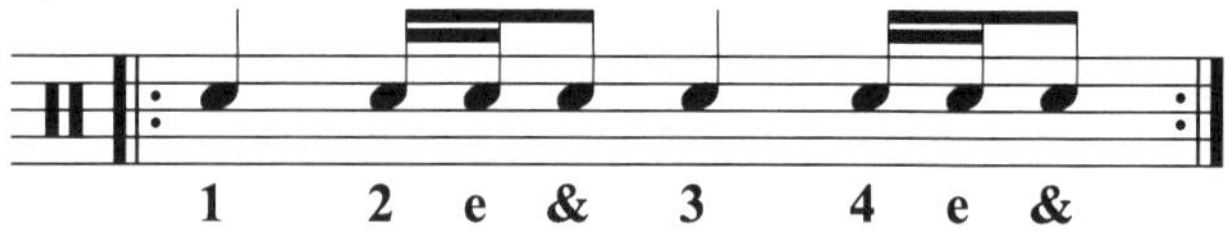
1 2 e & 3 4 e &

6

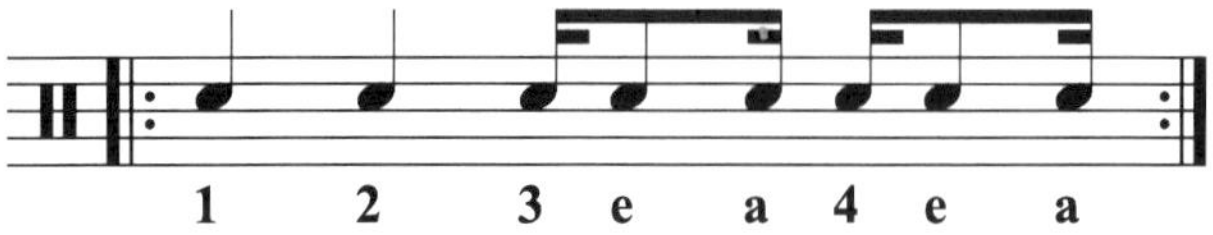
1 2 3 e a 4 e a

7

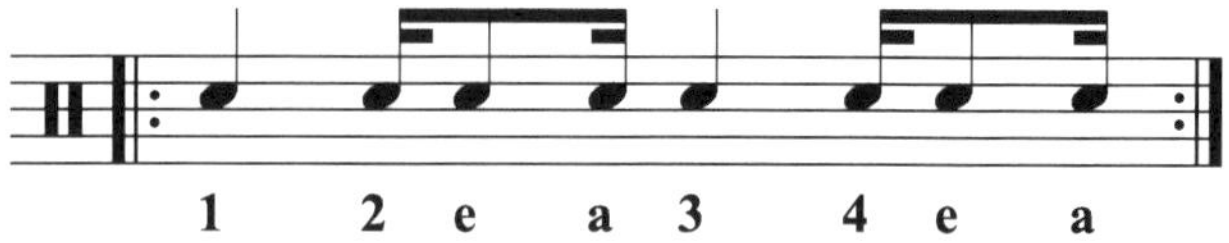
1 2 e a 3 4 e a

8

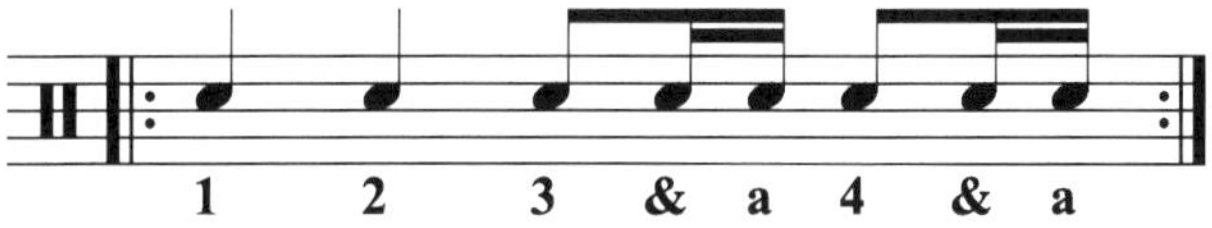
1 2 3 & a 4 & a

9

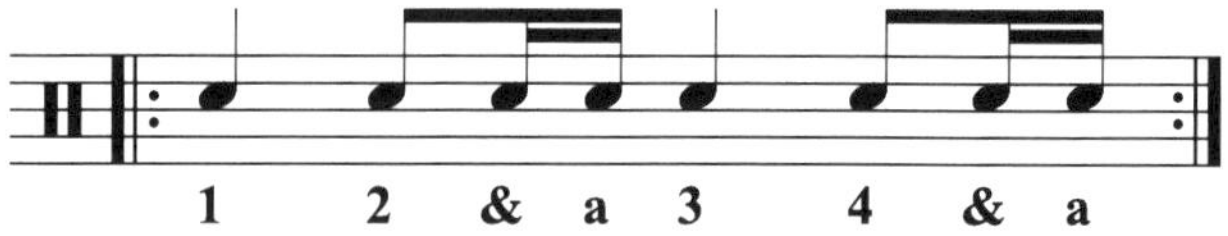
1 2 & a 3 4 & a

10

1 2 e & a e & a

11

1 e & a 3 e & a

12

1 2 3 e 4 e

13

1 2 e 3 4 e

14

1 2 e & e &

15

1 e & 3 e &

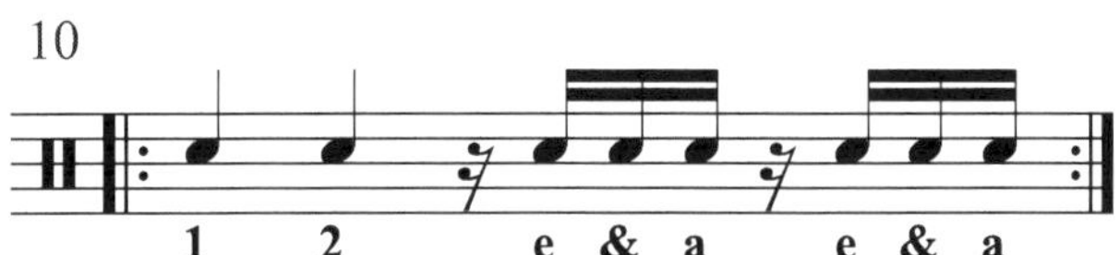

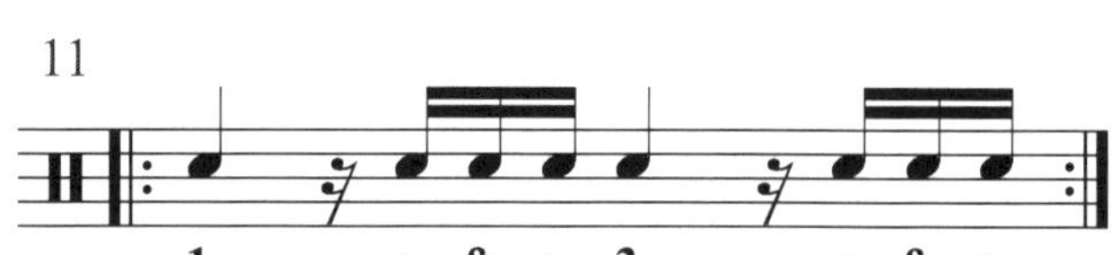

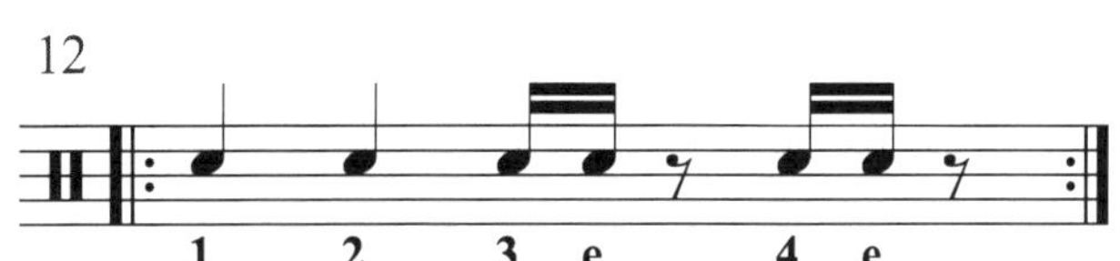

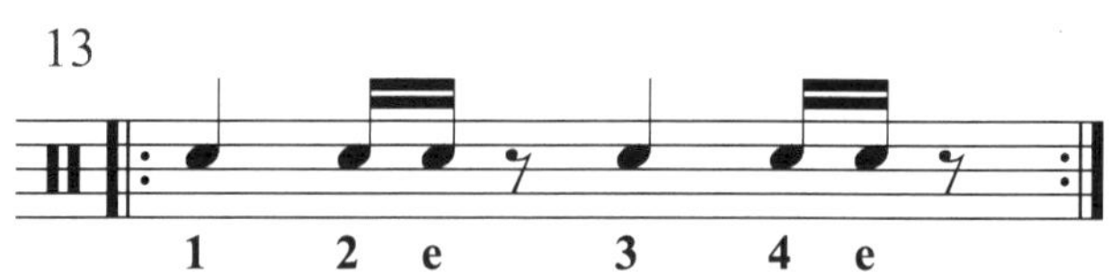

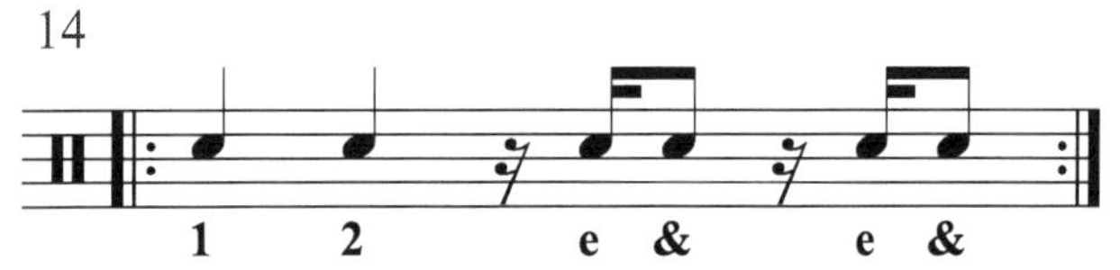

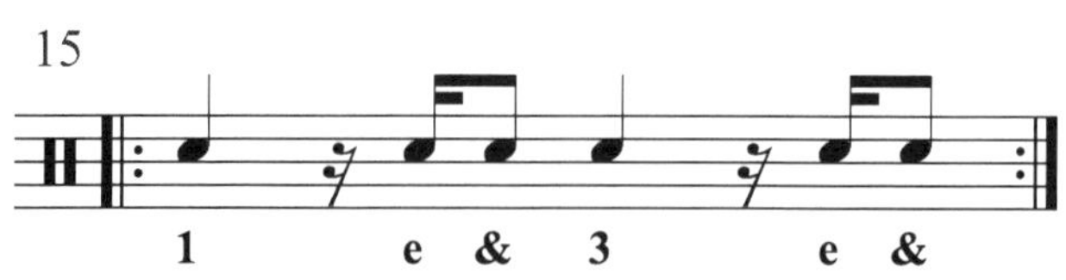

16th Note Rhythms

16th Note Rhythms

16th Note Rhythms

16th Note Rhythms

16th Note Rhythms

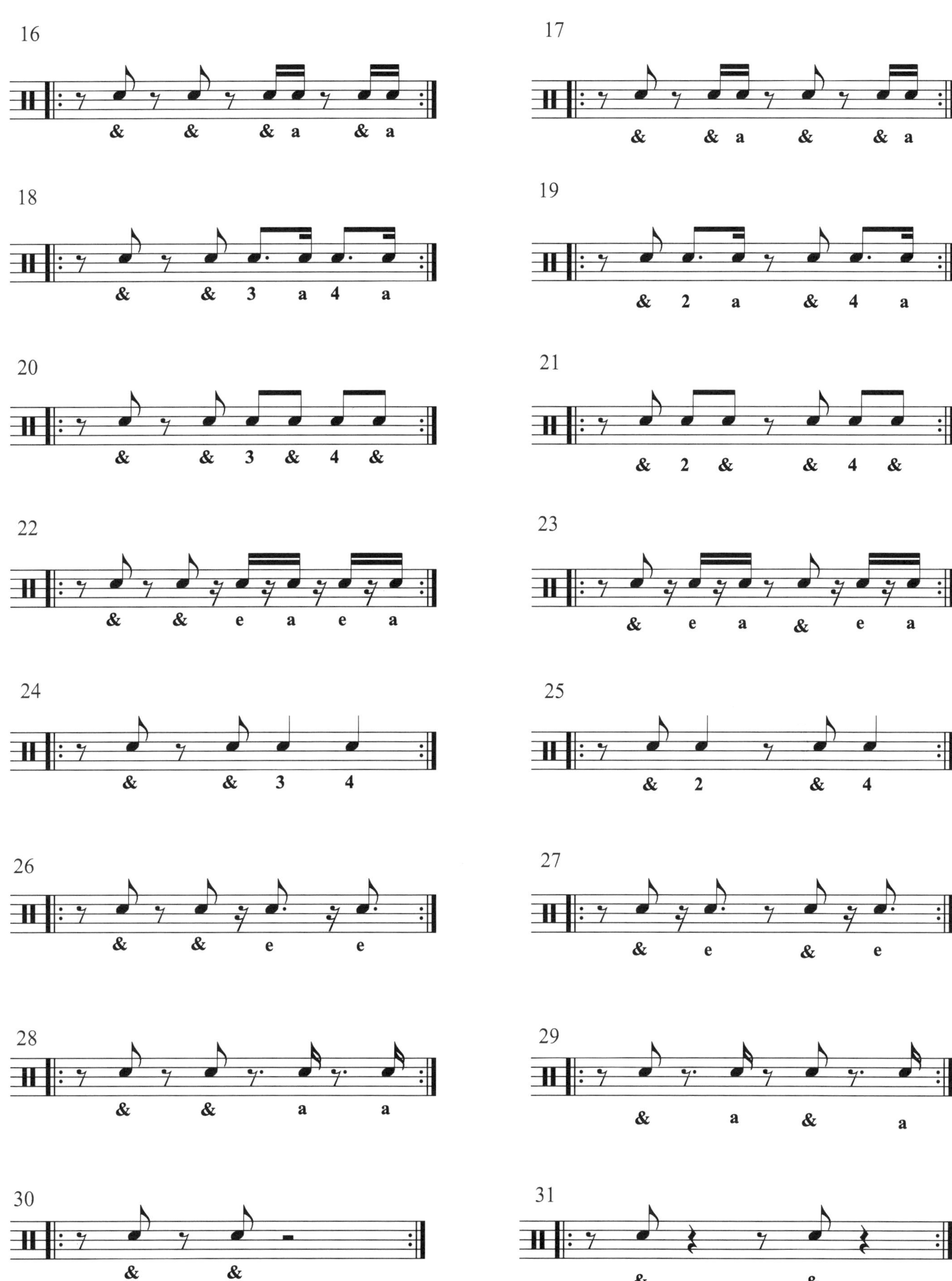

16th Note Rhythms

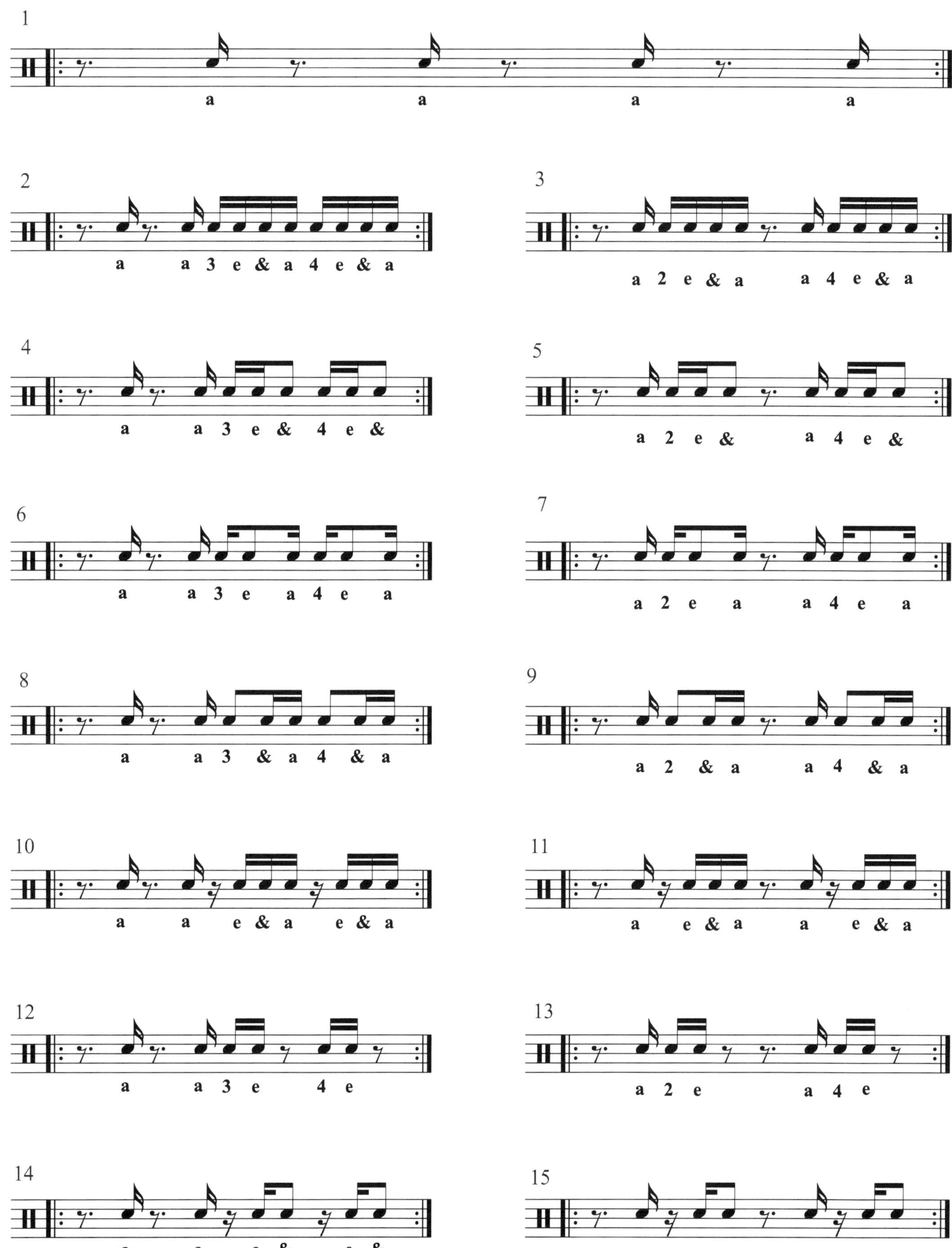

16th Note Rhythms

16th Note Rhythms

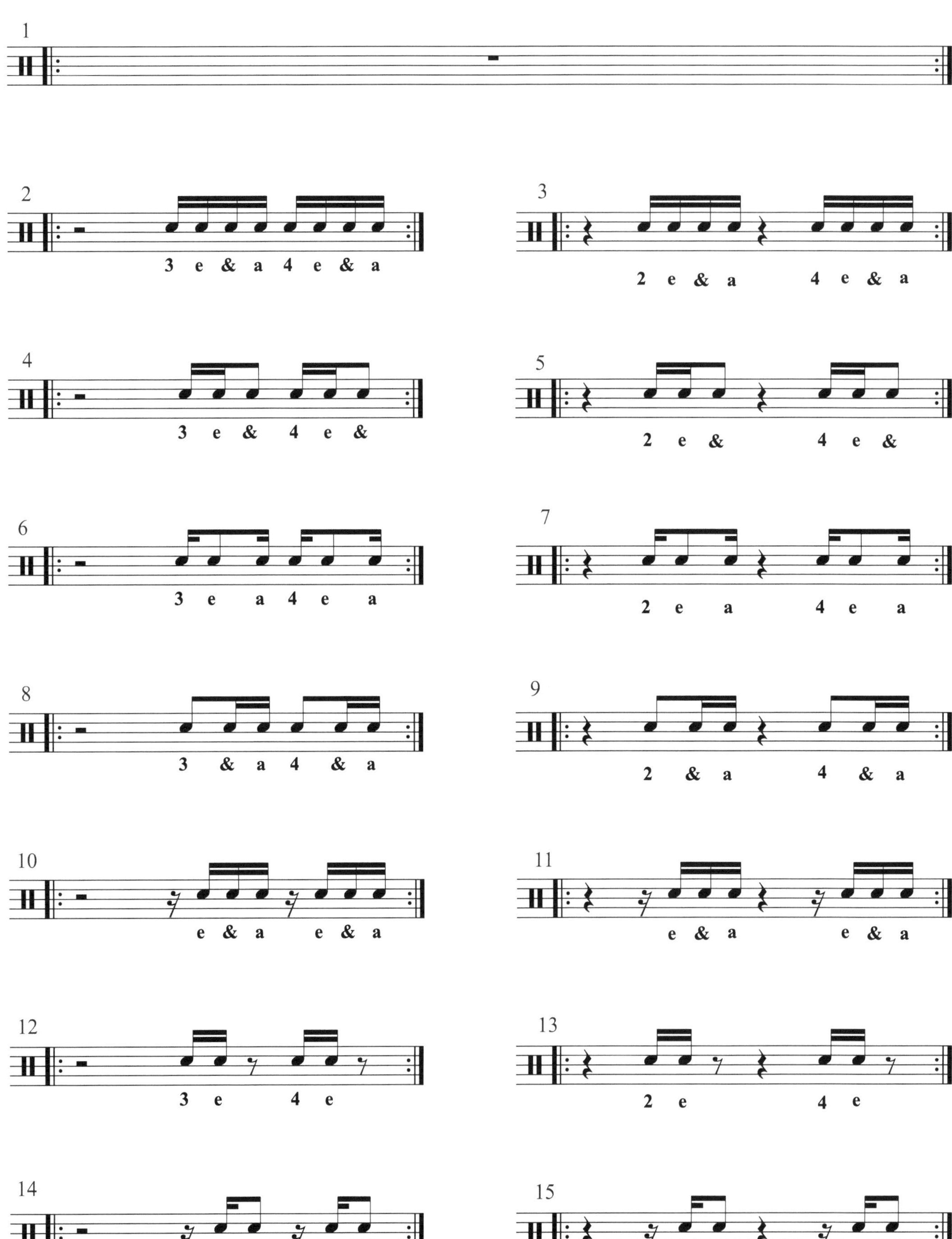

16th Note Rhythms

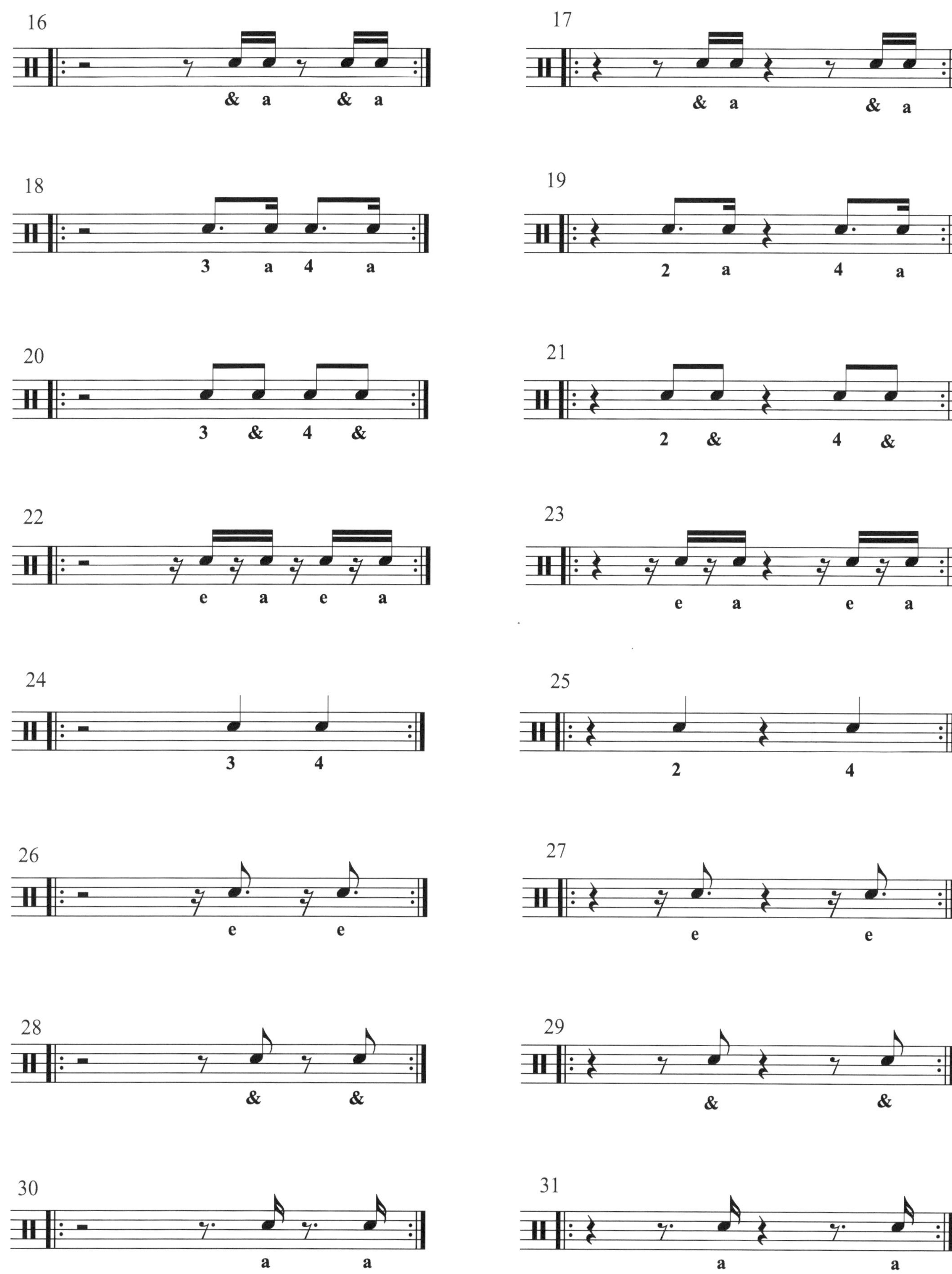

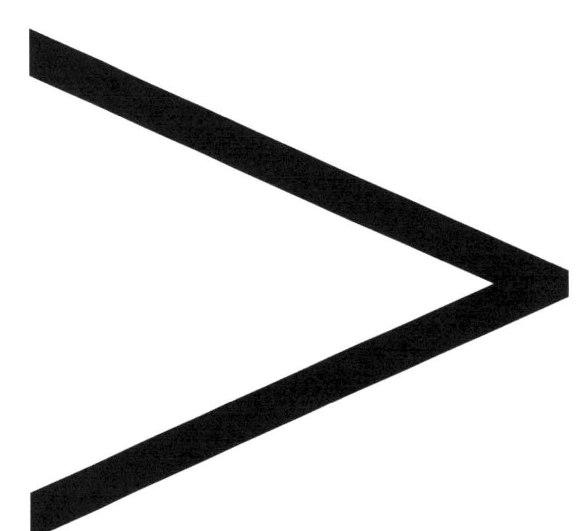

Adding Accents to the Rhythmic Alphabet

In the next section let's add accents to the broken rhythms. After you master these individually go back and play through the last section with one of the accented rhythms replacing the non-accented rhythm.

1
2
3
4
5
6
7
8
9
10
11
12
13
14
15
16
17
18

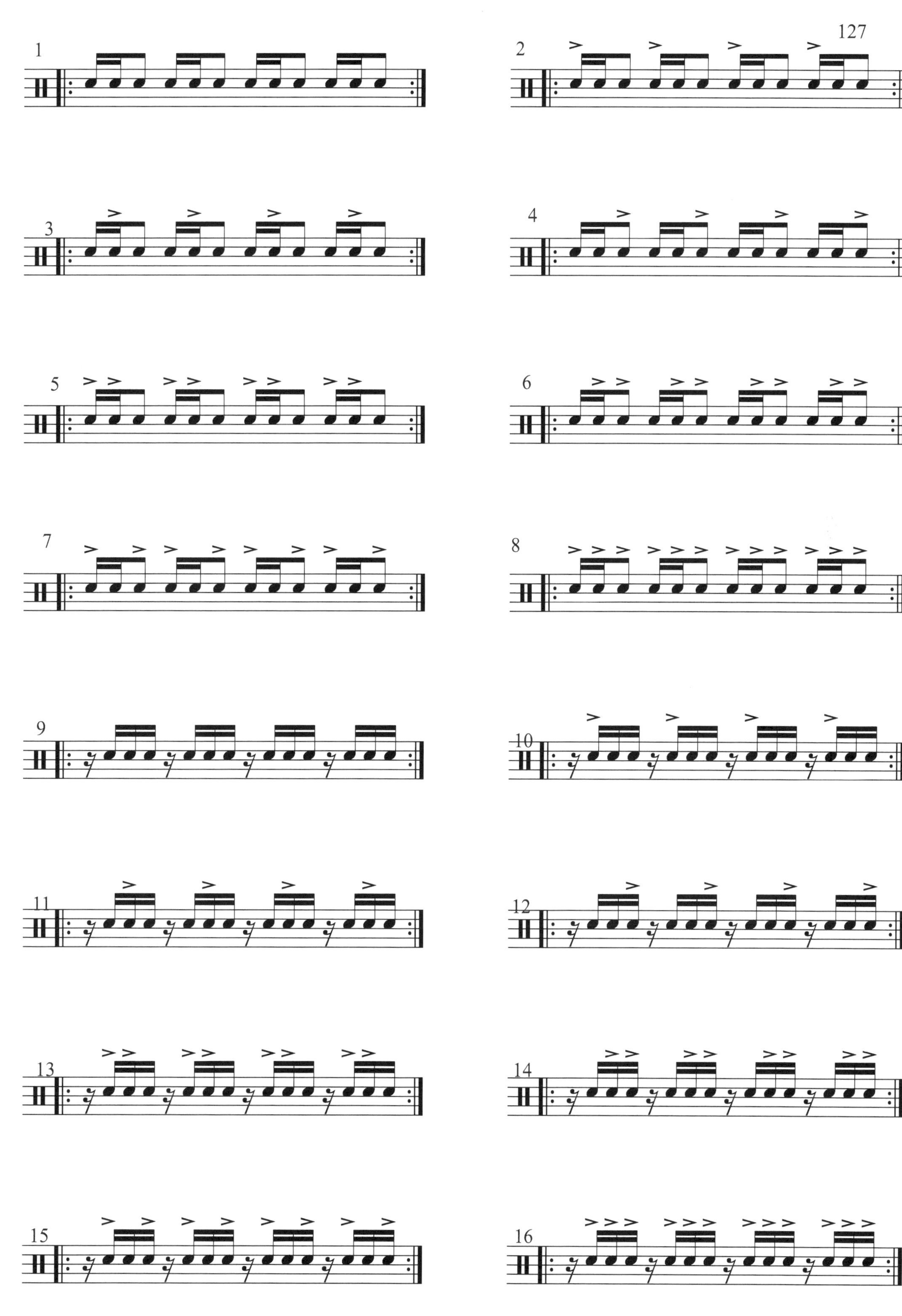
1
2
3
4
5
6
7
8
9
10
11
12
13
14
15
16

1
2
3
4
5
6
7
8
9
10
11
12
13
14
15
16

1
2
3
4
5
6
7
8
9
10
11
12
13
14
15
16

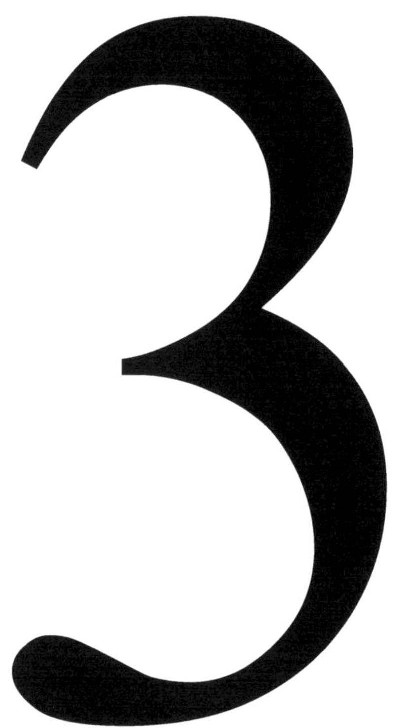

Subdivisions Per Beat

$2^3 = 8$ Rhythm Alphabet

Plus 2 Quater Note Triplet Rhythms for a total of 10

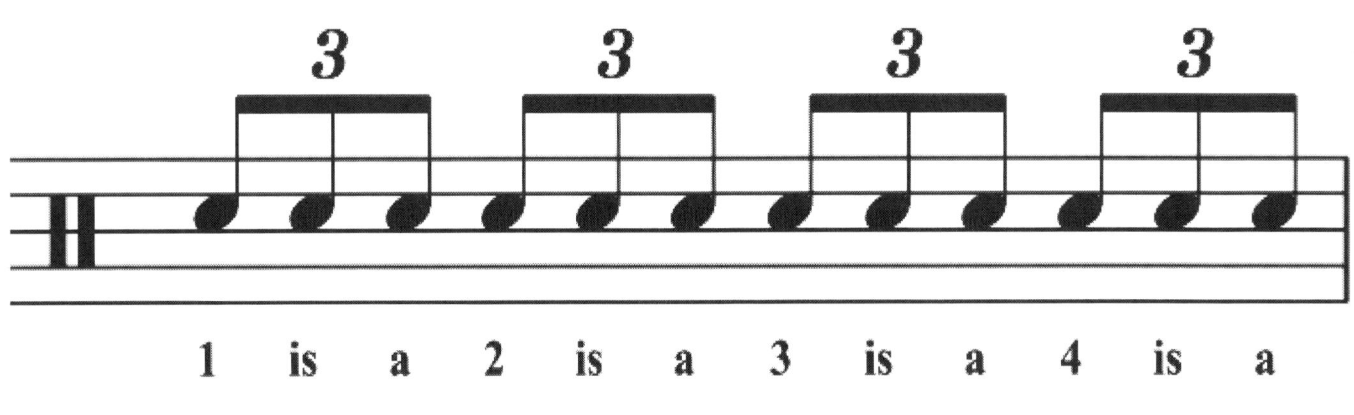

$2^{12} = 4{,}096$

Rhythmic Possibilities In One Measure

8th Note Triplets

The 8th note triplet divides the beat into three equal subdivisions. The 8th note triplet sustains for one third of a beat. In the next section we will explore the ternary, or triplet rhythmic alphabet. With three even subdivisions in one beat there are 8 rhythmic possibilities. In a measure of 4|4 time using only eighth note triplets there are 12 equal subdivisions for a total of 4,096 rhythmic possibilities in one measure. We do not do all 4,096, but we do cover all AAAABBBB, AABB and ABAB combinations.

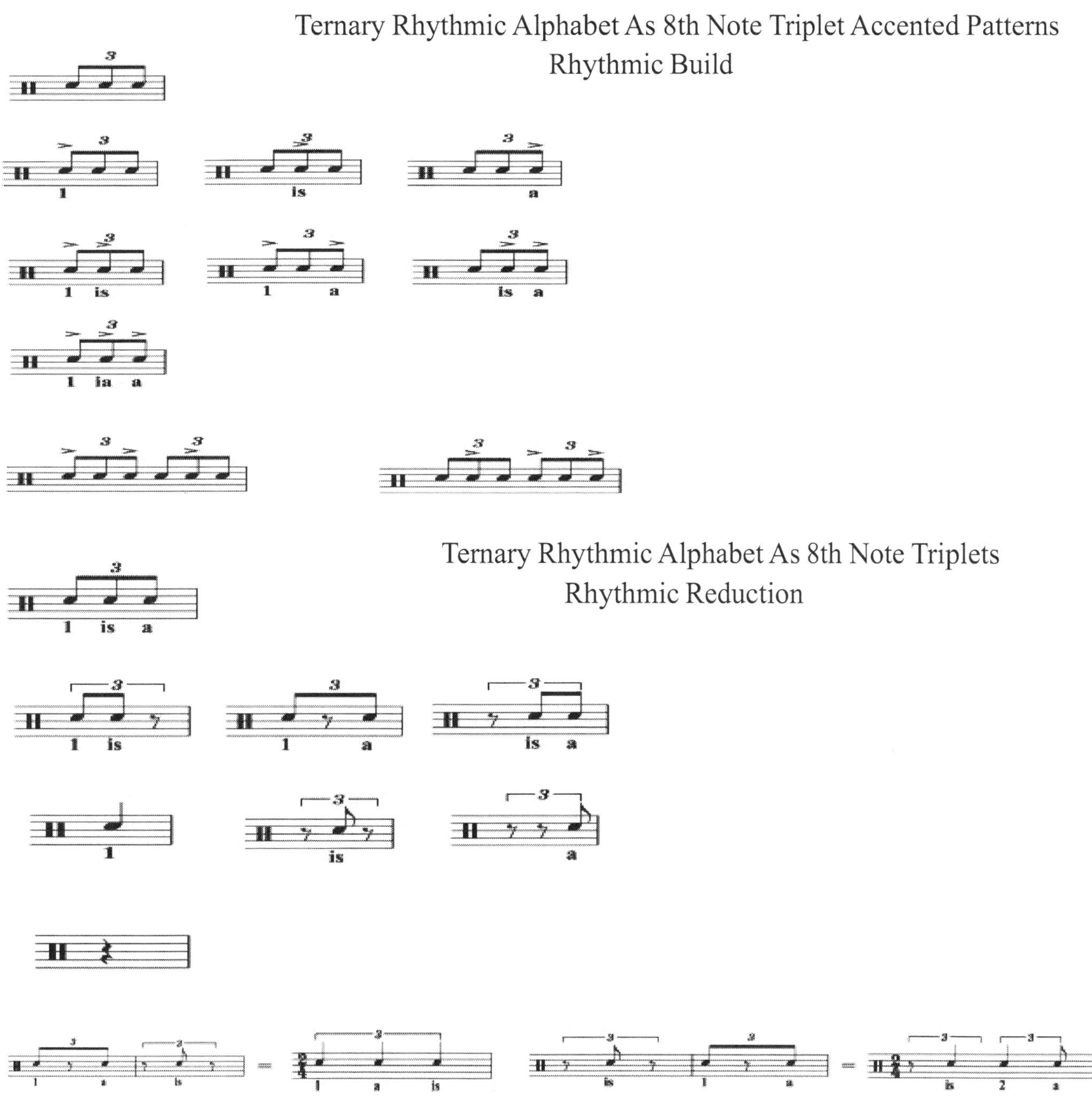

Natural Sticking Ternary Accent Patterns
Right Hand Lead

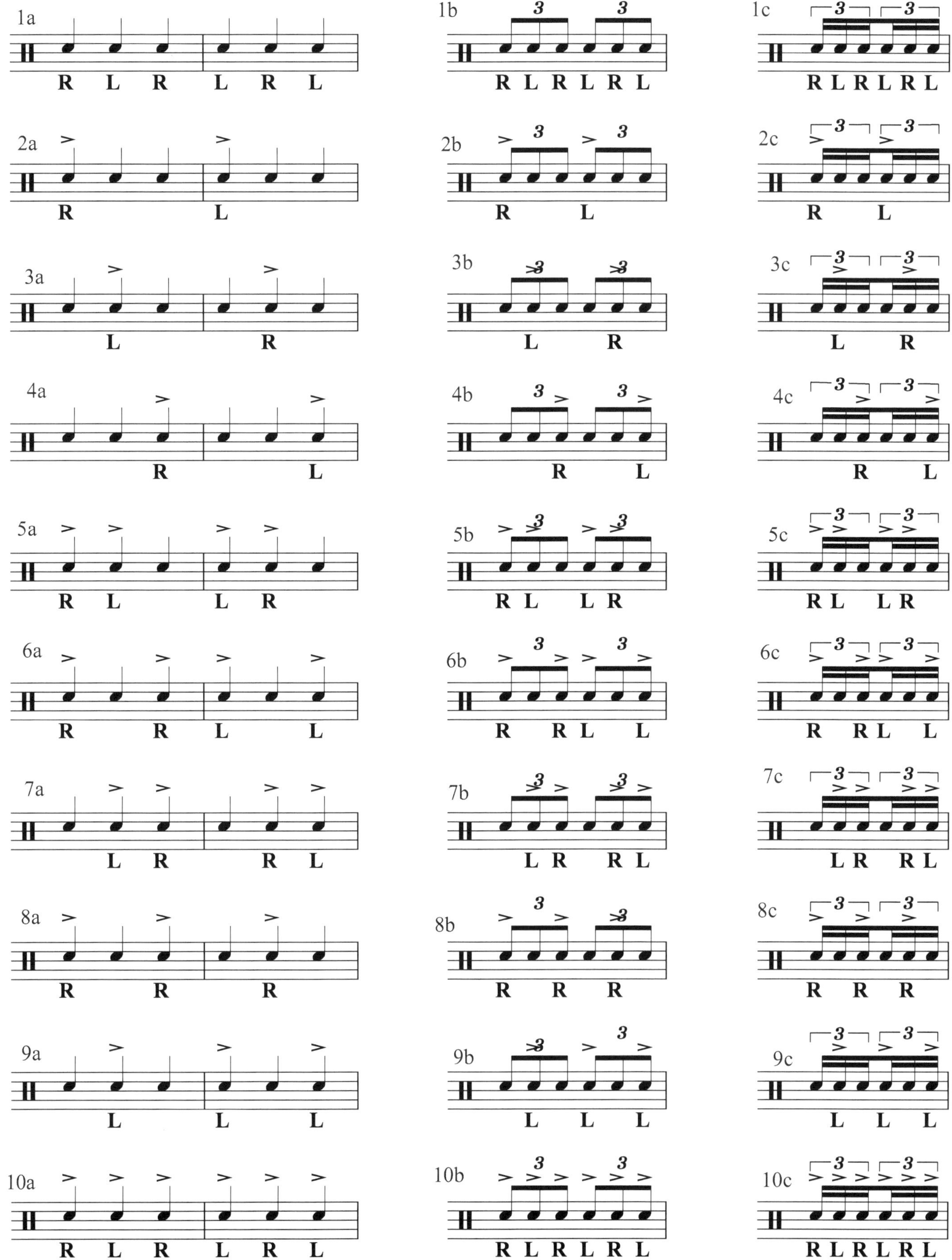

Natural Sticking Ternary Rhythms
Right Hand Lead

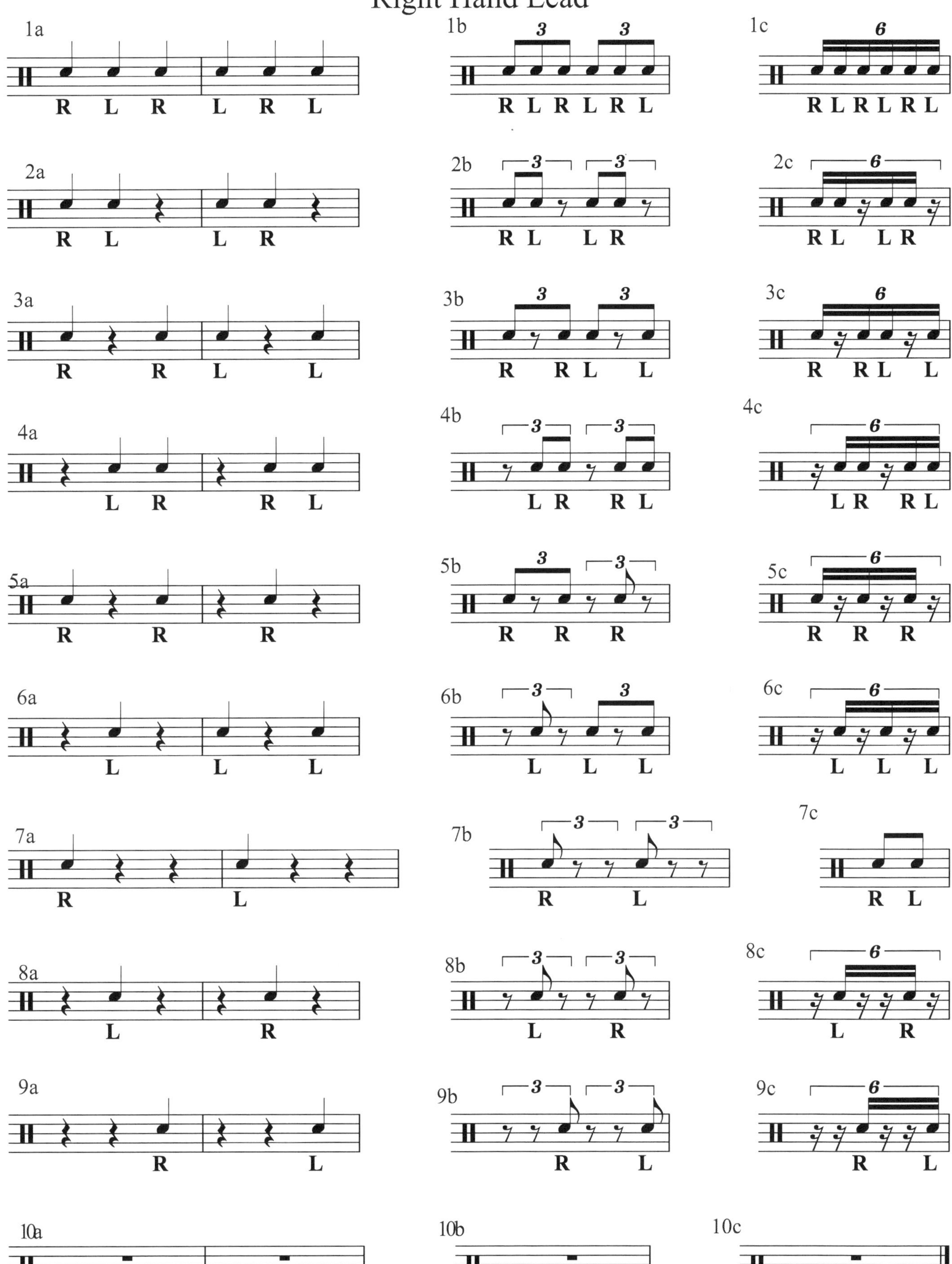

8th Note Triplet Rhythmic Alphabet Accented

1

2

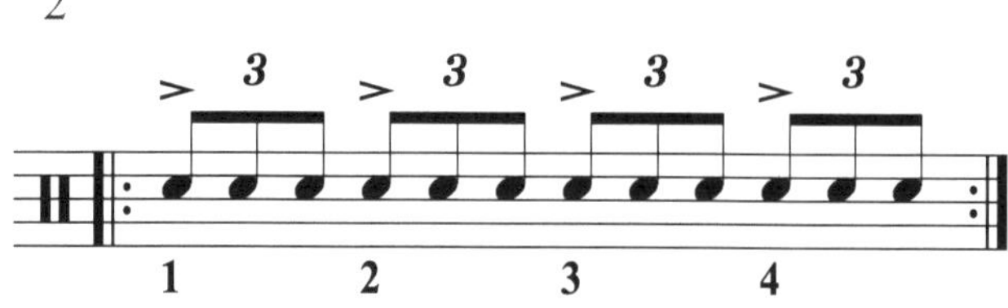

3

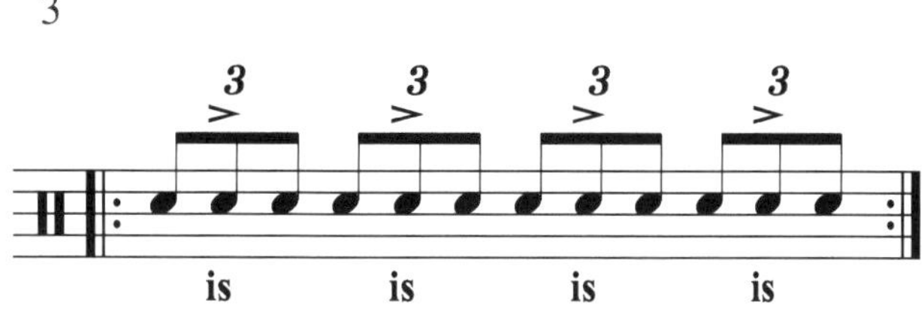

4

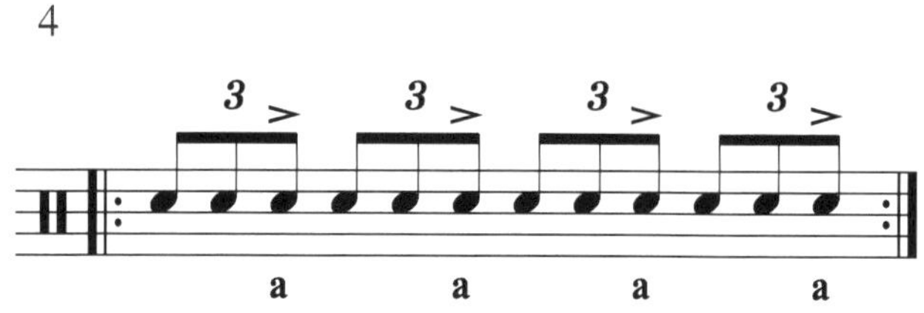

5

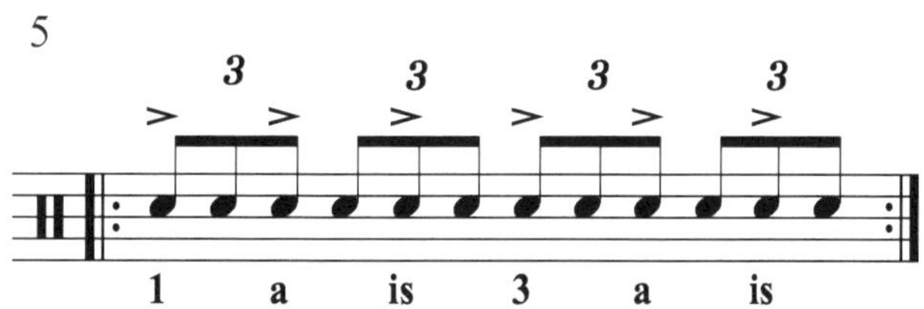

6

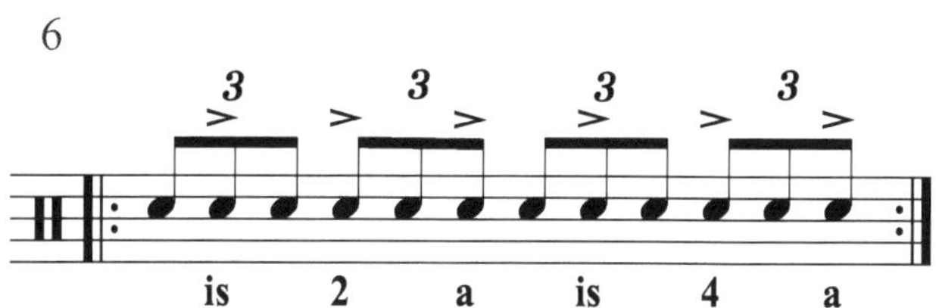

7

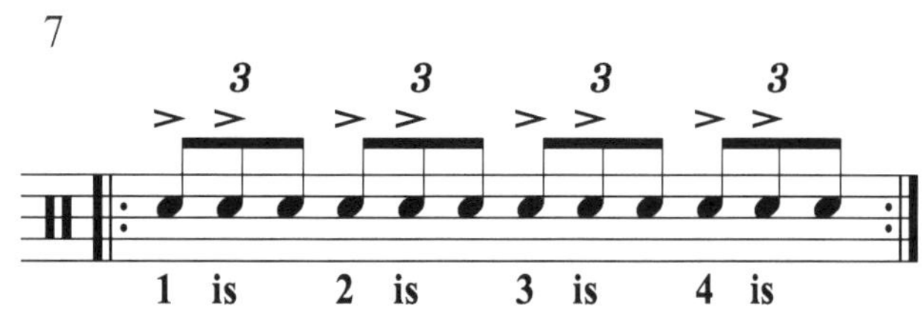

8

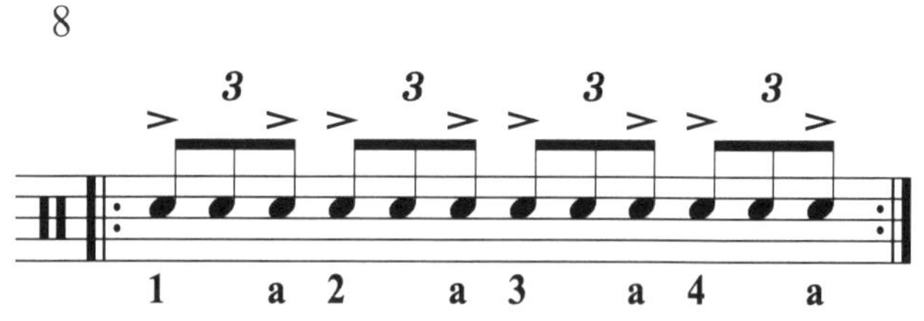

9

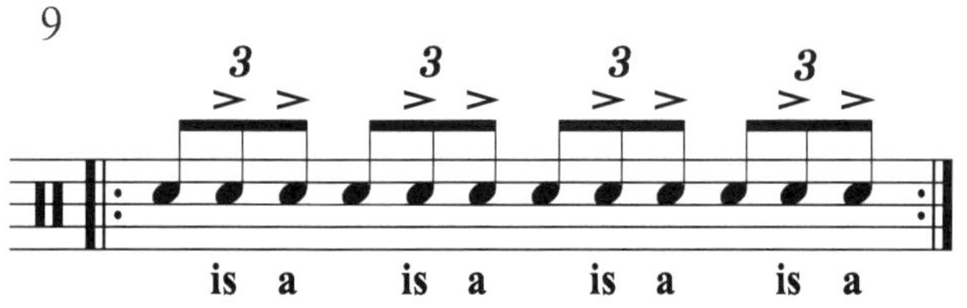

10

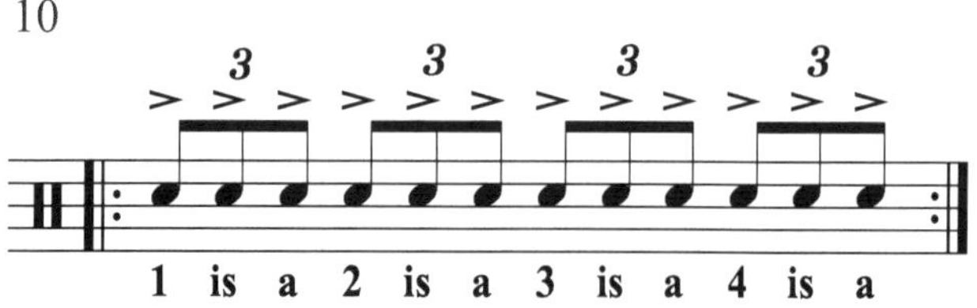

8th Note Triplet Rhythmic Alphabet

1

2

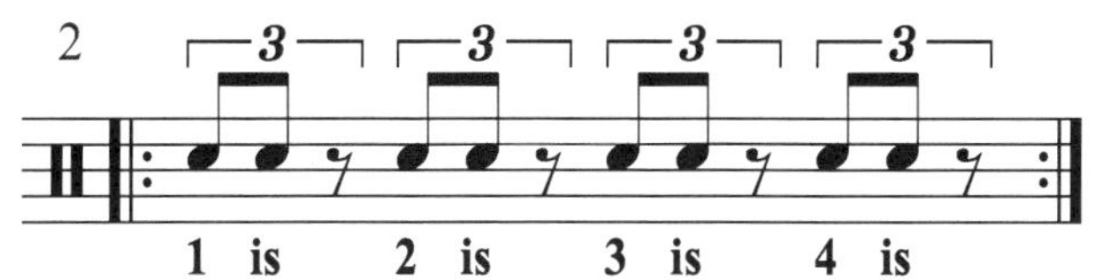

3

4

5

6

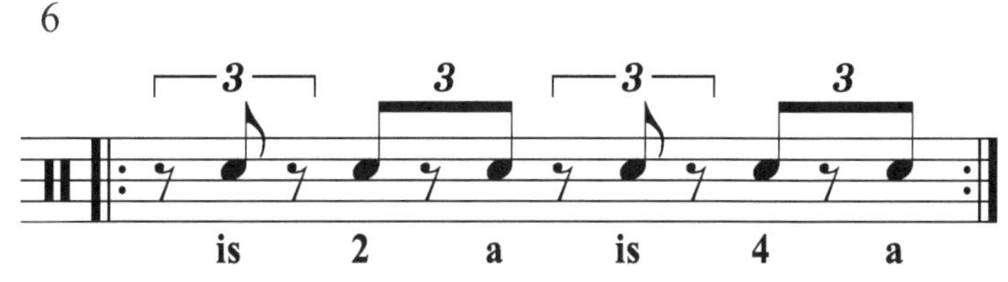

7

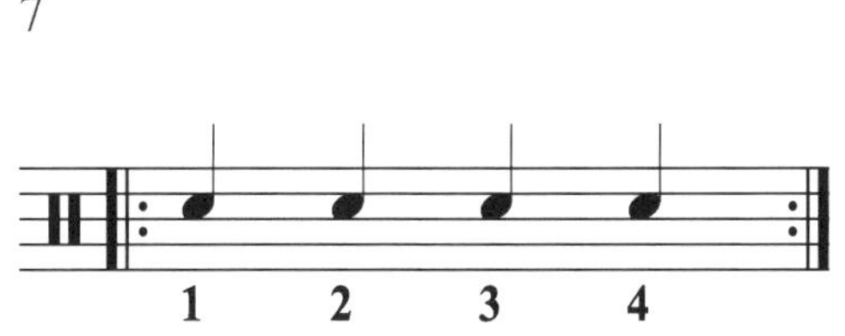

8

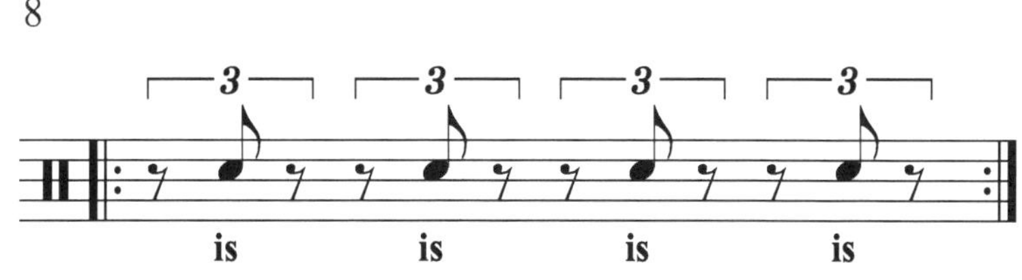

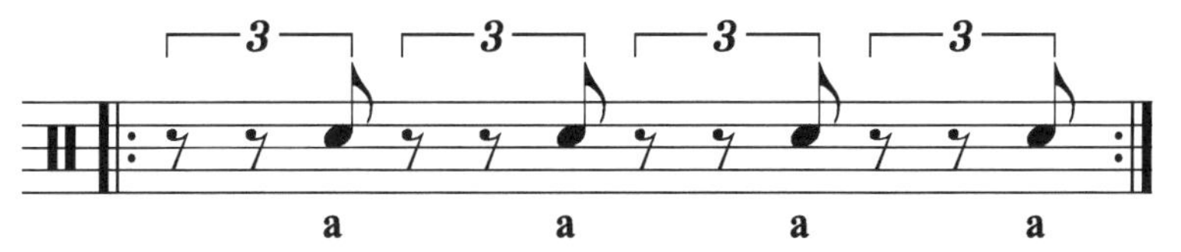

10

8th Note Triplet Accents

8th Note Triplet Accents

8th Note Triplet Accents

8th Note Triplet Accents

8th Note Triplet Accents

8th Note Triplet Accents

8th Note Triplet Accents

8th Note Triplet Accents

8th Note Triplet Accents

8th Note Triplet Accents

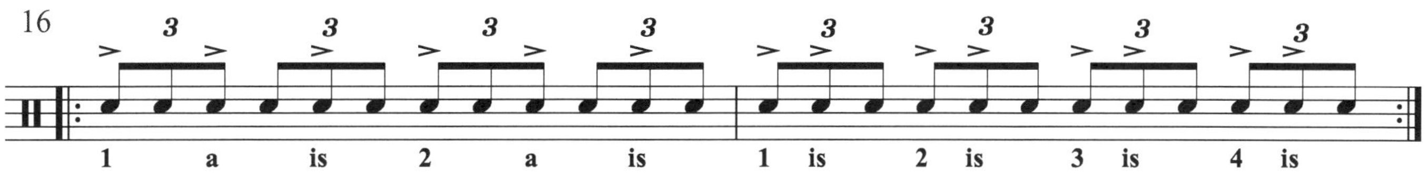

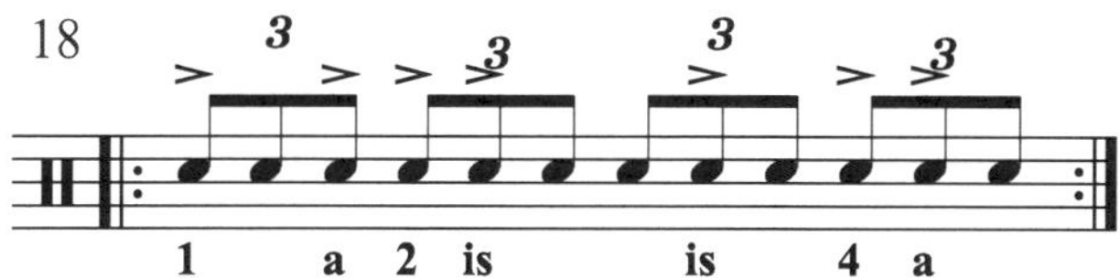

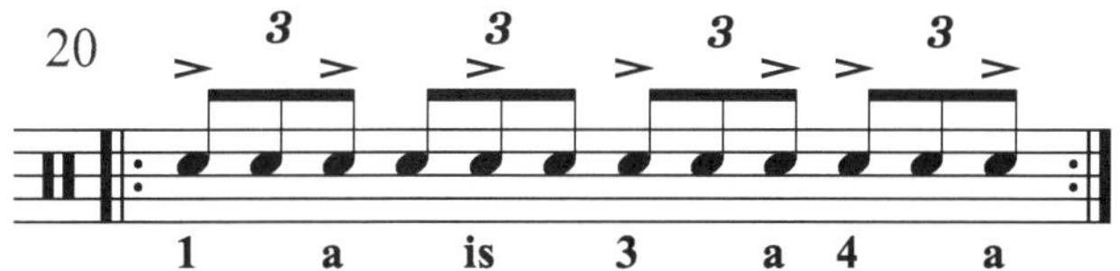

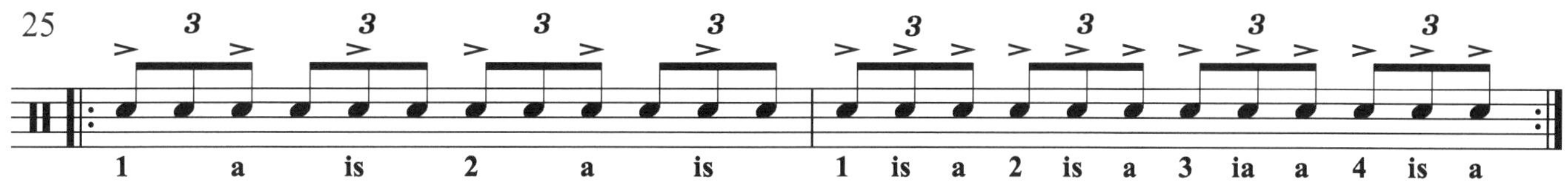

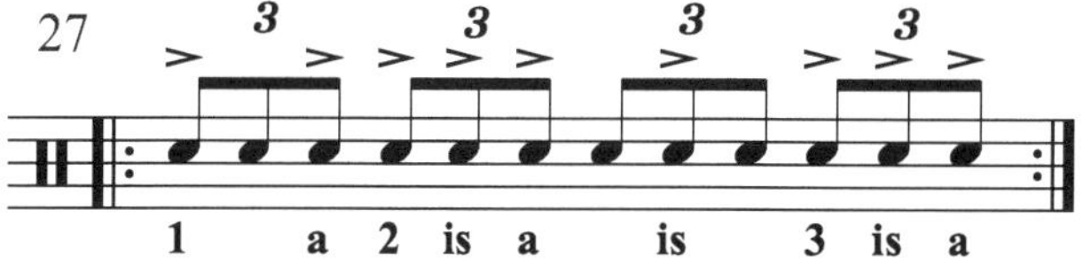

8th Note Triplet Accents

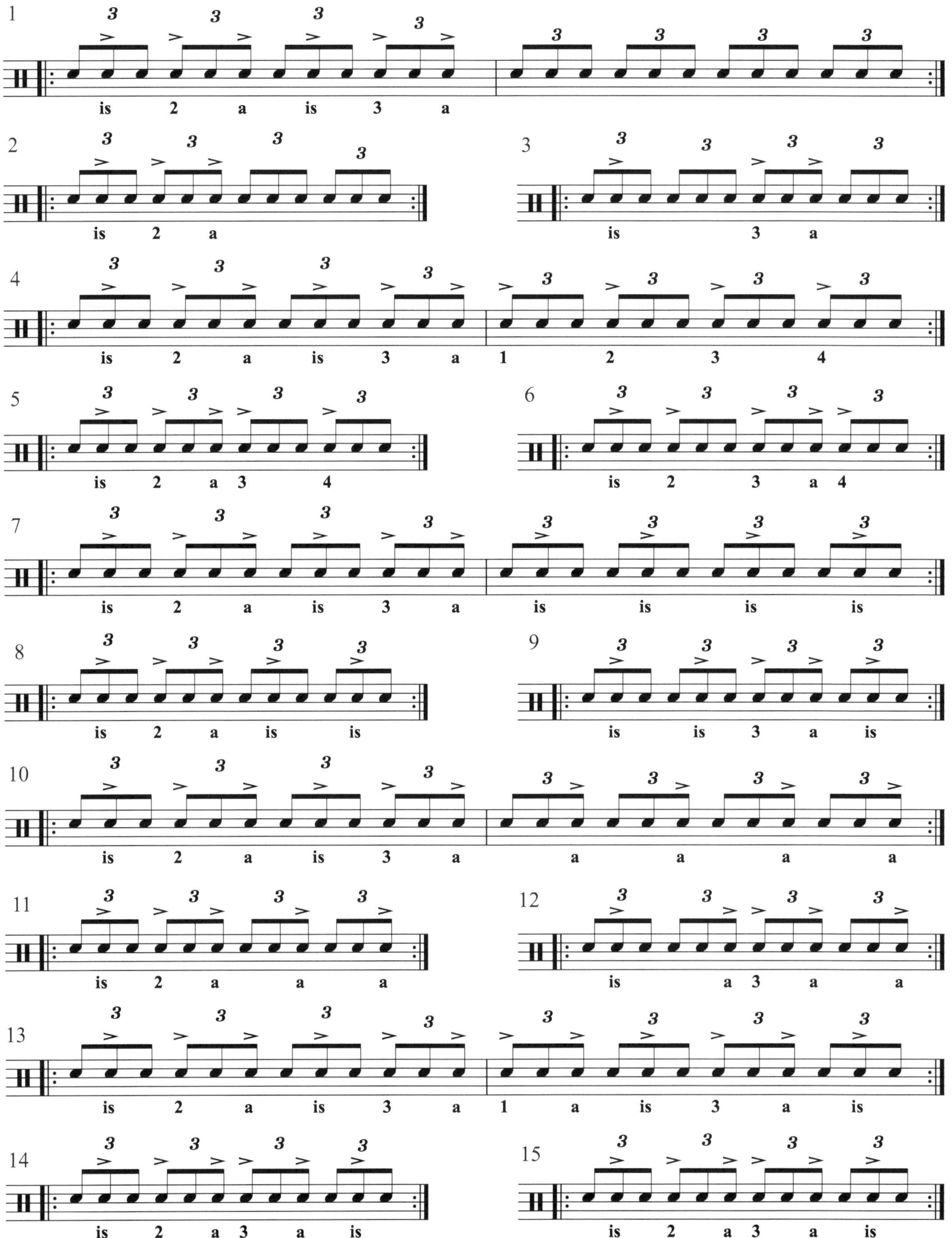

8th Note Triplet Accents

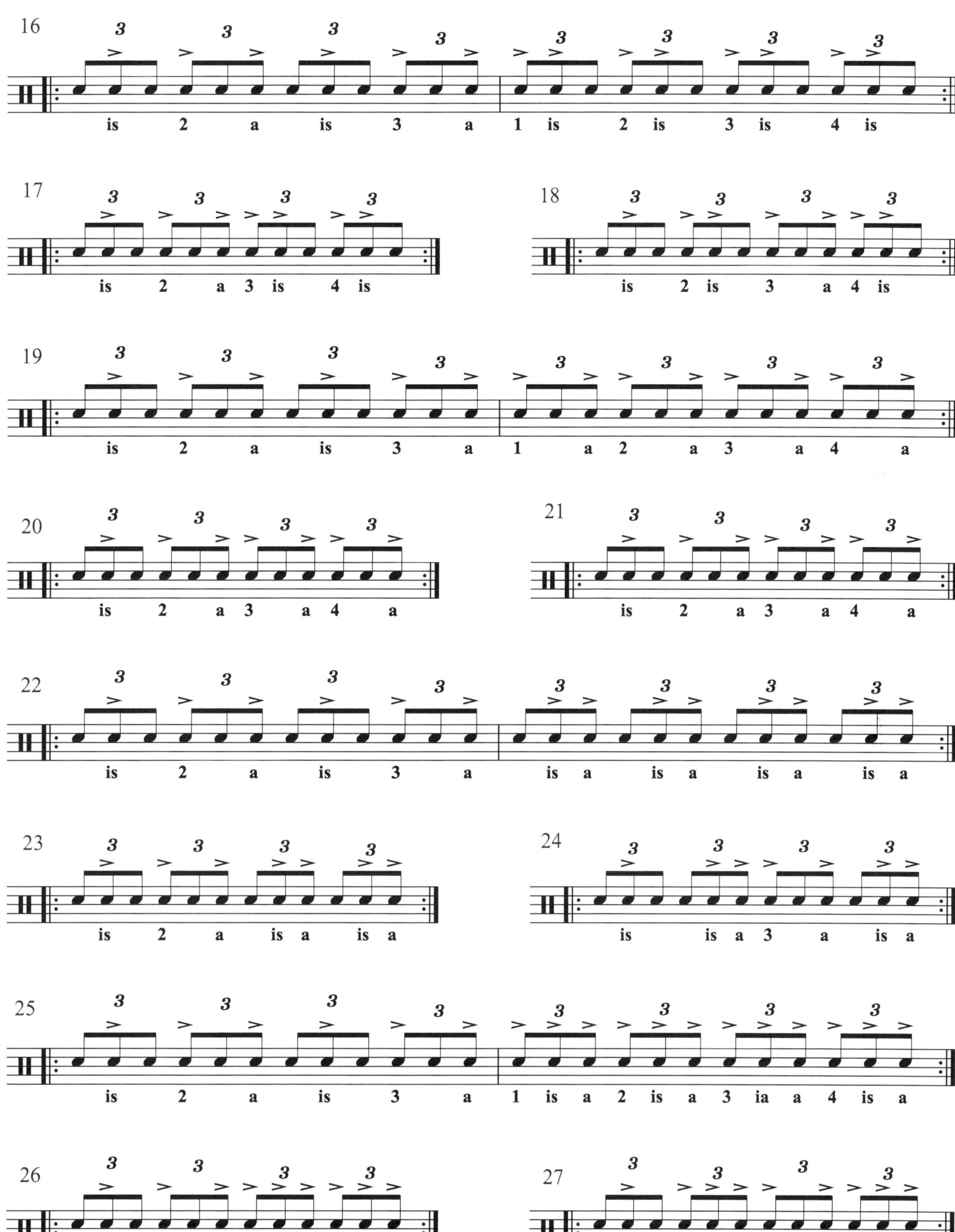

8th Note Triplet Accents

8th Note Triplet Accents

8th Note Triplet Accents

8th Note Triplet Accents

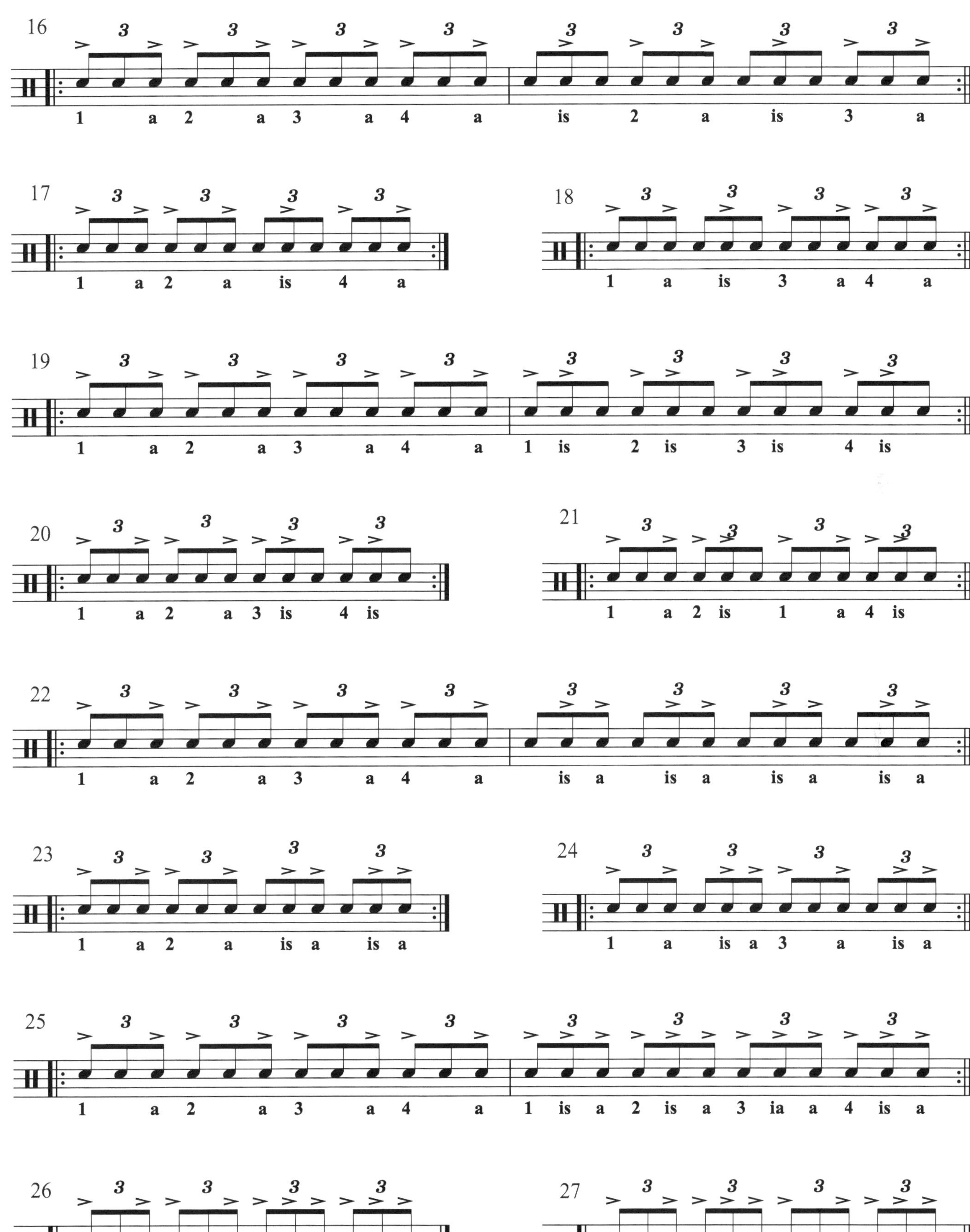

8th Note Triplet Accents

8th Note Triplet Accents

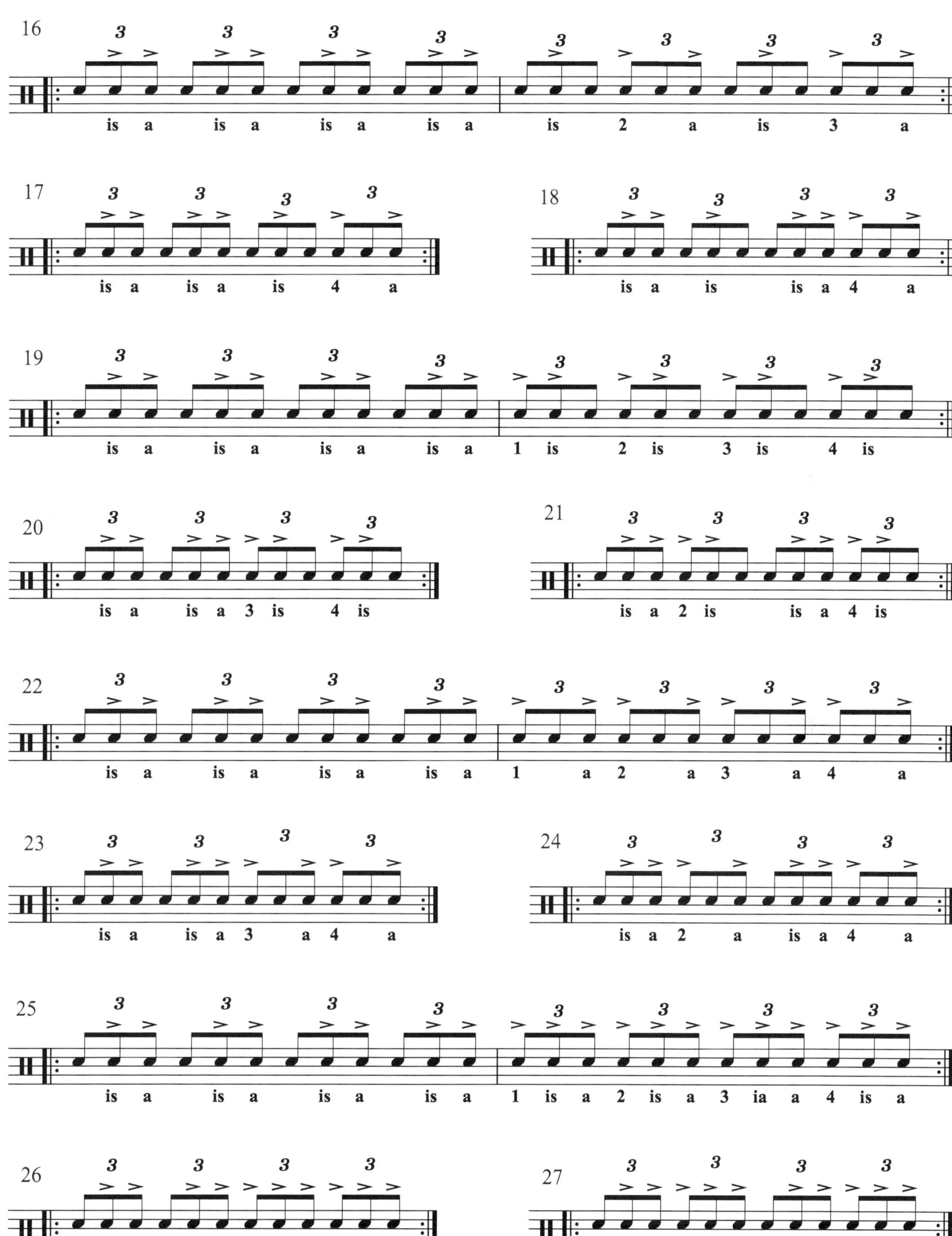

8th Note Triplet Accents

8th Note Triplet Accents

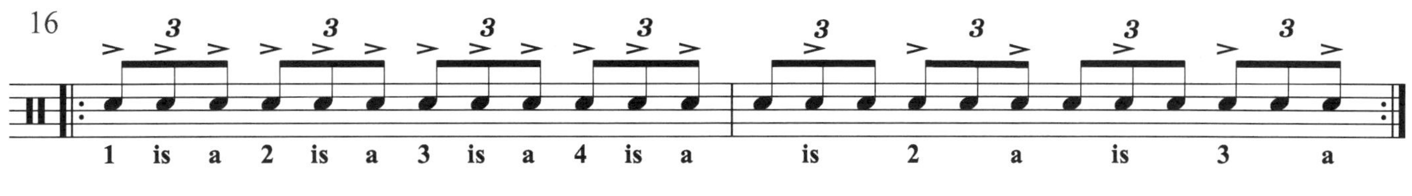

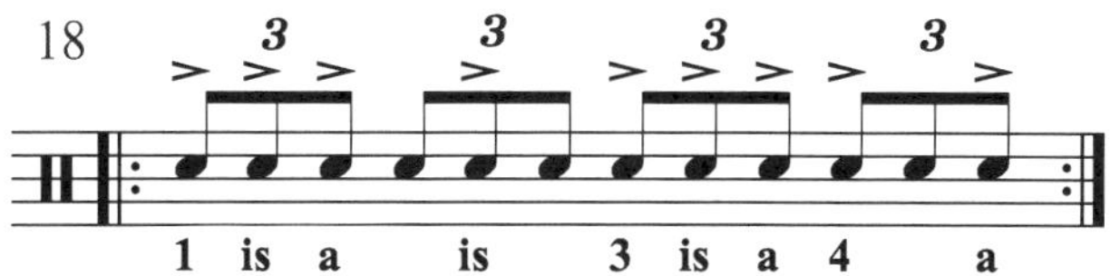

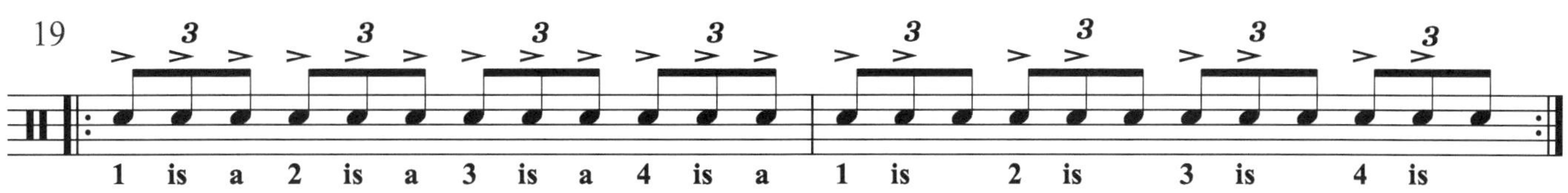

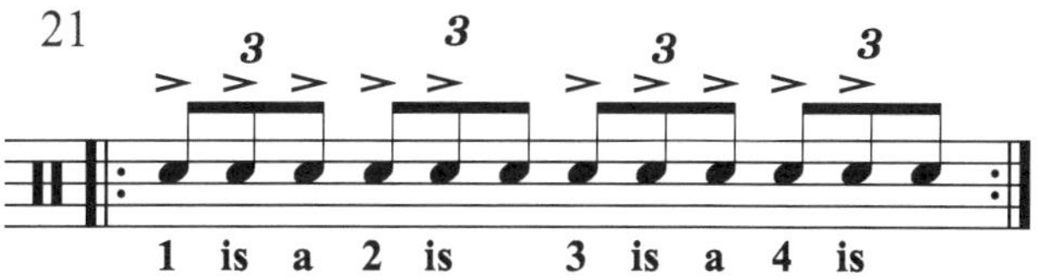

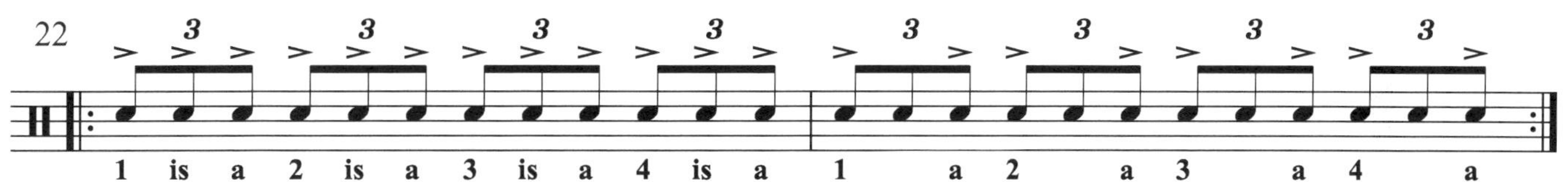

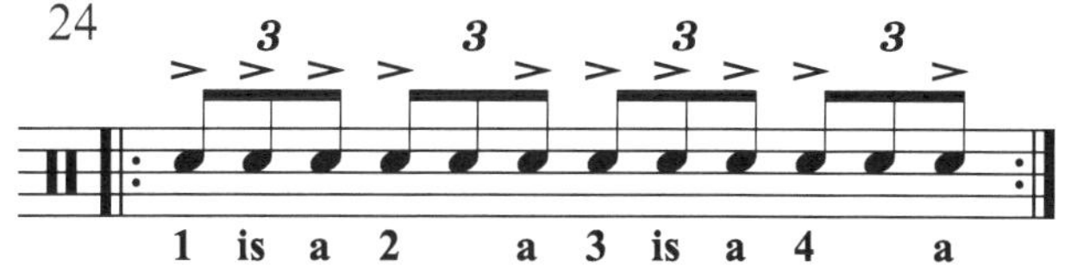

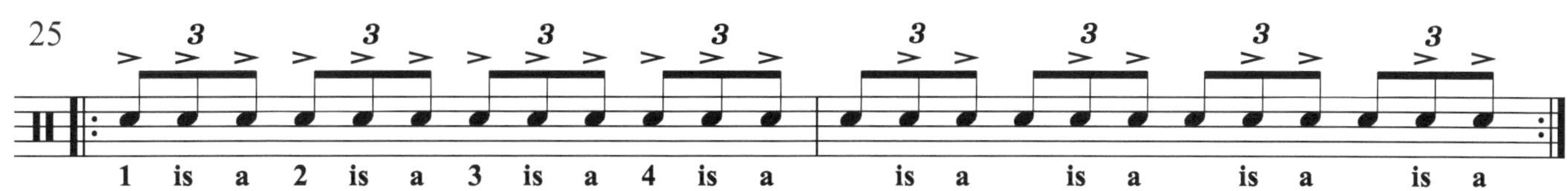

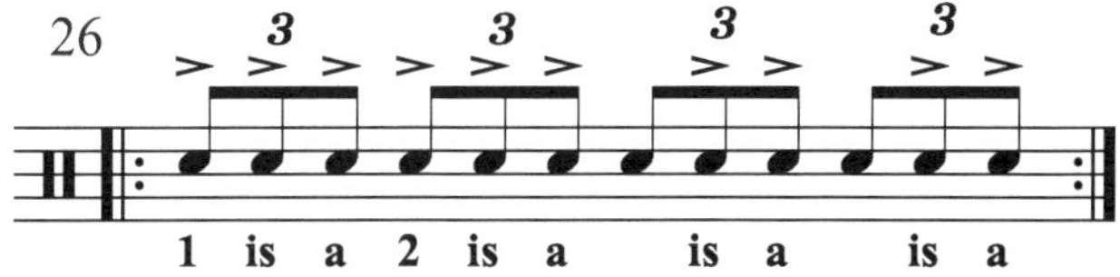

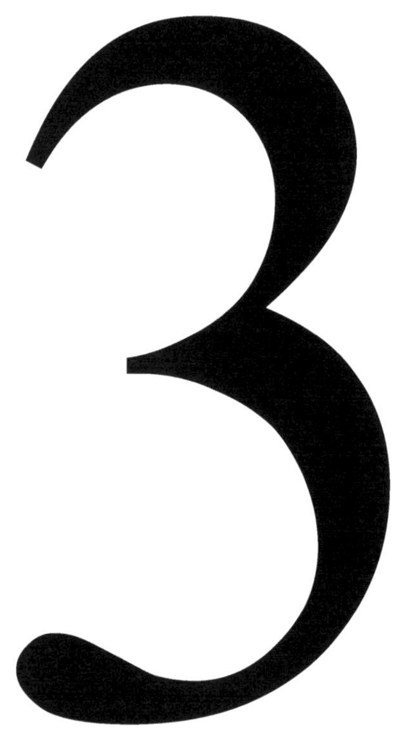

Subdivisions Per Beat

8th Note Triplet Rhythmic Alphabet

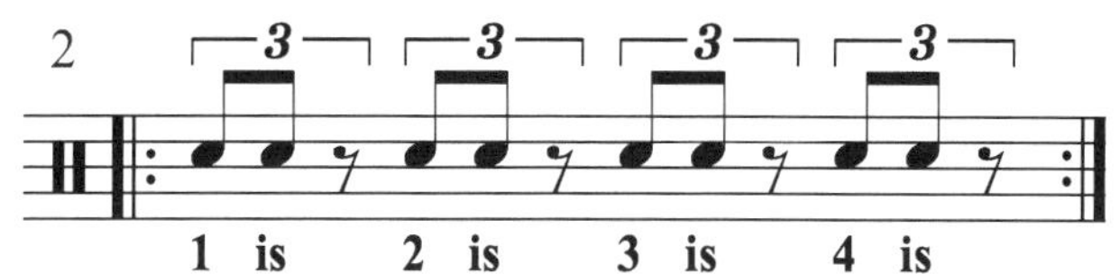

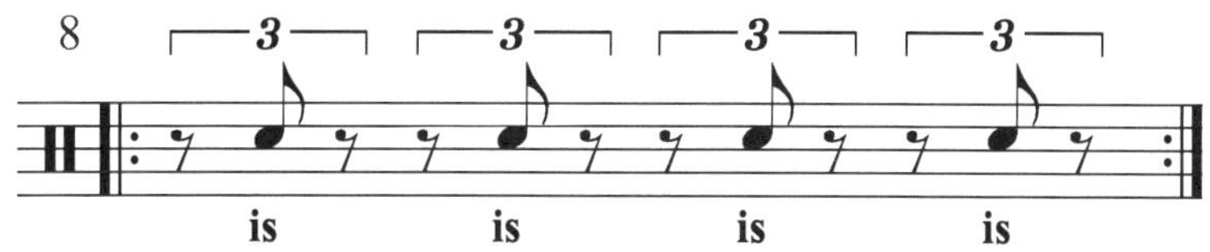

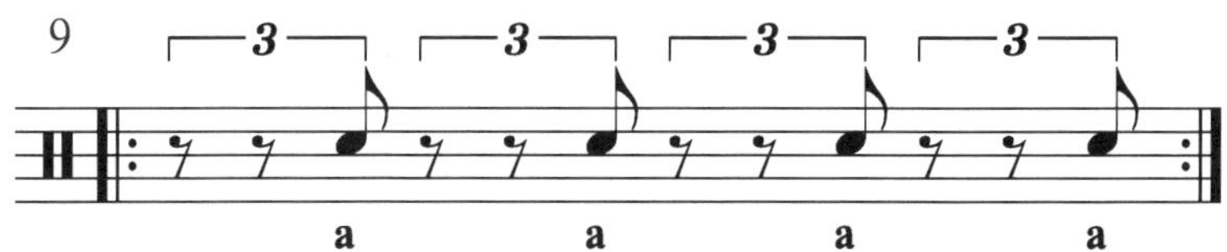

8th Note Triplet Rhythms

8th Note Triplet Rhythms

8th Note Triplet Rhythms

8th Note Triplet Rhythms

8th Note Triplet Rhythms

8th Note Triplet Rhythms

8th Note Triplet Rhythms

8th Note Triplet Rhythms

8th Note Triplet Rhythms

8th Note Triplet Rhythms

8th Note Triplet Rhythms

8th Note Triplet Rhythms

8th Note Triplet Rhythms

8th Note Triplet Rhythms

8th Note Triplet Rhythms

8th Note Triplet Rhythms

8th Note Triplet Rhythms

8th Note Triplet Rhythms

8th Note Triplet Rhythms

8th Note Triplet Rhythms

Adding Accents to the 8th Note Triplet Rhythmic Alphabet

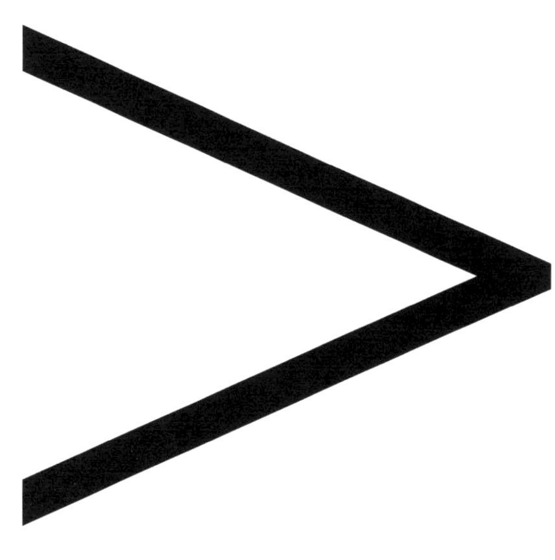

Now add accents to the broken triplet rhythms.
Once you feel comfortable with this go back and play the previous section substituting one of the accented rhythms for it's non-accented version.

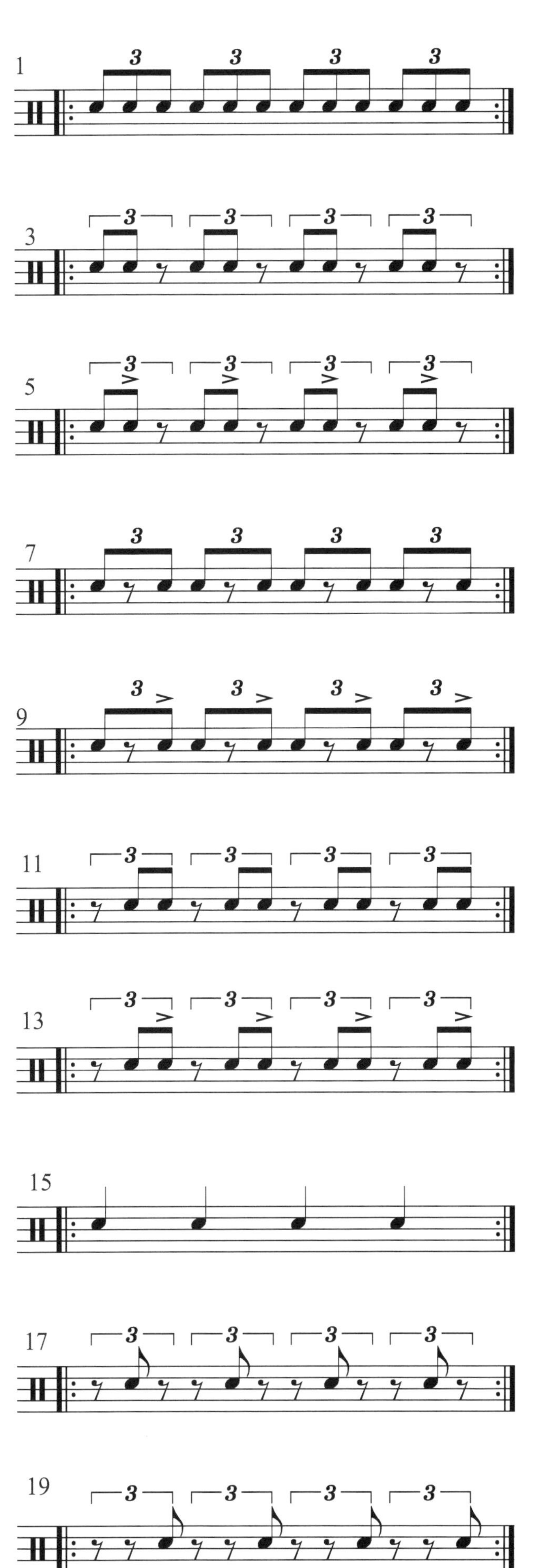

2

4

6

8

10

12

14

16

18

20

Subdivisions Per Beat

32nd Note Exercises

32nd notes in 4|4 time divide the beat in to eight equal sections, or four sections per 8th note. In 4|4 time 32nd notes give us the binary rhythmic alphabet expressed in half a beat, or an 8th note.

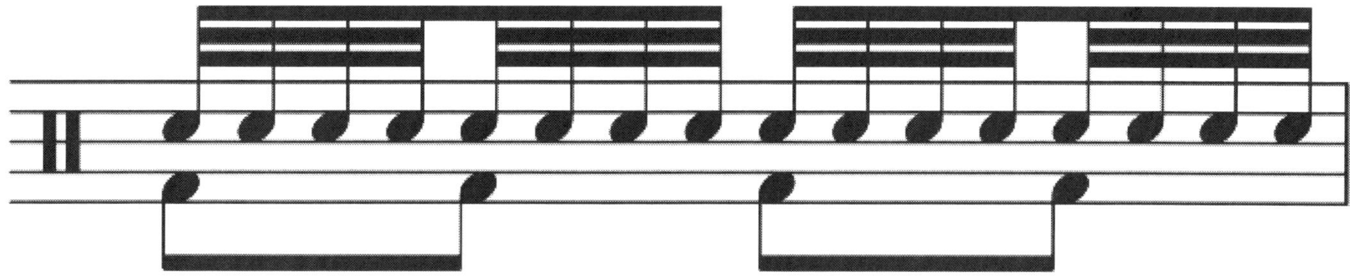

32nd Note Accents

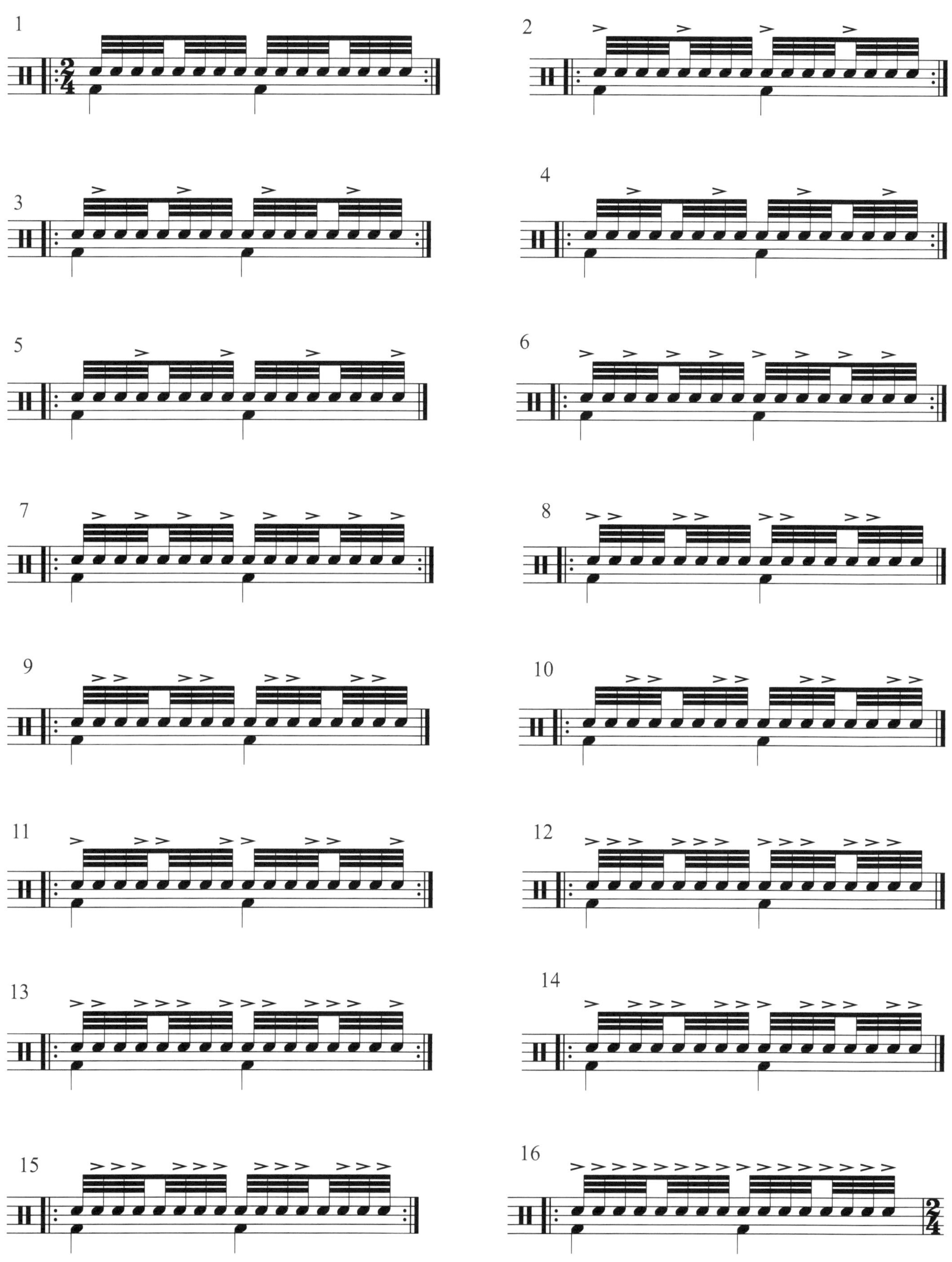

32nd Note Rhythms Rhythms

32nd Note Accents

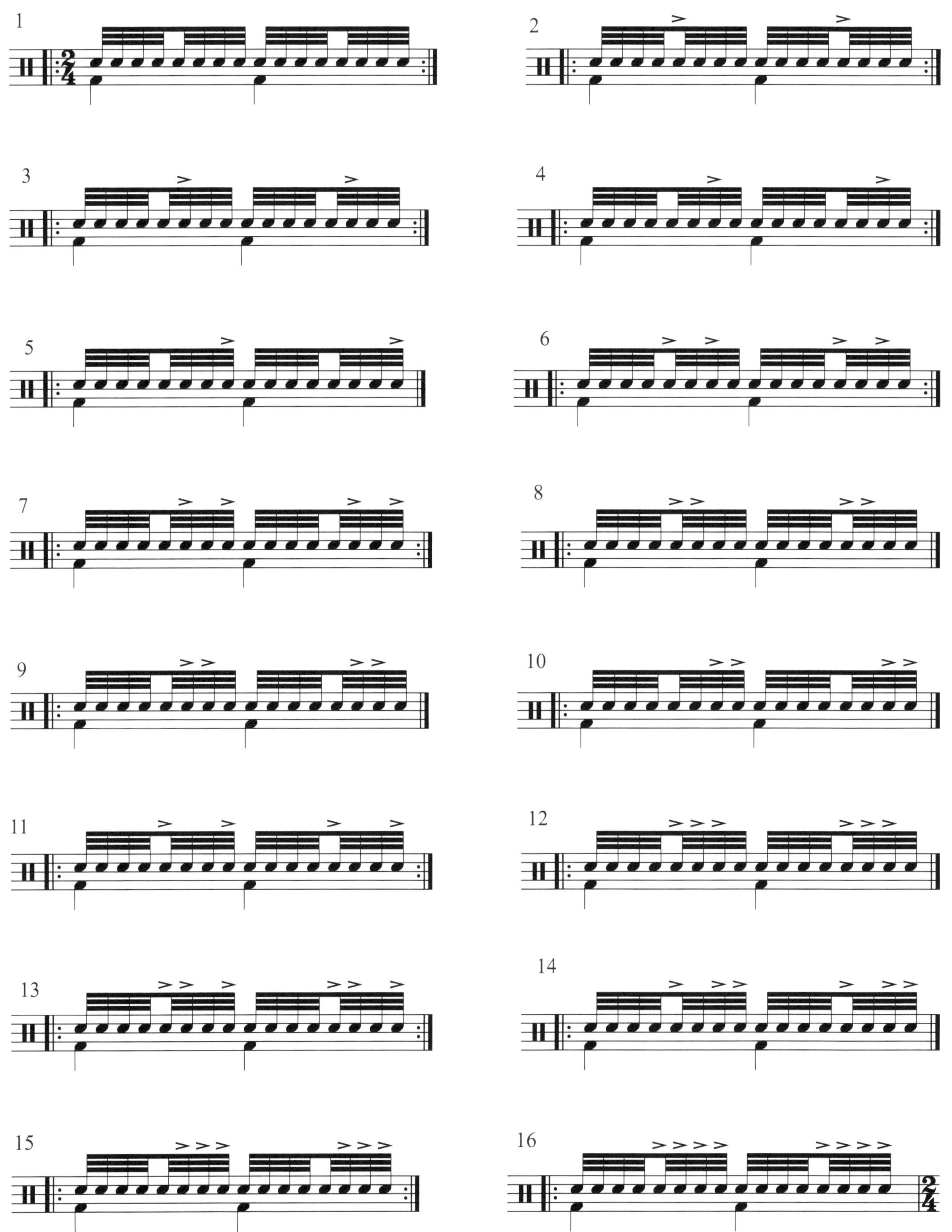

32nd Note Accents

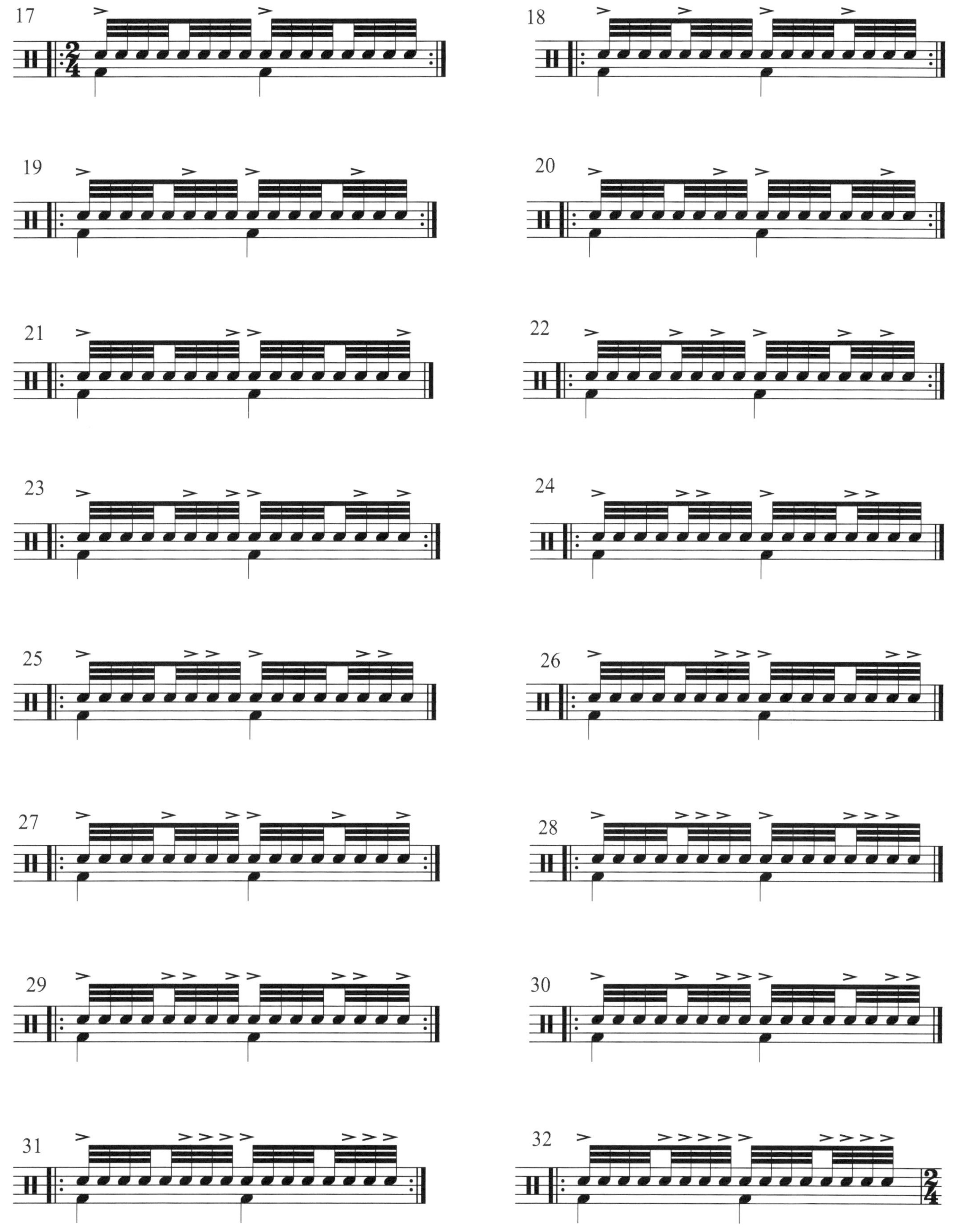

32nd Note Accents

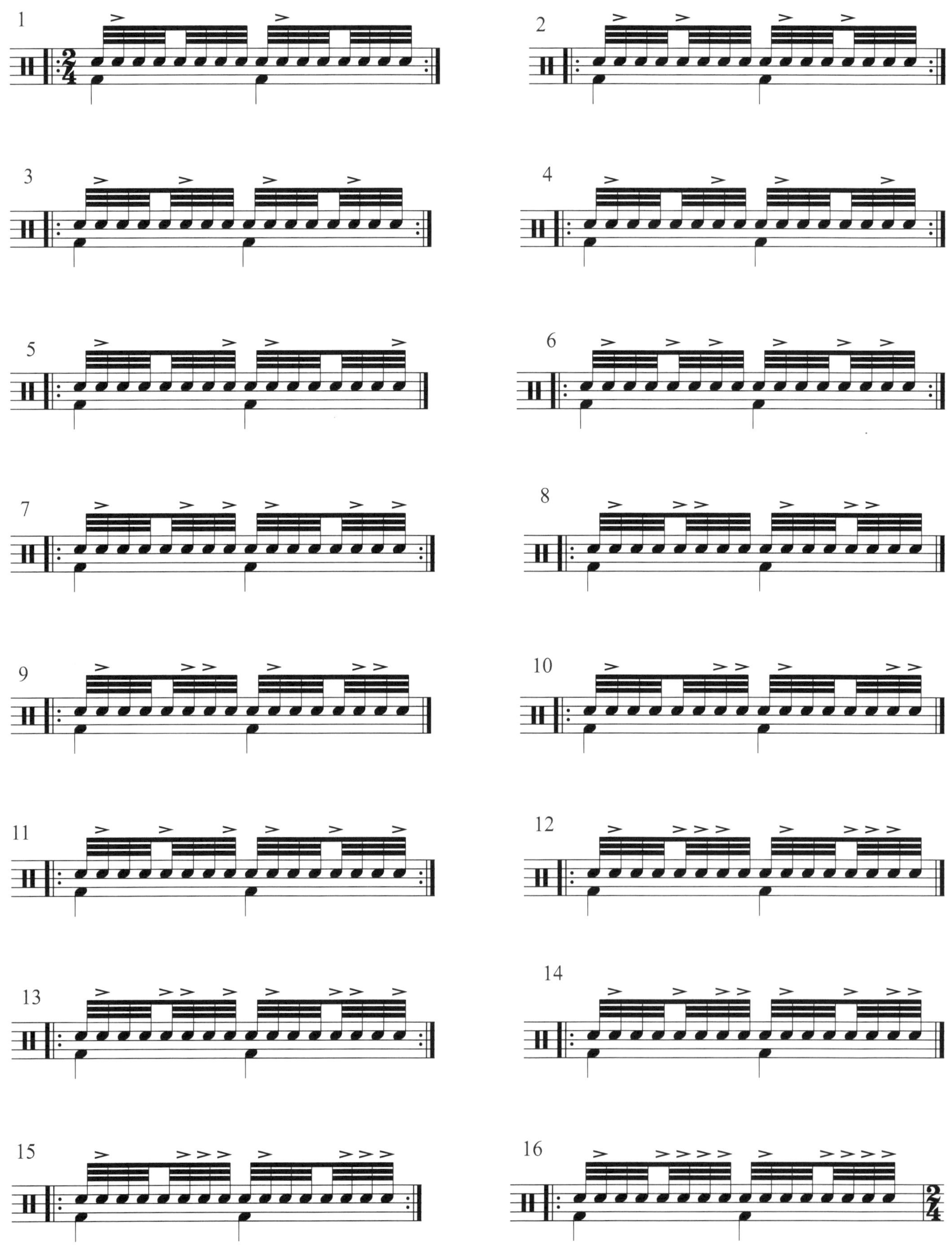

32nd Note Accents

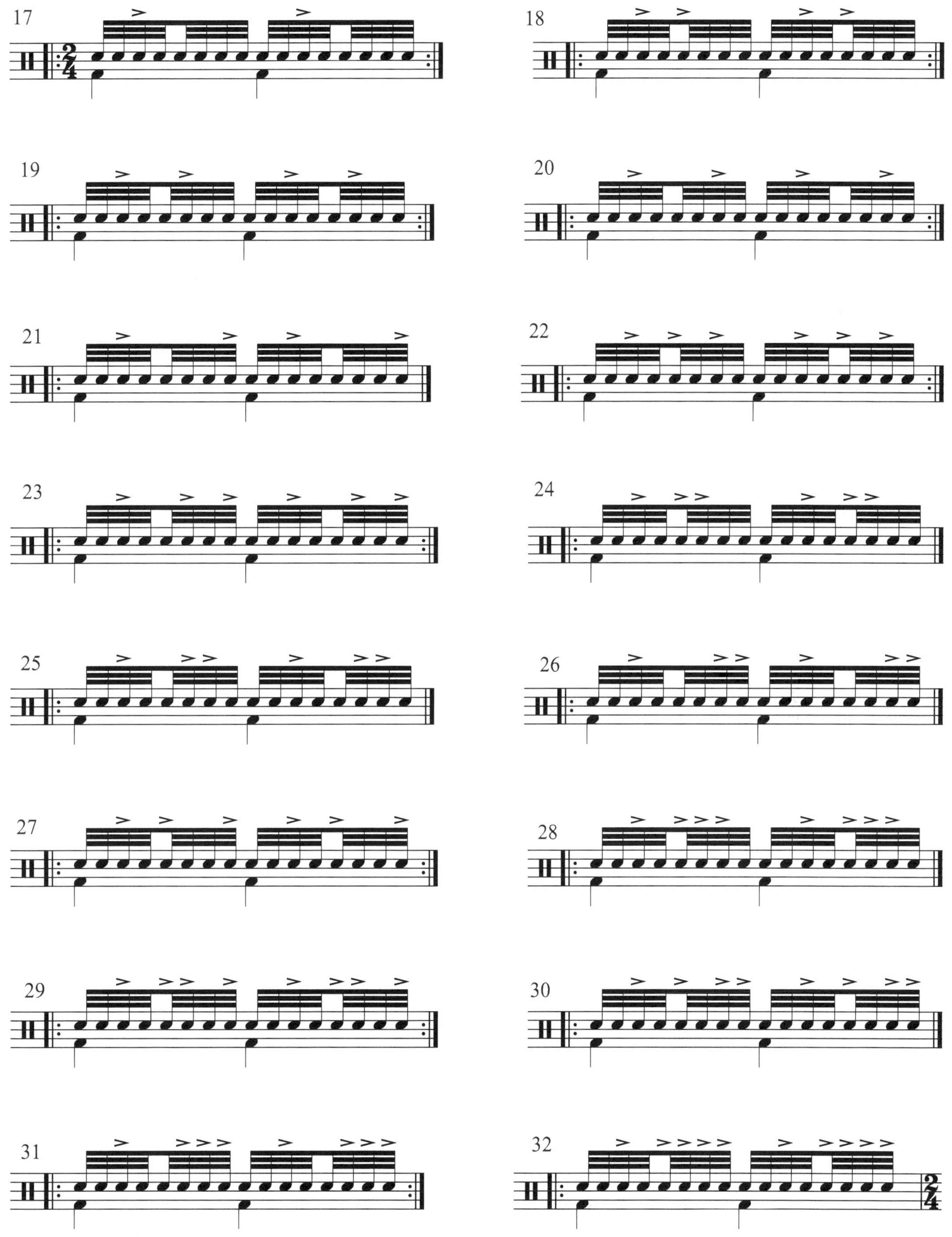

32nd Note Accents

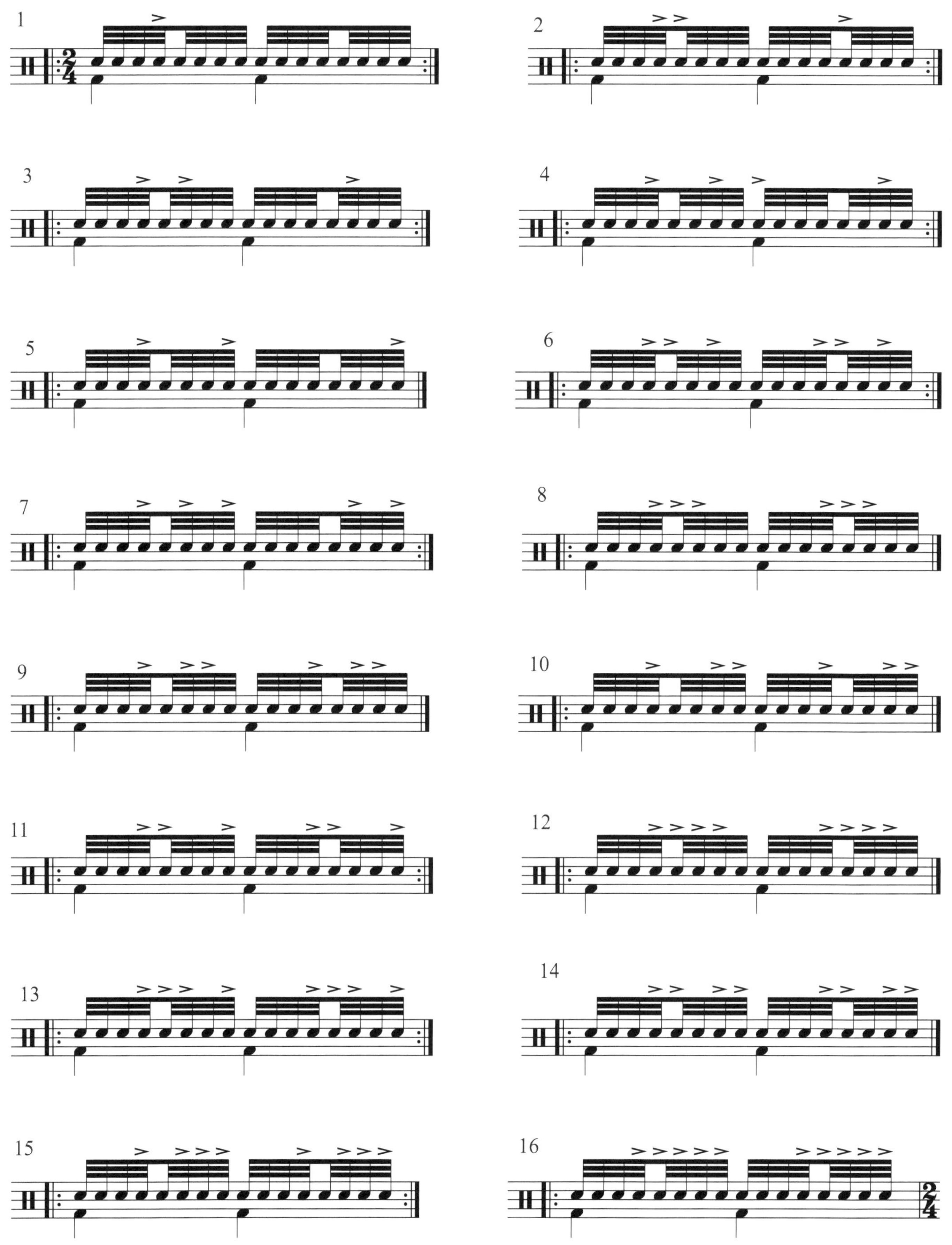

32nd Note Accents

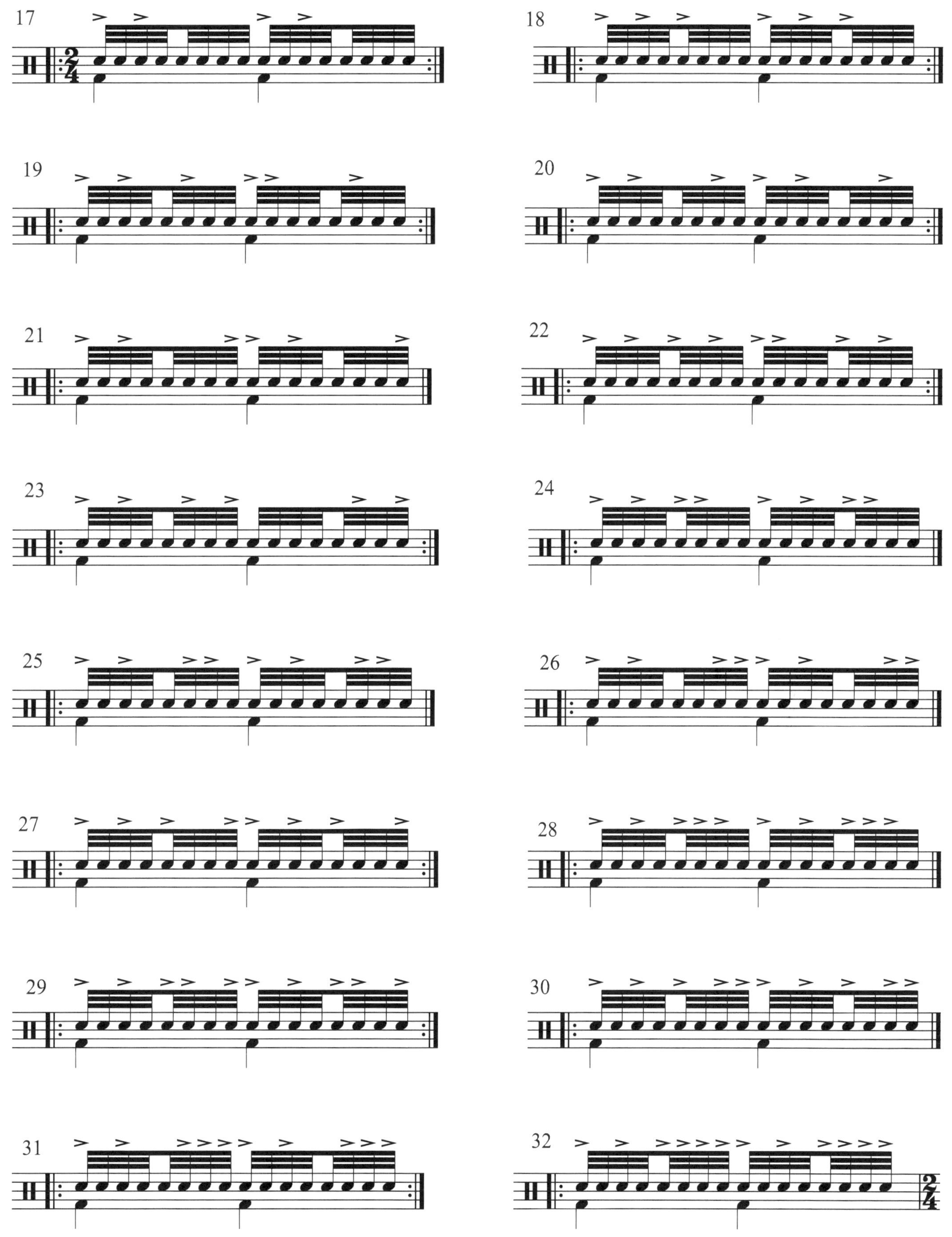

32nd Note Accents

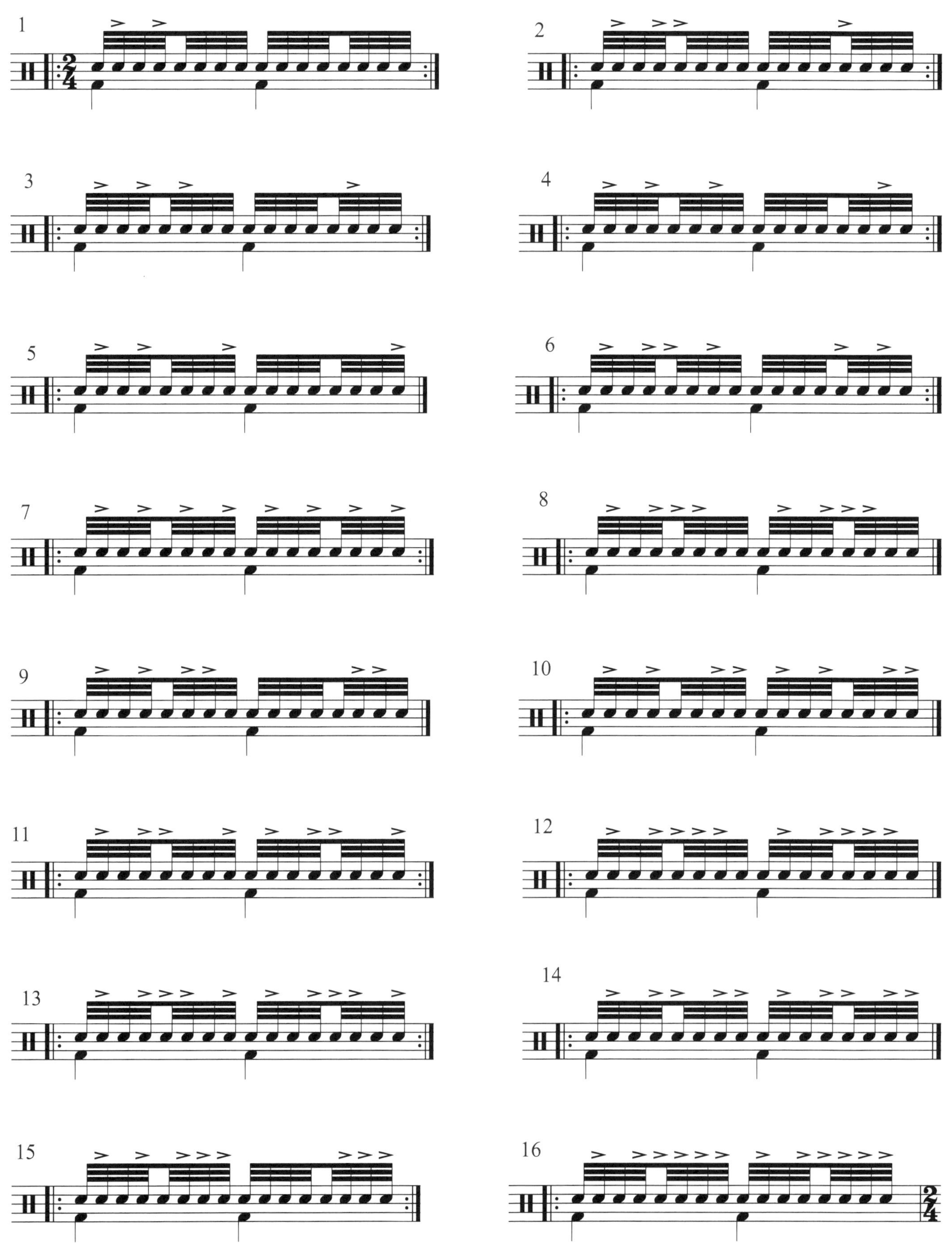

32nd Note Accents

32nd Note Accents

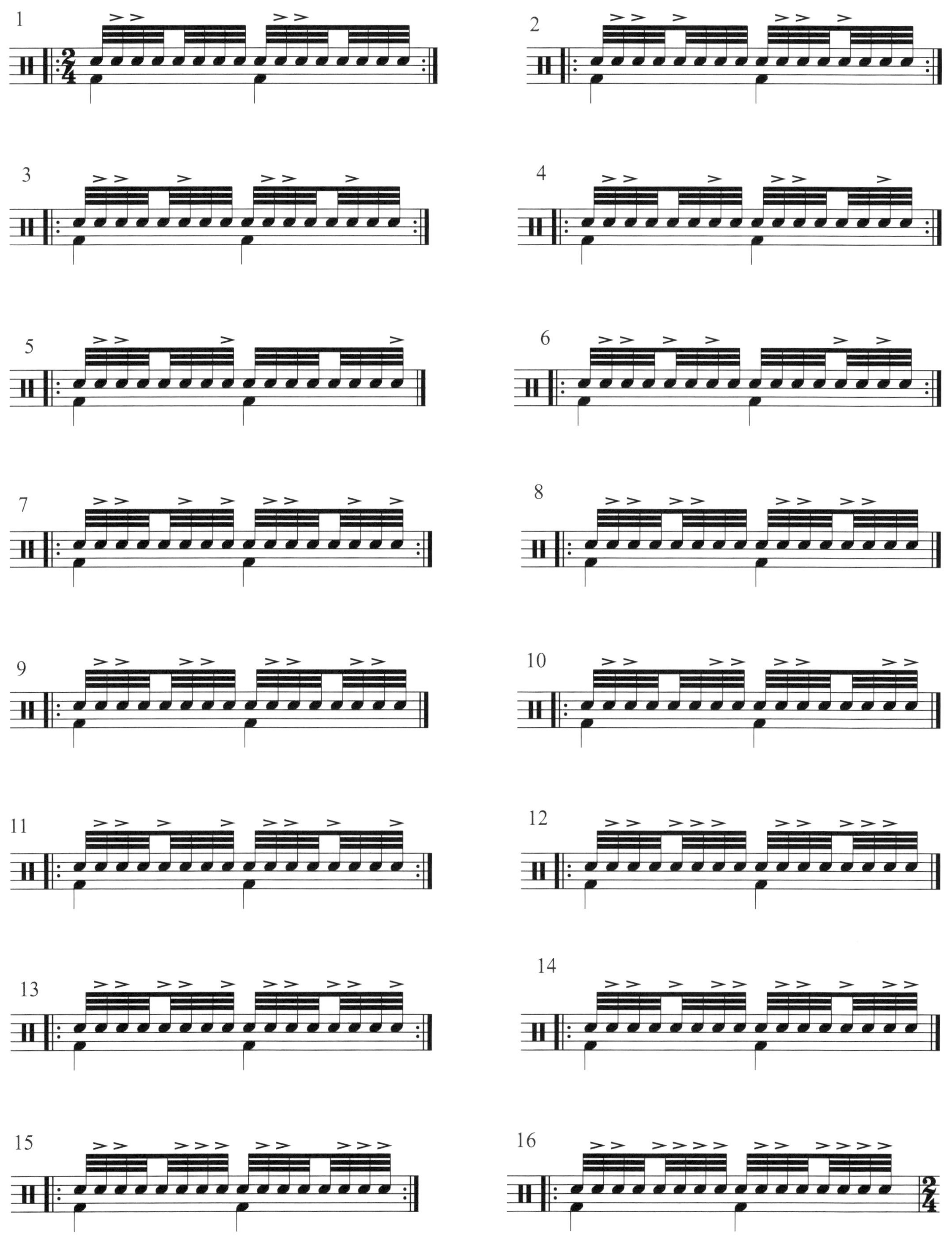

32nd Note Accents

32nd Note Accents

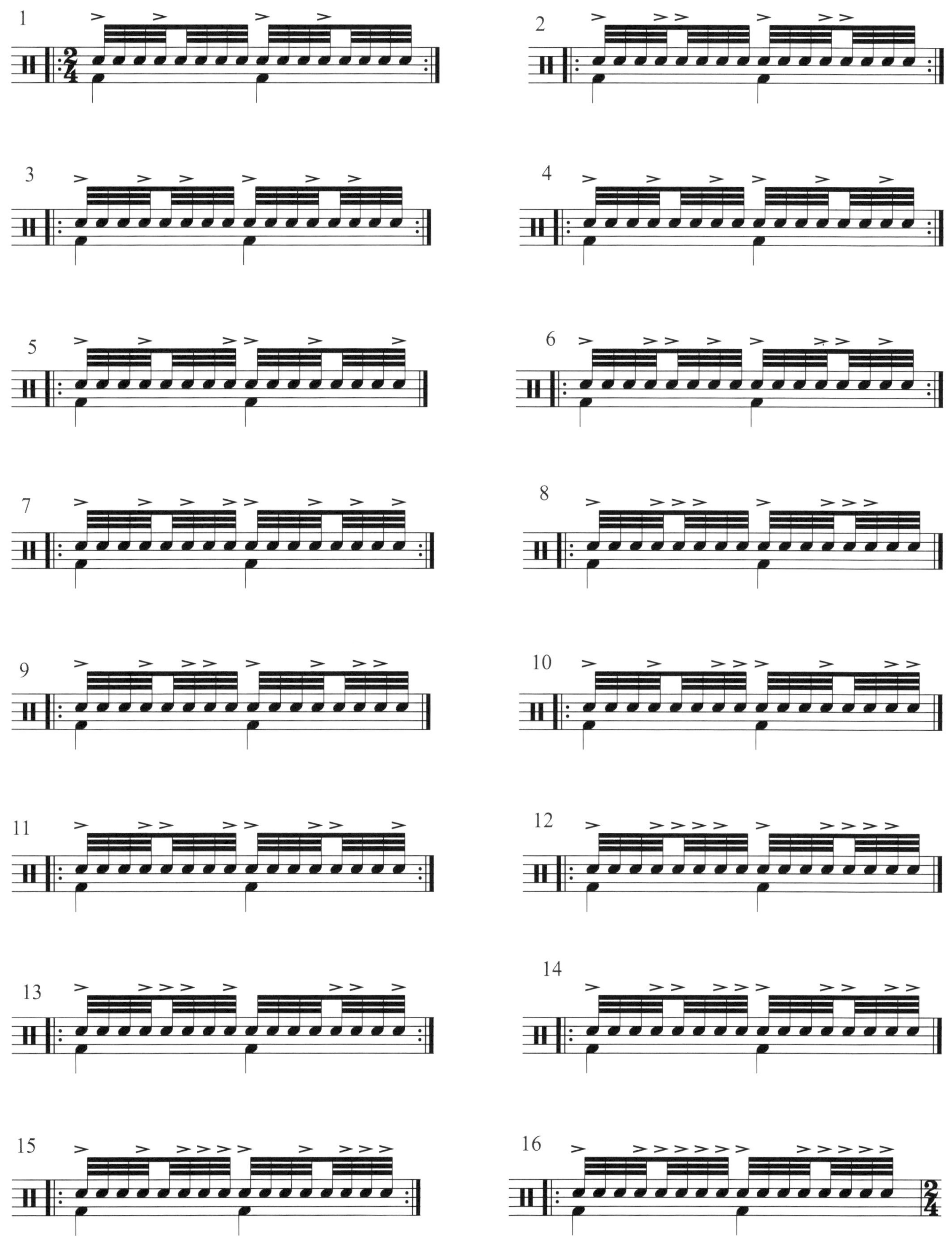

32nd Note Accents

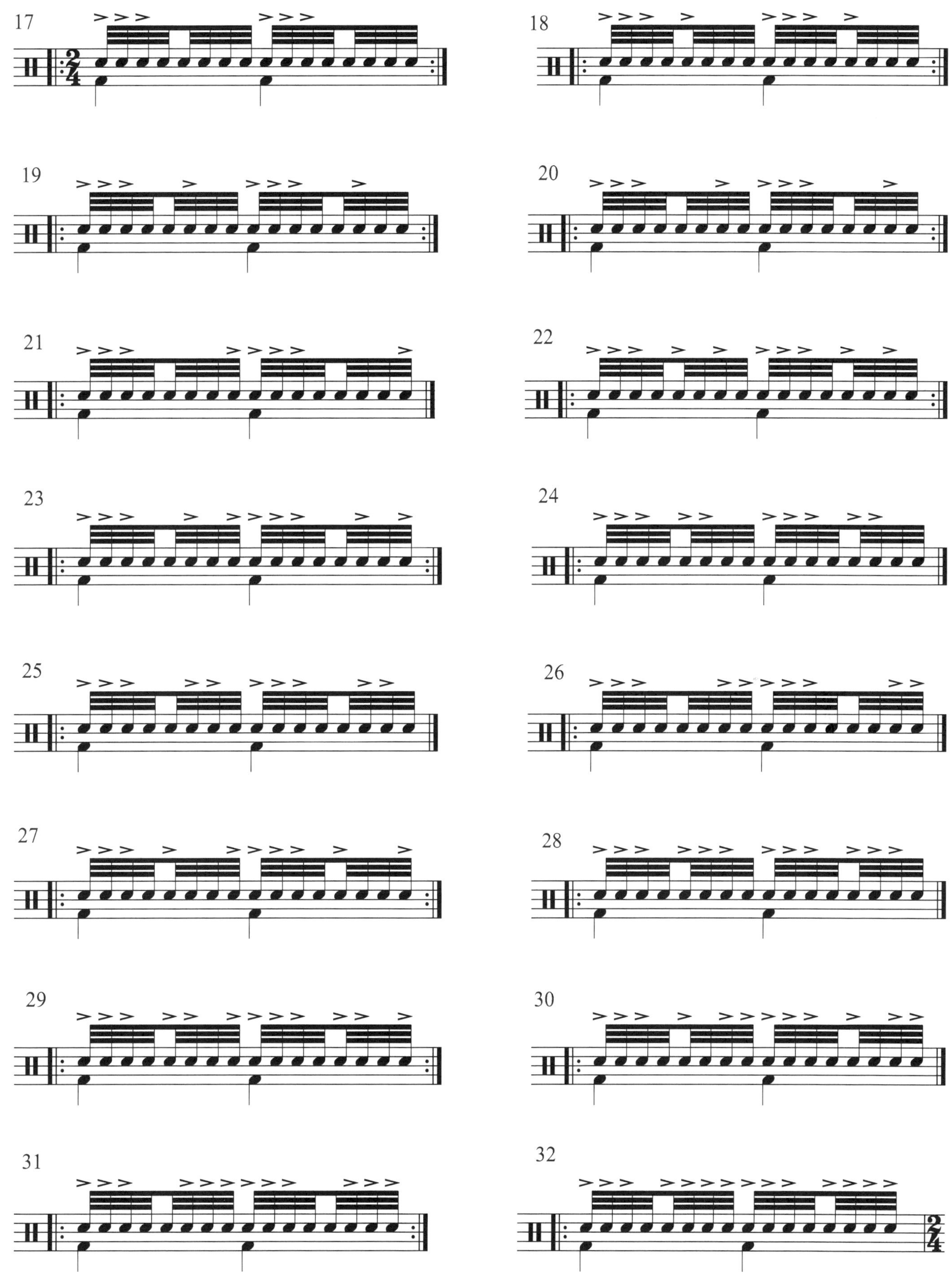

32nd Note Accents

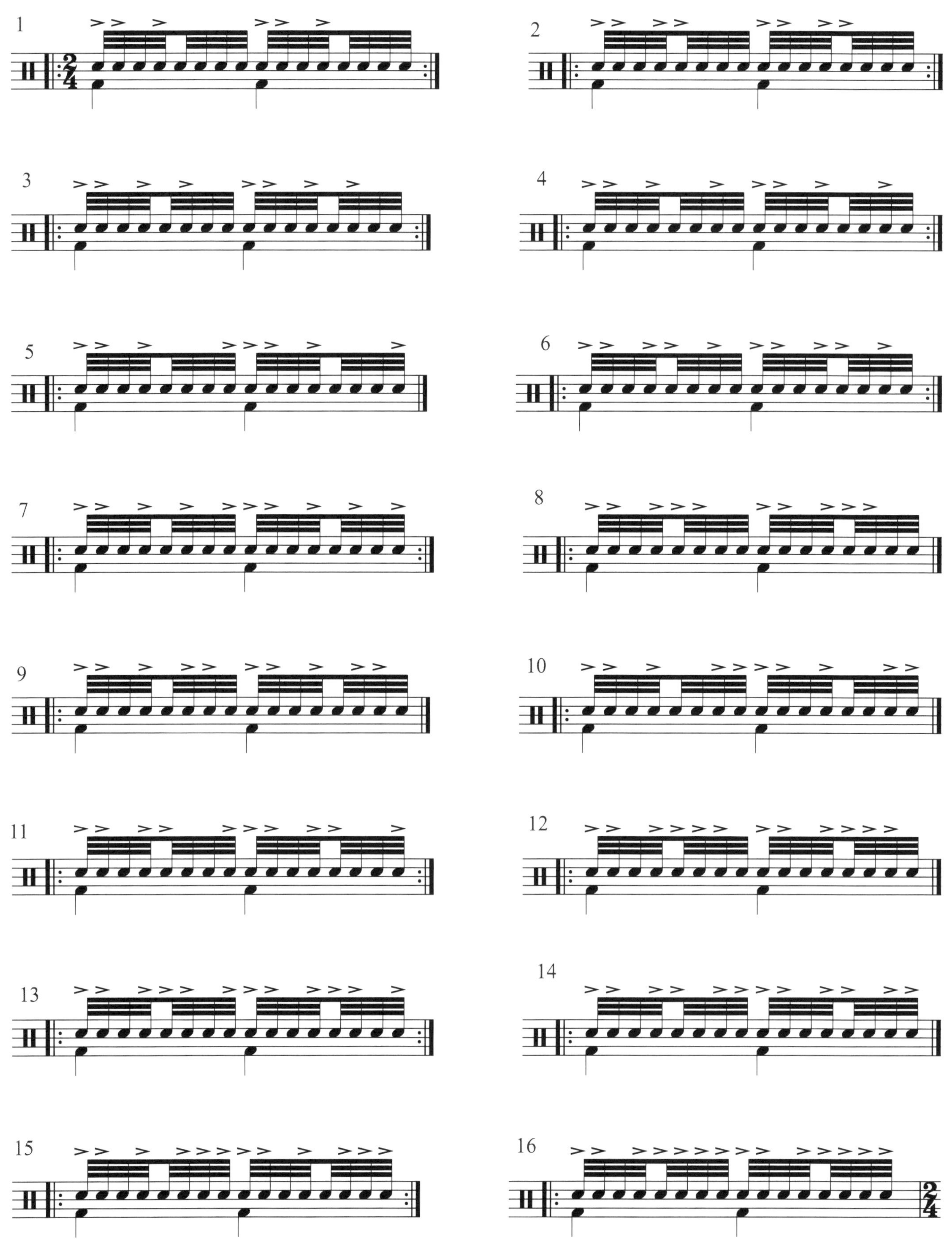

32nd Note Accents

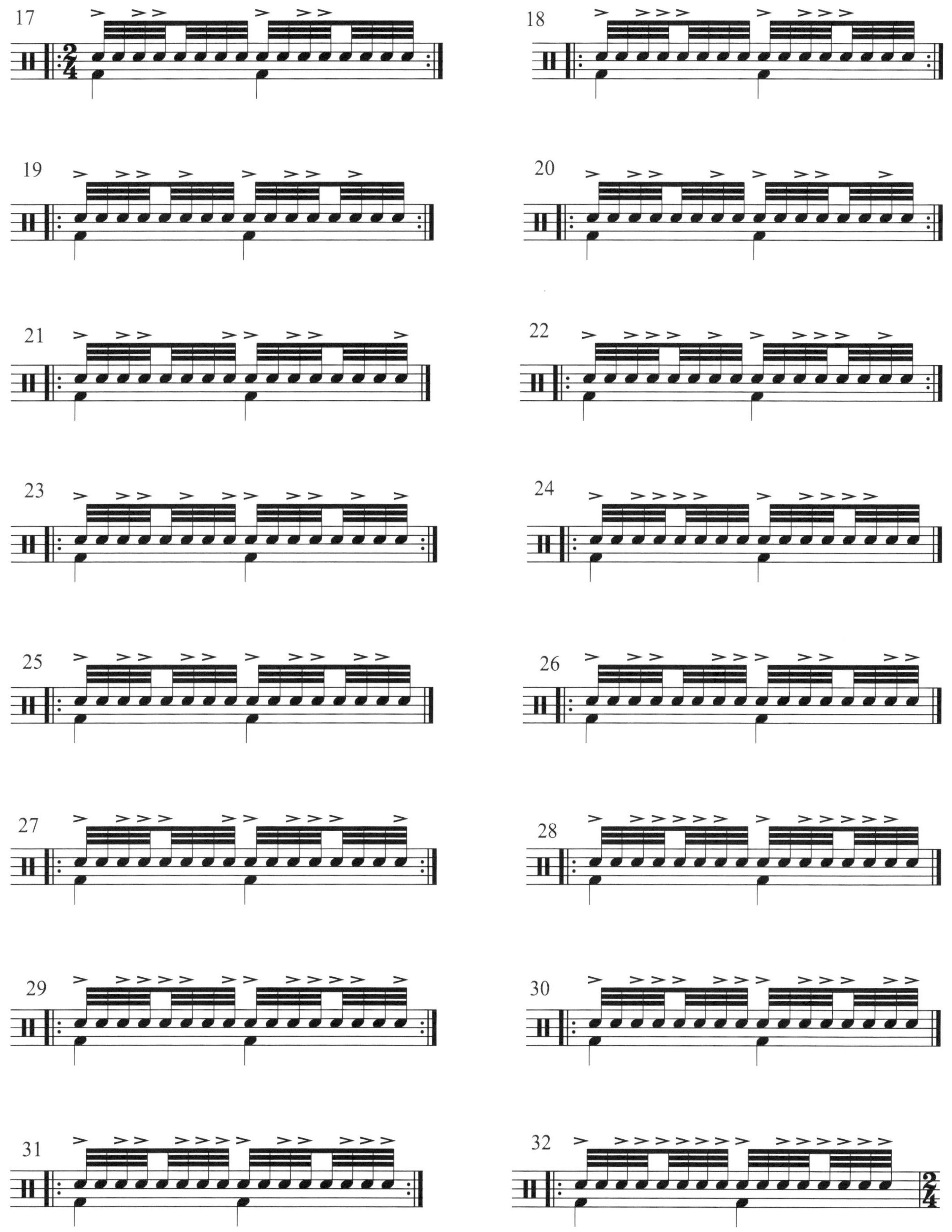

32nd Note Accents

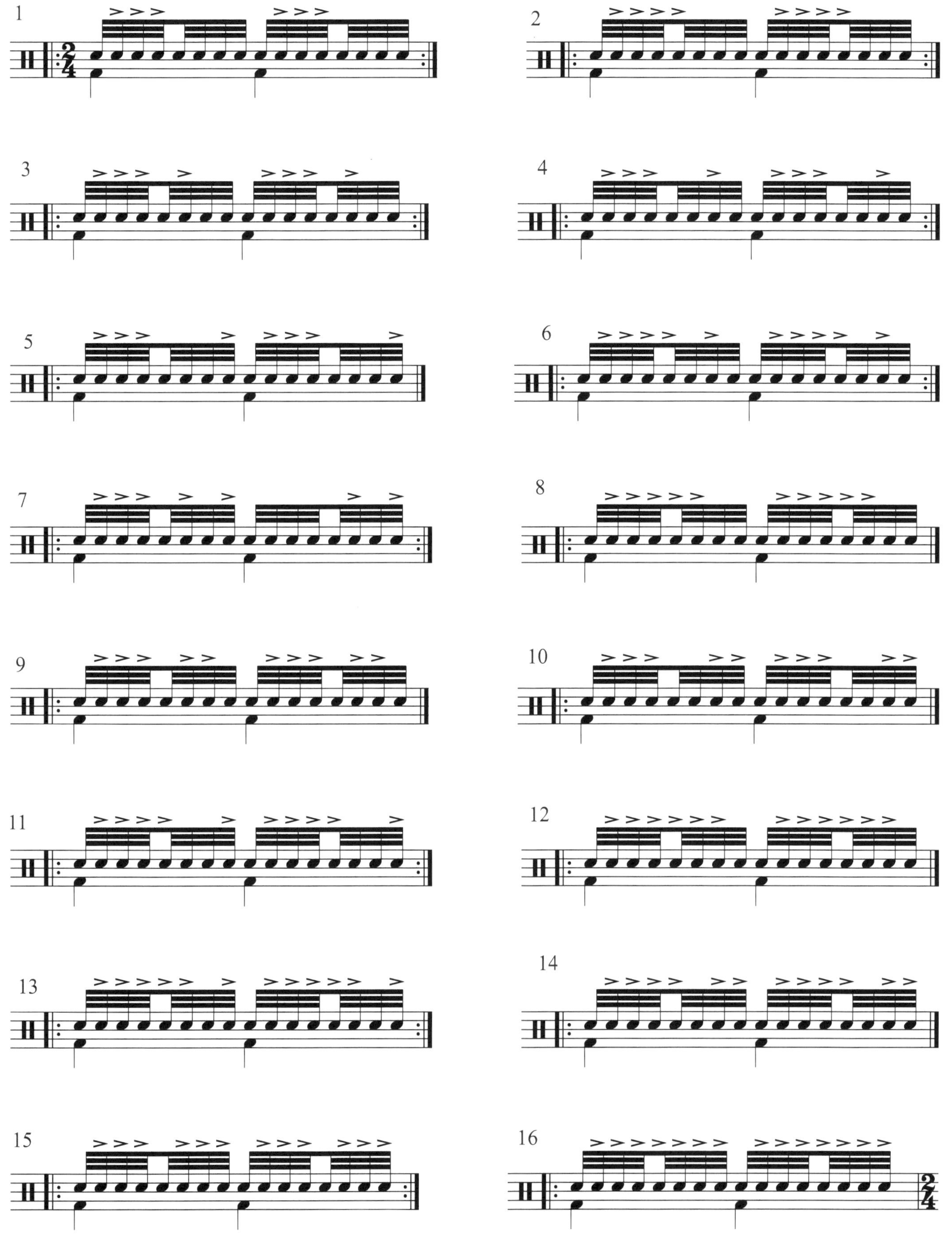

32nd Note Accents

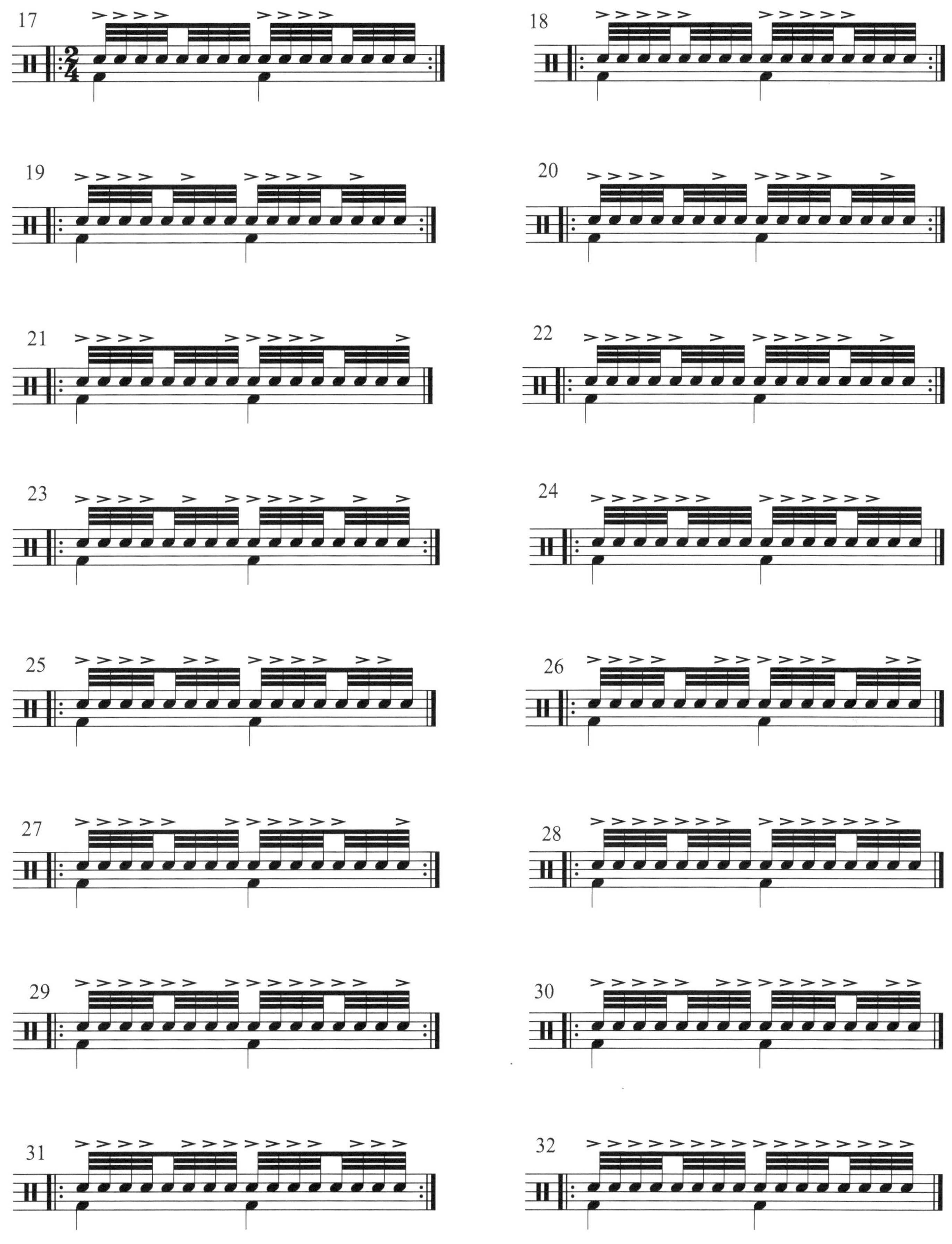

Subdivisions Per Beat

Now let's look at a brief overview of 32nd note rhythms, the binary rhythmic alphabet in half a beat of 4|4 time.

32nd Note Rhythms

32nd Note Rhythms

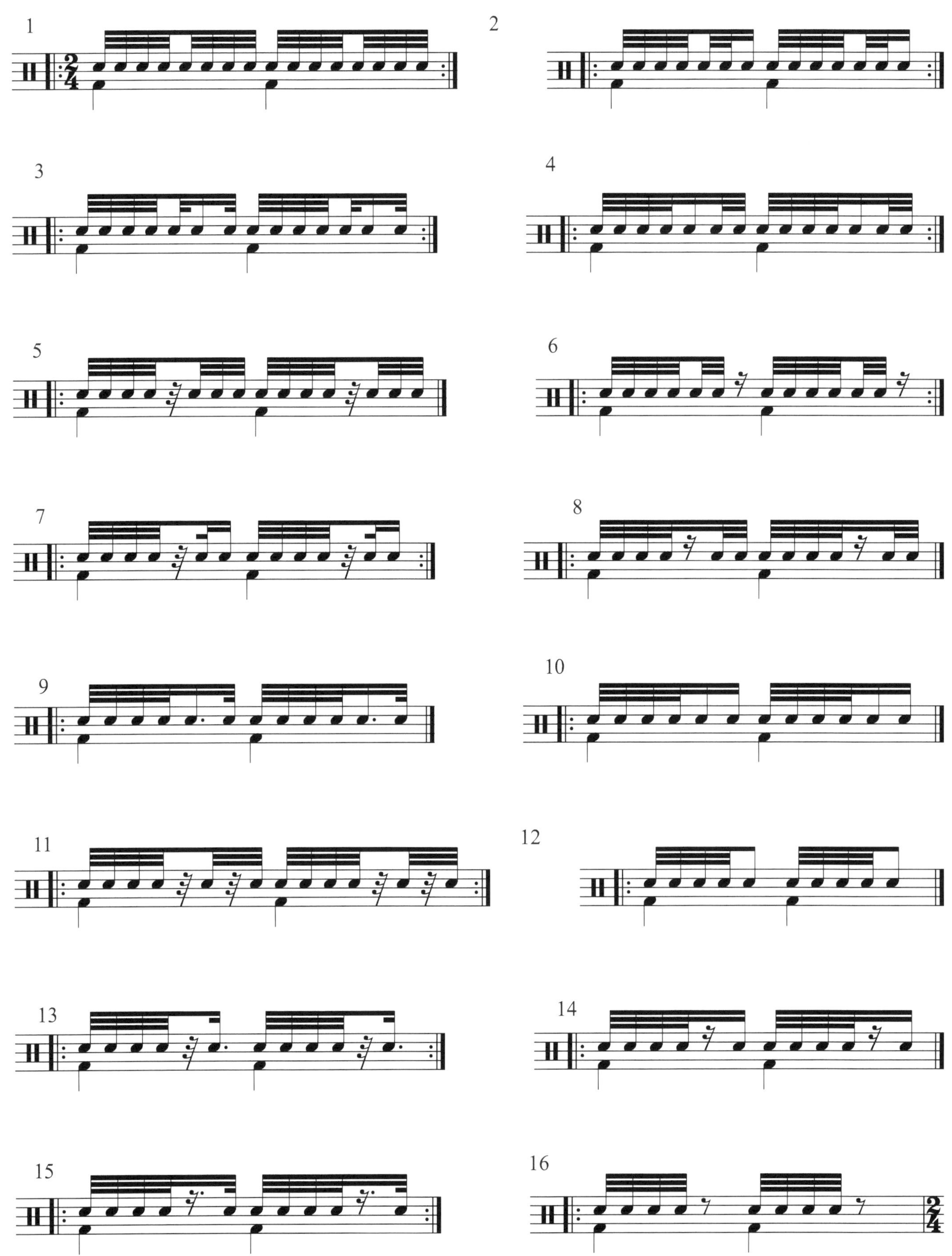

32nd Note Rhythms

32nd Note Rhythms

32nd Note Rhythms

32nd Note Rhythms

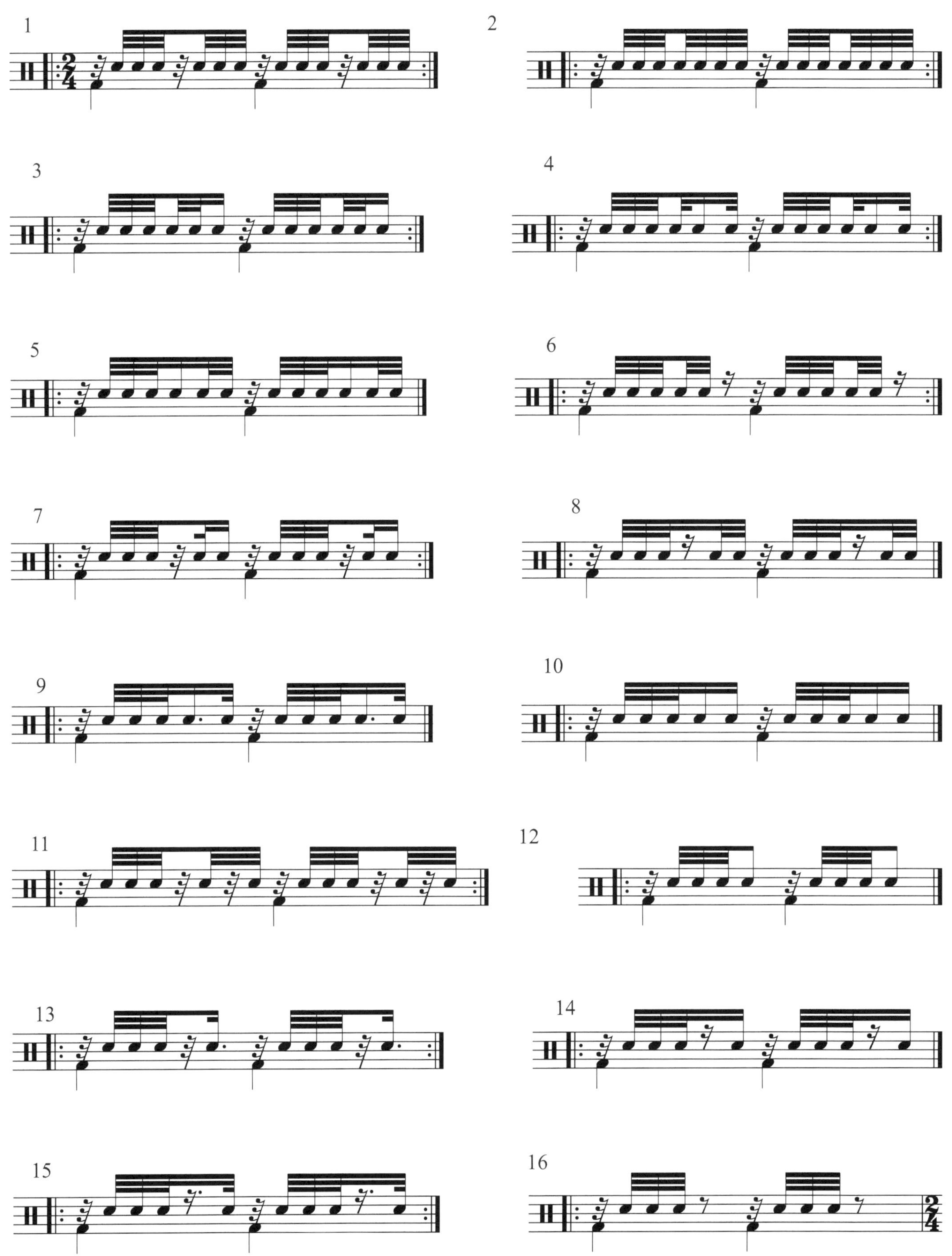

32nd Note Rhythms

32nd Note Rhythms

32nd Note Rhythms

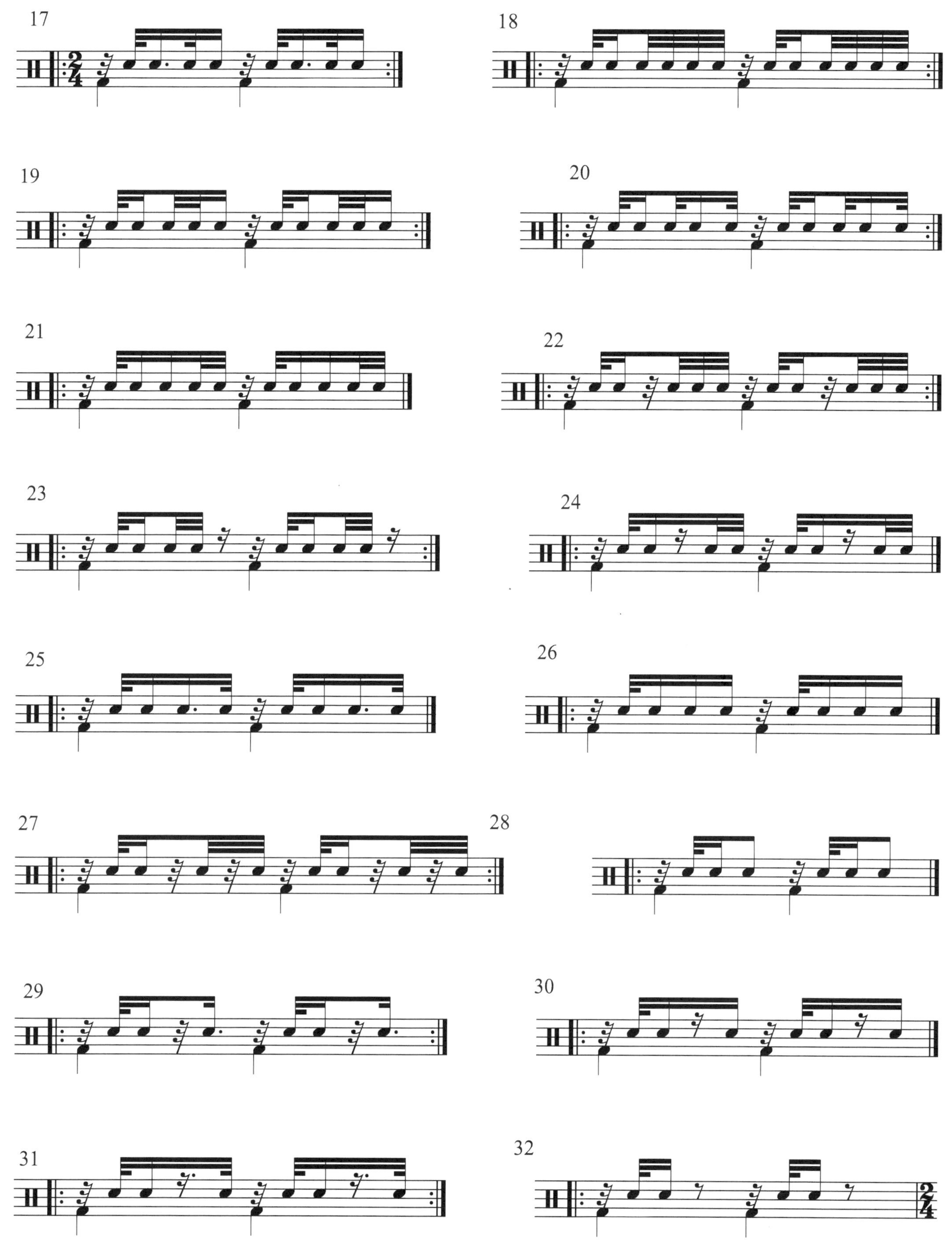

32nd Note Rhythms

32nd Note Rhythms

32nd Note Rhythms

32nd Note Rhythms

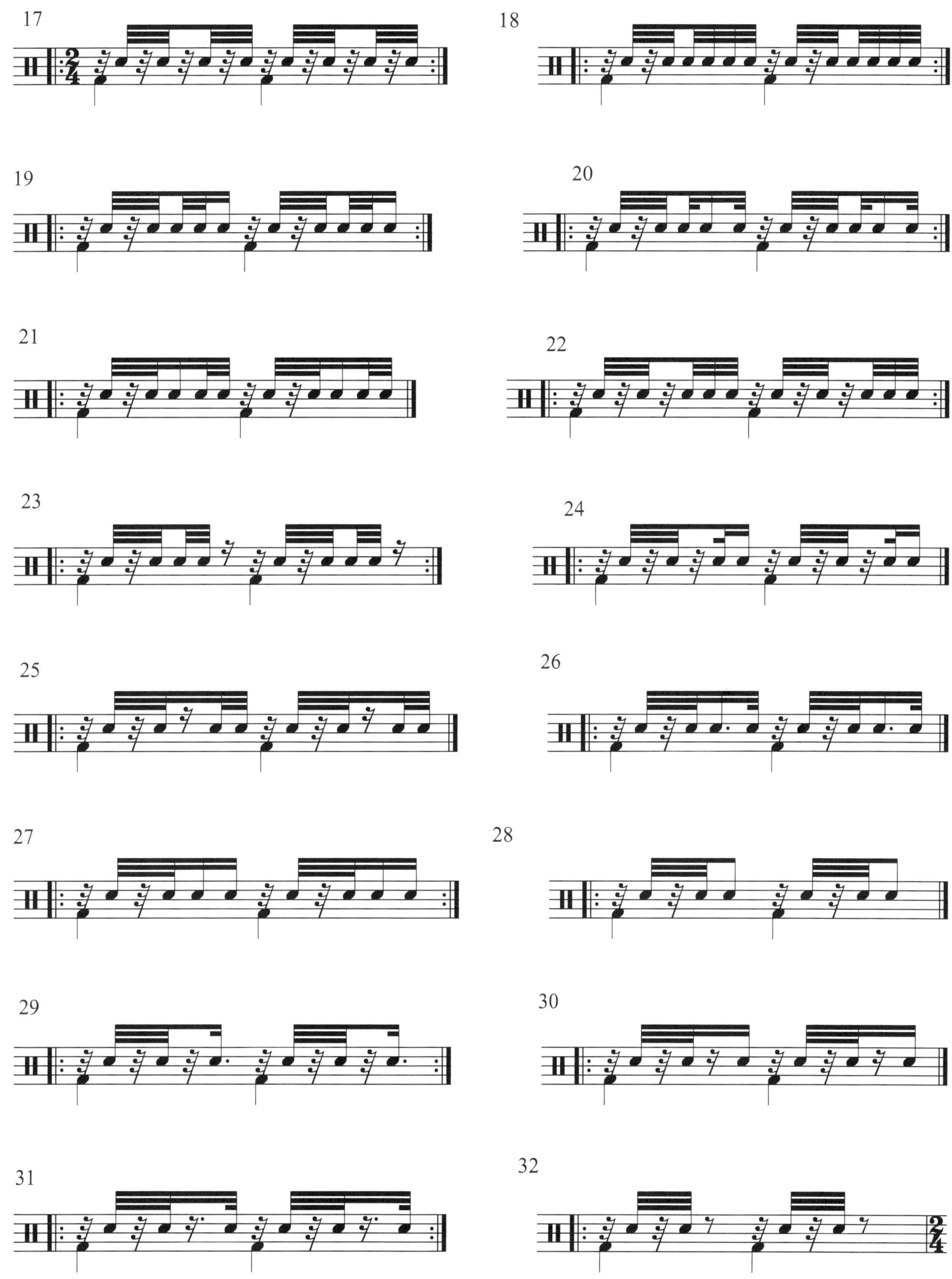

32nd Note Rhythms

32nd Note Rhythms

32nd Note Rhythms

32nd Note Rhythms

16th Note Triplets and Sextuplets

Now let's express the triplet alphabet in a smaller space, in half a beat instead of a whole beat. Sixteenth note triplets are three notes played evenly in the space of an eighth note. Sextuplets are six notes played evenly in the space of a quarter note. Both have 6 evenly spaced subdivisions in one beat. The difference in the two is where the emphasis placed, or how it grooves.

Here is a brief overview.

6s

Accents
1
6
6
2
6
6
3
6
6
4
6
6
5
6
6
6
6
6
7
6
6
8
6
6
9
6
6
10
6
6
Rhythms
1
6
6
2
6
6
3
6
6
4
6
6
5
3
3
6
6
6
7
8
6
6
9
6
6
10

6s Accents and Rhythms Overview

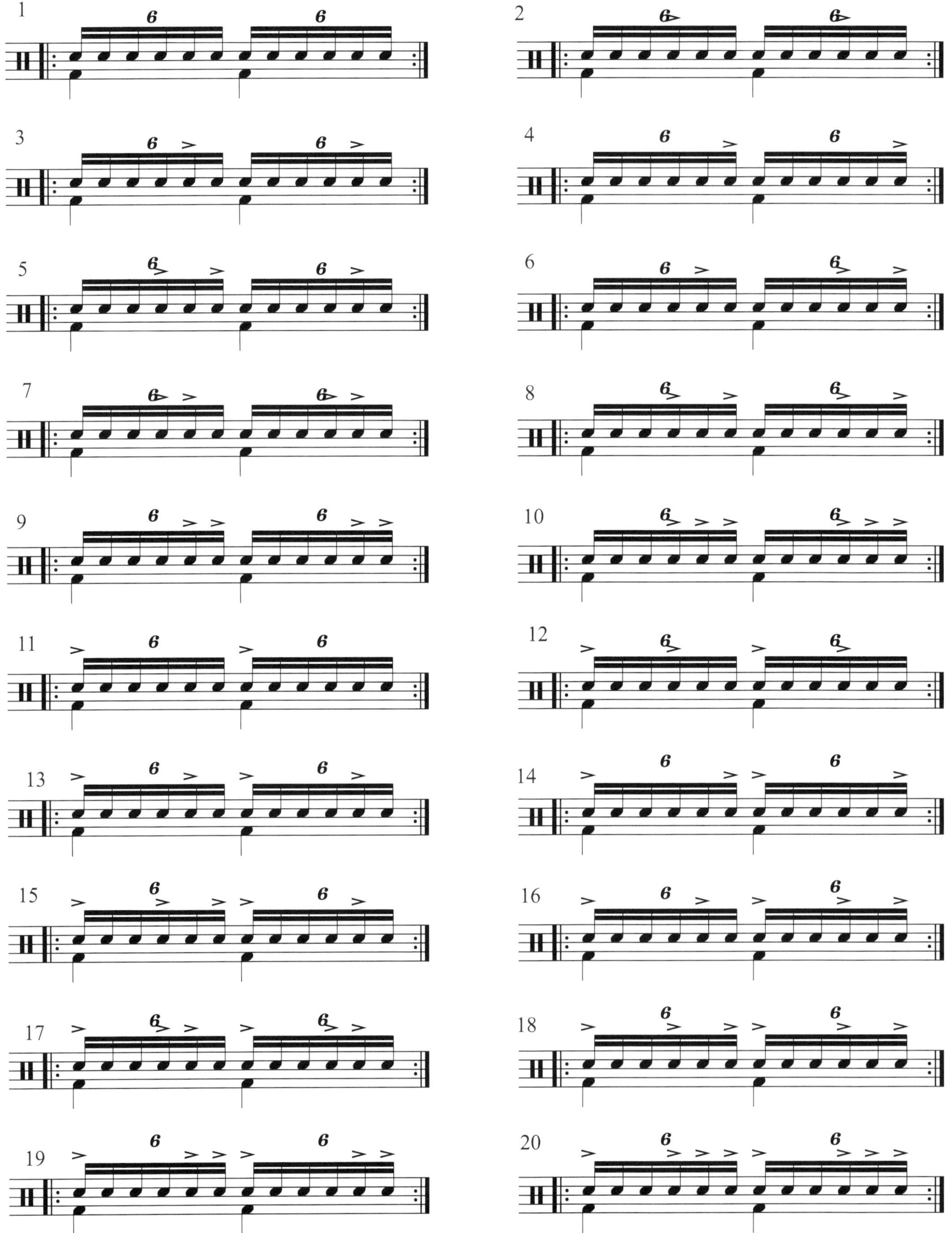

6s Accents and Rhythms Overview

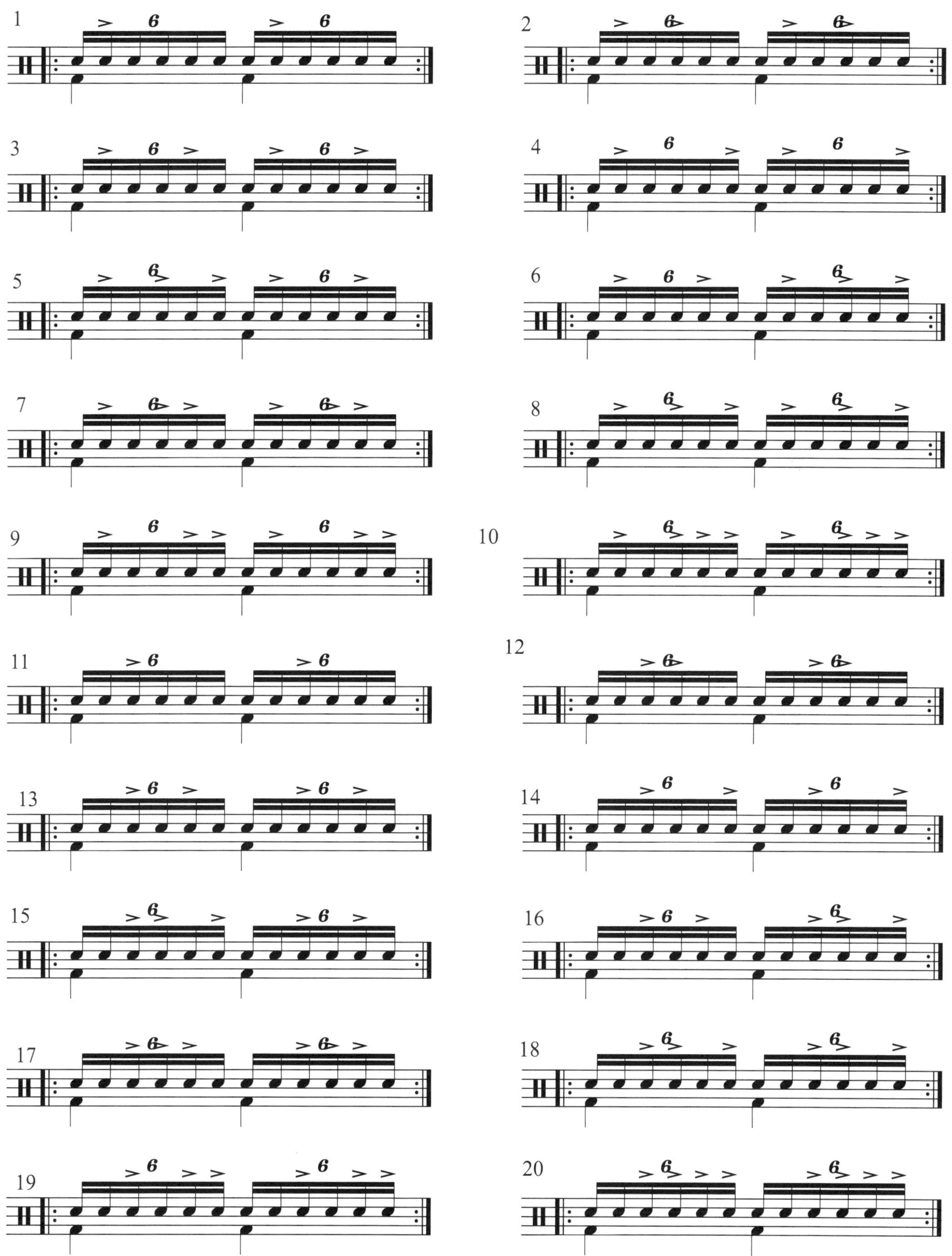

6s Accents and Rhythms Overview

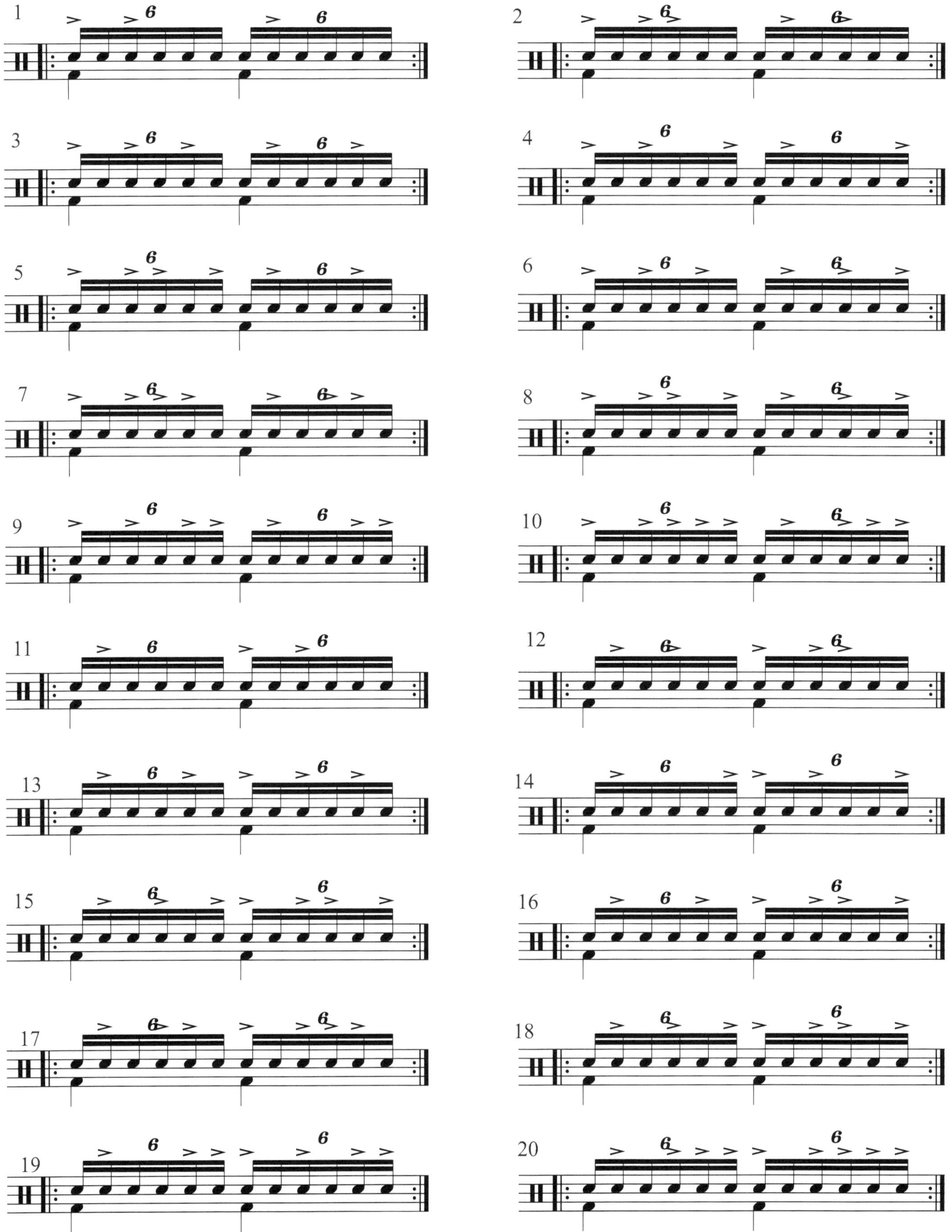

6s Accents and Rhythms Overview

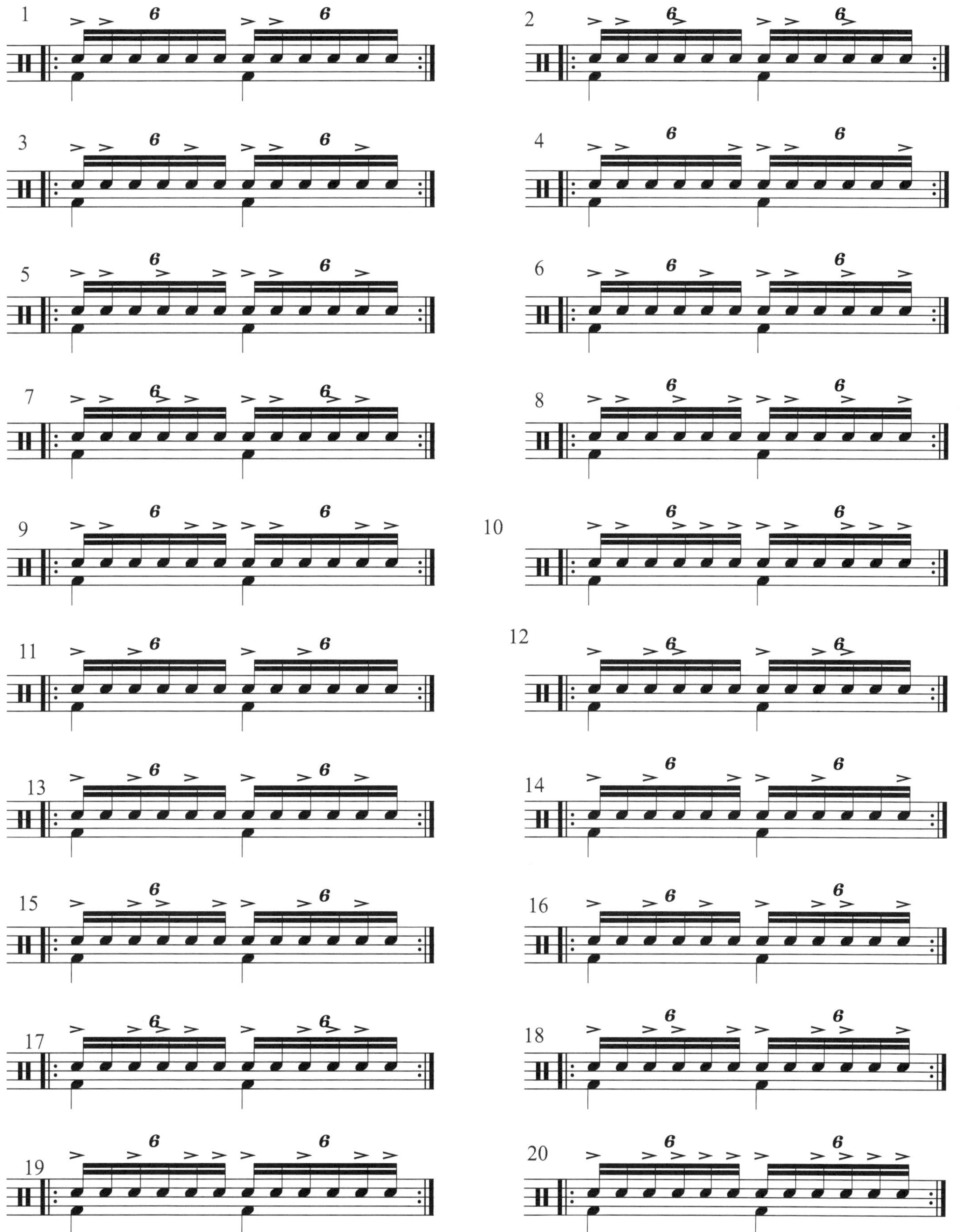

6s Accents and Rhythms Overview

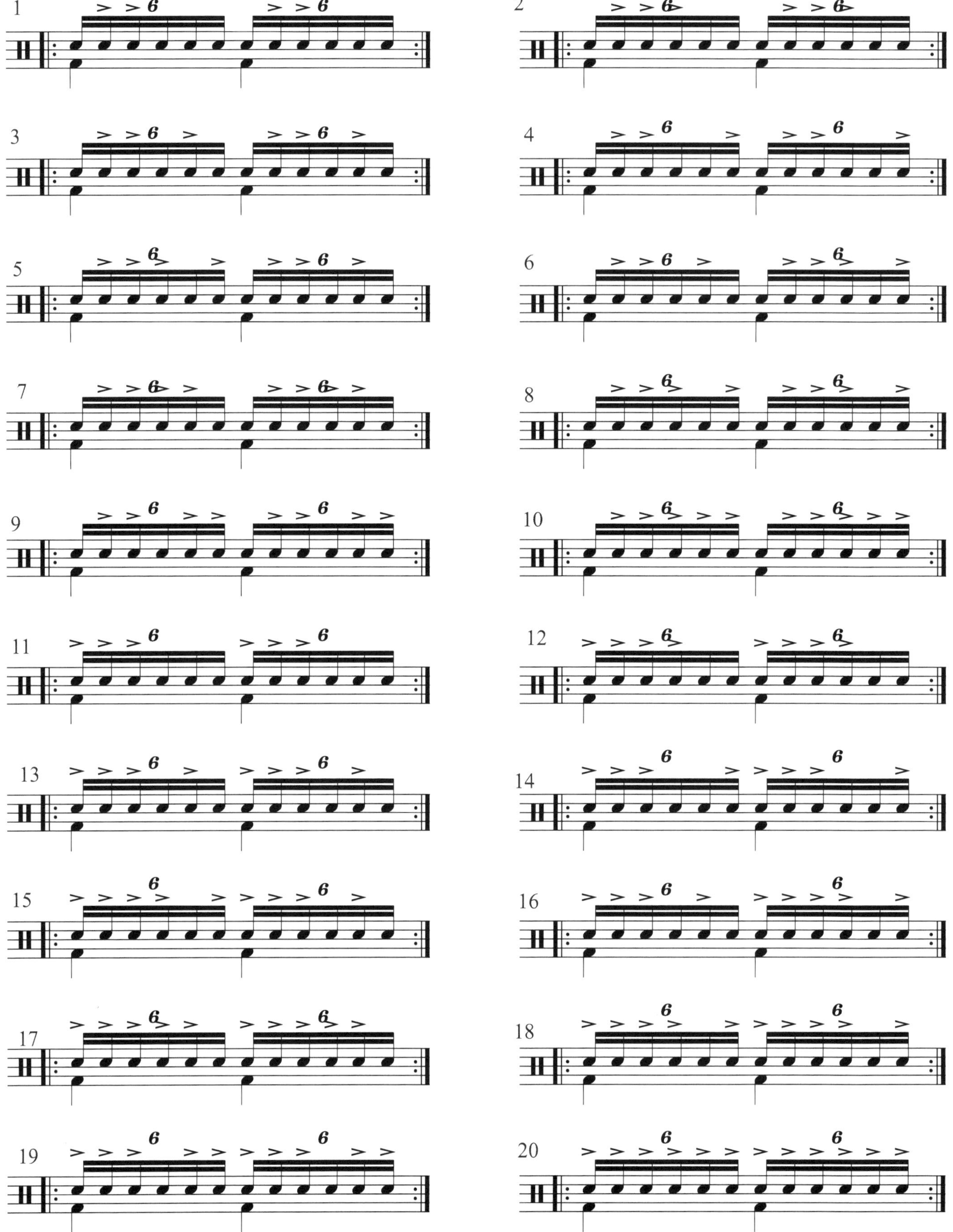

Subdivisions Per Beat

1

2

3

4

5

6

7

8

9

10

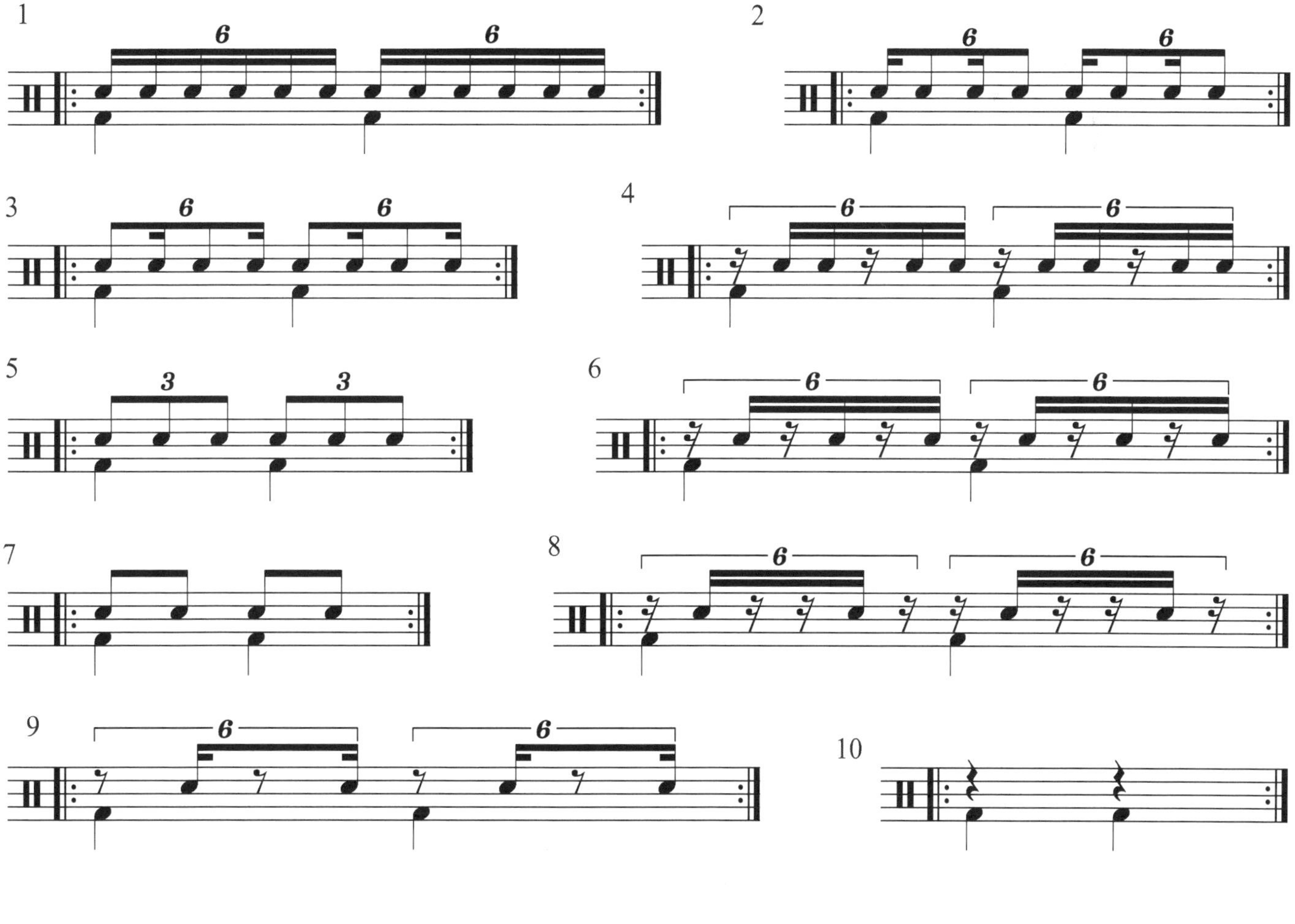

6s Accents and Rhythms Overview

6s Accents and Rhythms Overview

6s Accents and Rhythms Overview

6s Accents and Rhythms Overview

6s Accents and Rhythms Overview

Mixing Binary and Ternary Rhythms

In the next section we will briefly explore playing 8th notes, 8th note triplets, 16th notes and 16th note triplets in the same measure.

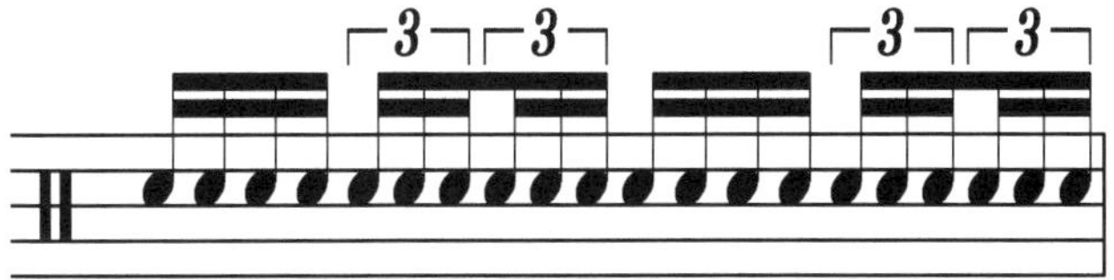

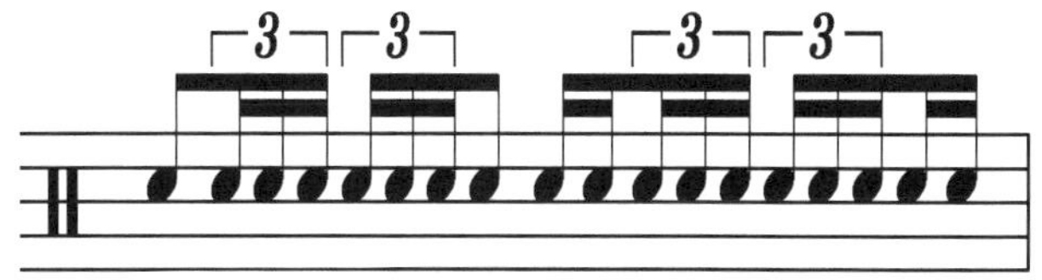

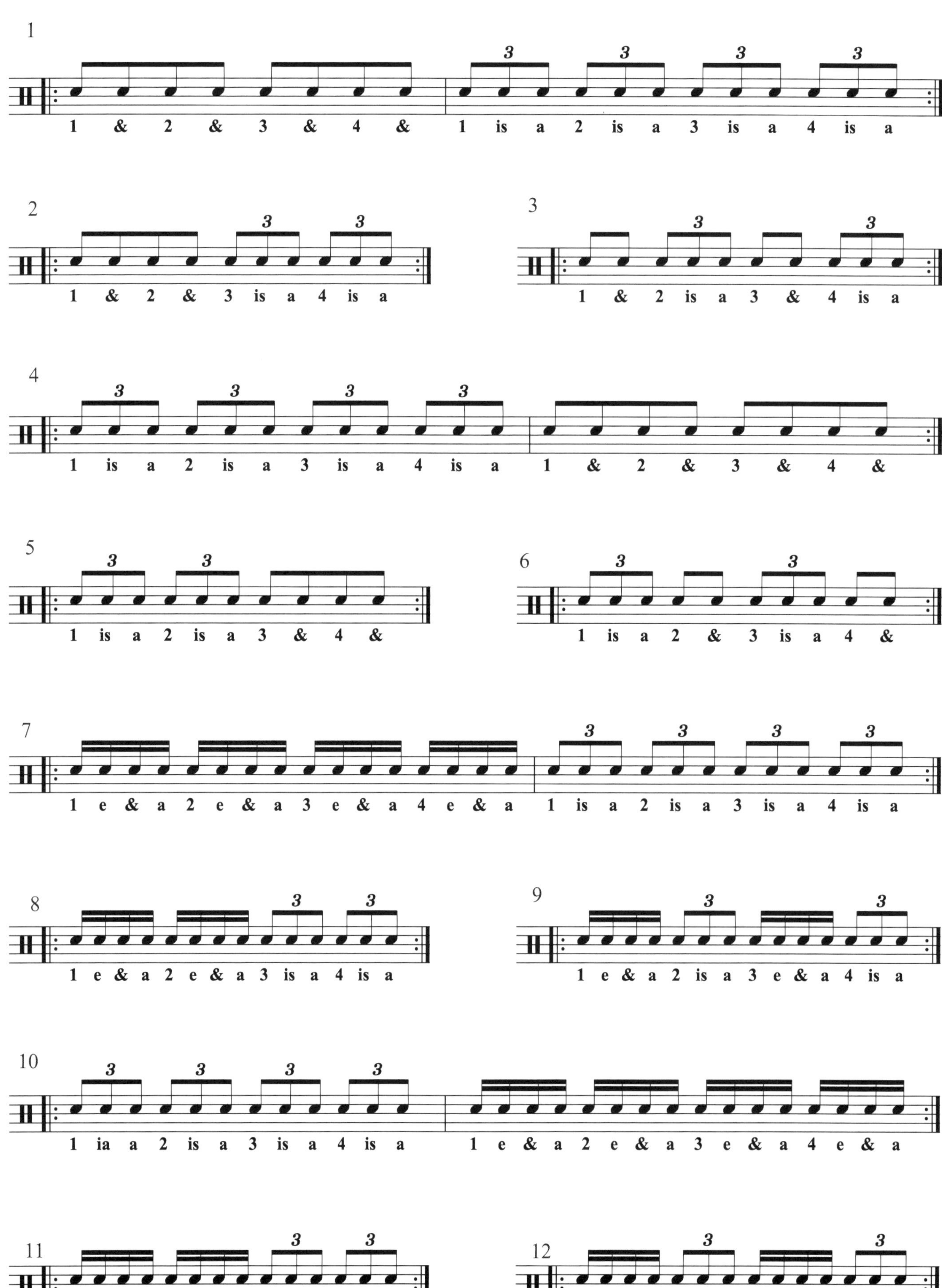
1
3 3 3 3
1 & 2 & 3 & 4 & 1 is a 2 is a 3 is a 4 is a
2
3 3
1 & 2 & 3 is a 4 is a
3
3 3
1 & 2 is a 3 & 4 is a
4
3 3 3 3
1 is a 2 is a 3 is a 4 is a 1 & 2 & 3 & 4 &
5
3 3
1 is a 2 is a 3 & 4 &
6
3 3
1 is a 2 & 3 is a 4 &
7
3 3 3 3
1 e & a 2 e & a 3 e & a 4 e & a 1 is a 2 is a 3 is a 4 is a
8
3 3
1 e & a 2 e & a 3 is a 4 is a
9
3 3
1 e & a 2 is a 3 e & a 4 is a
10
3 3 3 3
1 ia a 2 is a 3 is a 4 is a 1 e & a 2 e & a 3 e & a 4 e & a
11
3 3
1 e & a 2 e & a 3 is a 4 is a
12
3 3
1 e & a 2 is a 3 e & a 4 is a

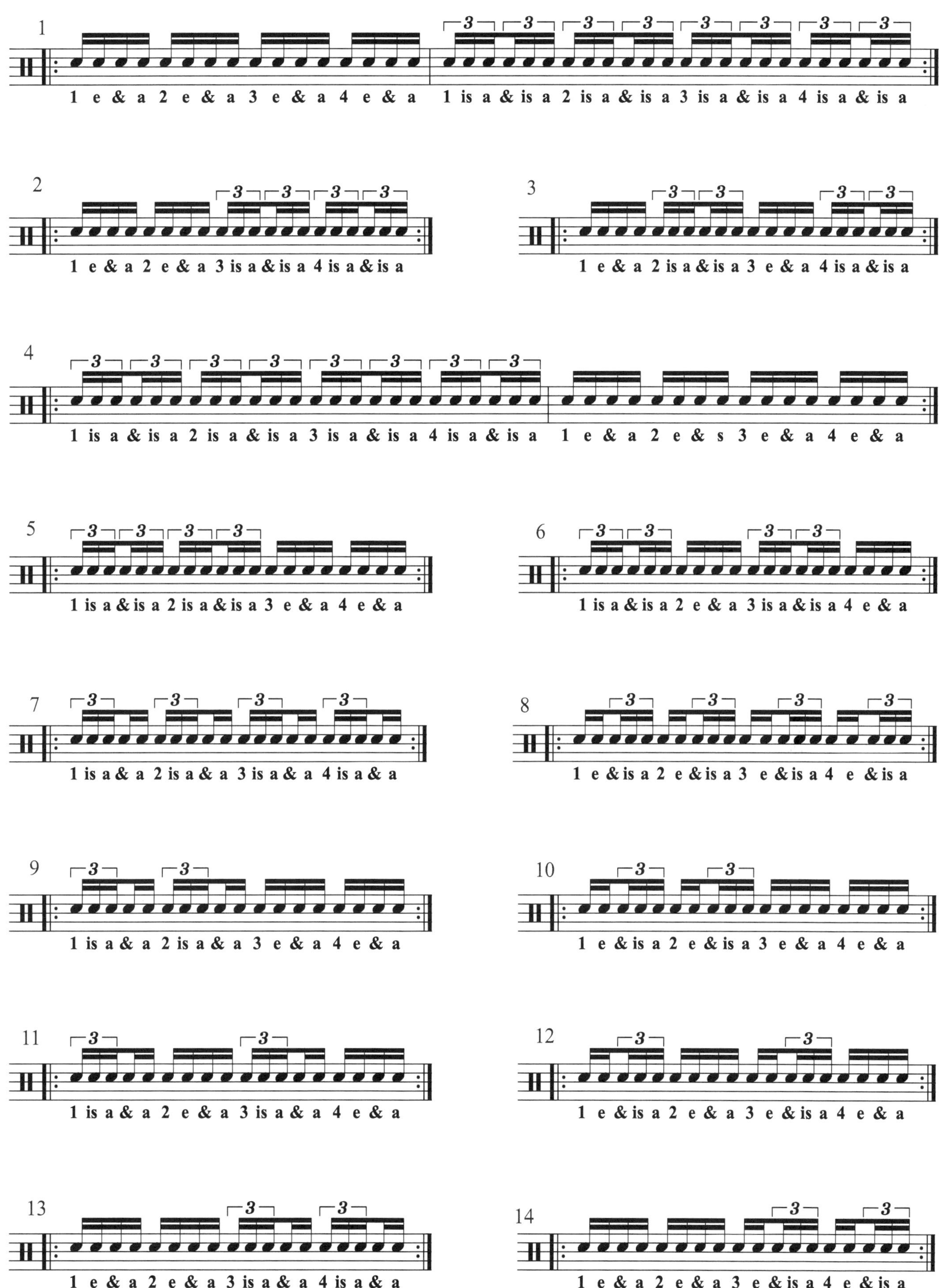
1
1 e & a 2 e & a 3 e & a 4 e & a 1 is a & is a 2 is a & is a 3 is a & is a 4 is a & is a
2
1 e & a 2 e & a 3 is a & is a 4 is a & is a
3
1 e & a 2 is a & is a 3 e & a 4 is a & is a
4
1 is a & is a 2 is a & is a 3 is a & is a 4 is a & is a 1 e & a 2 e & s 3 e & a 4 e & a
5
1 is a & is a 2 is a & is a 3 e & a 4 e & a
6
1 is a & is a 2 e & a 3 is a & is a 4 e & a
7
1 is a & a 2 is a & a 3 is a & a 4 is a & a
8
1 e & is a 2 e & is a 3 e & is a 4 e & is a
9
1 is a & a 2 is a & a 3 e & a 4 e & a
10
1 e & is a 2 e & is a 3 e & a 4 e & a
11
1 is a & a 2 e & a 3 is a & a 4 e & a
12
1 e & is a 2 e & a 3 e & is a 4 e & a
13
1 e & a 2 e & a 3 is a & a 4 is a & a
14
1 e & a 2 e & a 3 e & is a 4 e & is a

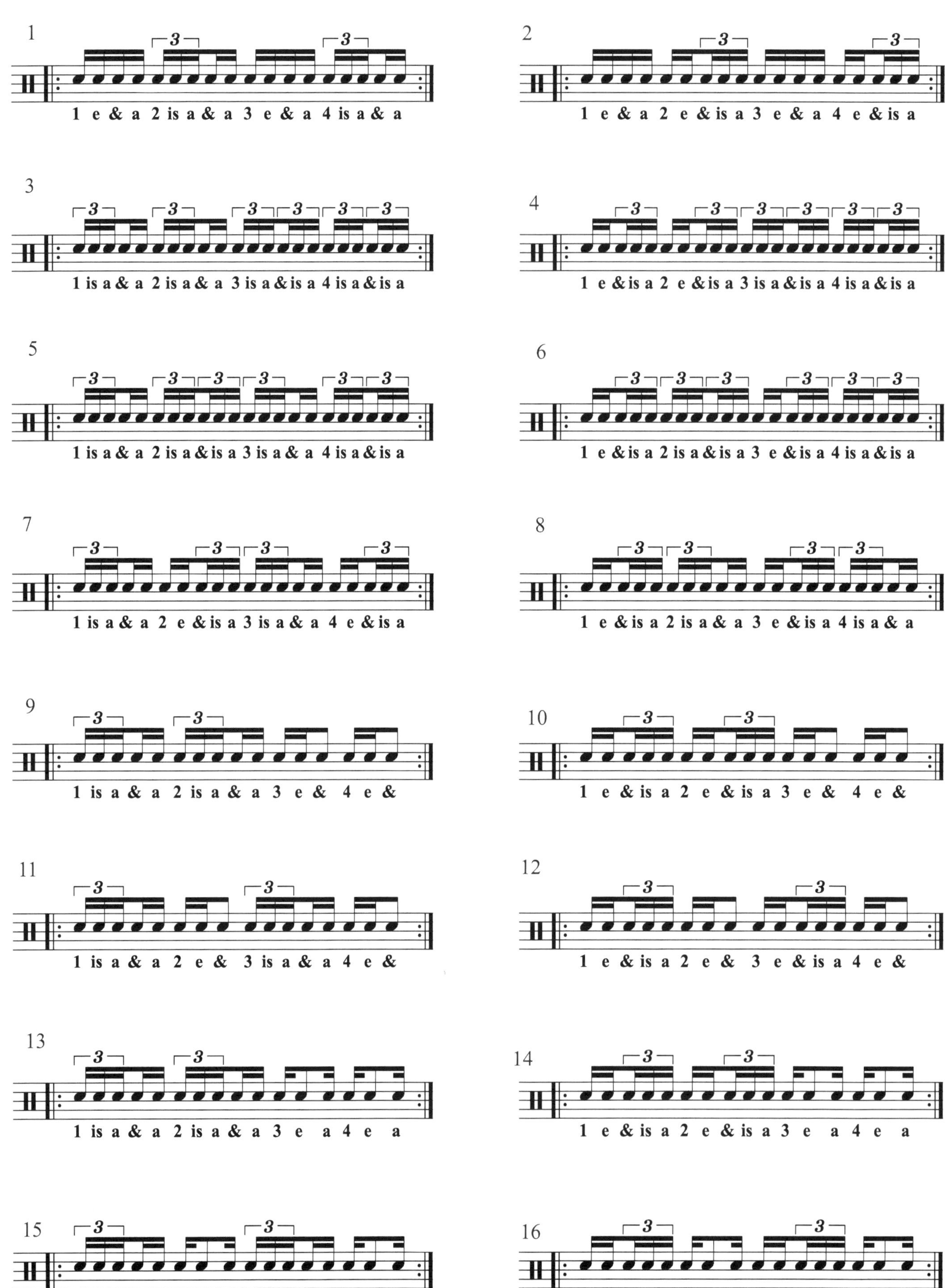
1
1 e & a 2 is a & a 3 e & a 4 is a & a
2
1 e & a 2 e & is a 3 e & a 4 e & is a
3
1 is a & a 2 is a & a 3 is a & is a 4 is a & is a
4
1 e & is a 2 e & is a 3 is a & is a 4 is a & is a
5
1 is a & a 2 is a & is a 3 is a & a 4 is a & is a
6
1 e & is a 2 is a & is a 3 e & is a 4 is a & is a
7
1 is a & a 2 e & is a 3 is a & a 4 e & is a
8
1 e & is a 2 is a & a 3 e & is a 4 is a & a
9
1 is a & a 2 is a & a 3 e & 4 e &
10
1 e & is a 2 e & is a 3 e & 4 e &
11
1 is a & a 2 e & 3 is a & a 4 e &
12
1 e & is a 2 e & 3 e & is a 4 e &
13
1 is a & a 2 is a & a 3 e a 4 e a
14
1 e & is a 2 e & is a 3 e a 4 e a
15
1 is a & a 2 e a 3 is a & a 4 e a
16
1 e & is a 2 e a 3 e & is a 4 e a

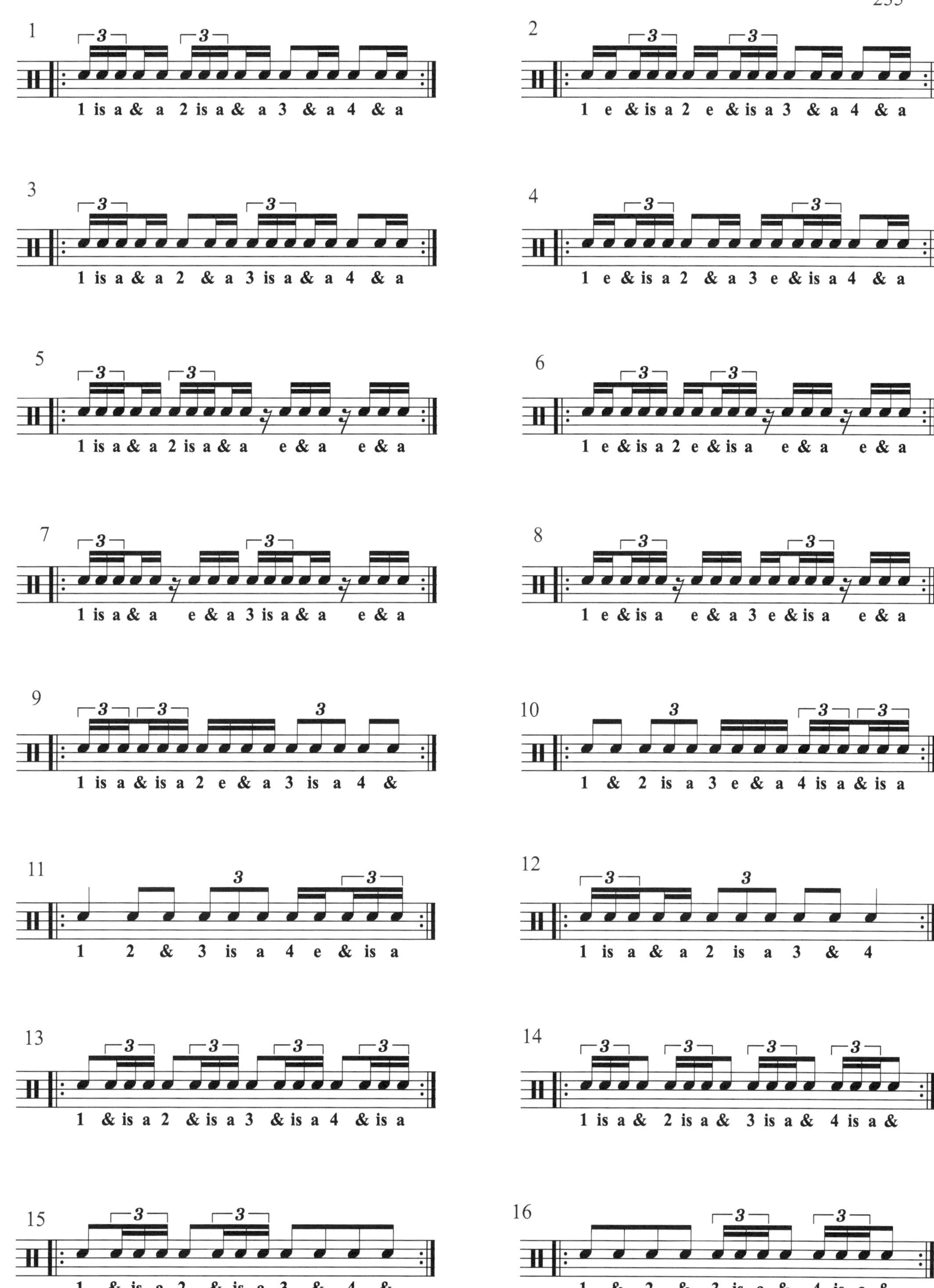
1
1 is a & a 2 is a & a 3 & a 4 & a
2
1 e & is a 2 e & is a 3 & a 4 & a
3
1 is a & a 2 & a 3 is a & a 4 & a
4
1 e & is a 2 & a 3 e & is a 4 & a
5
1 is a & a 2 is a & a e & a e & a
6
1 e & is a 2 e & is a e & a e & a
7
1 is a & a e & a 3 is a & a e & a
8
1 e & is a e & a 3 e & is a e & a
9
1 is a & is a 2 e & a 3 is a 4 &
10
1 & 2 is a 3 e & a 4 is a & is a
11
1 2 & 3 is a 4 e & is a
12
1 is a & a 2 is a 3 & 4
13
1 & is a 2 & is a 3 & is a 4 & is a
14
1 is a & 2 is a & 3 is a & 4 is a &
15
1 & is a 2 & is a 3 & 4 &
16
1 & 2 & 3 is a & 4 is a &

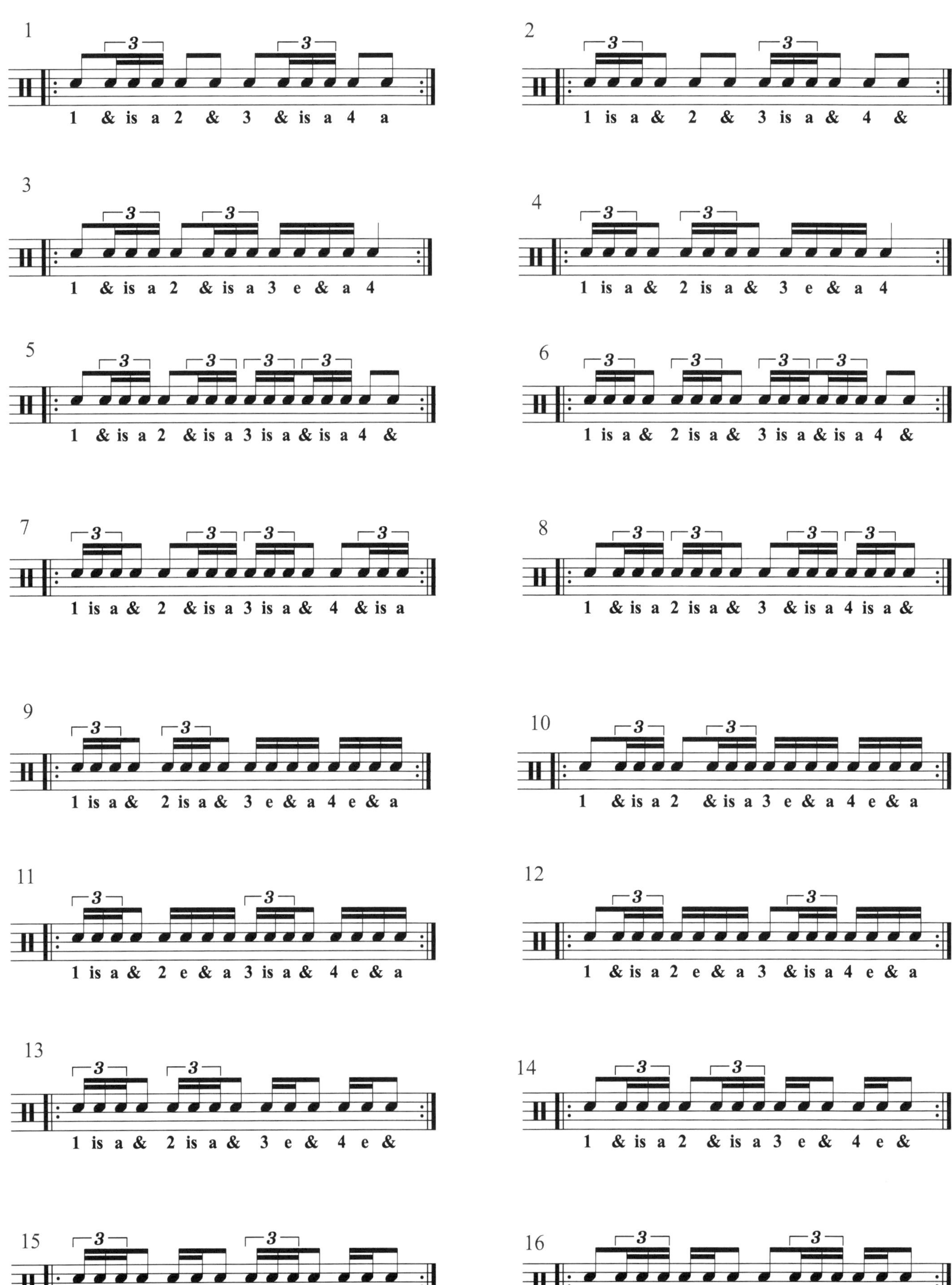
1
1 & is a 2 & 3 & is a 4 a
2
1 is a & 2 & 3 is a & 4 &
3
1 & is a 2 & is a 3 e & a 4
4
1 is a & 2 is a & 3 e & a 4
5
1 & is a 2 & is a 3 is a & is a 4 &
6
1 is a & 2 is a & 3 is a & is a 4 &
7
1 is a & 2 & is a 3 is a & 4 & is a
8
1 & is a 2 is a & 3 & is a 4 is a &
9
1 is a & 2 is a & 3 e & a 4 e & a
10
1 & is a 2 & is a 3 e & a 4 e & a
11
1 is a & 2 e & a 3 is a & 4 e & a
12
1 & is a 2 e & a 3 & is a 4 e & a
13
1 is a & 2 is a & 3 e & 4 e &
14
1 & is a 2 & is a 3 e & 4 e &
15
1 is a & 2 e & 3 is a & 4 e &
16
1 & is a 2 e & 3 & is a 4 e &

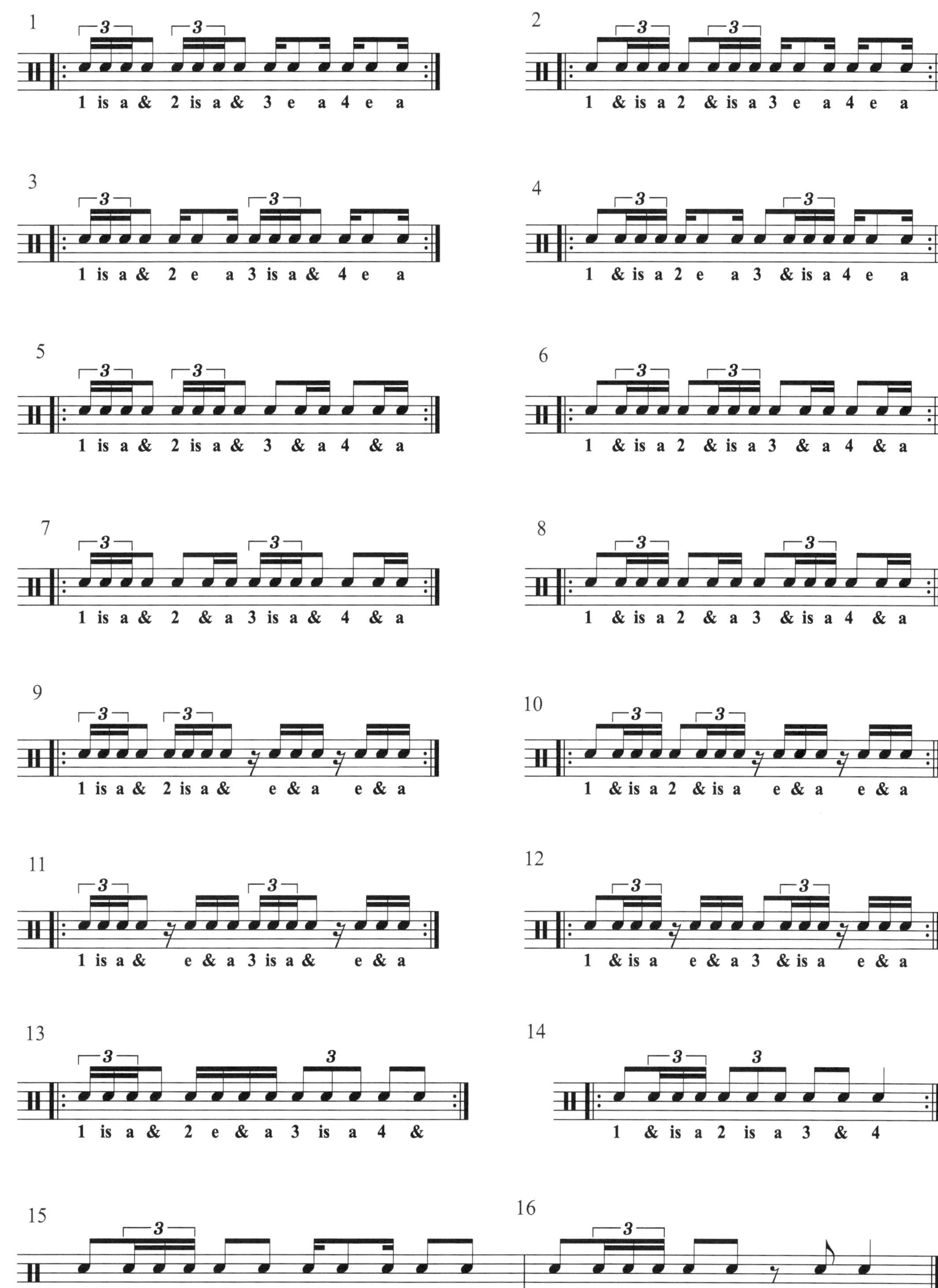
1
3
3
1 is a & 2 is a & 3 e a 4 e a
2
3
3
1 & is a 2 & is a 3 e a 4 e a
3
3
3
1 is a & 2 e a 3 is a & 4 e a
4
3
3
1 & is a 2 e a 3 & is a 4 e a
5
3
3
1 is a & 2 is a & 3 & a 4 & a
6
3
3
1 & is a 2 & is a 3 & a 4 & a
7
3
3
1 is a & 2 & a 3 is a & 4 & a
8
3
3
1 & is a 2 & a 3 & is a 4 & a
9
3
3
1 is a & 2 is a & e & a e & a
10
3
3
1 & is a 2 & is a e & a e & a
11
3
3
1 is a & e & a 3 is a & e & a
12
3
3
1 & is a e & a 3 & is a e & a
13
3
3
1 is a & 2 e & a 3 is a 4 &
14
3
3
1 & is a 2 is a 3 & 4
15
3
16
3

4s in 3s

Expressing Binary Rhythms in Ternary Spaces

In the next section we will look at expressing the binary rhythmic alphabet with triplets. Four sets of triplets gives us twelve even subdivisions that can be phrased as three groups of four.. Once you've established groups of four you can express the binary rhythmic alphabet. Instead of one beat, or half a beat this time the binary rhythms will be expressed in a beat and a third.

We will use two measures of triplets for six even groups of four. This will allow us to play three complete sets of rhythmic phrases containing two binary rhythms in each.

4s in 3s

1a
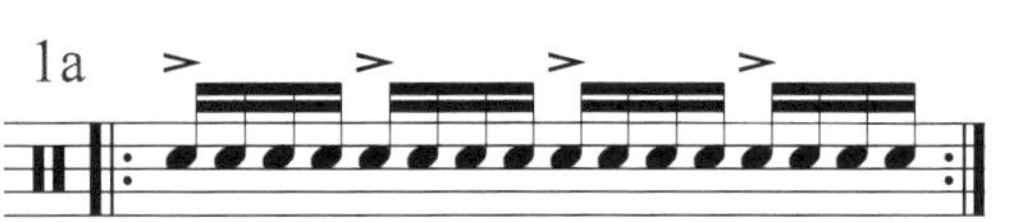

1b
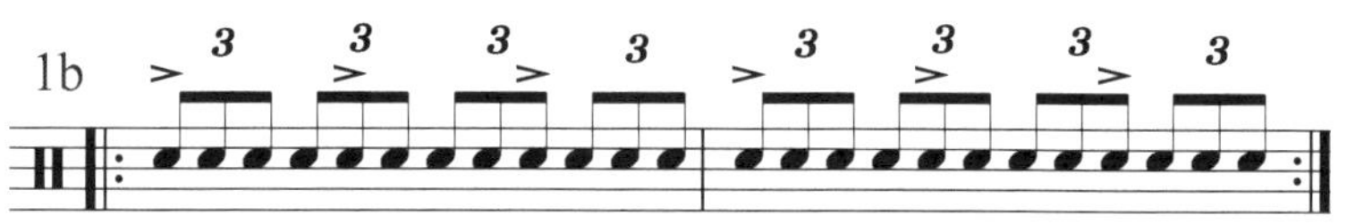

2a

2b

3a

3b

4a

4b

5a

5b
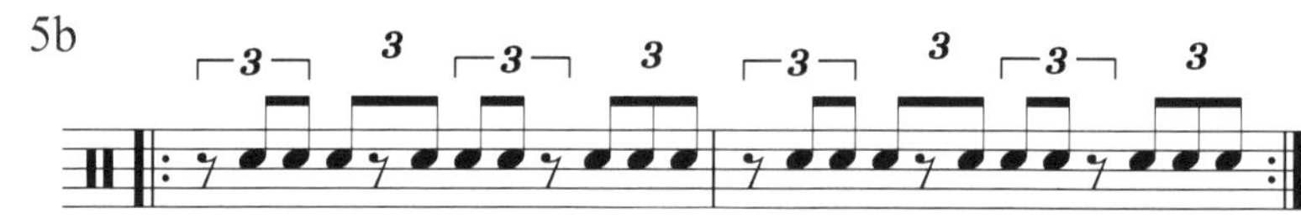

6a

6b

7a

7b

8a

8b

4s in 3s

4s in 3s

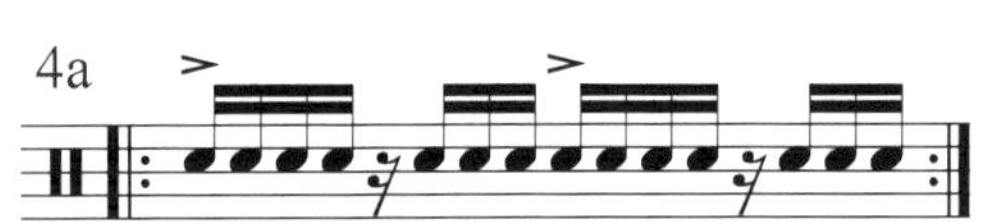

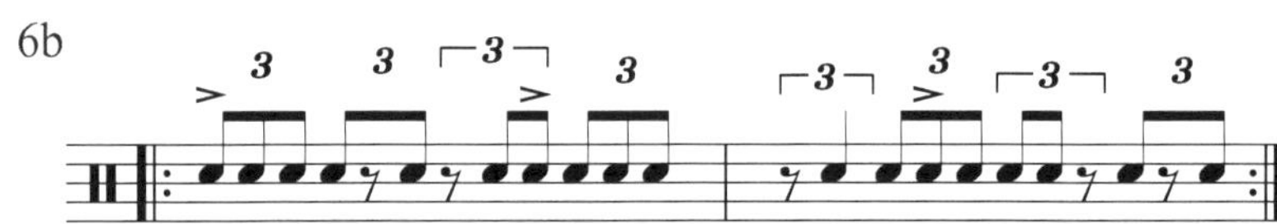

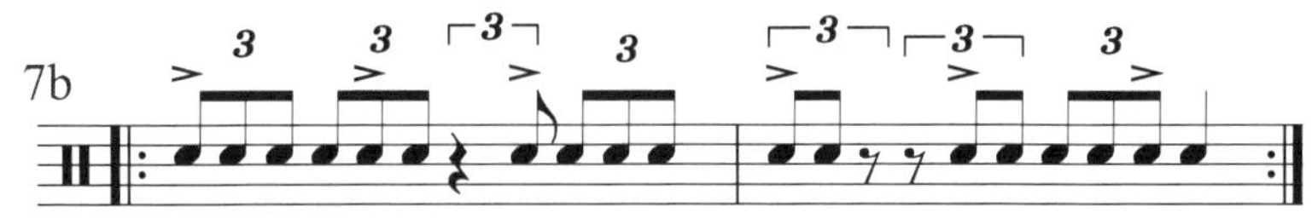

4s in 3s

4s in 3s

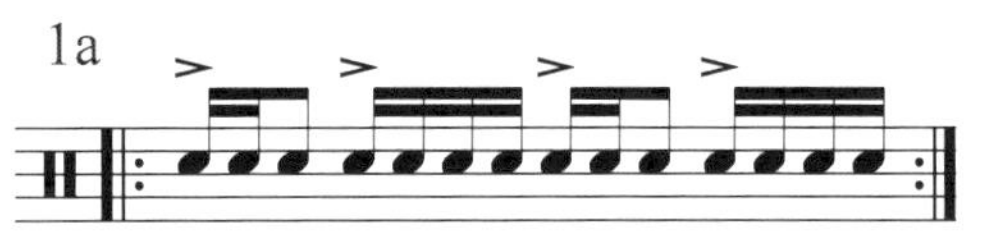

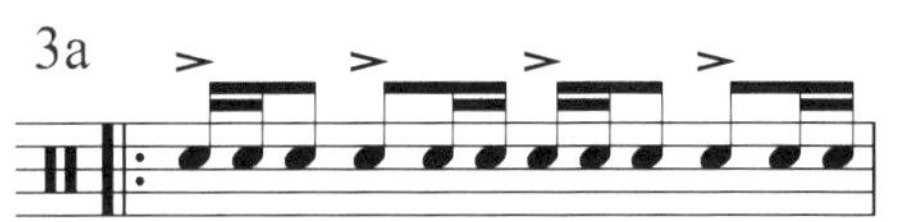

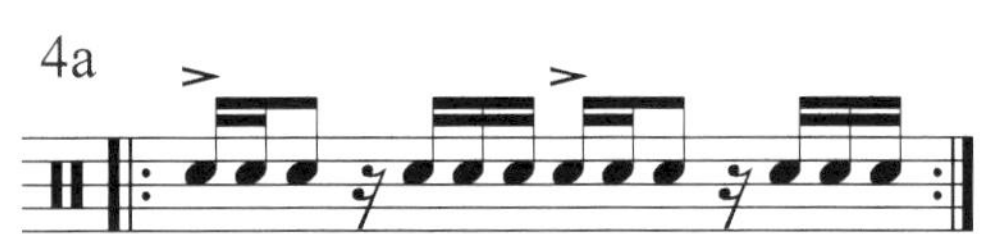

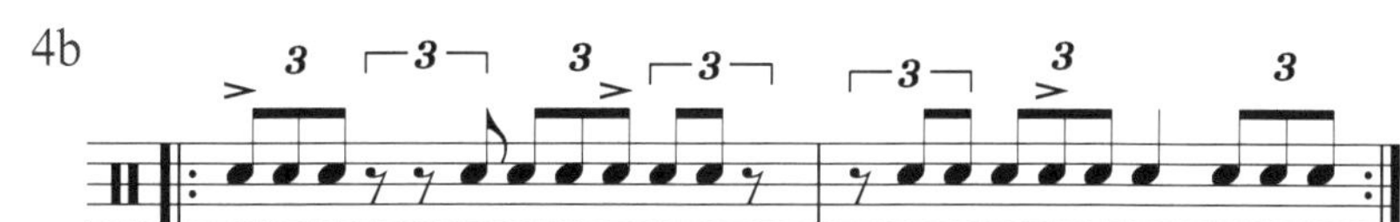

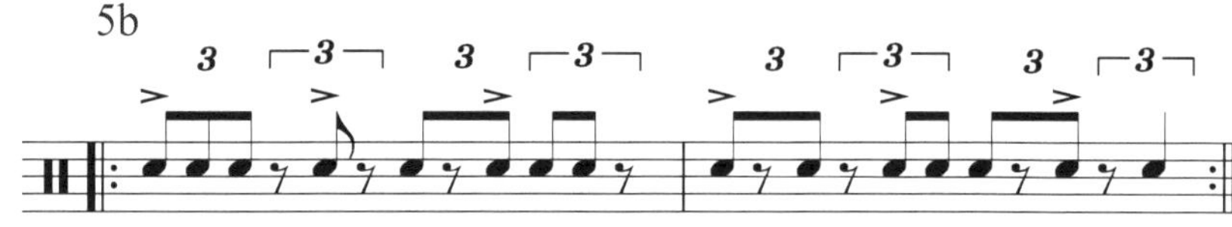

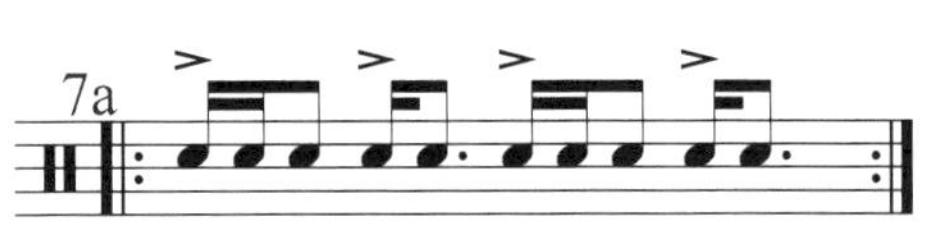

4s in 3s

4s in 3s

4s in 3s

4s in 3s

1a

1b

2a

2b

3a

3b

4a

4b

5a

5b

6a

6b

7a

7b

8a

8b

4s in 3s

4s in 3s

1a

1b

2a

2b

3a

3b

4a

4b

5a

5b

6a

6b

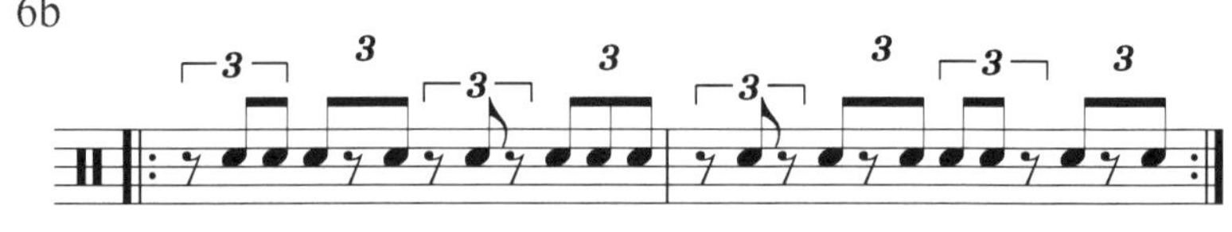

7a

7b

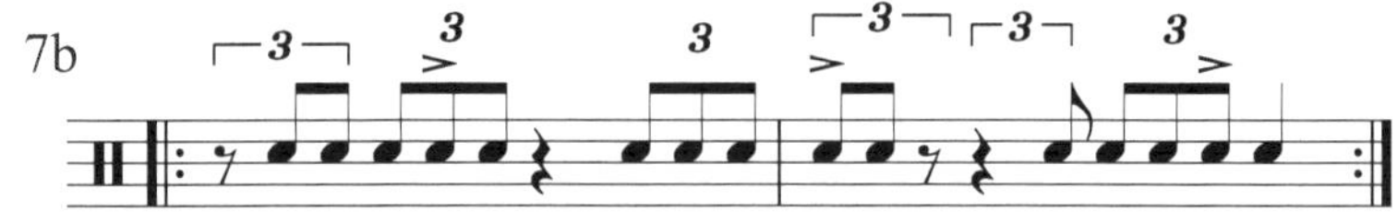

8a

8b

4s in 3s

4s in 3s

1a

1b

2a

2b

3a

3b

4a

4b

5a

5b

6a

6b

7a

7b

8a

8b

4s in 3s

9a
9b
3
3
3
3
3
3
10a
10b
3
3
3
3
3
3
3
3
11a
11b
3
3
3
3
3
3
12a
12b
3
3
3
3
3
3
13a
13b
3
3
3
3
3
3
14a
14b
3
3
3
3
3
15a
15b
3
3
3
3
16a
16b

4s in 3s

1a

1b

2a

2b

3a

3b

4a

4b

5a

5b

6a

6b

7a

7b

8a

8b

4s in 3s

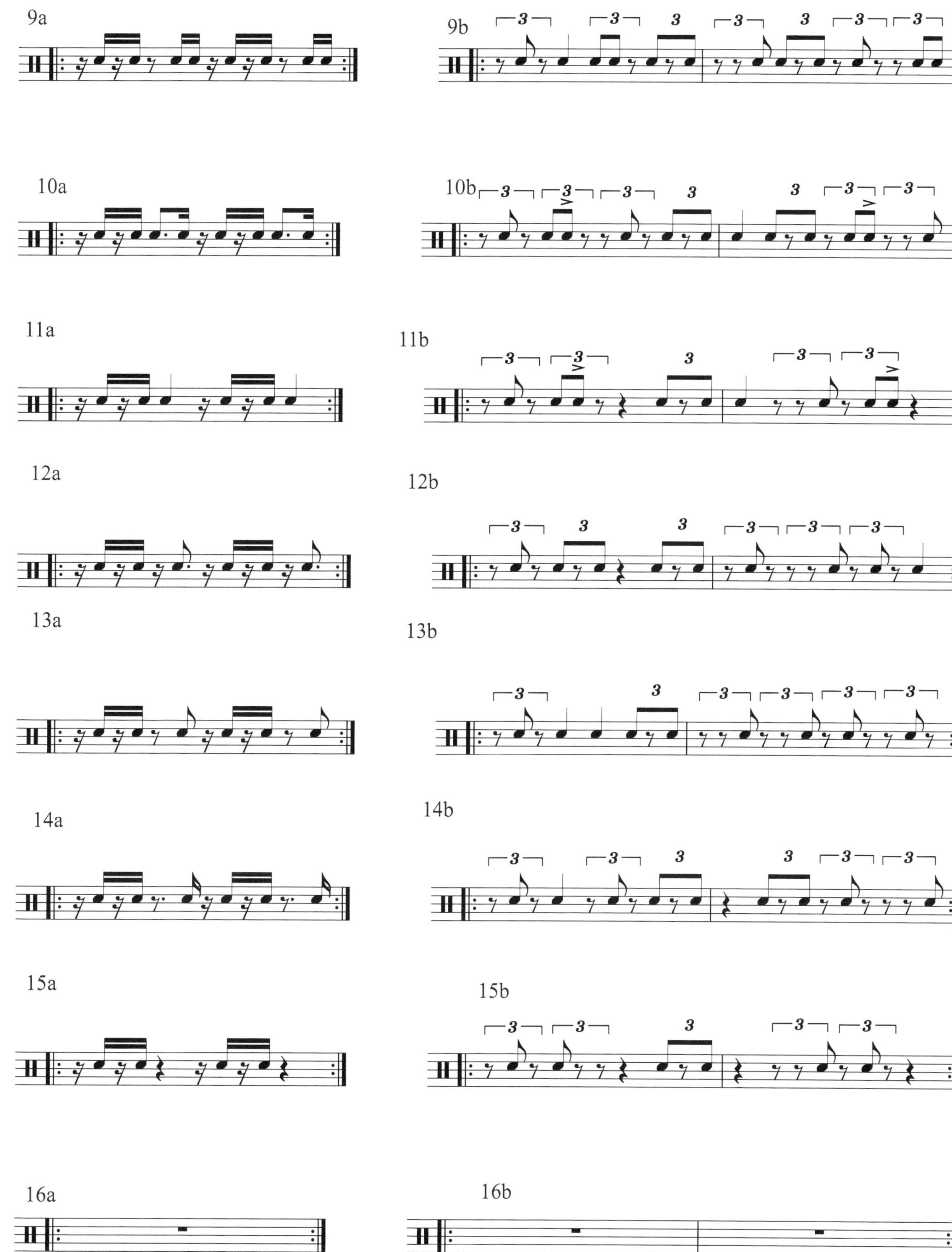

4s in 3s

1a

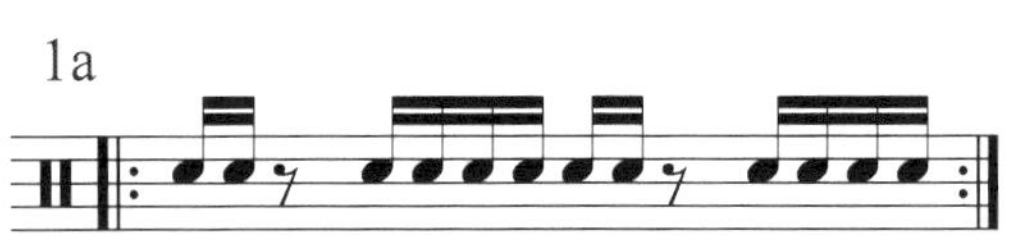

1b

2a

2b

3a

3b

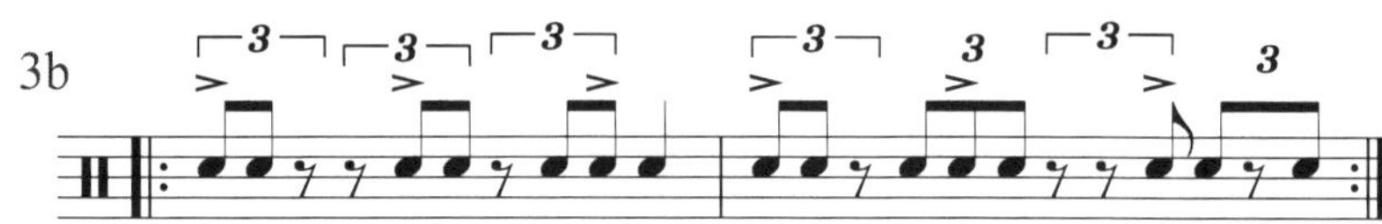

4a

4b

5a

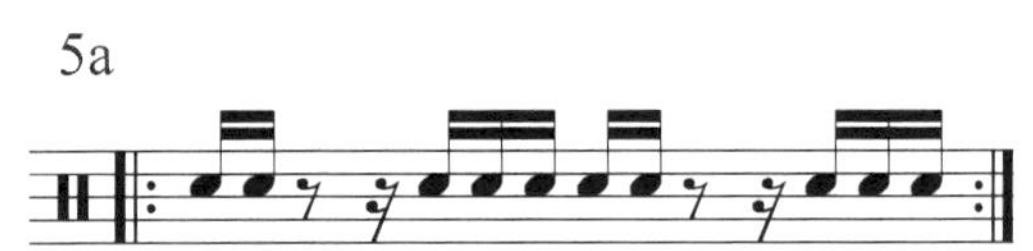

5b

6a

6b

7a

7b

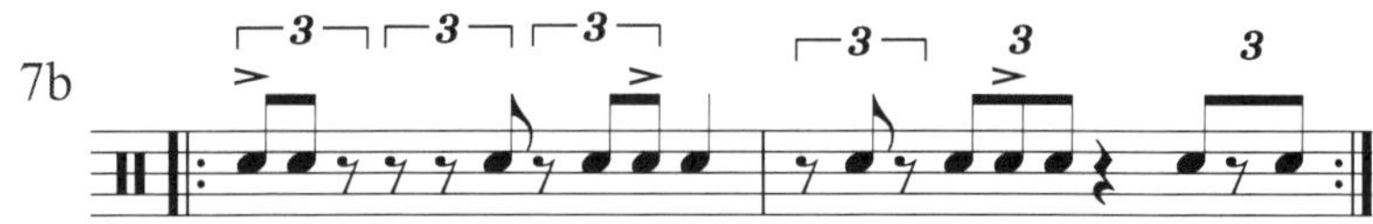

8a

8b

4s in 3s

4s in 3s

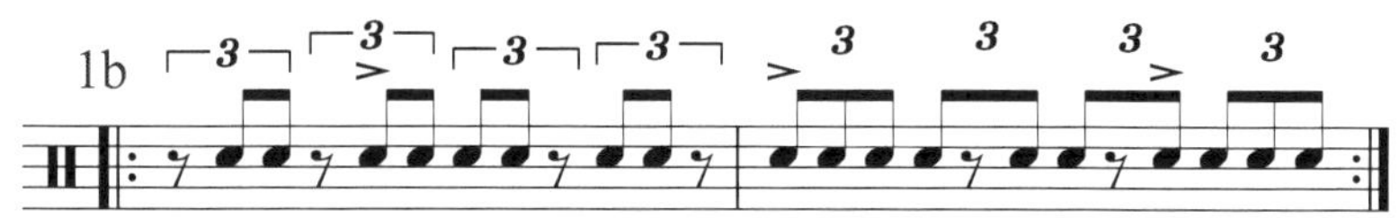

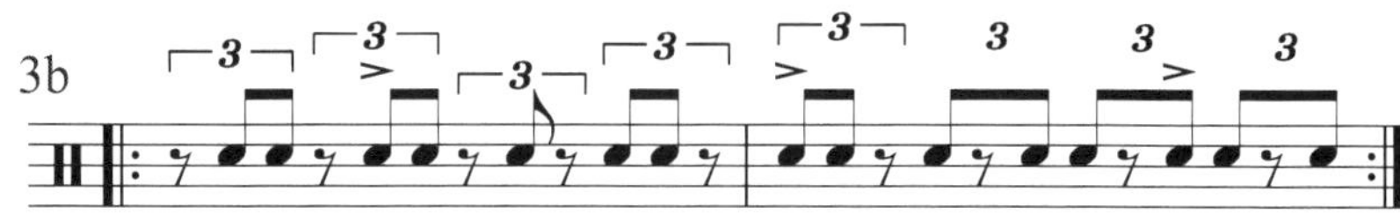

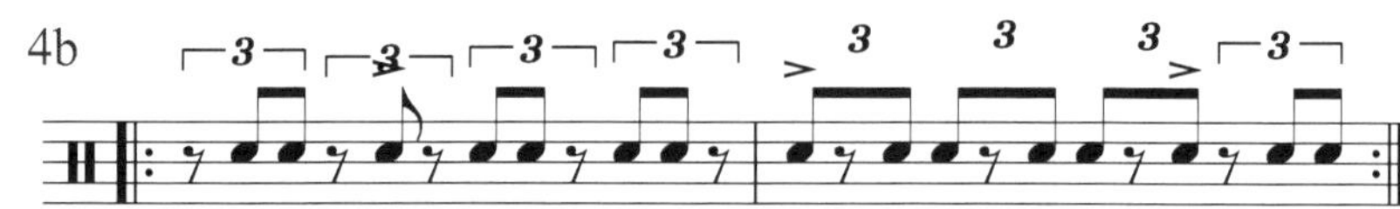

4s in 3s

4s in 3s

1a

1b

2a

2b

3a

3b

4a

4b

5a

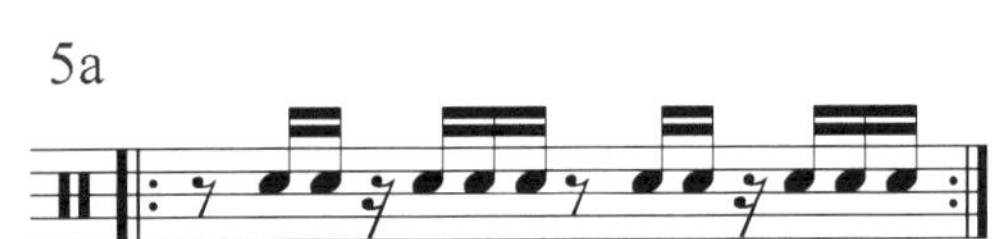

5b

6a

6b

7a

7b

8a

8b

4s in 3s

4s in 3s

1a

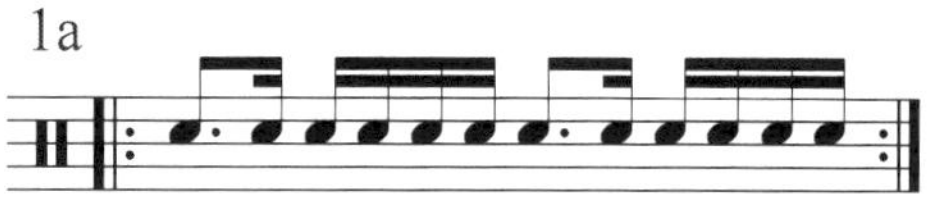

1b

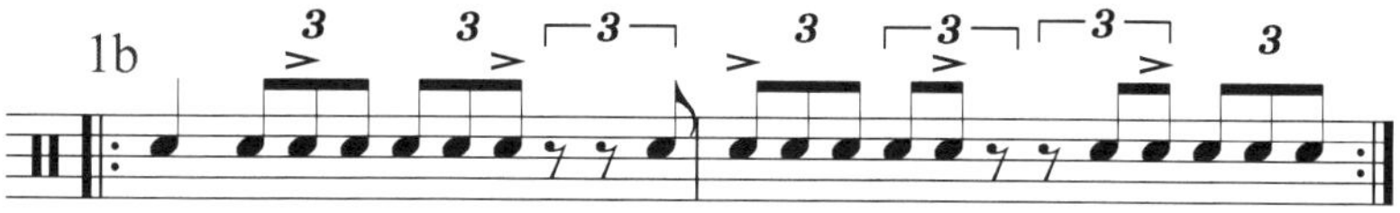

2a

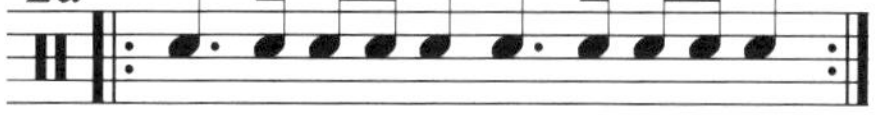

2b

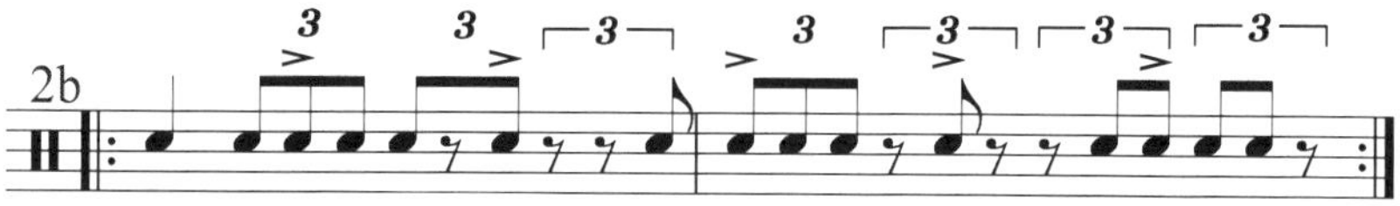

3a

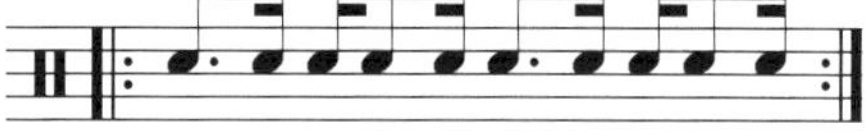

3b

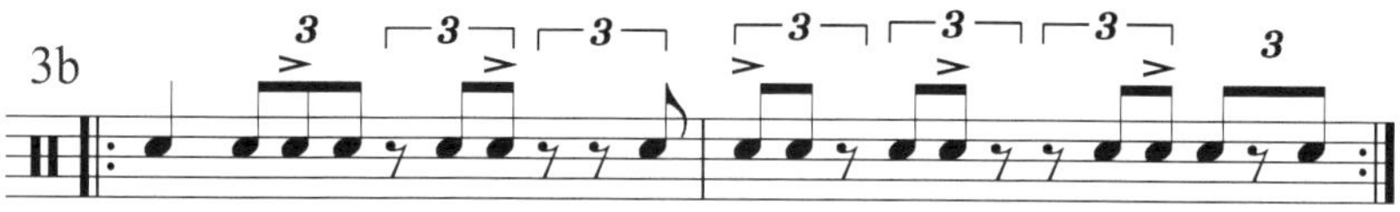

4a

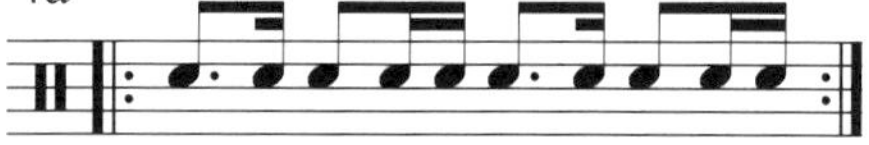

4b

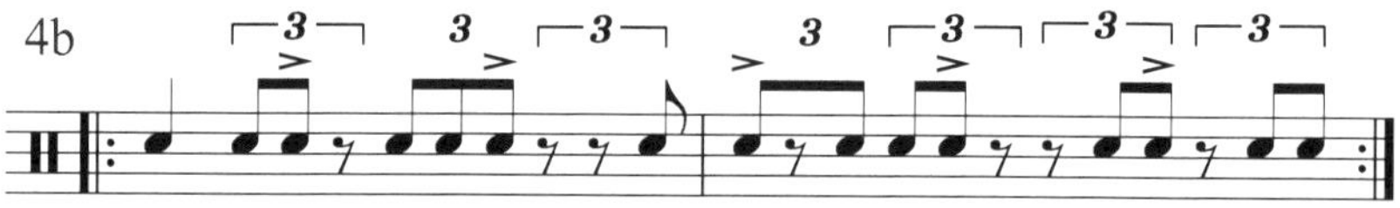

5a

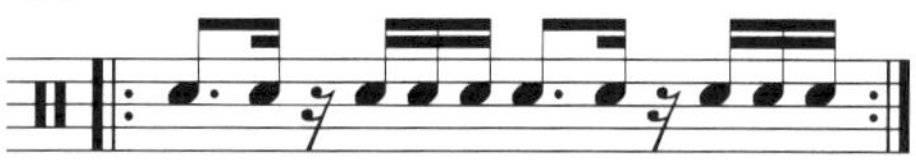

5b

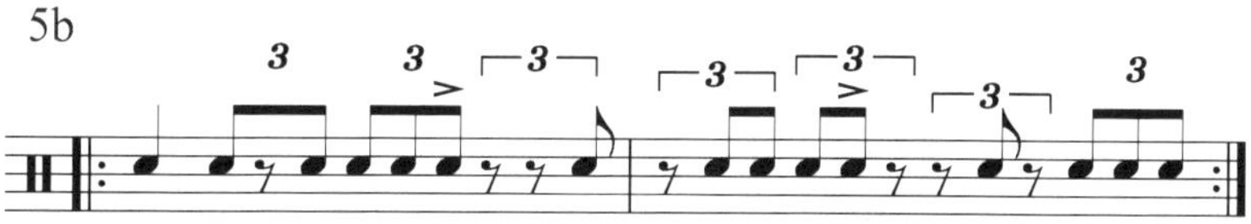

6a

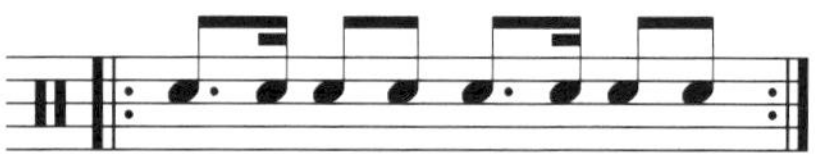

6b

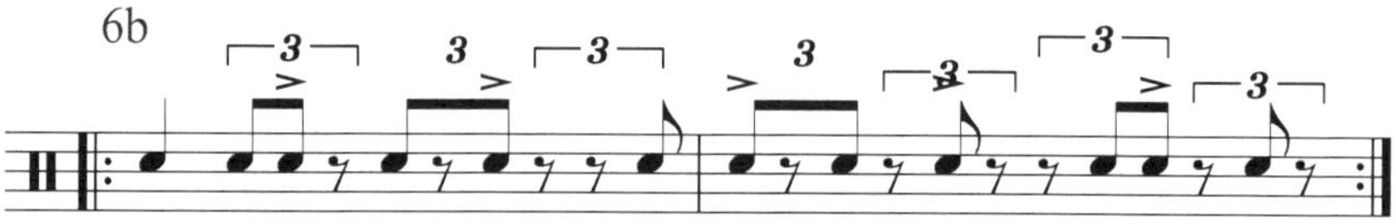

7a

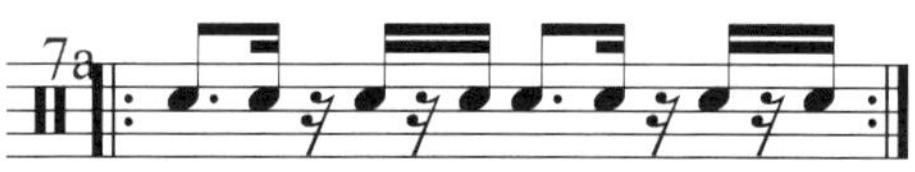

7b

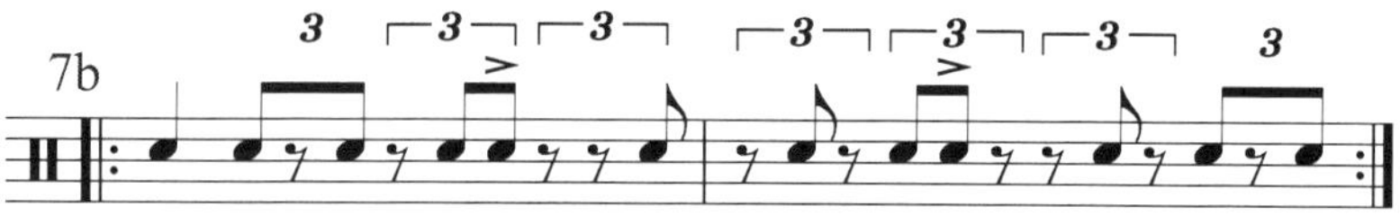

8a

8b

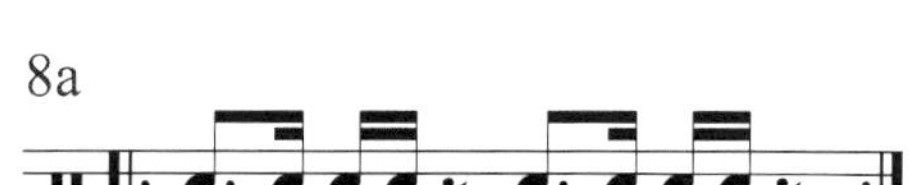

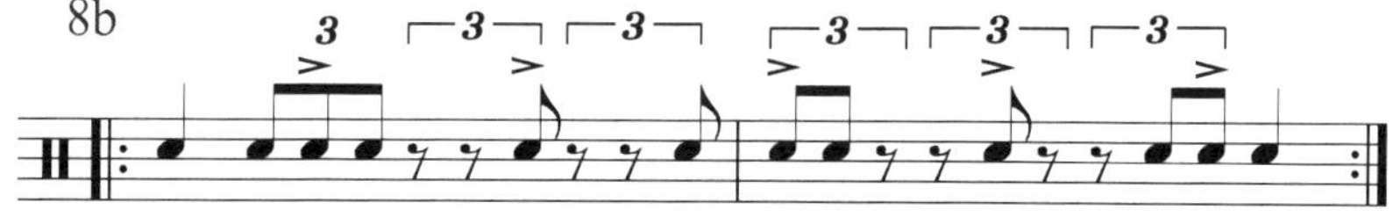

4s in 3s

4s in 3s

4s in 3s

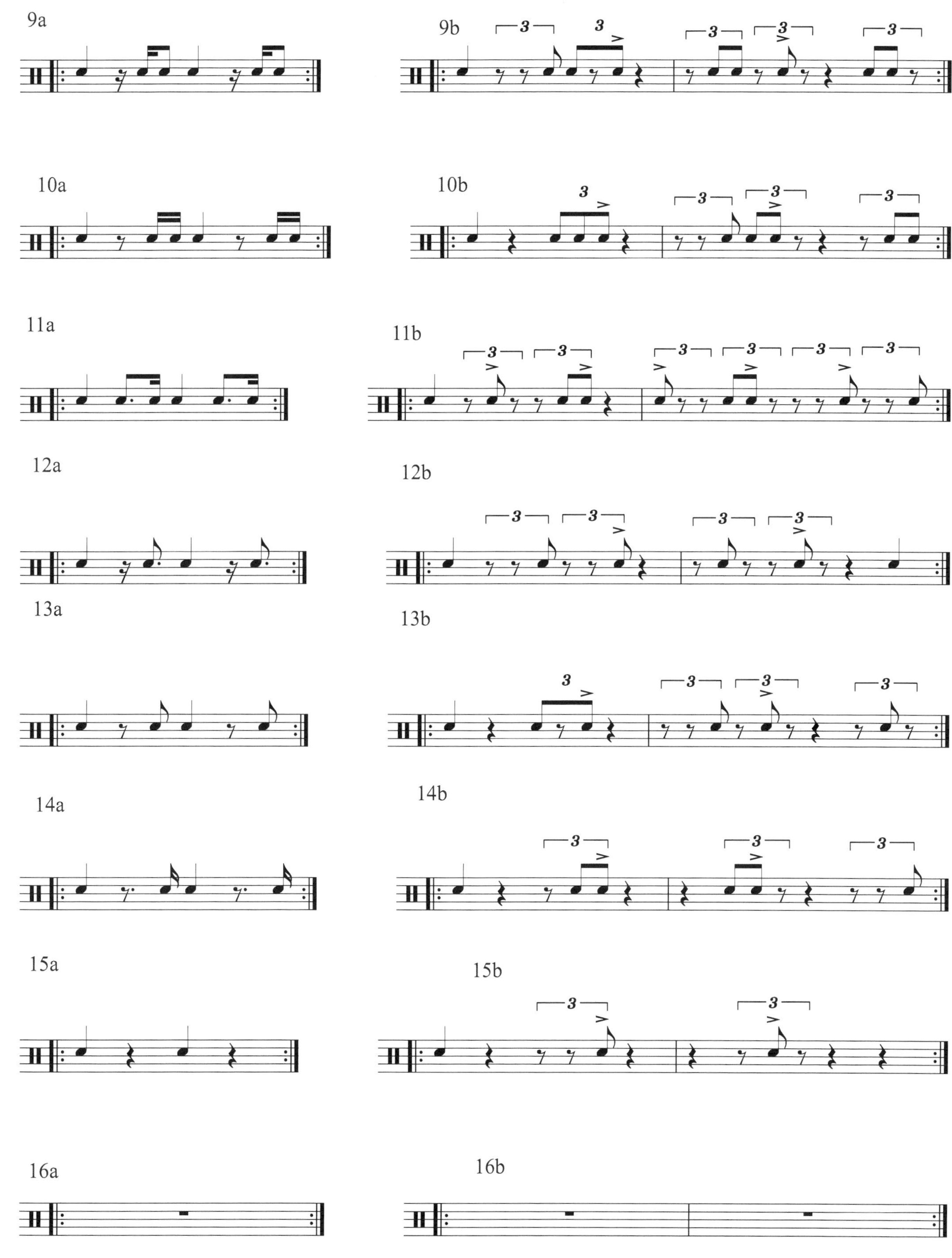

9a
9b
3
3
3
3
3
10a
10b
3
3
3
3
11a
11b
3
3
3
3
3
3
12a
12b
3
3
3
3
13a
13b
3
3
3
3
14a
14b
3
3
3
15a
15b
3
3
16a
16b

4s in 3s

4s in 3s

4s in 3s

4s in 3s

4s in 3s

4s in 3s

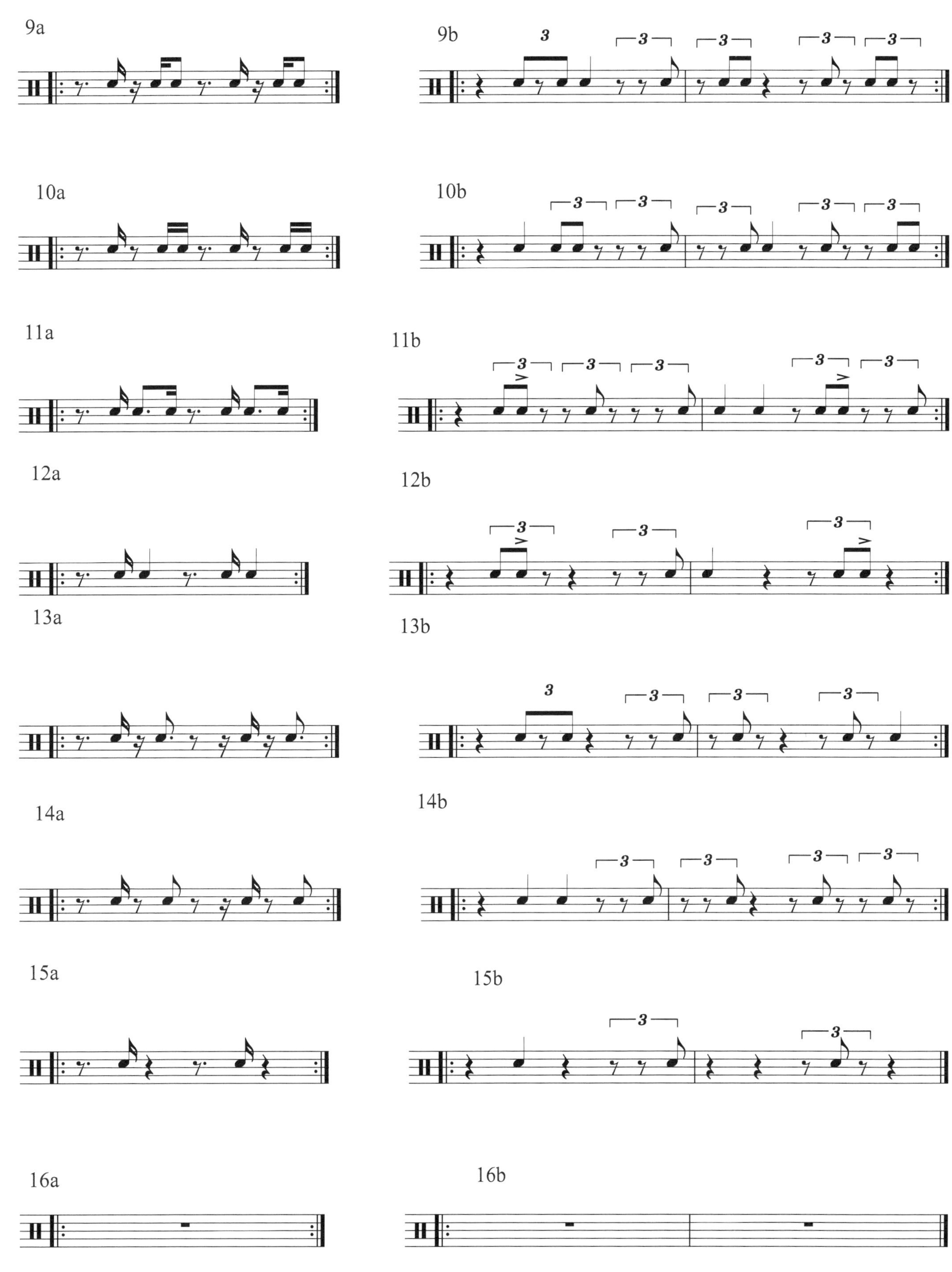

3s in 4s

Triplet Rhythms Expressed in Binary Structures

There are several ways to express triplet rhythms in a binary structure. On page 265 we accent 16th notes in groups of three for the first three beats of the measure. This gives us four even sets of three. Beat four will be used as 8th notes to reset the pattern to start again on beat one of the next measure.

On page 266 we use the same idea, but over two measures. We take the groups of three across the bar into the second measure.

One page 267 we use the same idea in 3|4 time. In 3|4 we will have four even groups of three.

Three 16th notes are equal to one doted 8th note.

3s in 4s

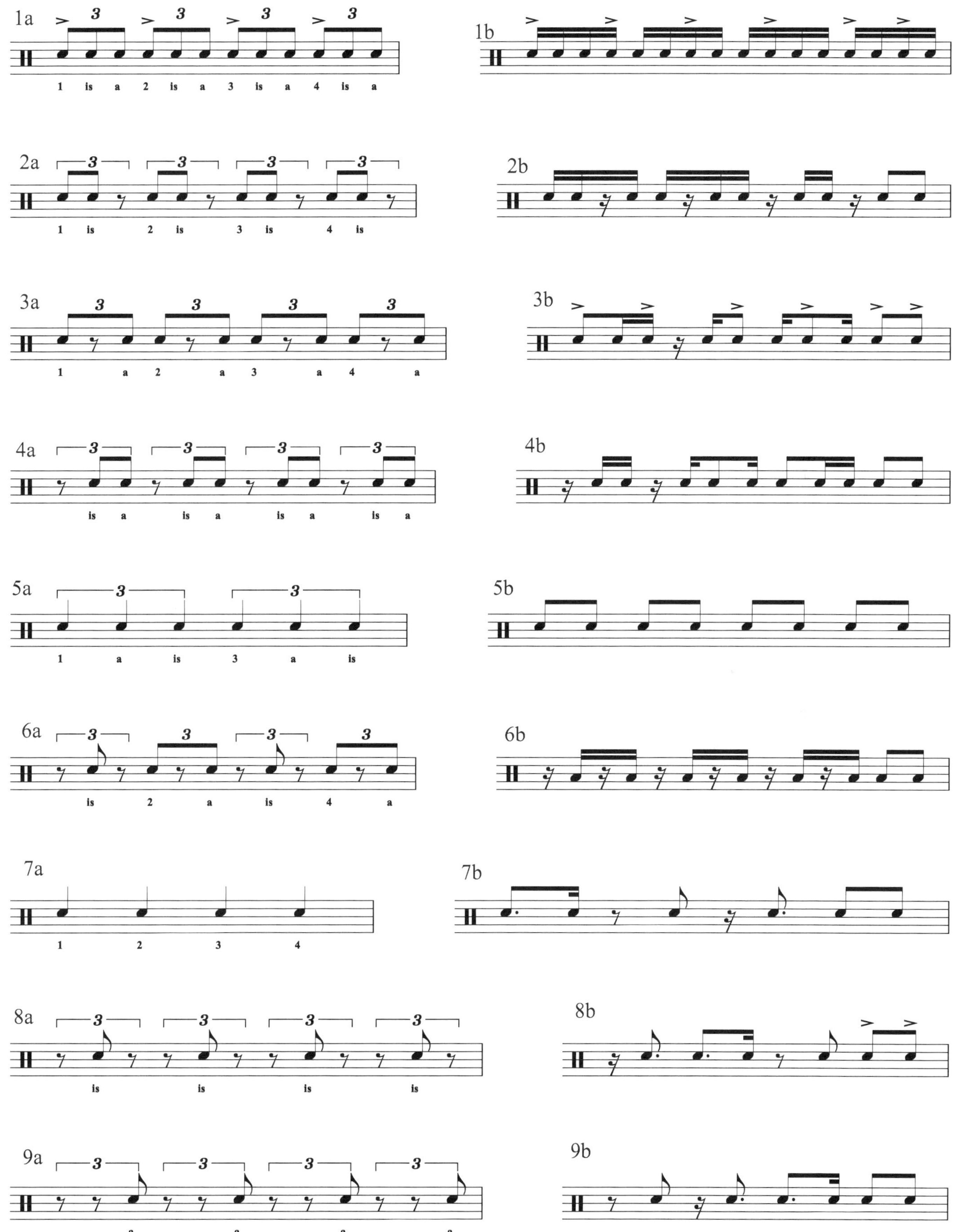
1a
1 is a 2 is a 3 is a 4 is a
1b
2a
1 is 2 is 3 is 4 is
2b
3a
1 a 2 a 3 a 4 a
3b
4a
is a is a is a is a
4b
5a
1 a is 3 a is
5b
6a
is 2 a is 4 a
6b
7a
1 2 3 4
7b
8a
is is is is
8b
9a
a a a a
9b

Two Measures 3s in 4s

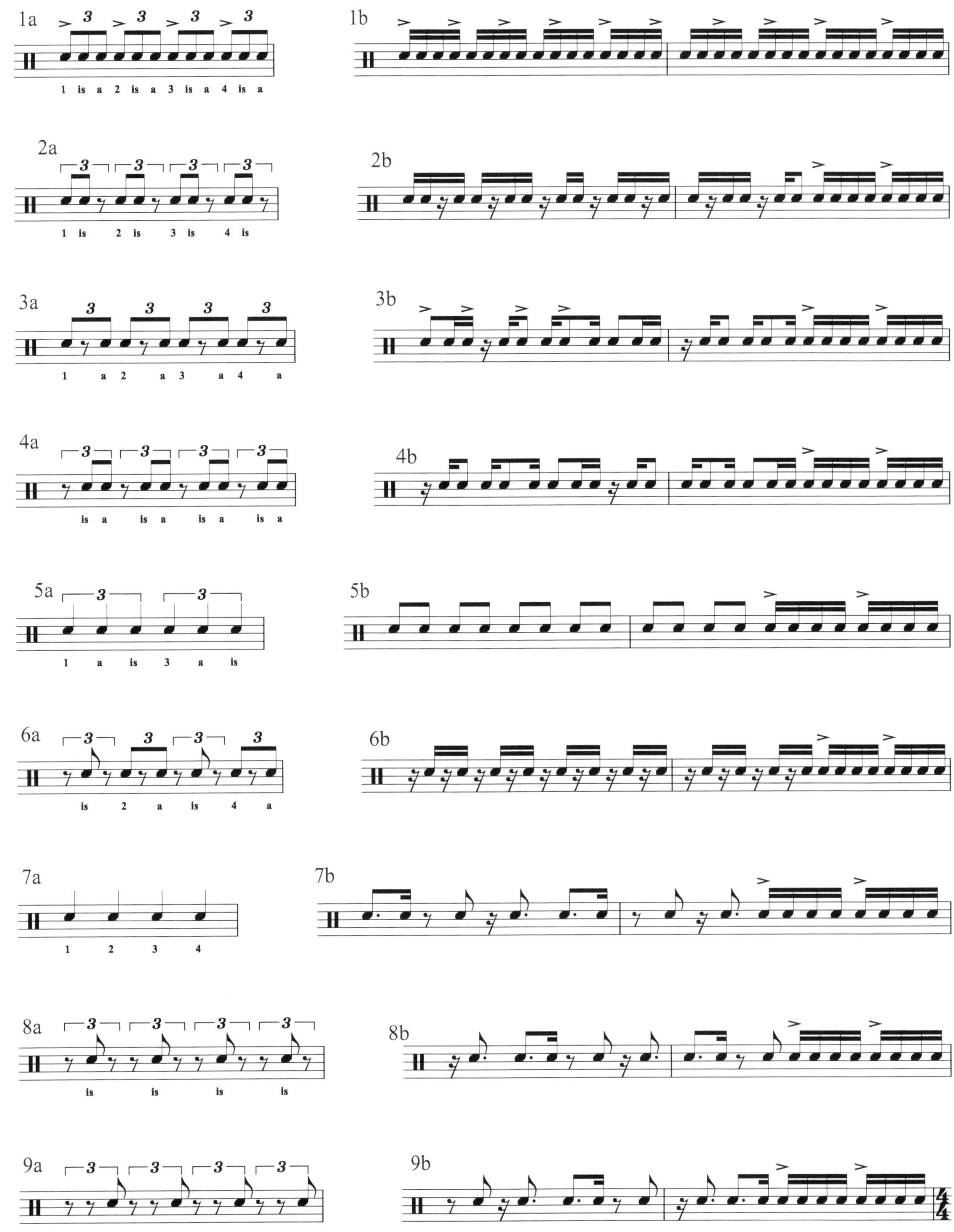

3s in 4s 3|4

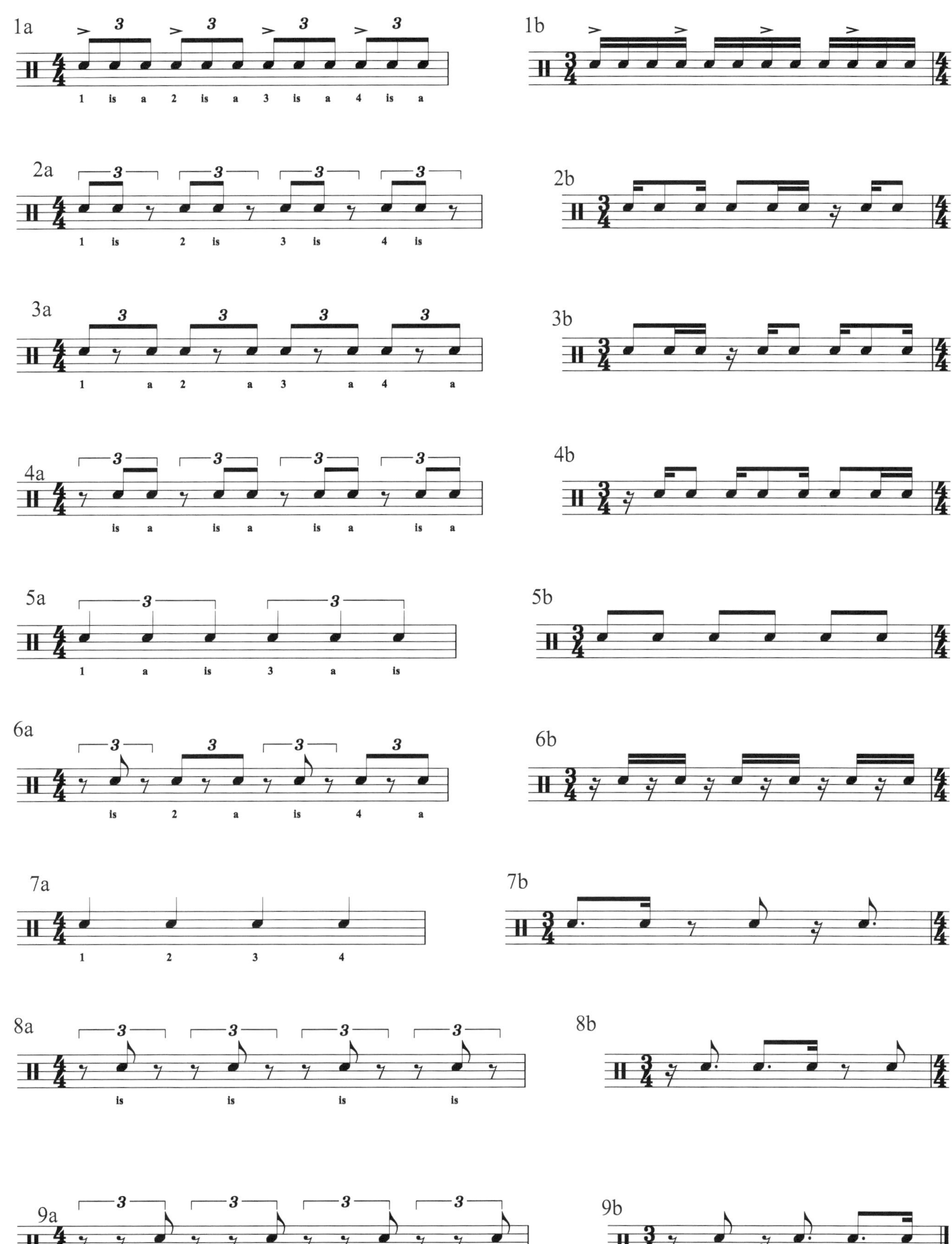
1a
1 is a 2 is a 3 is a 4 is a
1b
2a
1 is 2 is 3 is 4 is
2b
3a
1 a 2 a 3 a 4 a
3b
4a
is a is a is a is a
4b
5a
1 a is 3 a is
5b
6a
is 2 a is 4 a
6b
7a
1 2 3 4
7b
8a
is is is is
8b
9a
a a a a
9b

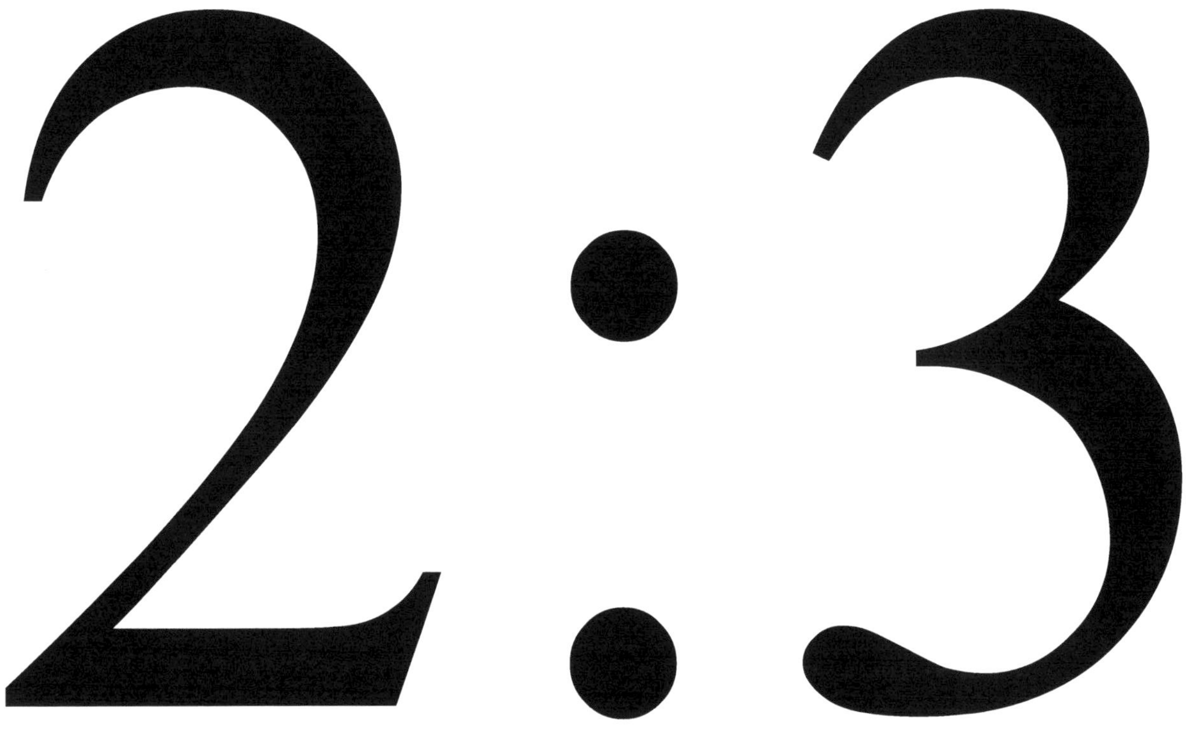

Two Equal Subdivisions and Three Equal Subdivisions in the Same Beat

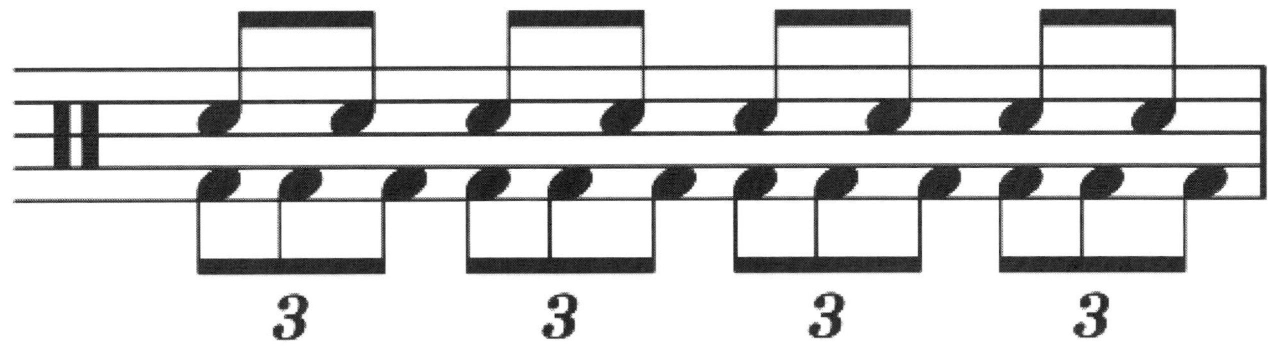

2:3 Polyrhythmic Alphabet

Using rhythmic reduction we can take a polyrhythm and reduce it to a polyrhythmic alphabet.

In this section will work with 8th notes and 8th note triplets in the same space.

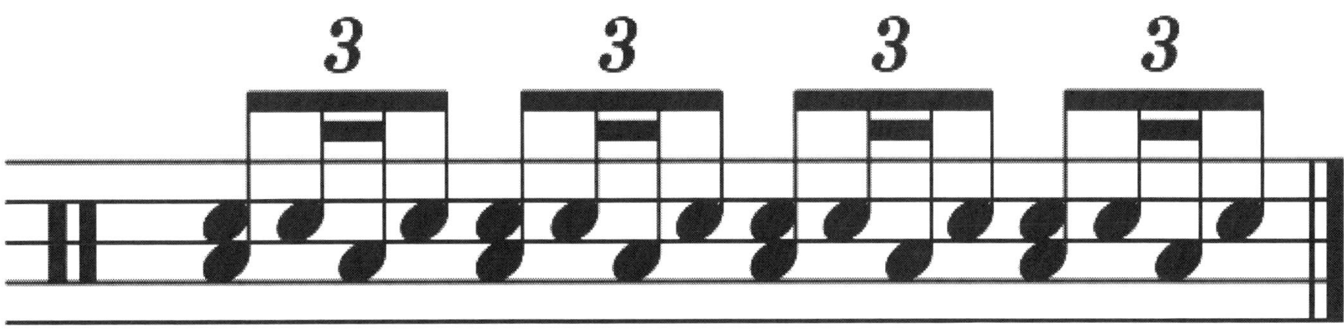

2:3 Polyrhythmic Alphabet

2:3 Polyrhythmic Alphabet

3:2 Polyrhythmic Alphabet

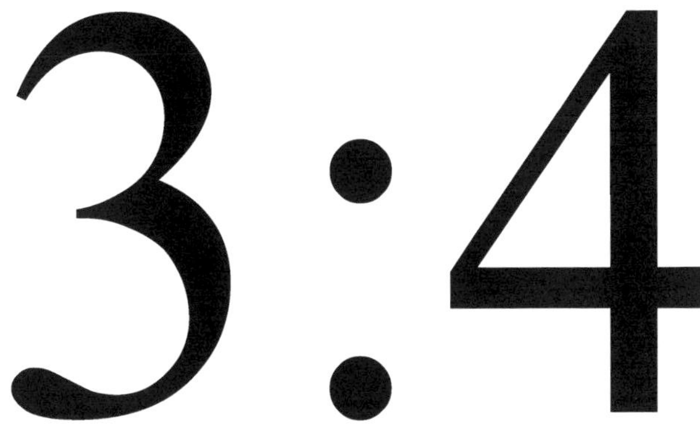

Three Equal Subdivisions and Four Equal Subdivisions in the Same Space

3:4 Polyrhythmic Alphabet Level I

In this section we will use quarter note triplets and 8th notes, three evenly spaced notes, and four evenly spaced notes over two beats for level one of the three against four polyrhythmic alphabet.

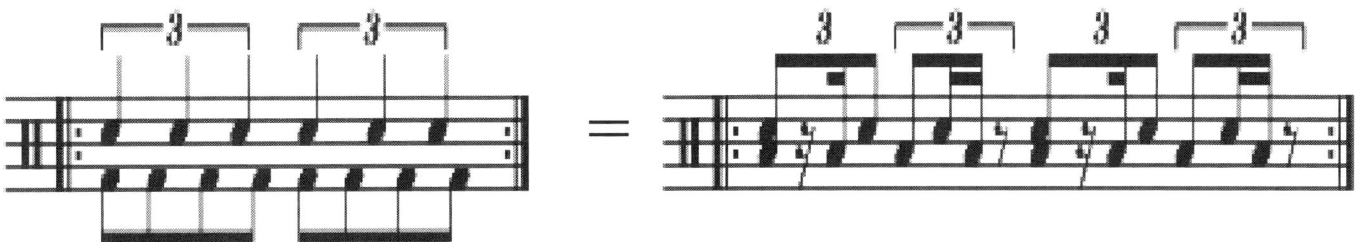

3:4 Polyrhythmic Alphabet Level I

3:4 Polyrhythmic Alphabet Level I

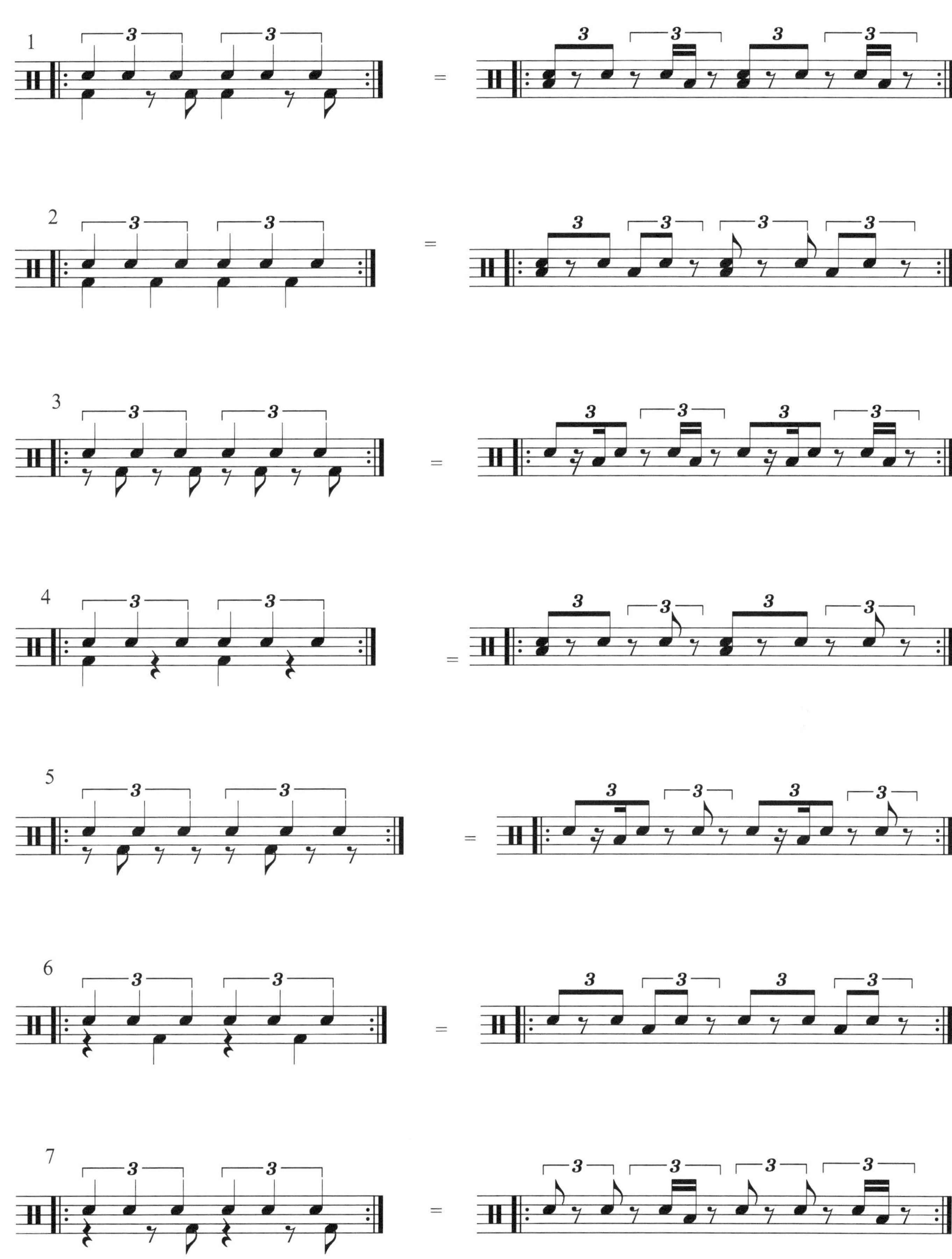

3:4 Polyrhythmic Alphabet Level I

3:4 Polyrhythmic Alphabet Level I

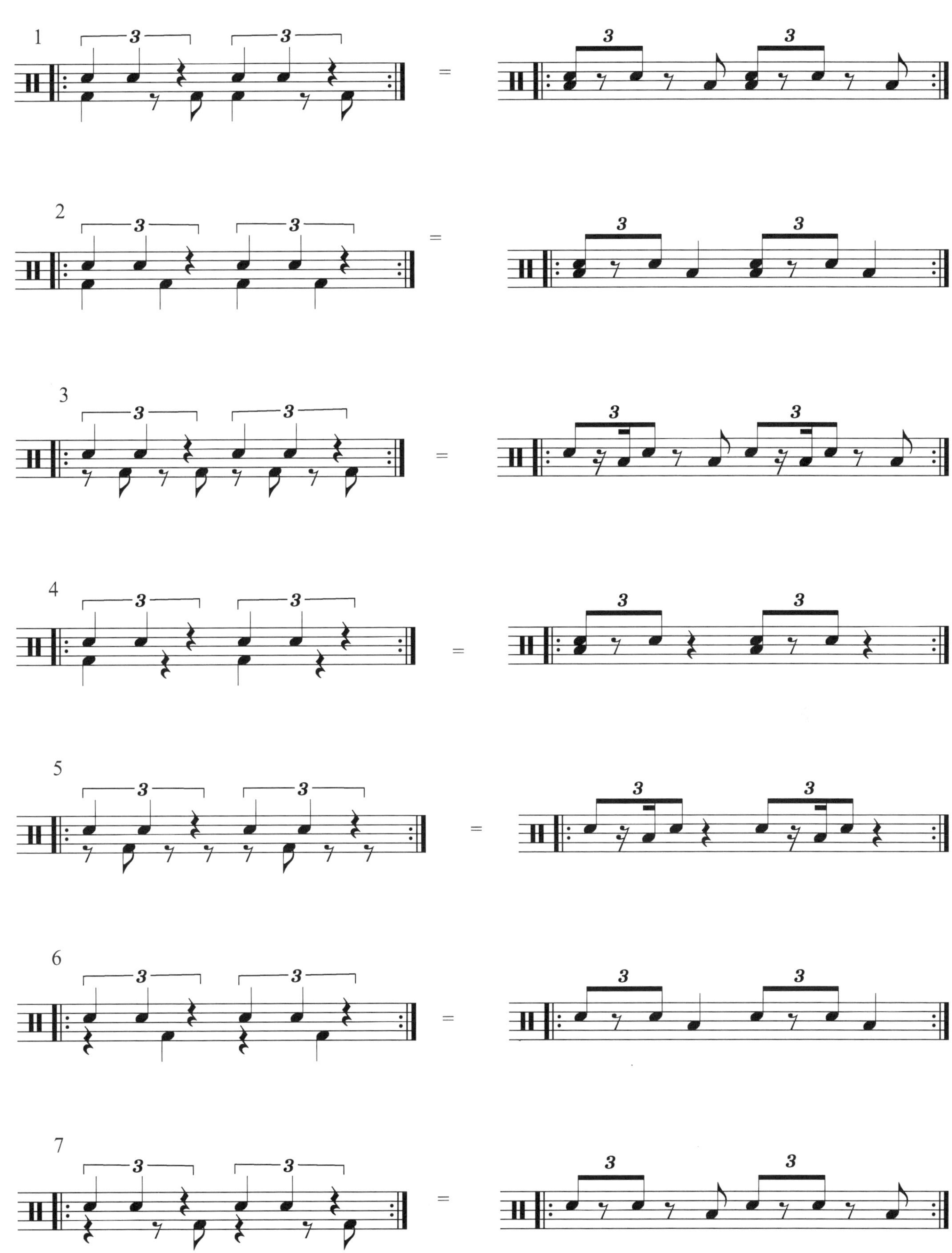

3:4 Polyrhythmic Alphabet Level I

3:4 Polyrhythmic Alphabet Level I

3:4 Polyrhythmic Alphabet Level I

3:4 Polyrhythmic Alphabet Level I

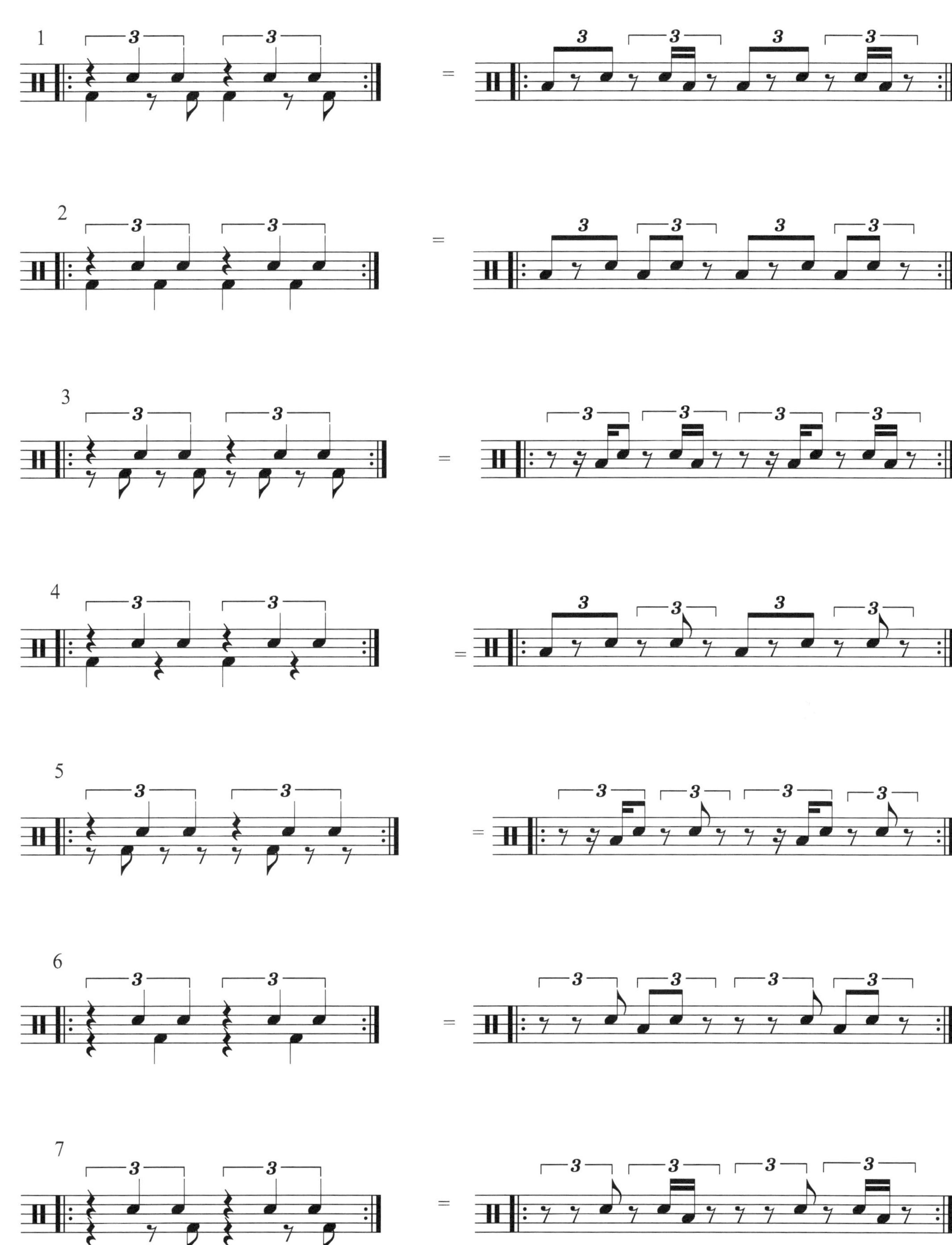

3:4 Polyrhythmic Alphabet Level I

3:4 Polyrhythmic Alphabet Level I

3:4 Polyrhythmic Alphabet Level I

3:4 Polyrhythmic Alphabet Level I

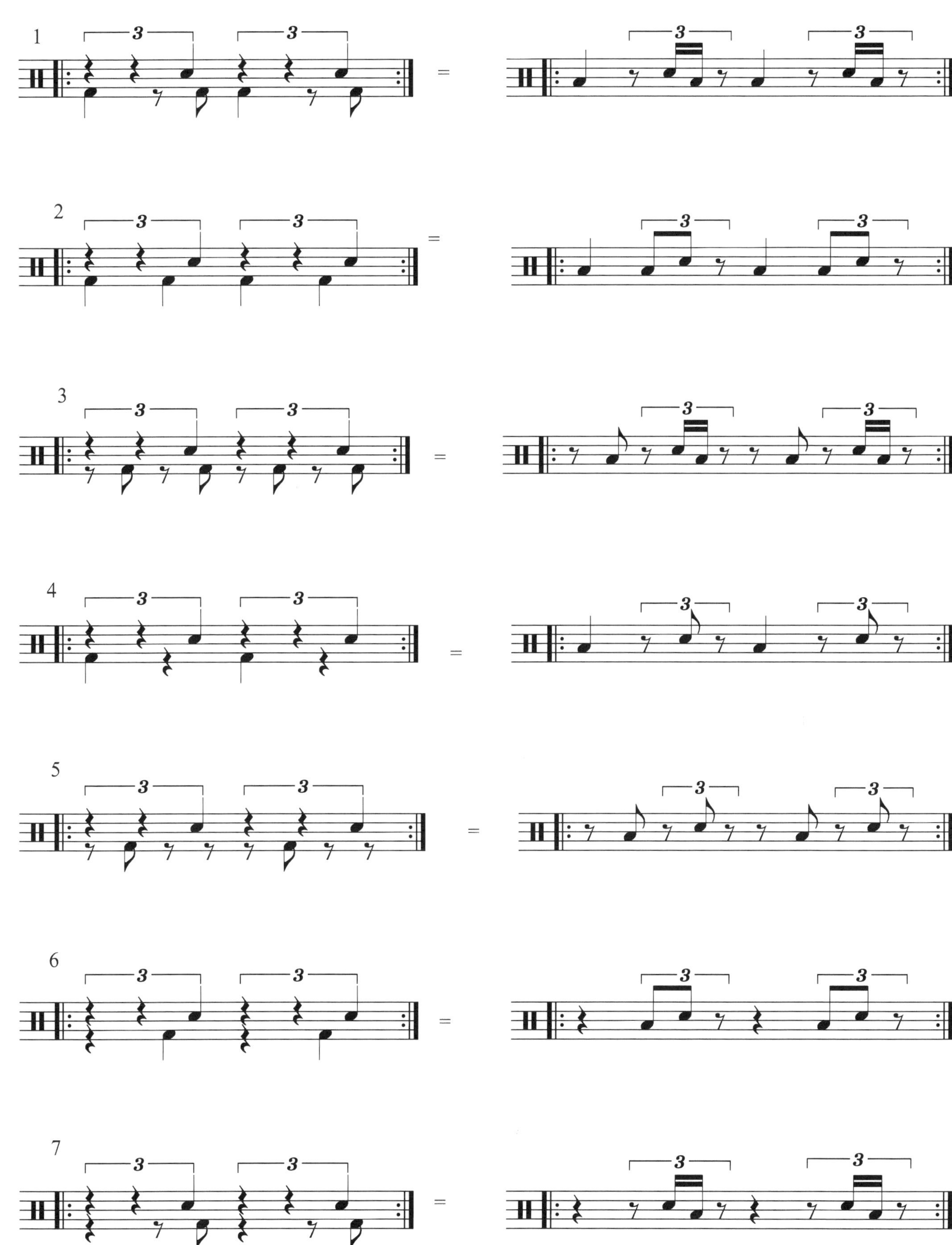

3:4 Polyrhythmic Alphabet Level I

3:4 Polyrhythmic Alphabet Level I

3:4 Polyrhythmic Alphabet Level I

3:4 Polyrhythmic Alphabet Level I

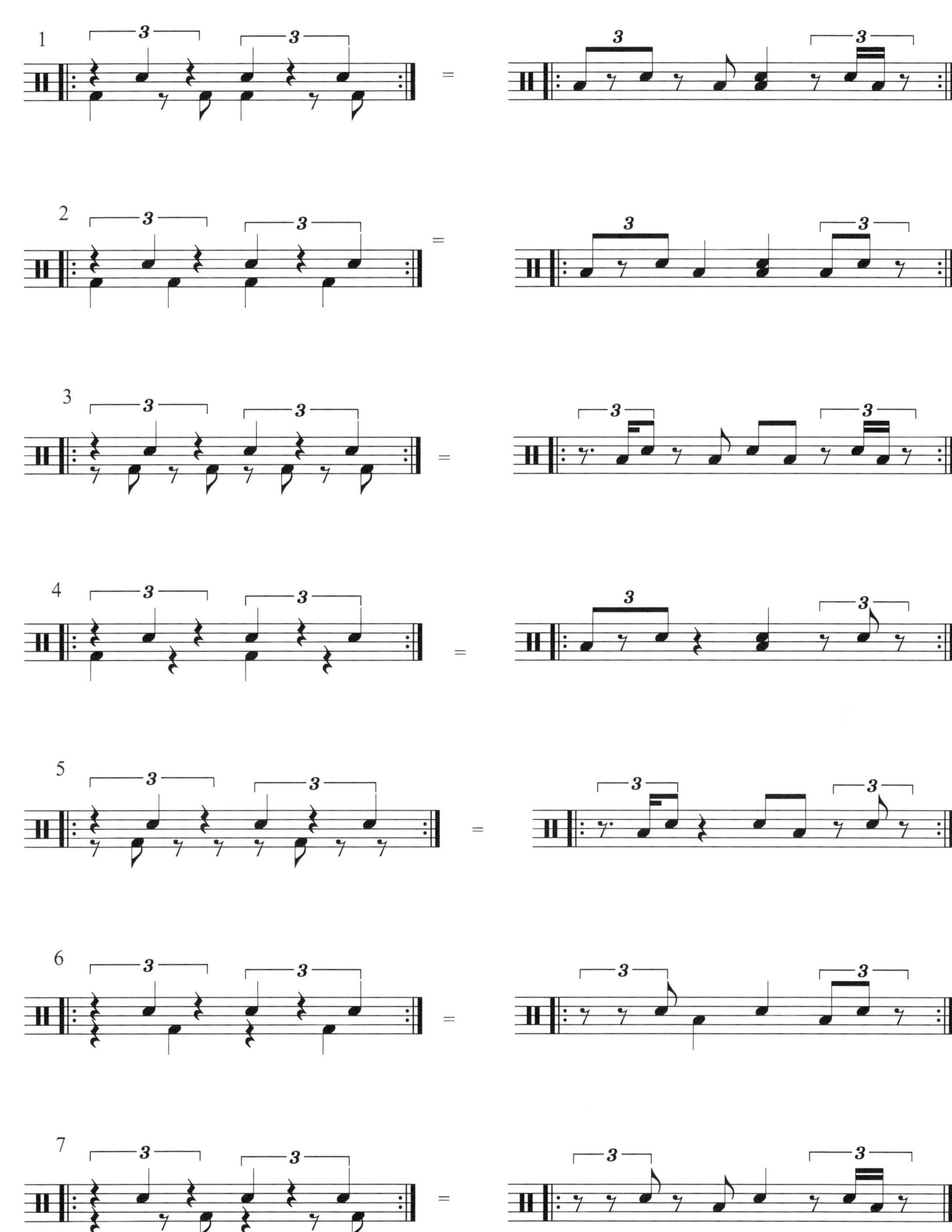

Subdivisions Per Beat

Quintuplets - 5s - Fivelets

So far we have only explored rhythms based on groups of two or three. Now let's take a brief look at quintuplet rhythms. Quintuplets divide the beat into five equal subdivisions.

First we explore the rhythmic build with accents, then the rhythmic reduction with the quintuplet rhythms.

$$2^5 = 32$$ Rhythm Alphabet.

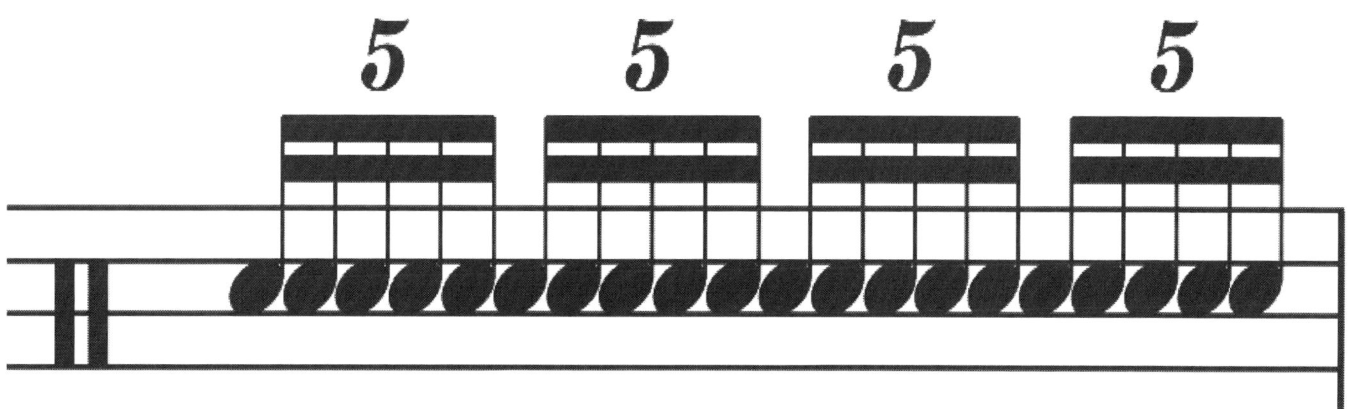

Quintuplets

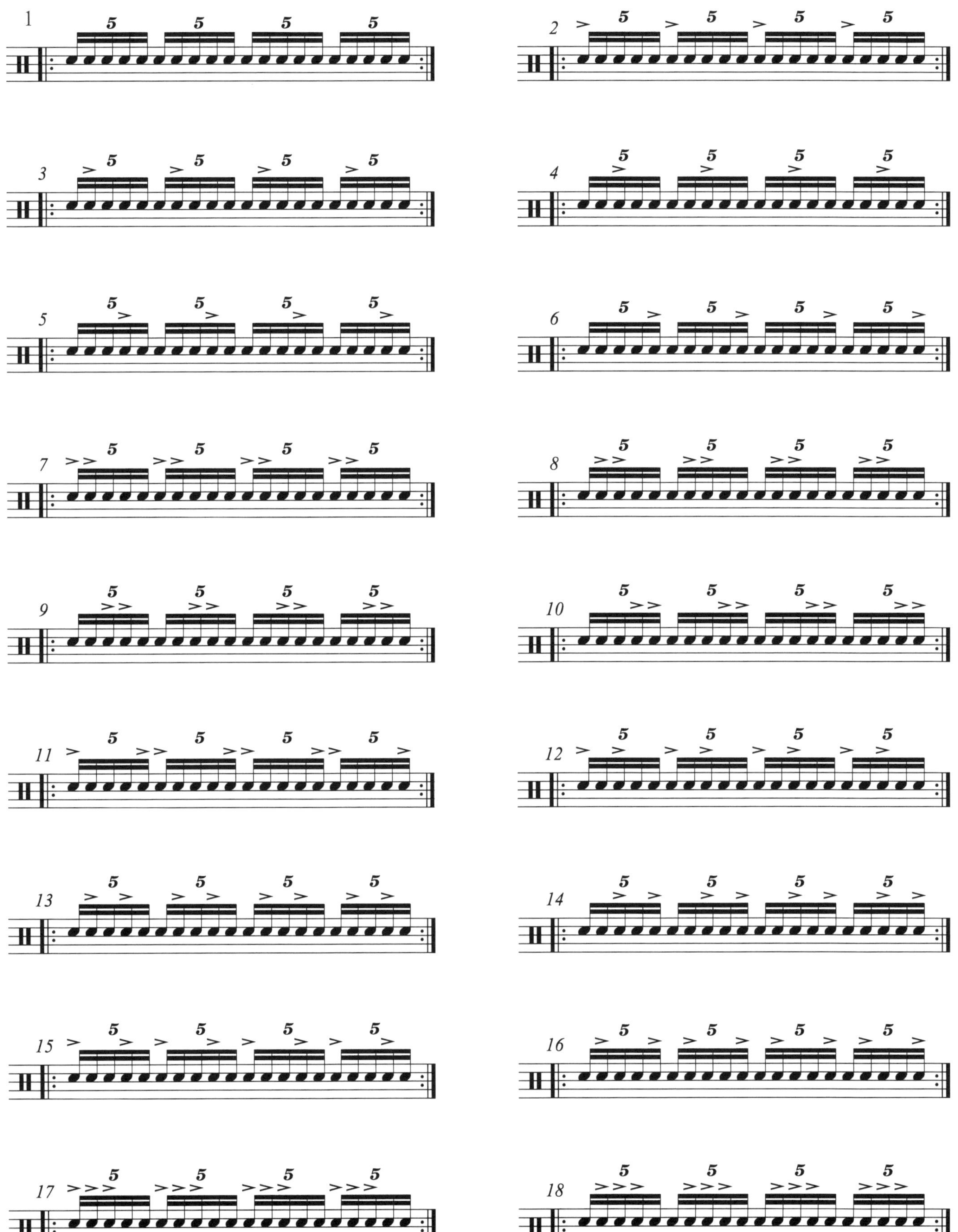

Quintuplets

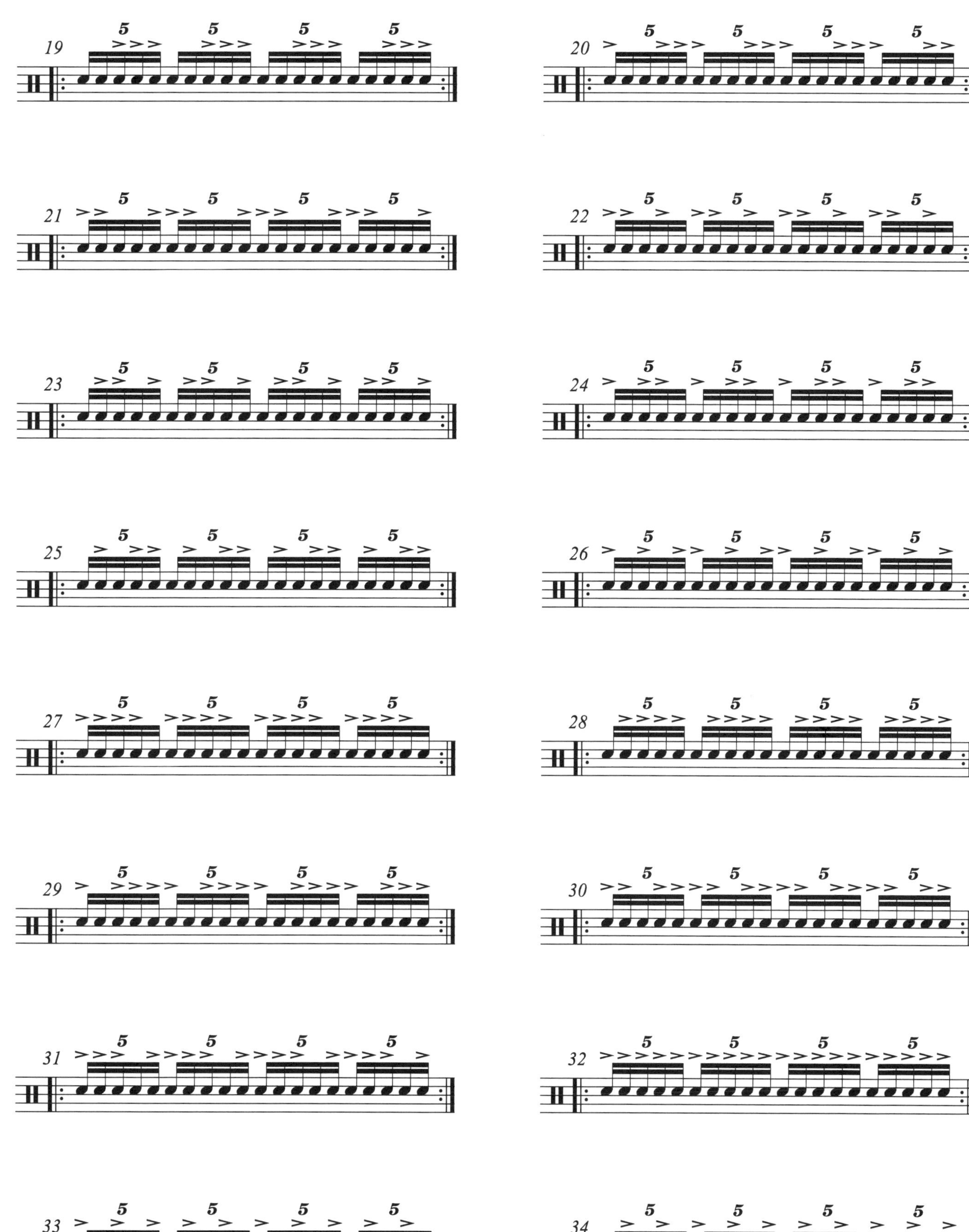

Quintuplets

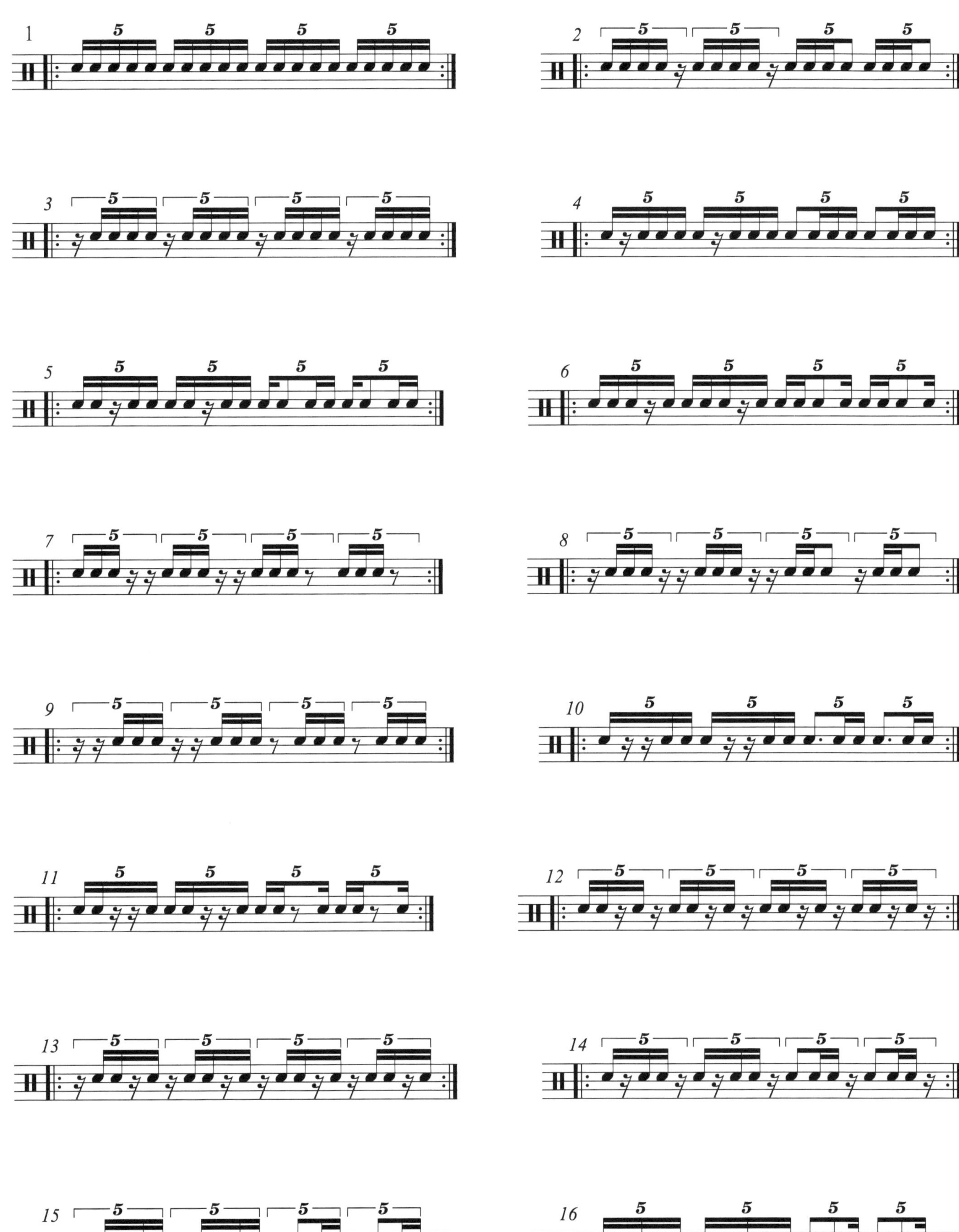

Quintuplets

Subdivisions Per Beat

Septuplets - 7s

A brief look at septuplet rhythms. Septuplets divide the beat into seven equal subdivisions.

First we explore the rhythmic build with accents, then the rhythmic reduction with the septuplet rhythms.

$2^7 = 128$ Rhythm Alphabet

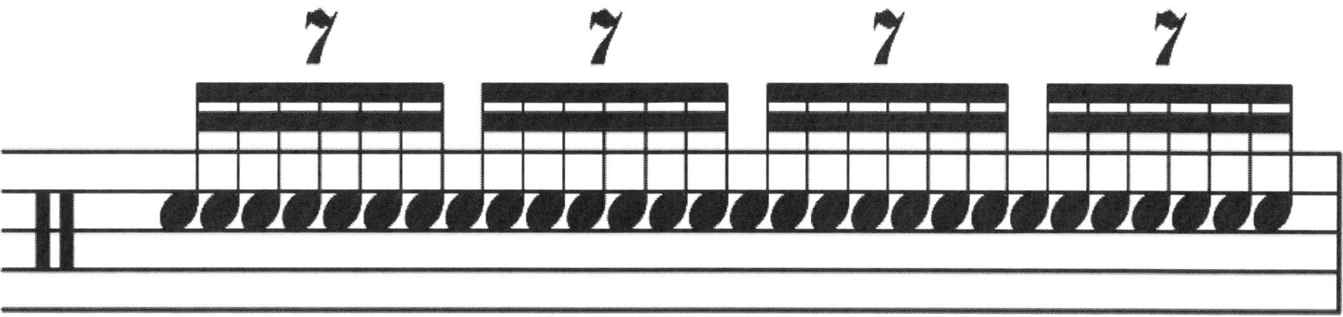

Septuplets (7s)

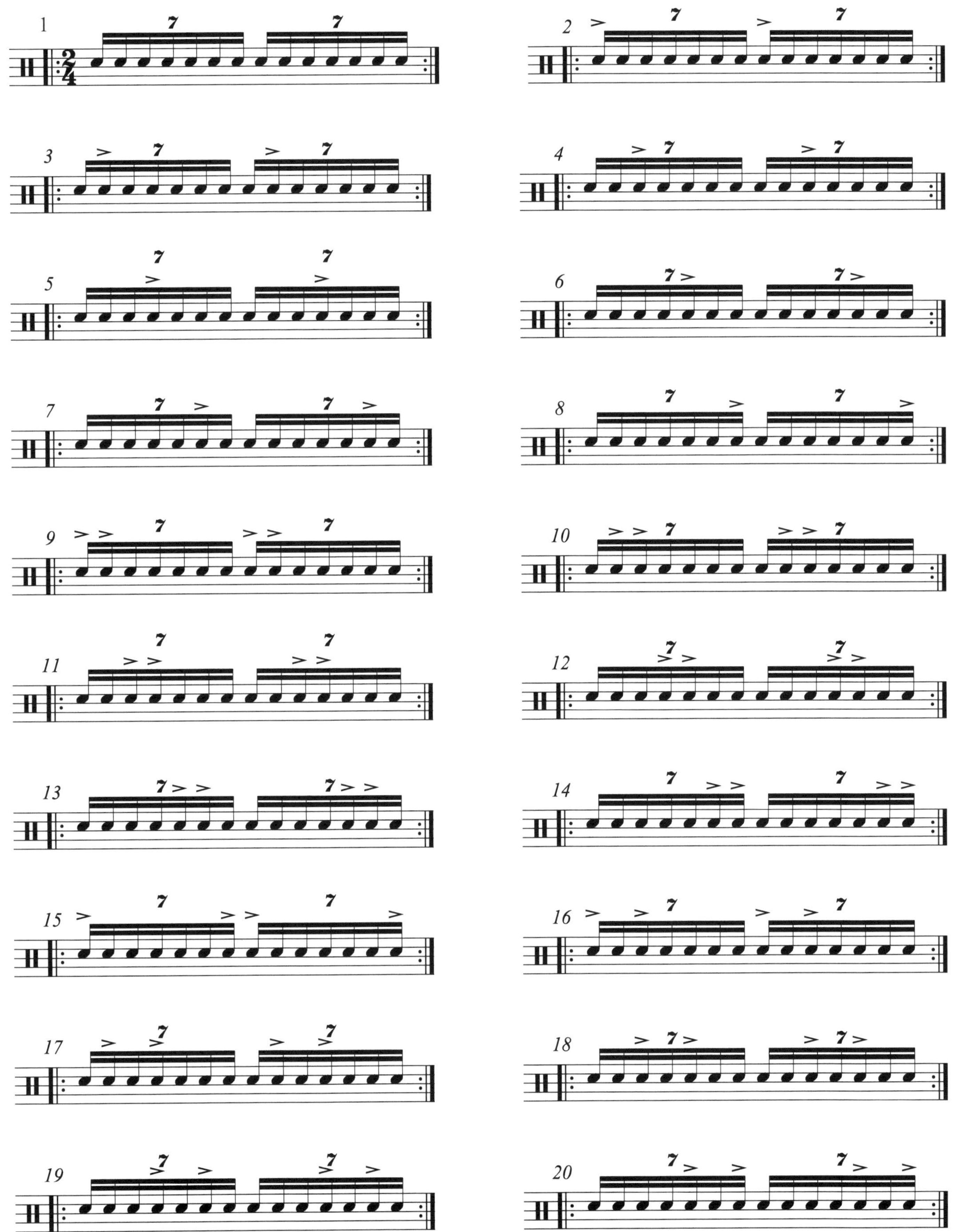

Septuplets (7s)

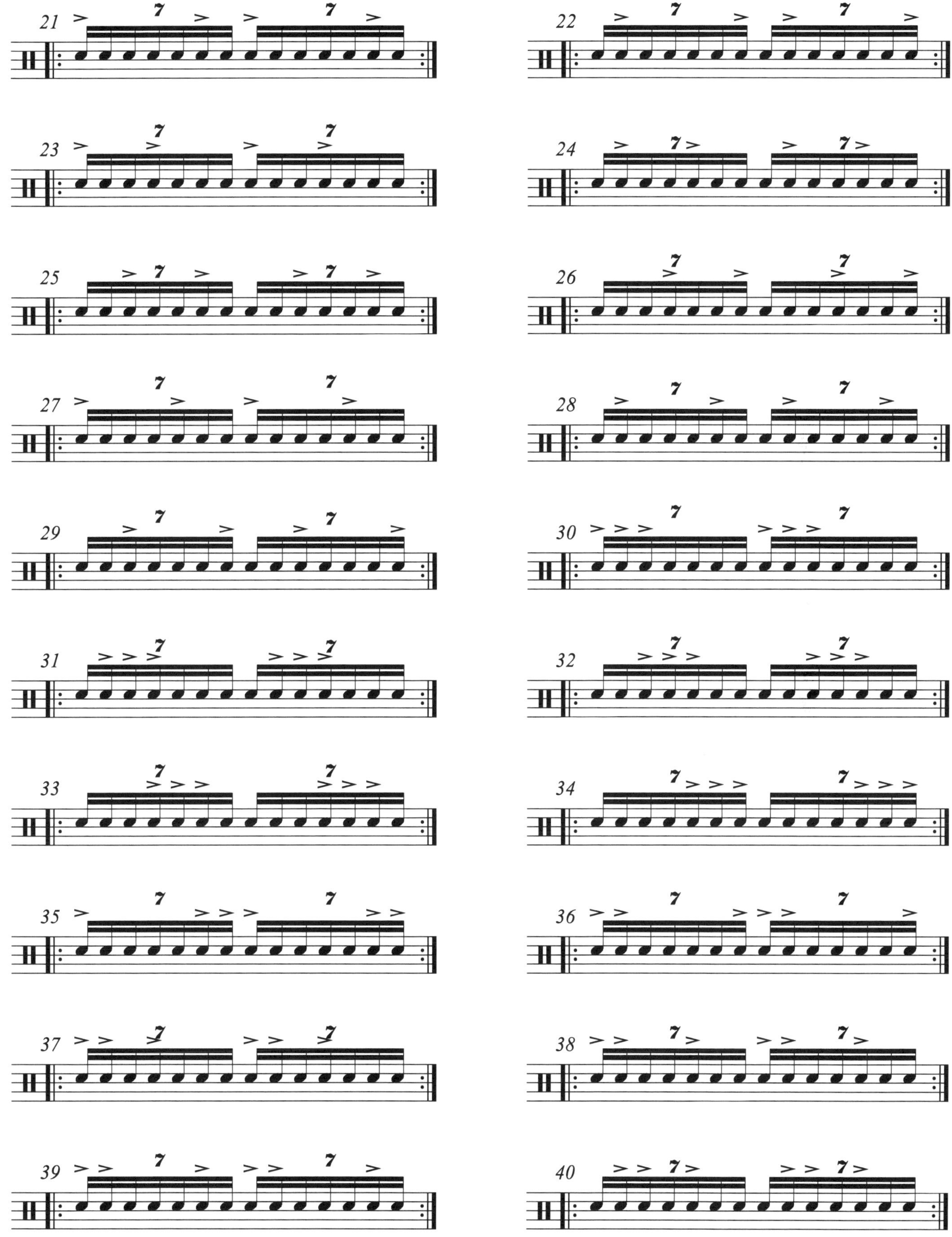

Septuplets (7s)

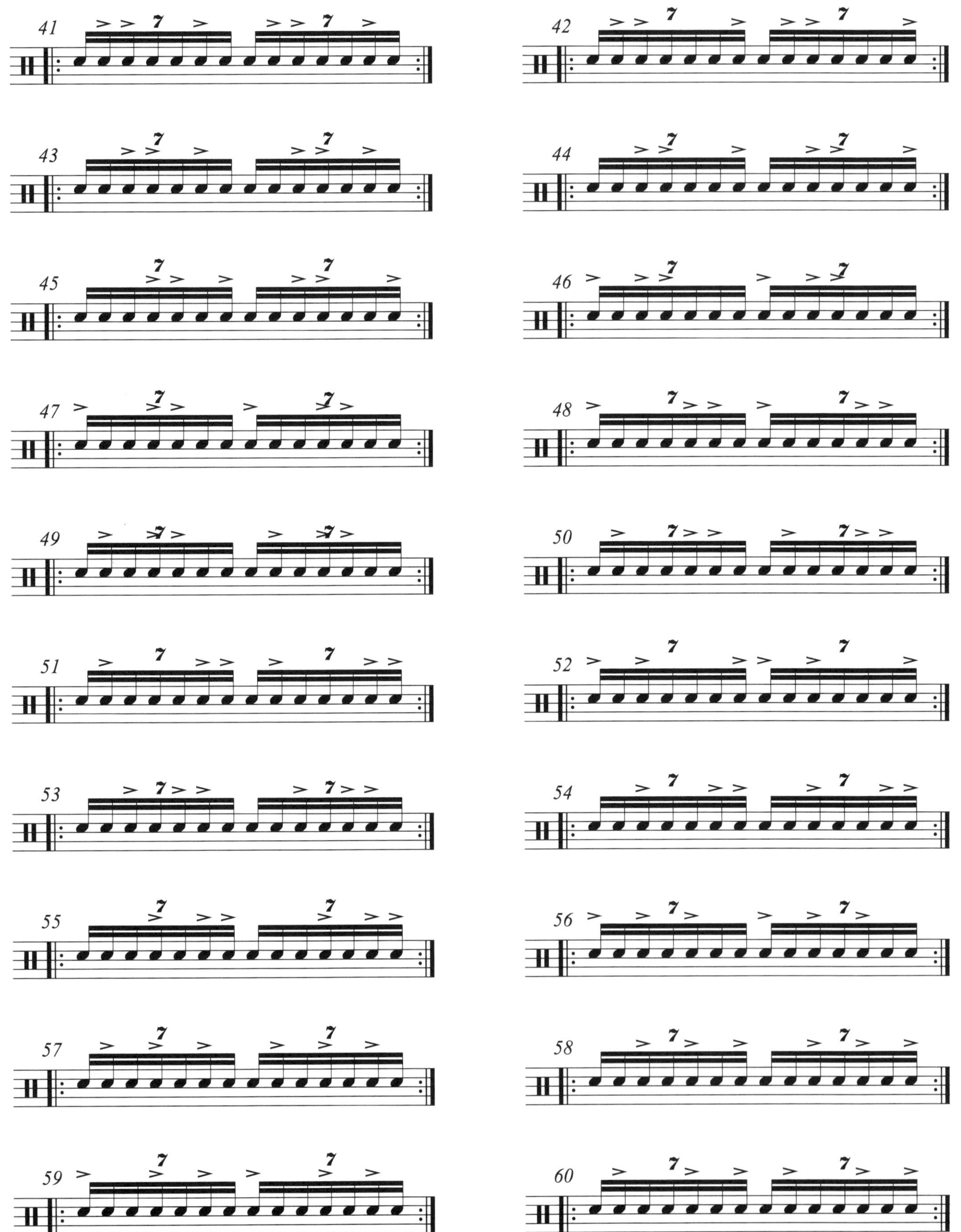

Septuplets (7s)

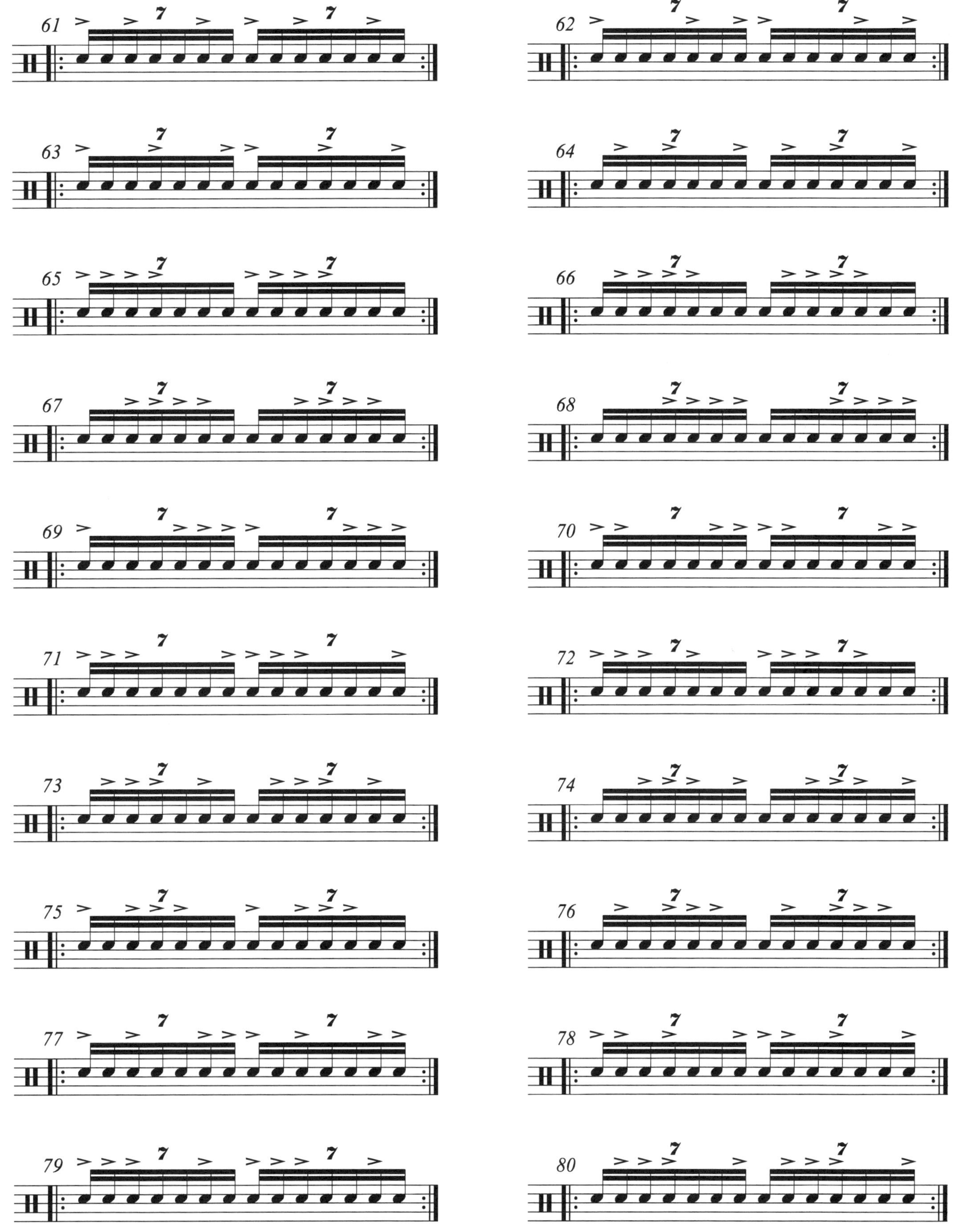

Septuplets (7s)

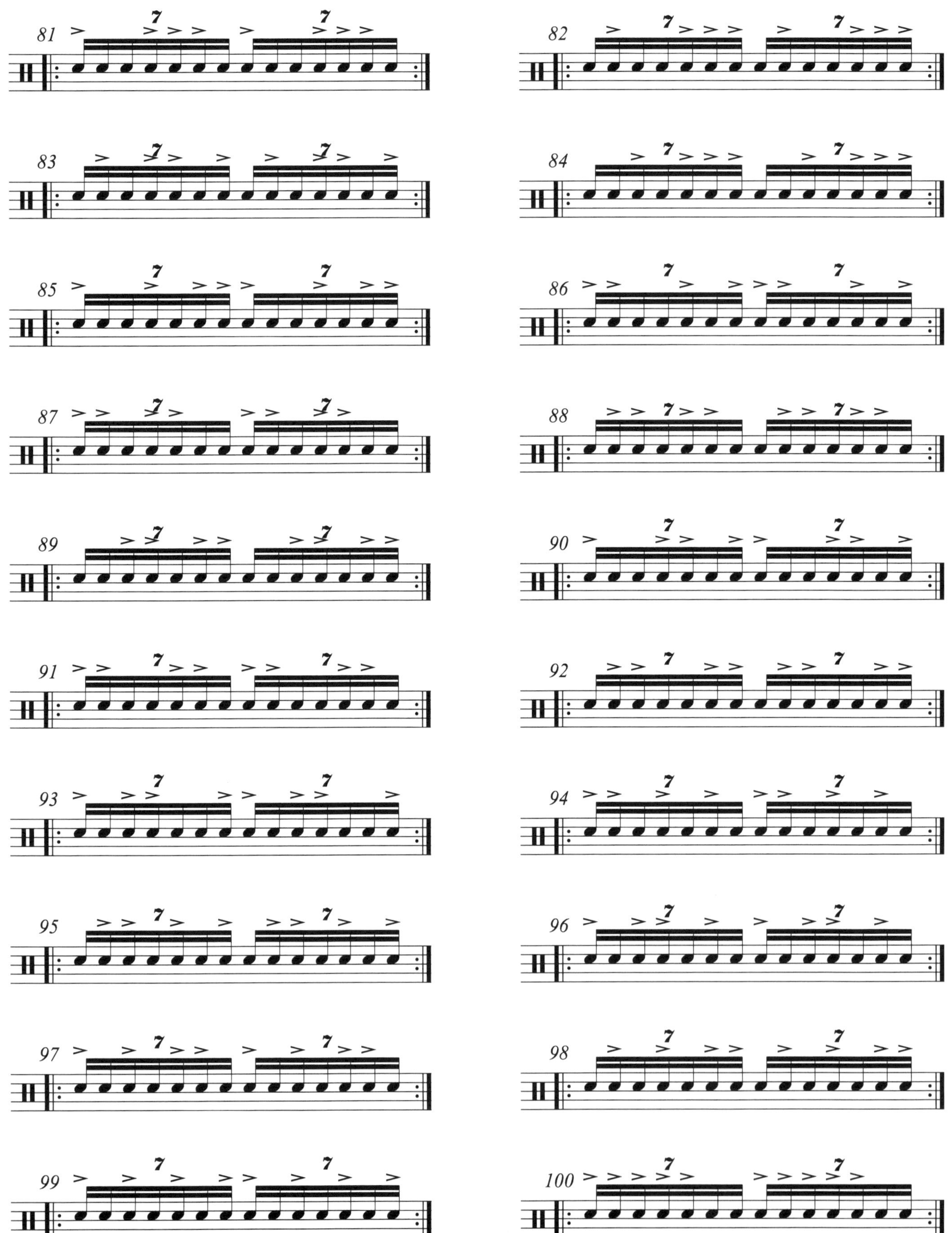

Septuplets (7s)

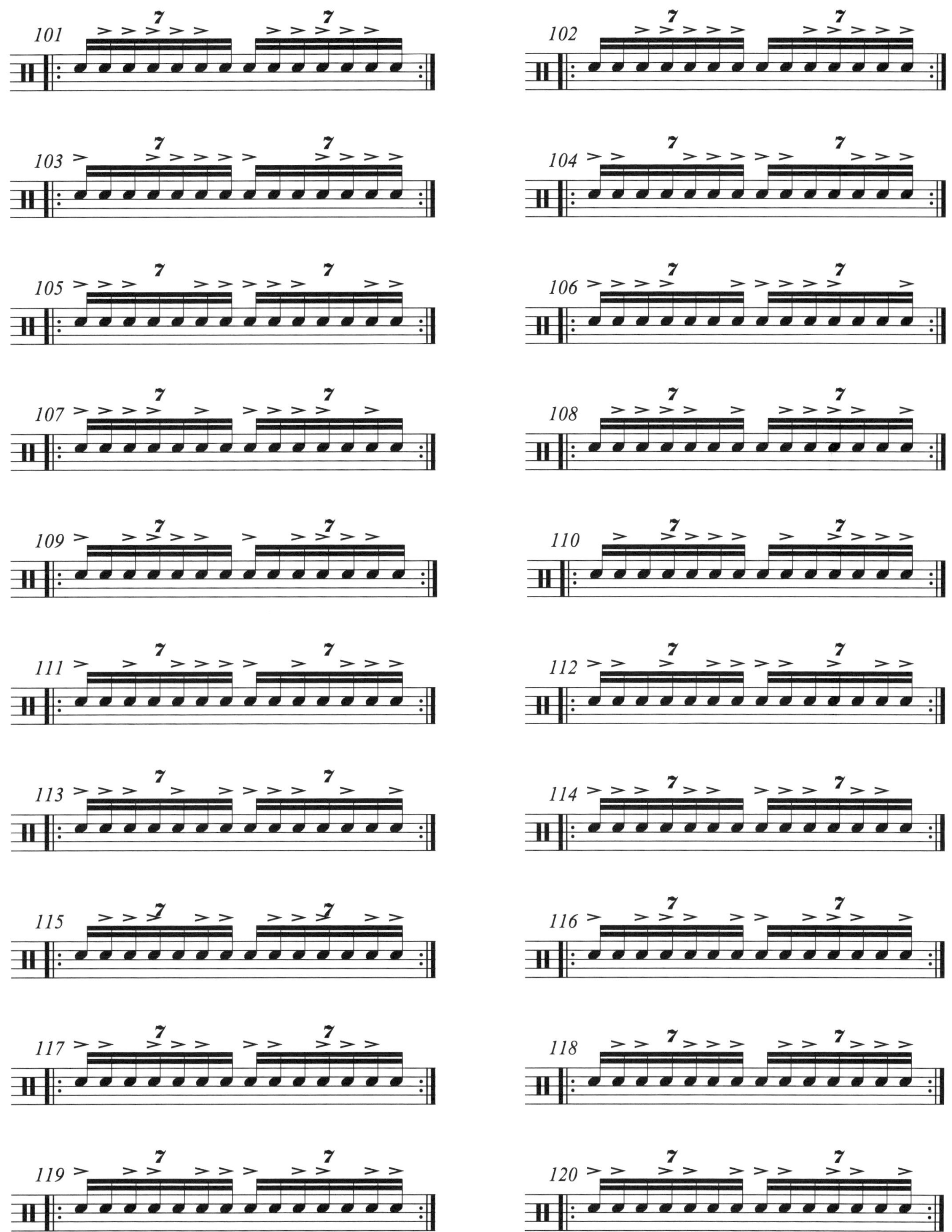

Septuplets (7s)

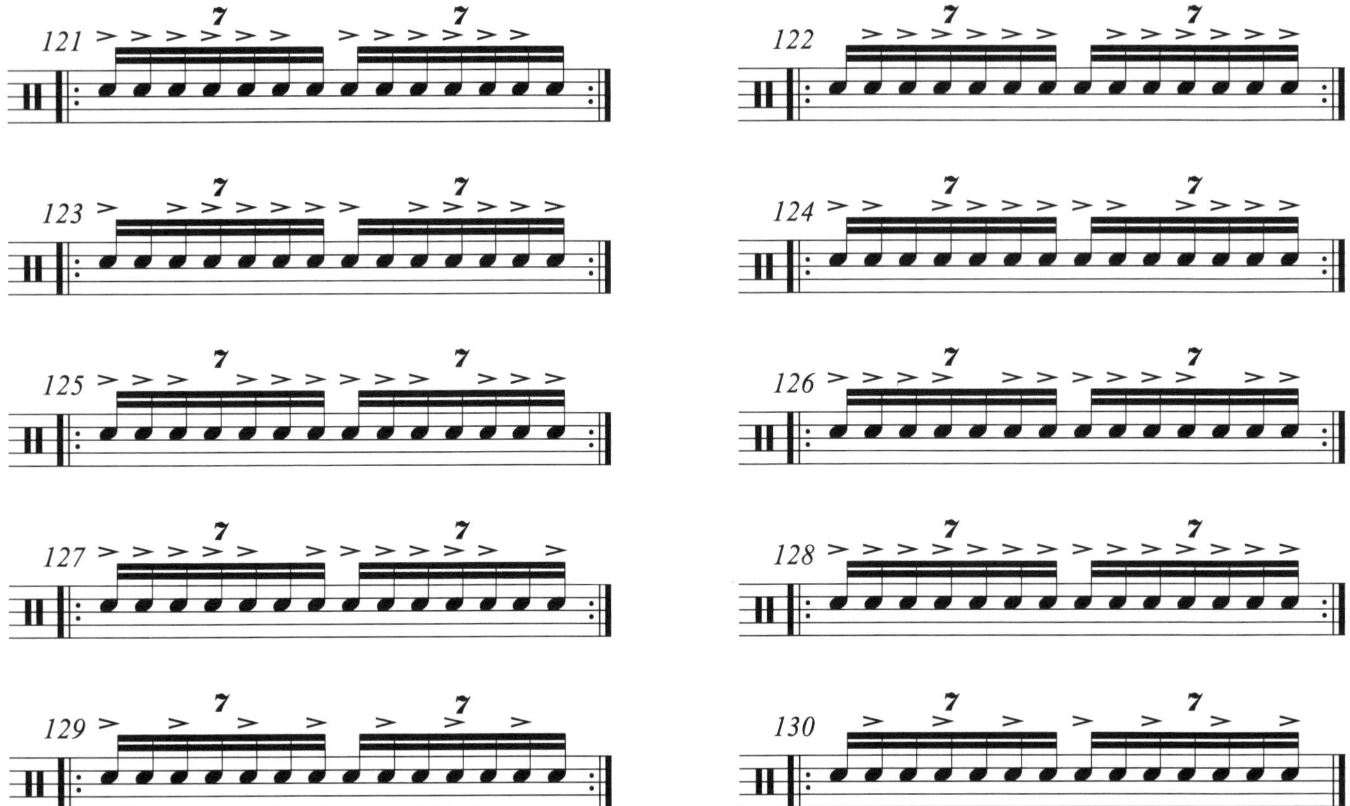

Septuplets (7s)

Subdivisions Per Beat

$2^7 = 128$ Rhythm Alphabet

Rhythmic Reduction

Septuplets (7s)

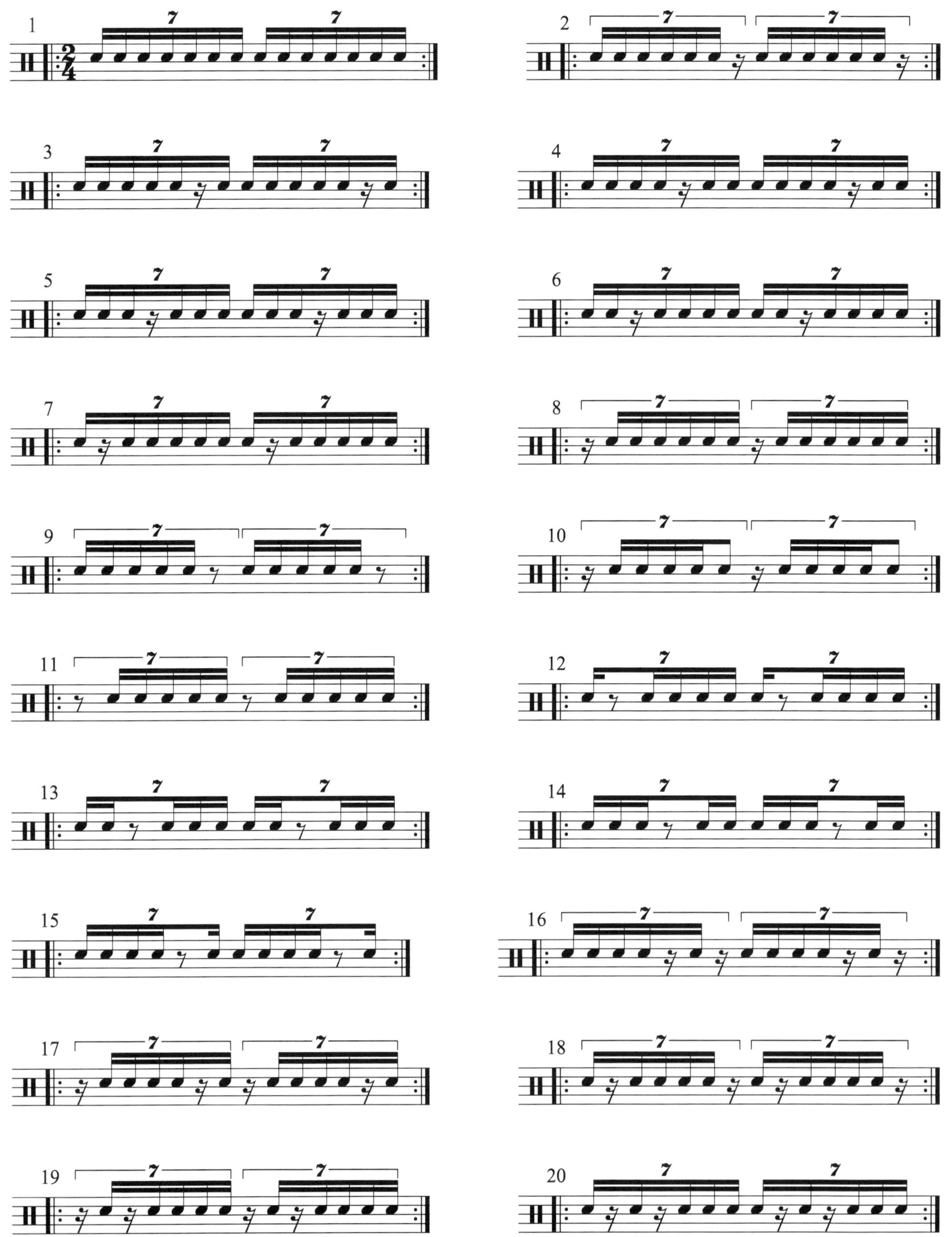

Septuplets (7s)

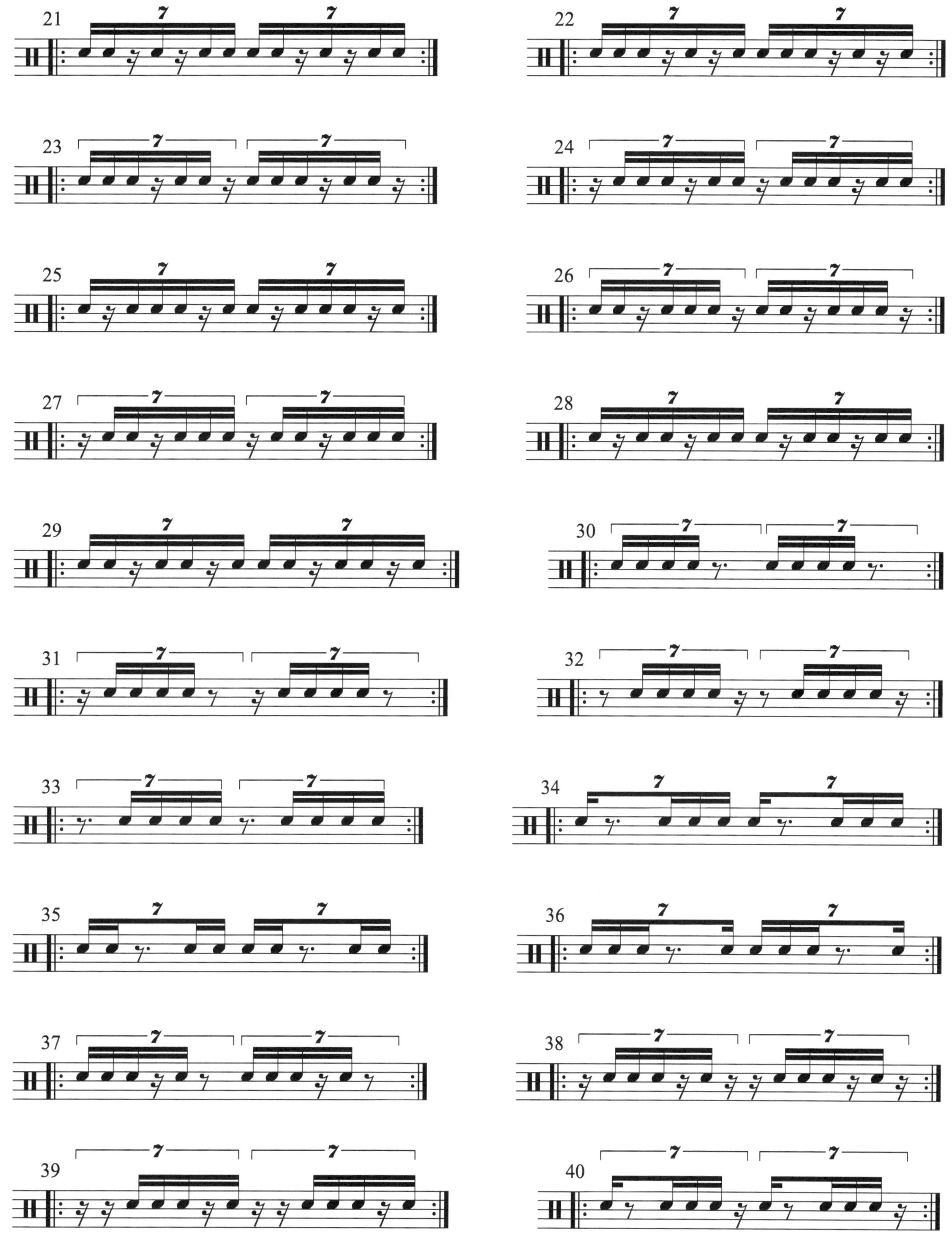

Septuplets (7s)

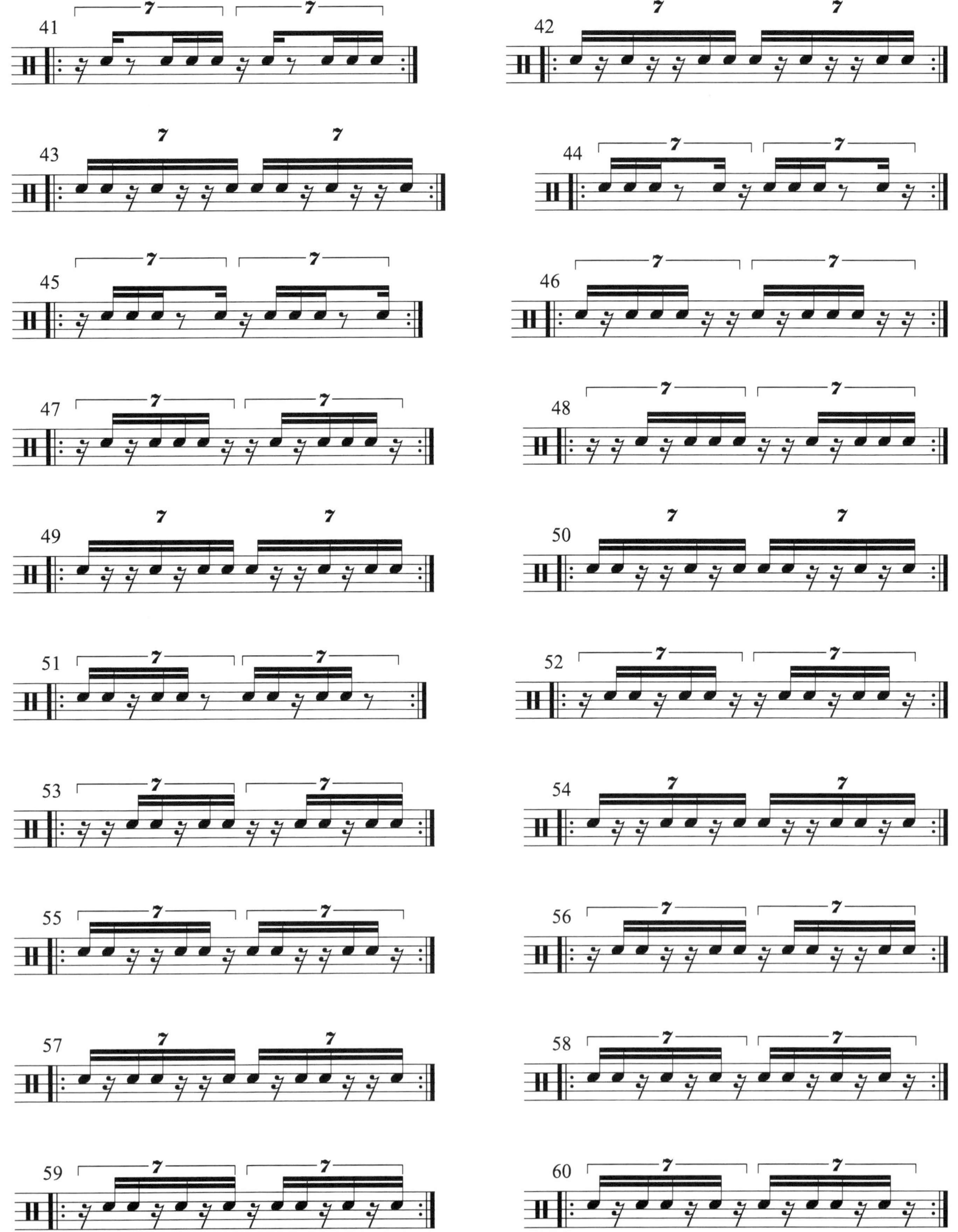

Septuplets (7s)

Septuplets (7s)

Septuplets (7s)

Septuplets (7s)

The Multipurpose Section

Here are just a few of the many uses for the exercises in this book.

Play the accents as doubles, or buzzes.

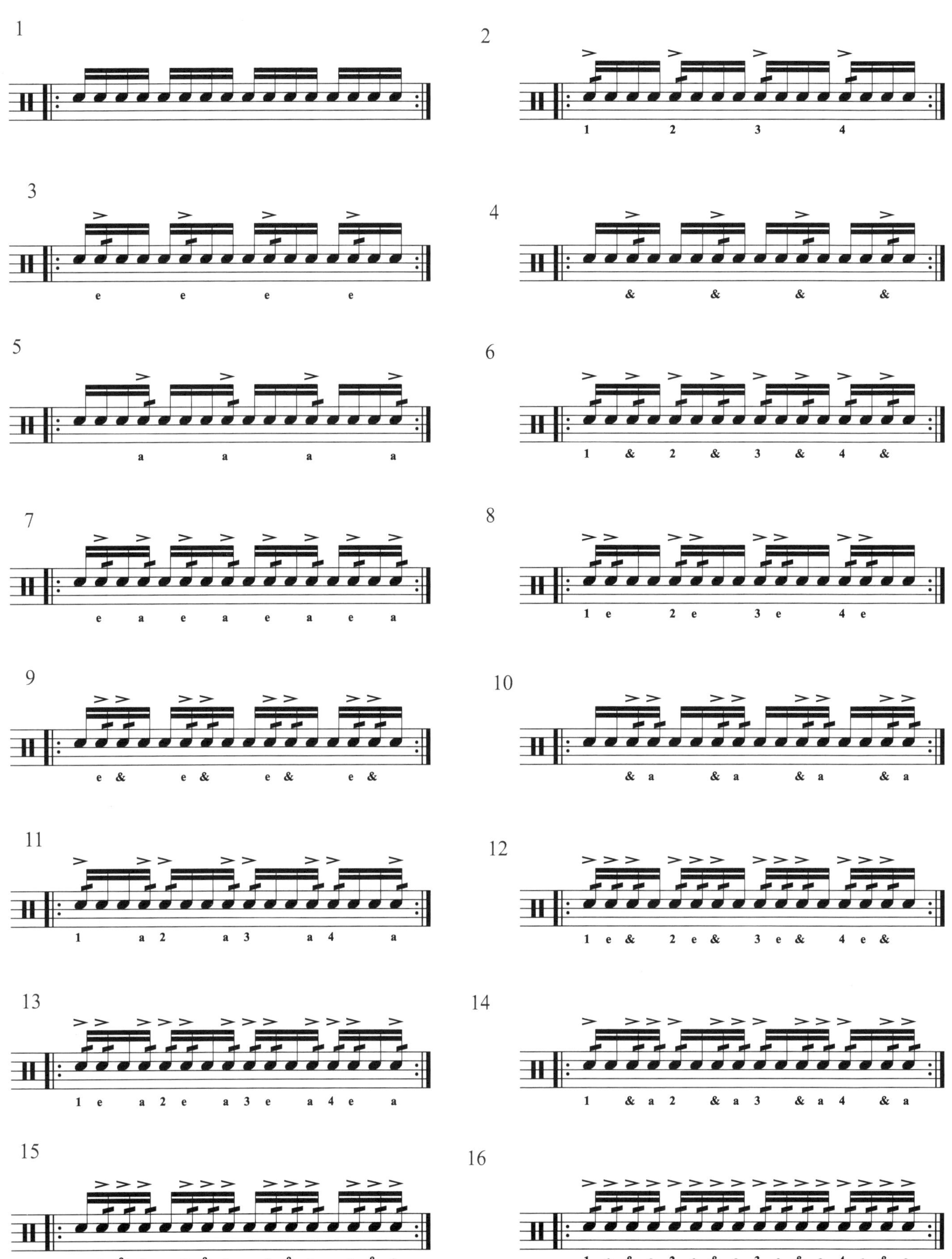

Double, or buzz the non-accented notes at tap the accents.

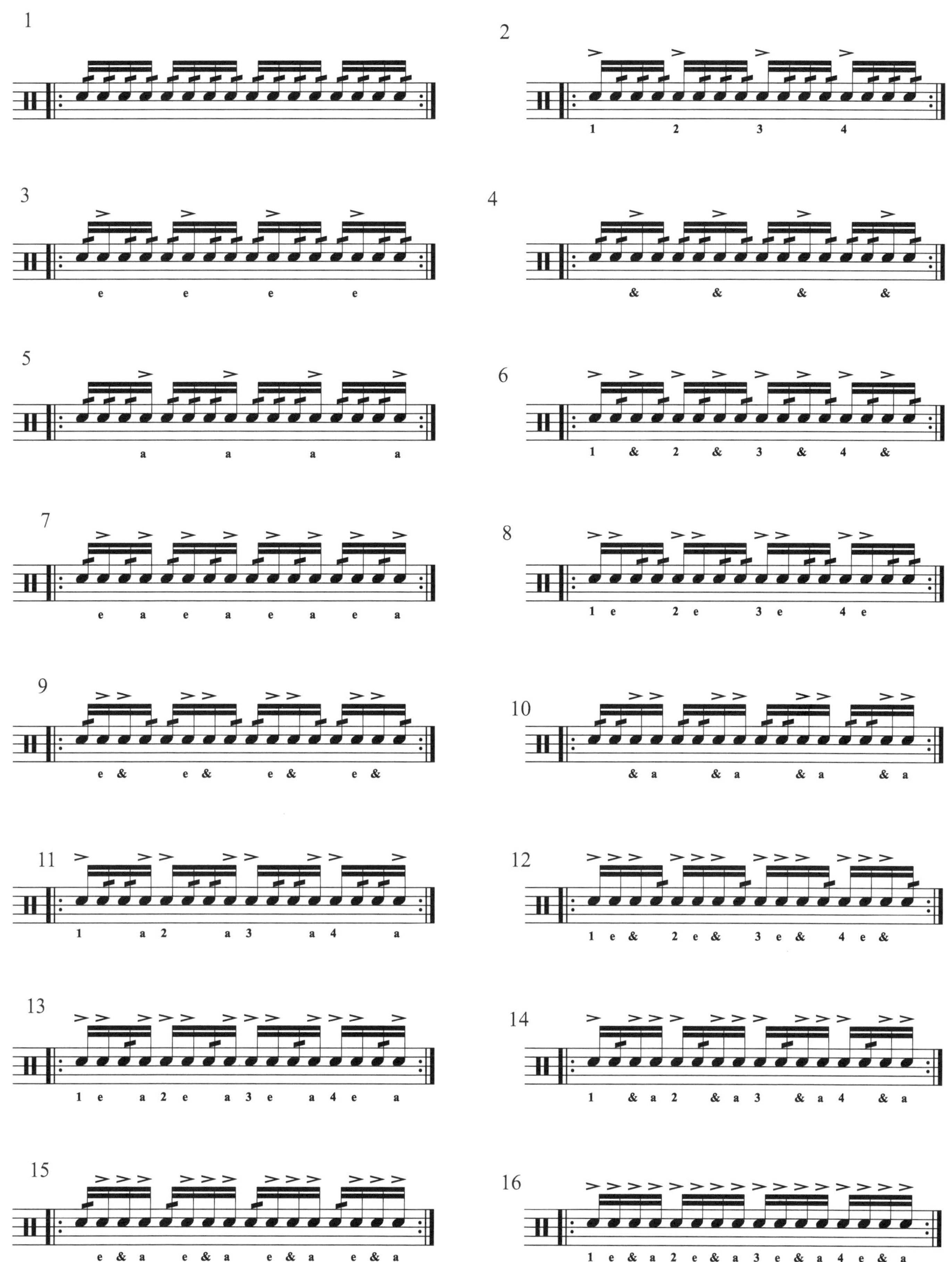

Play the accented notes as flams.

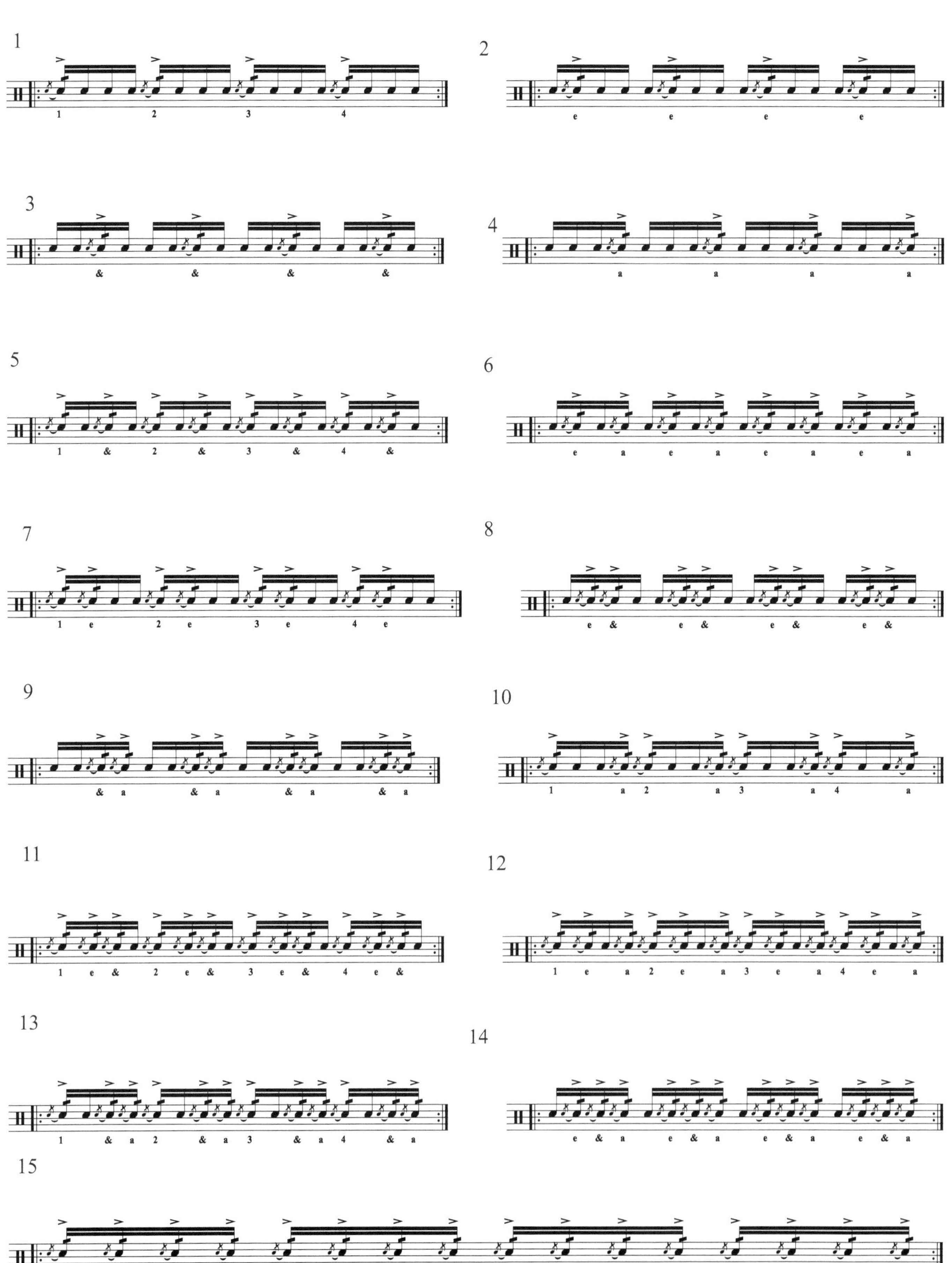

Cheese: Double the primary note of the flam.

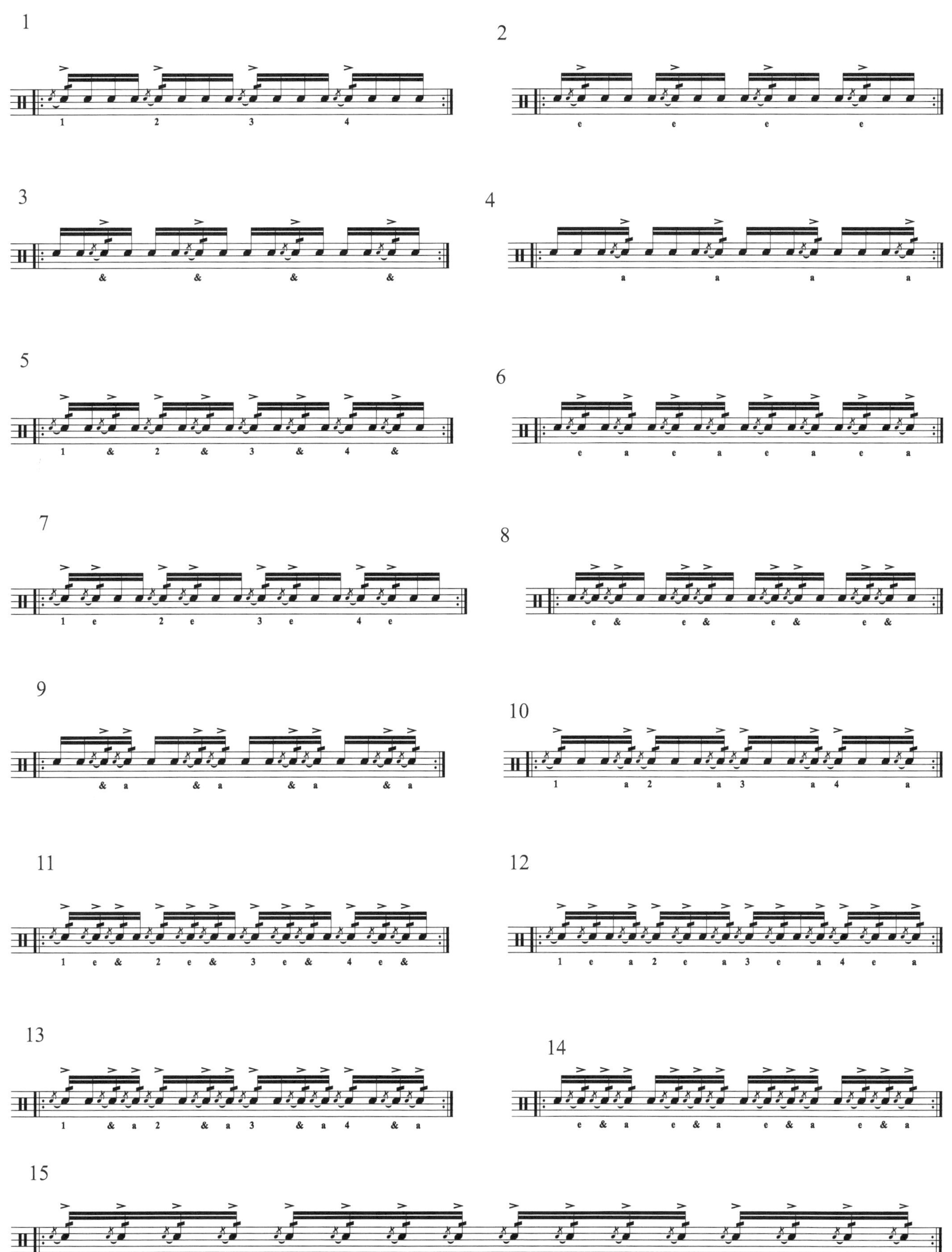

Play the accents as drags.

Do the same with the triplet exercises.

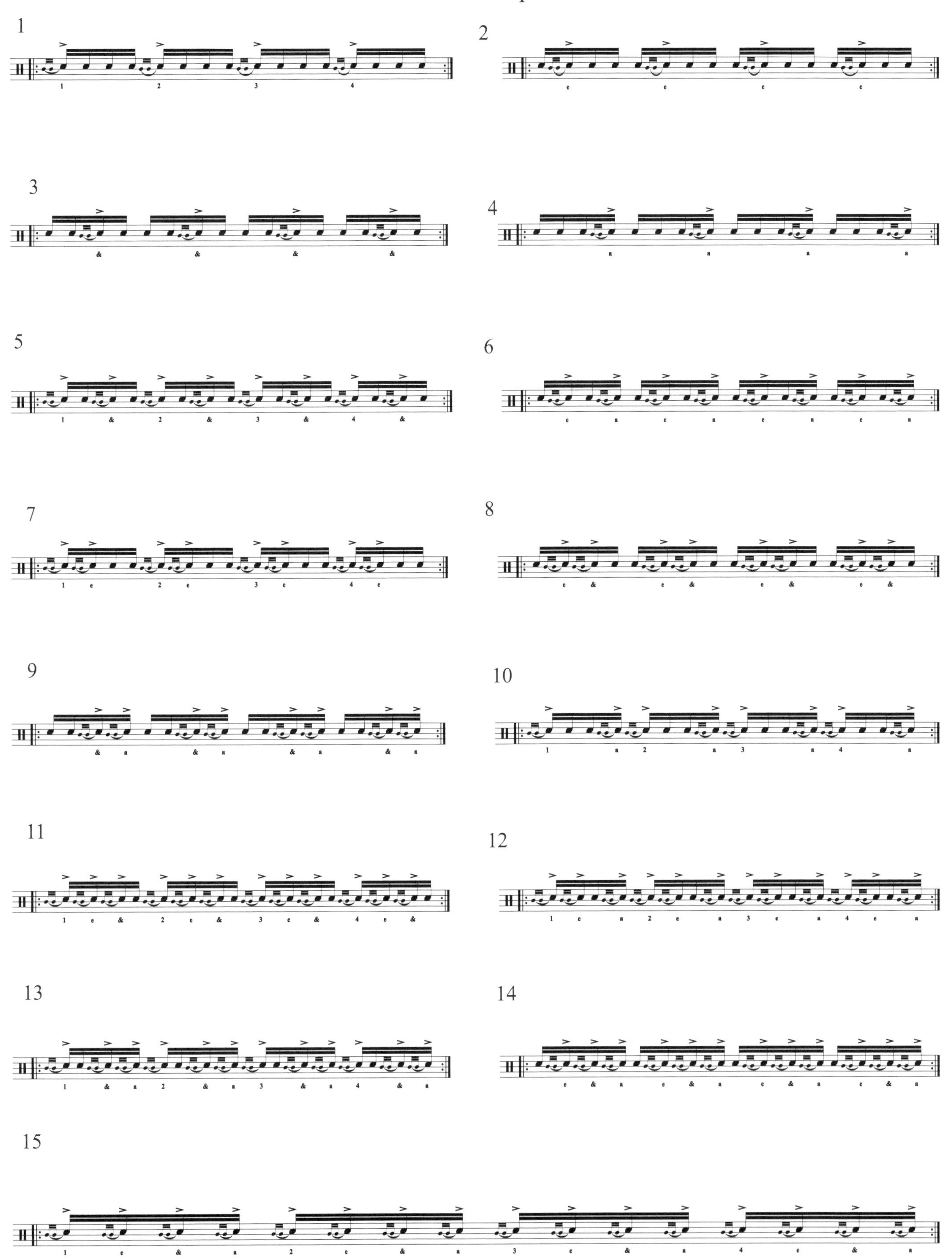

Play the bass drum with the accents.

Come back and add the hi hat on the down beats. (1,2,3,4,) - Play the hi hat on the up beats. (&)
Do the same with the triplet exercises. Play the hi hat on the down beats, or 2 and 4.

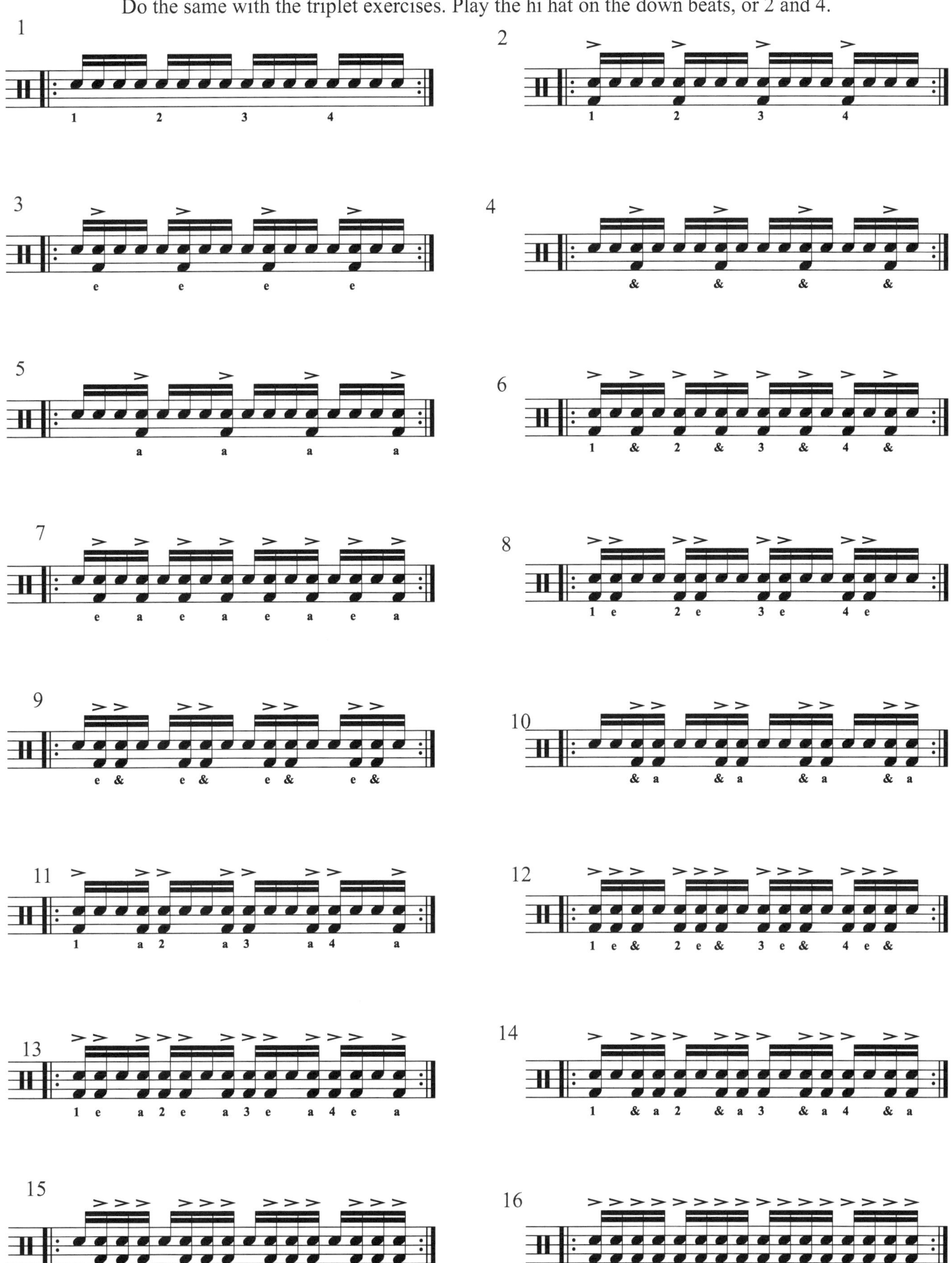

Play the accents over bass drum and hi hat ostinato patterns.

Change the accents to doubles. Double the non-accented notes and tap the accents.

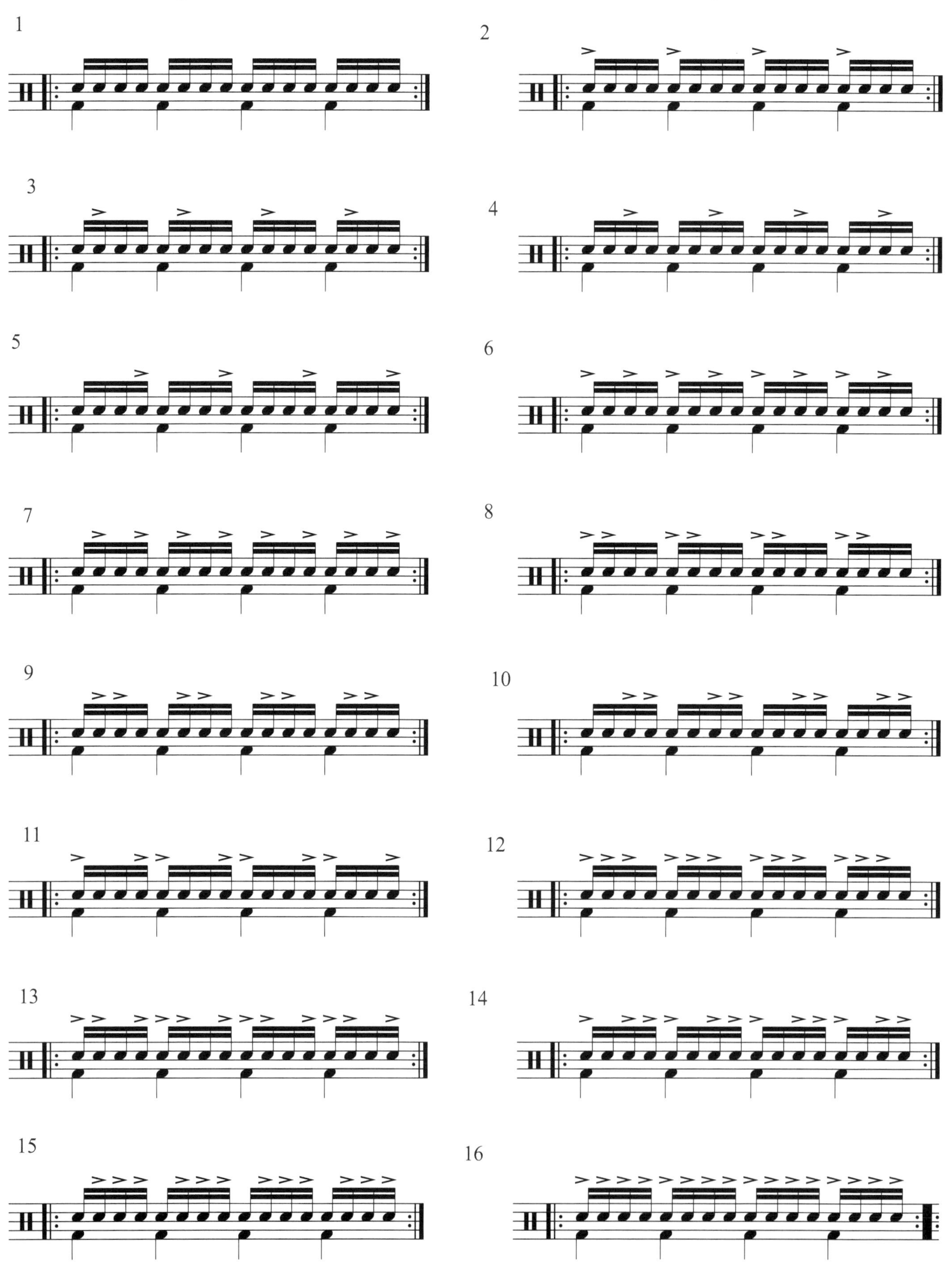

Play the accents over bass drum and hi hat ostinato patterns.

Change the accents to doubles. Double the non-accented notes and tap the accents.

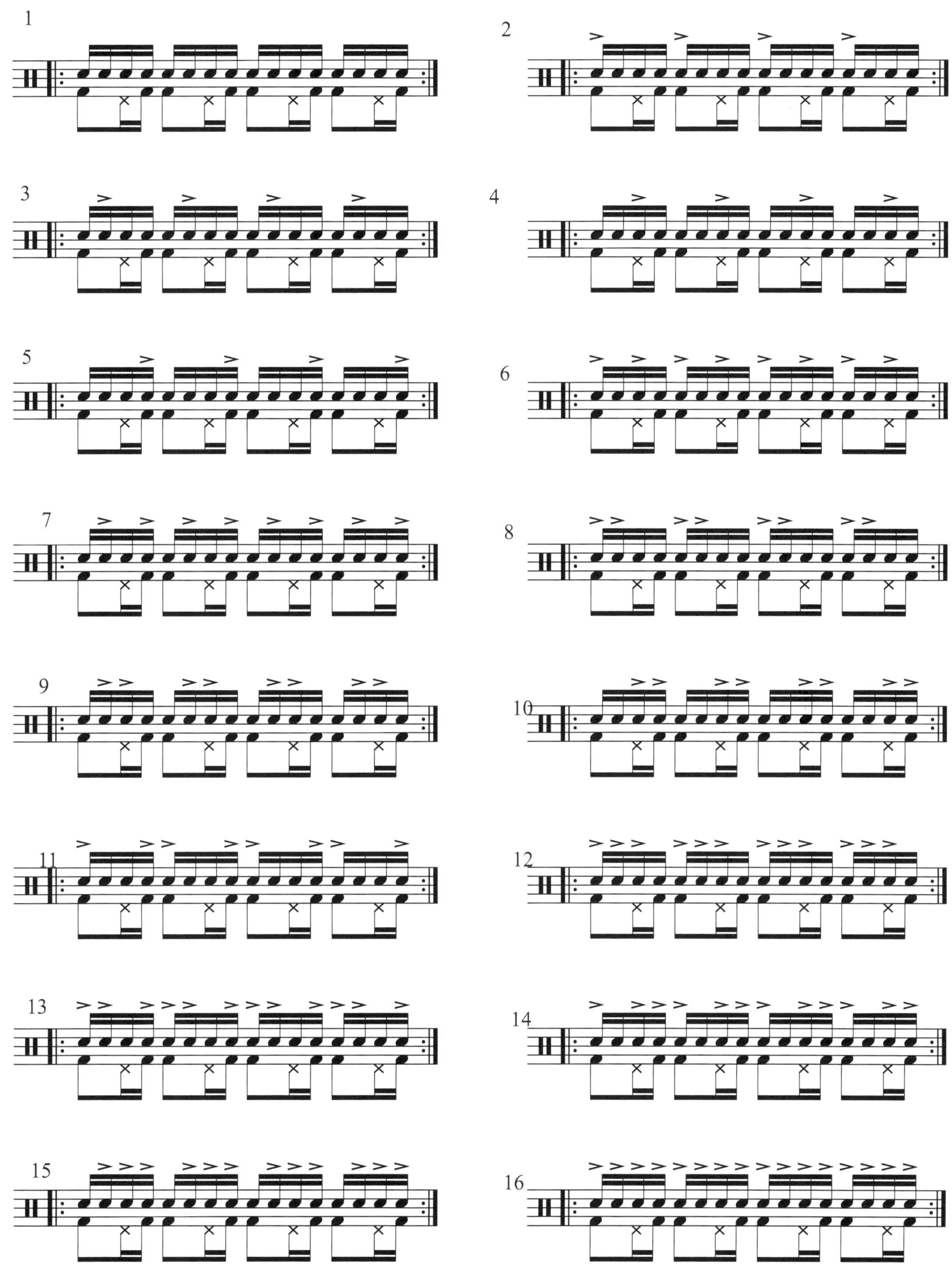

Play the accents over bass drum and hi hat ostinato patterns.

Change the accents to doubles. Double the non-accented notes and tap the accents.

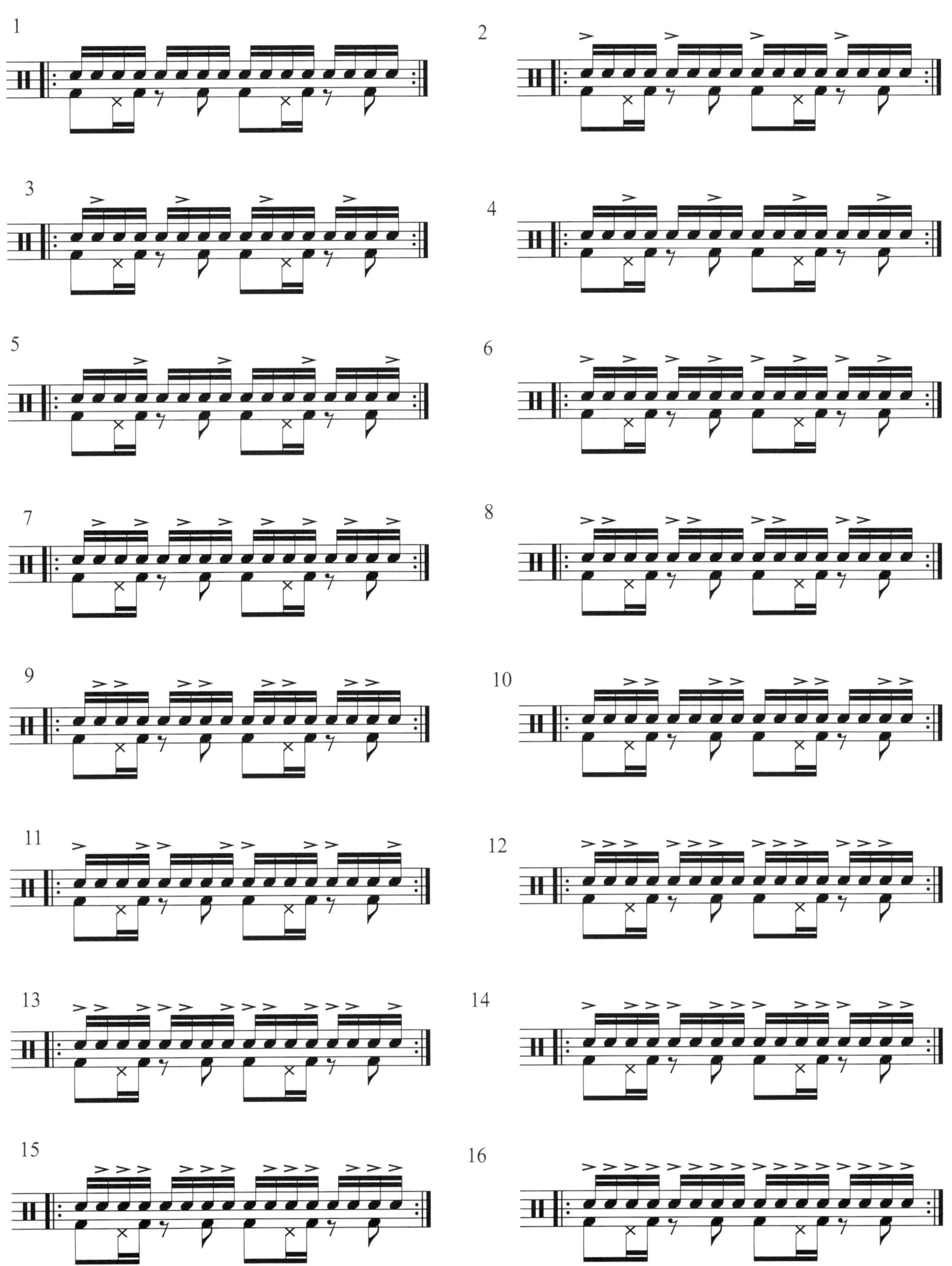

Play the non-accented notes on the snare and the accents on the toms.

Change the accents to doubles. Double the non-accented notes and tap the accents on the toms.

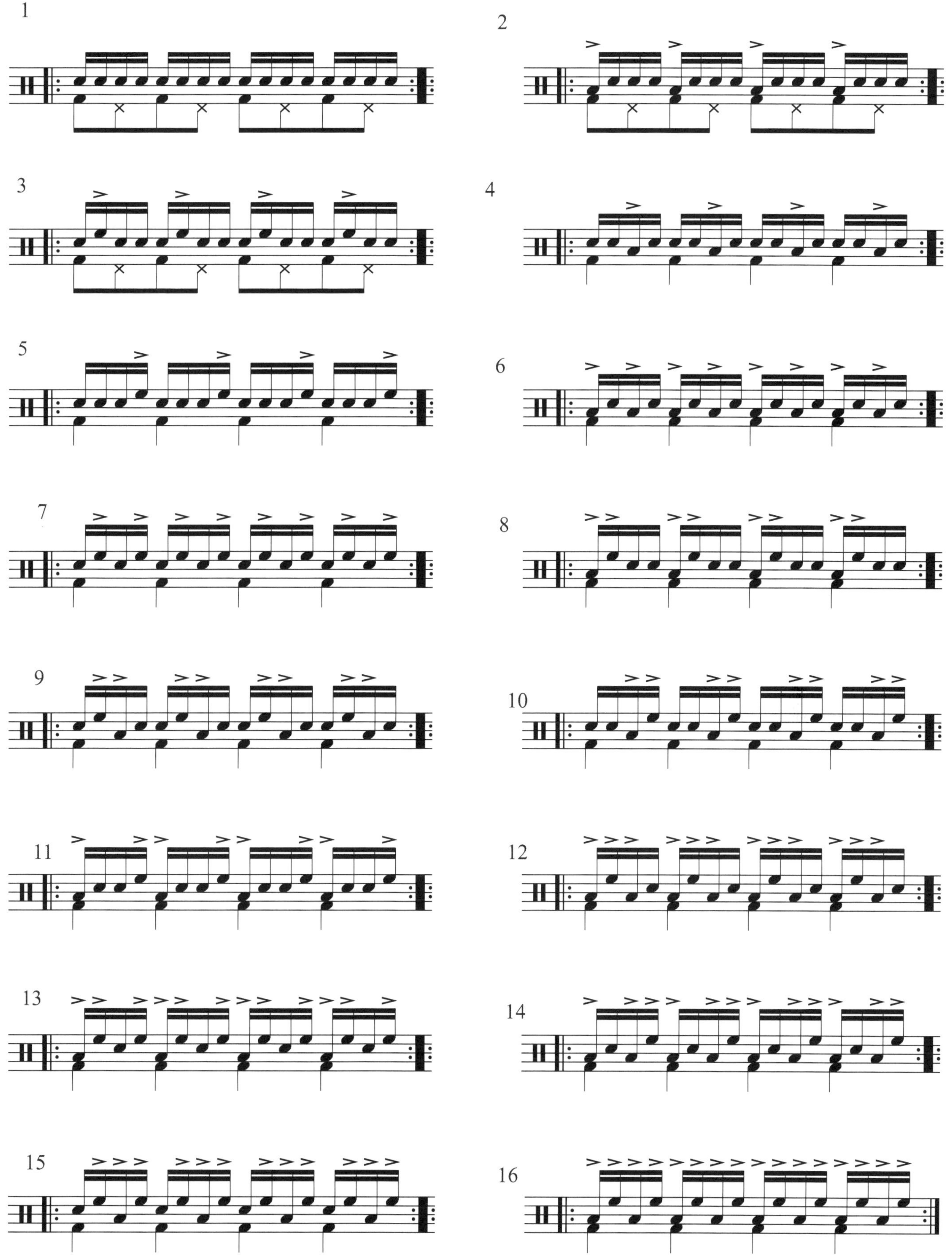

Play the 8th note rhythms on the bass drum with a hi hat and snare drum ostinato.

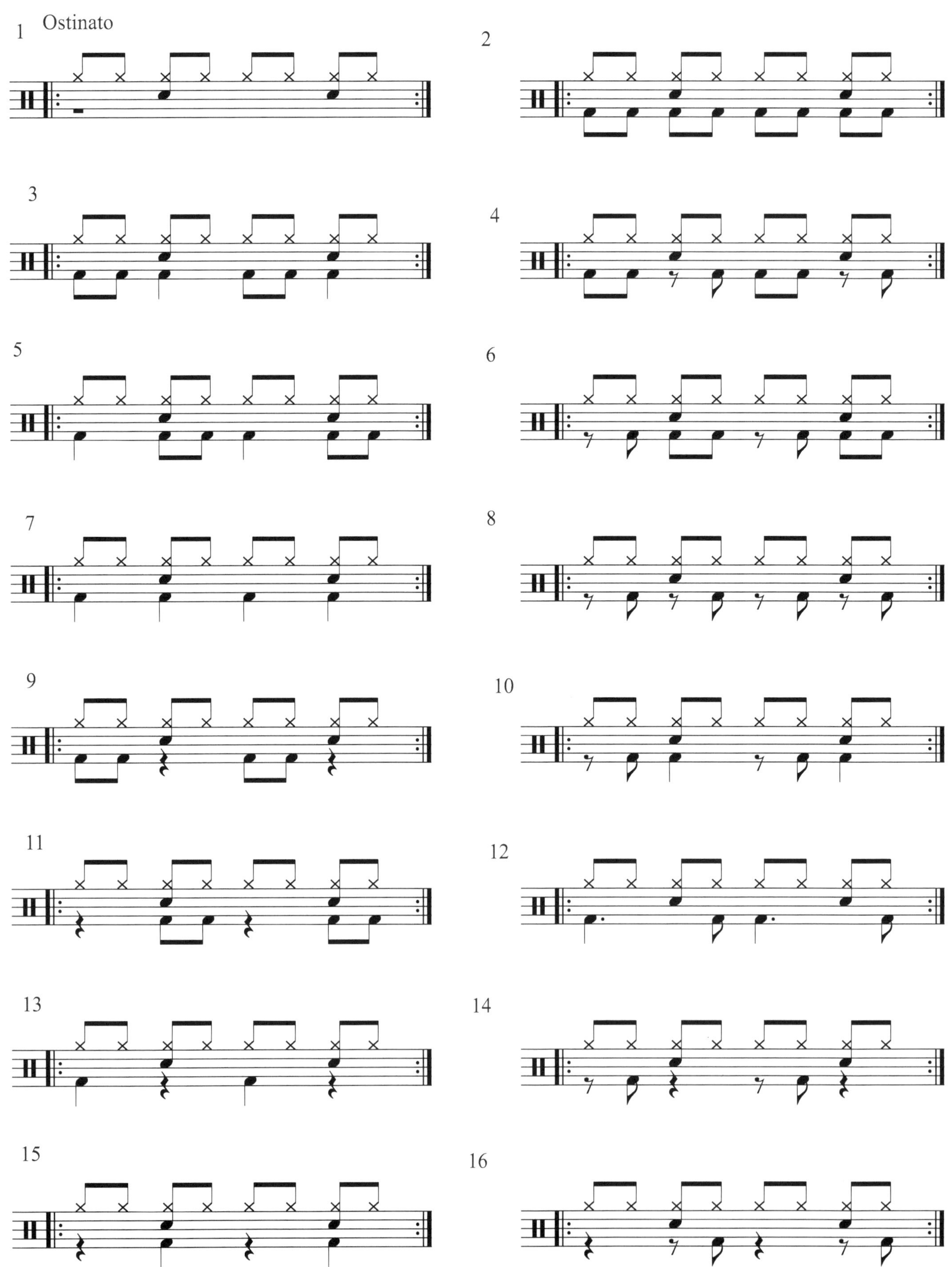

Play the 16th note rhythms on the bass drum with a hi hat and snare drum ostinato.

Use each of the binary rhythms as an ostinato on the hi hat, or ride cymbal with 2 and 4 on the snare. Play the 8th and 16th note rhythms on the bass drum.

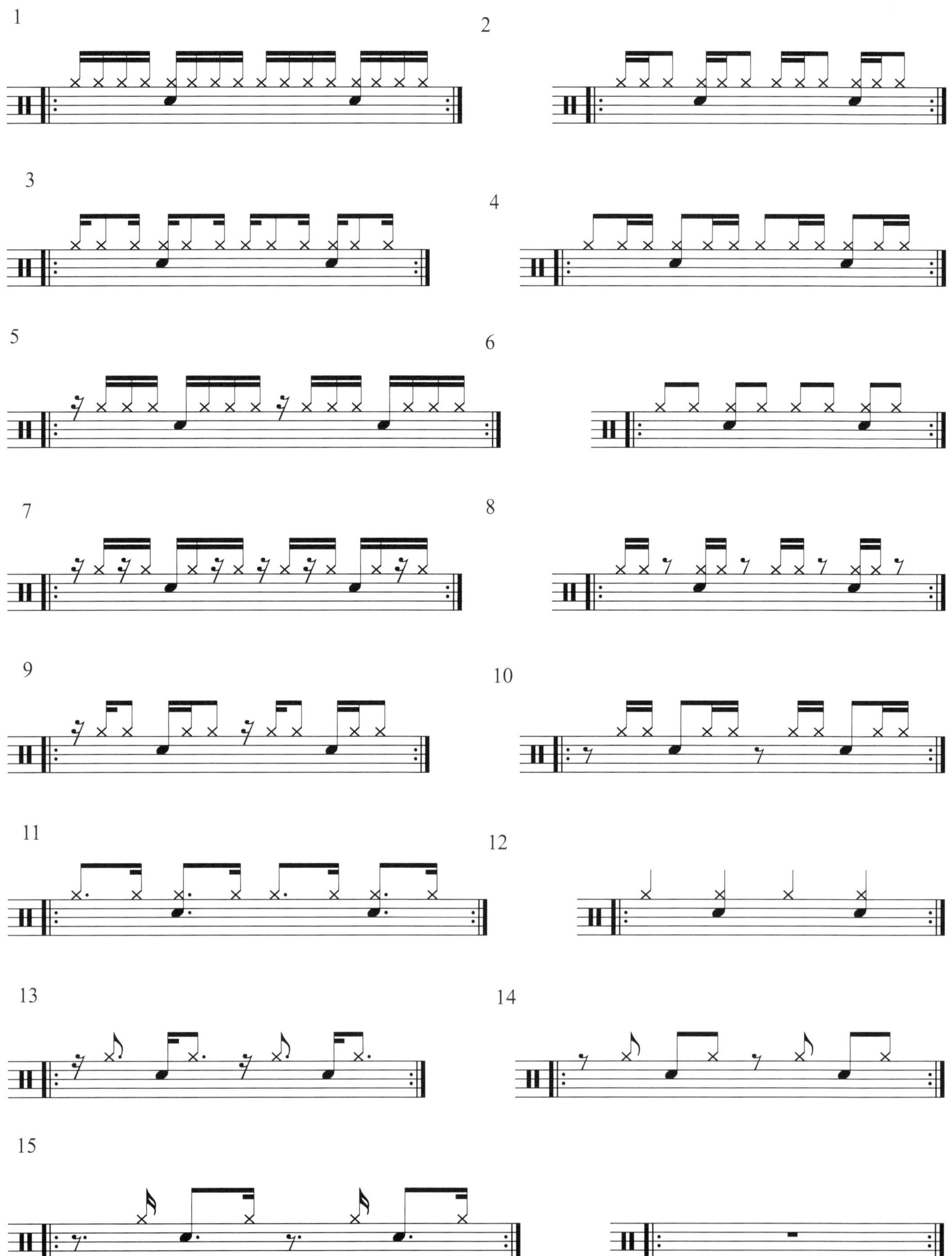

Play the 16th rhythms on the snare with a bass drum and hit hat ostinato.

Play with right hand lead, left hand lead, right hand only, left hand only.

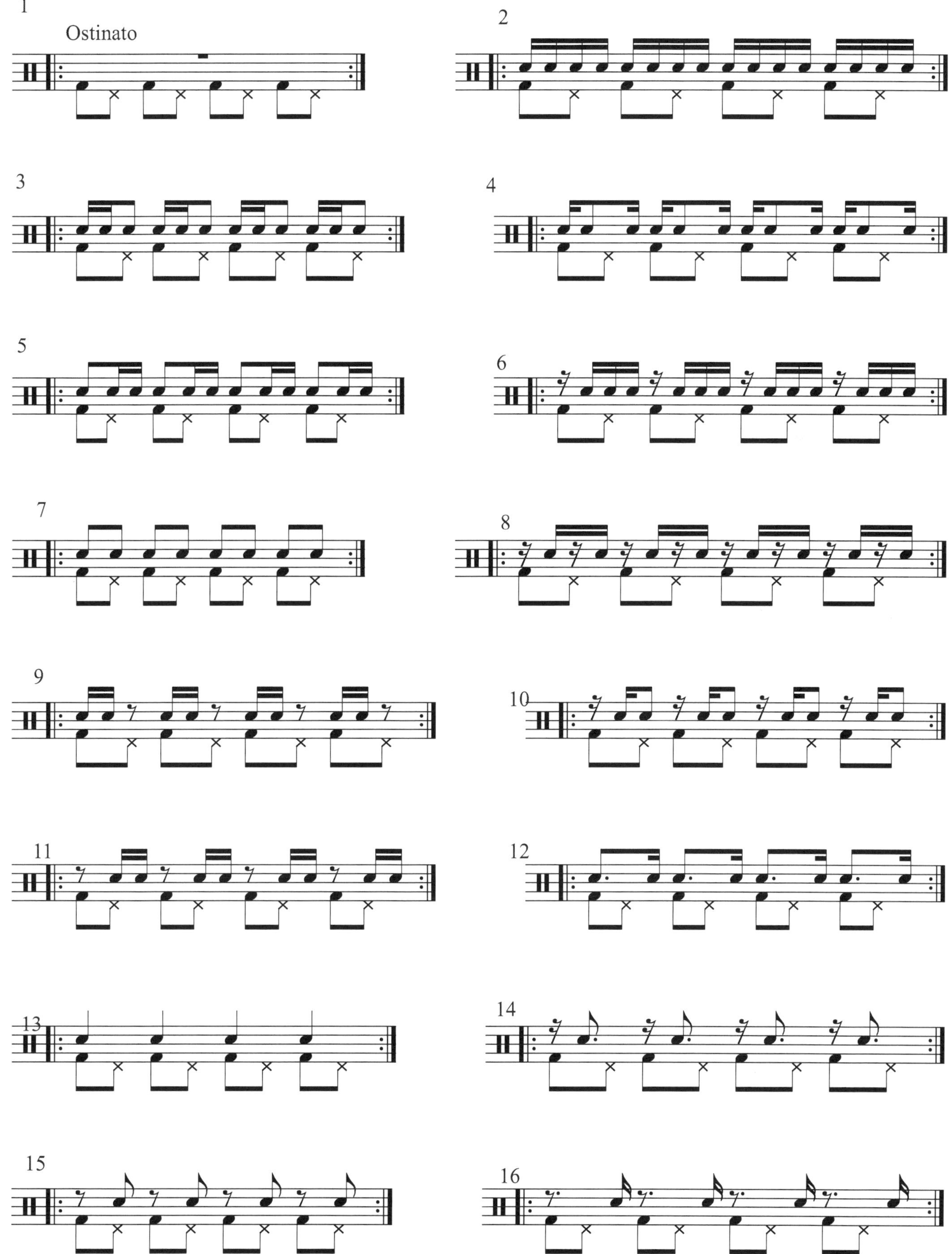

Play the 16th note rhythms on the snare
with a ride cymbal and bass drum ostinato.

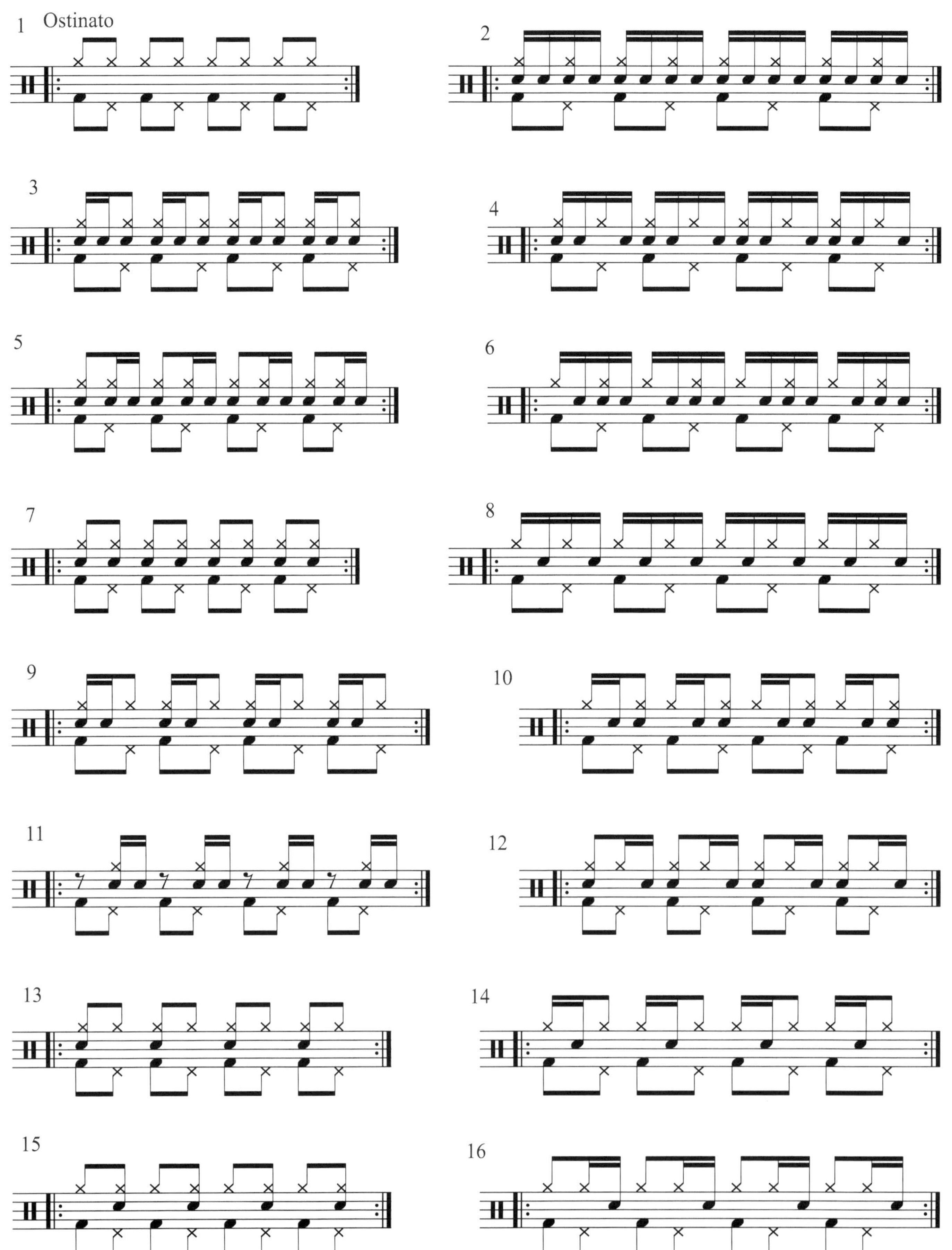

Play the 16th note rhythms on the snare

with a ride cymbal and bass drum ostinato.

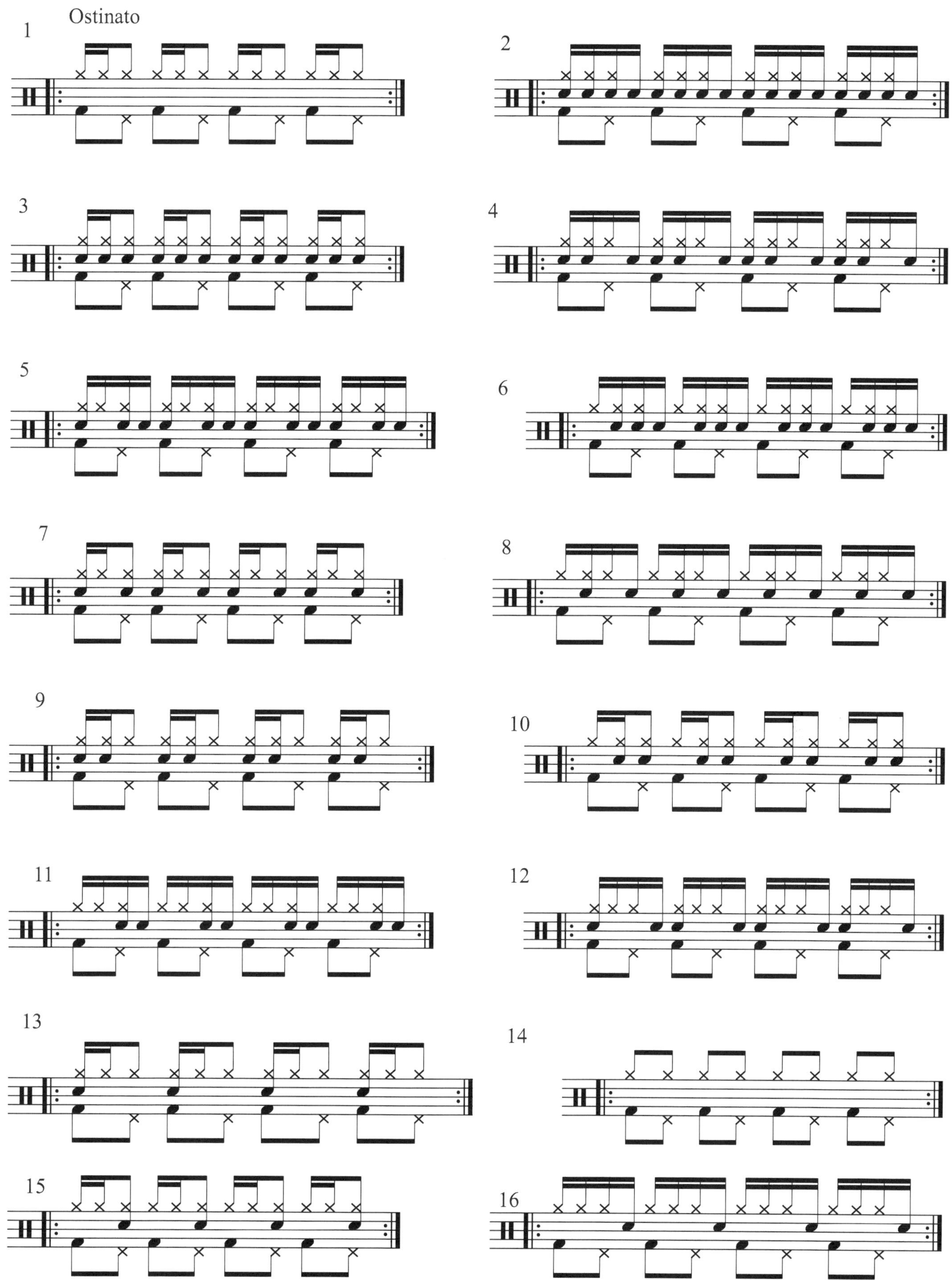

Swing the 8th Note Rhythmic Alphabet

Play the 8th note binary rhythms as triplets. The down beat remains the same, but the & is played in the space of the third triplet, the (a).

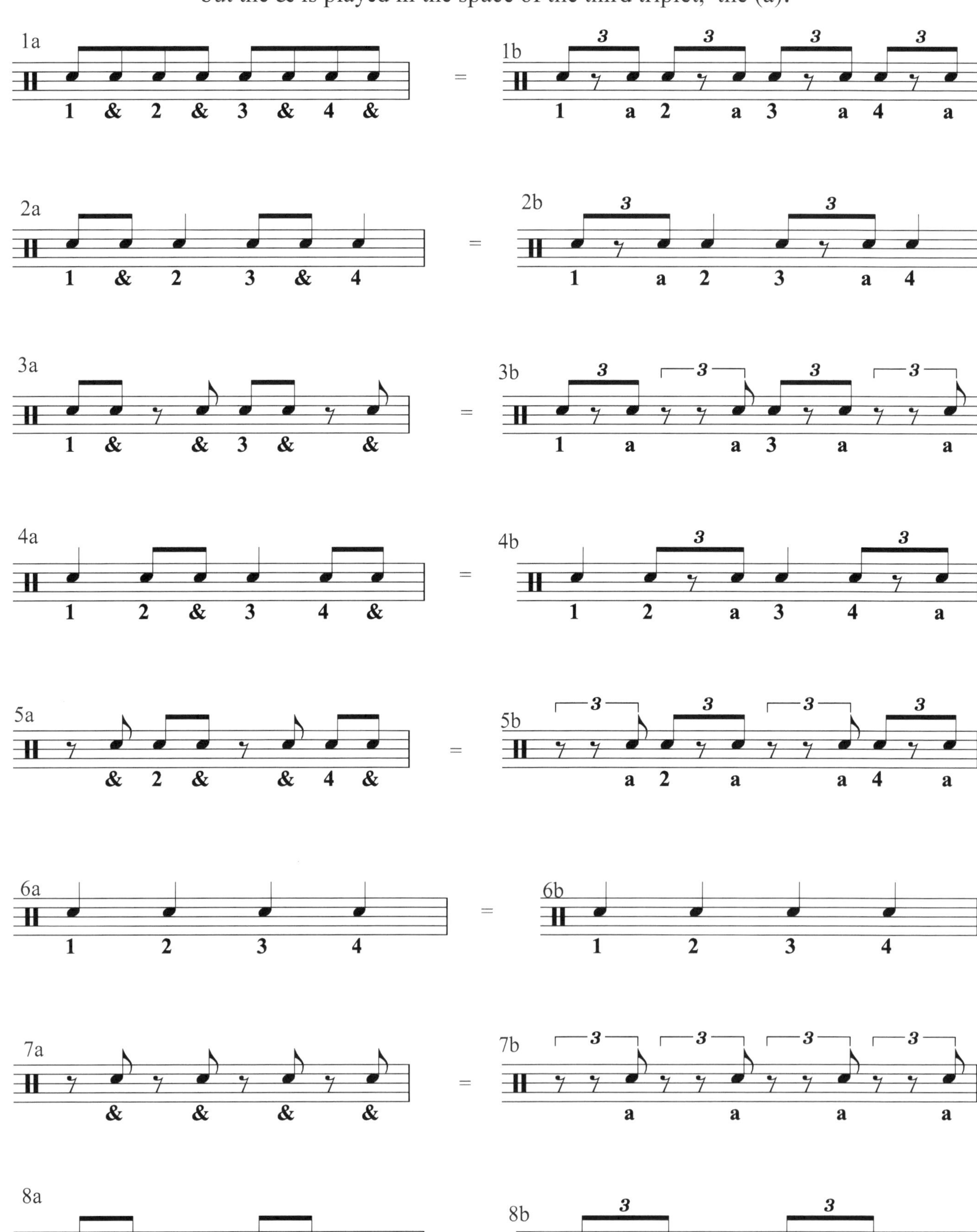

Swing the 8th Note Rhythmic Alphabet.

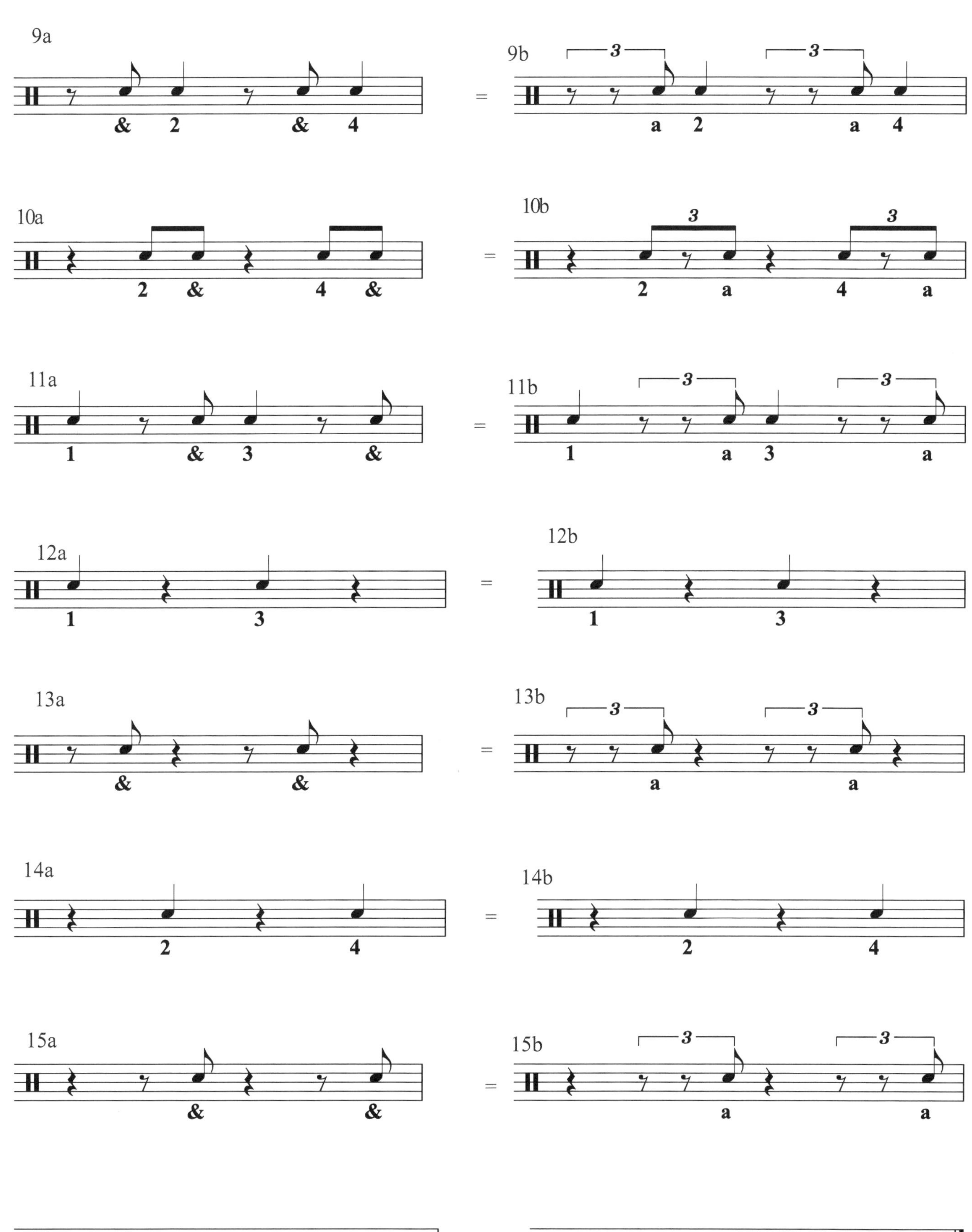

Swing the 8th note rhythmic alphabet on the bass drum.

Shuffle Ostinato

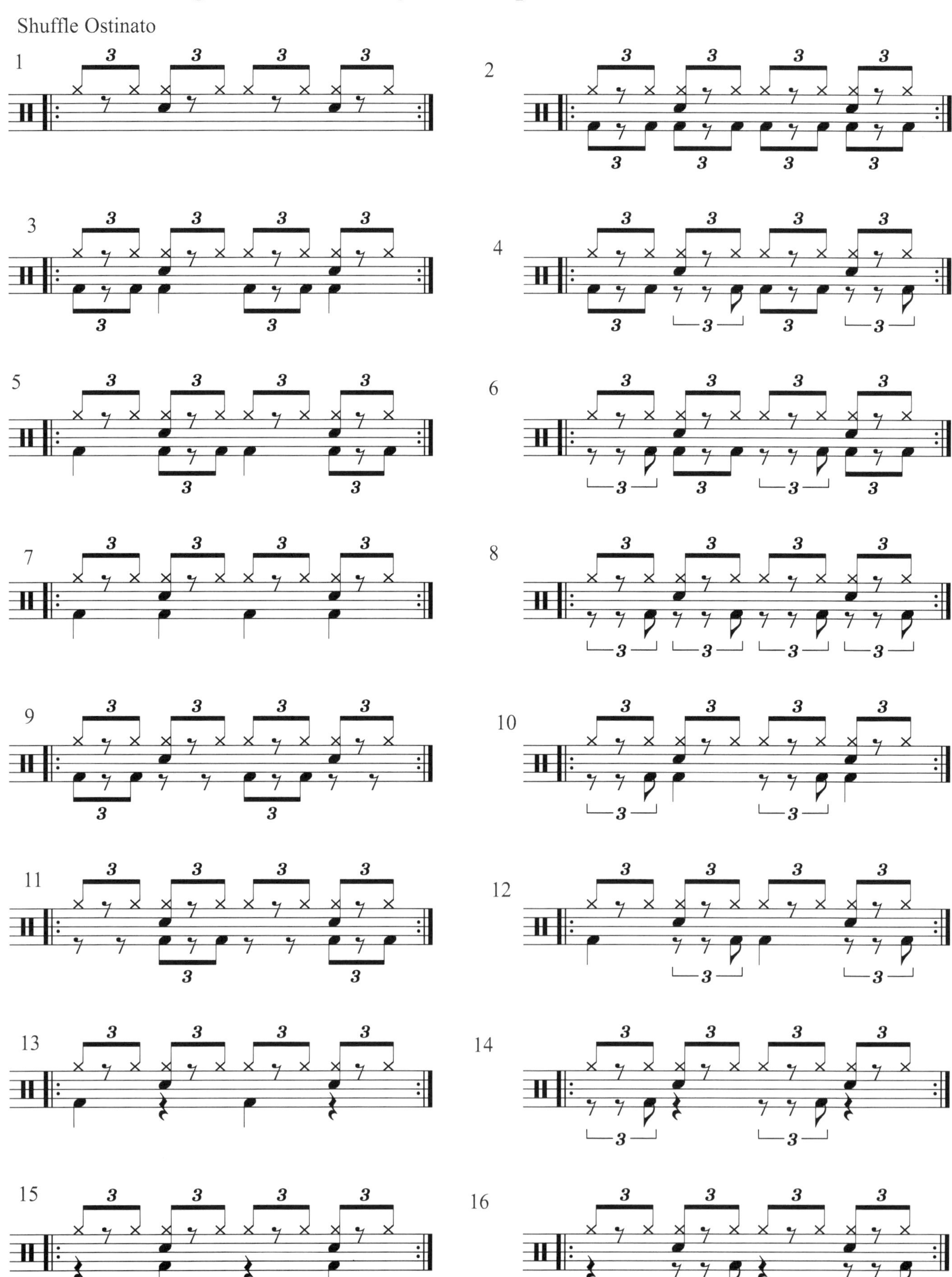

Swing the 8th note rhythmic alphabet on the bass drum.

Half Time Shuffle

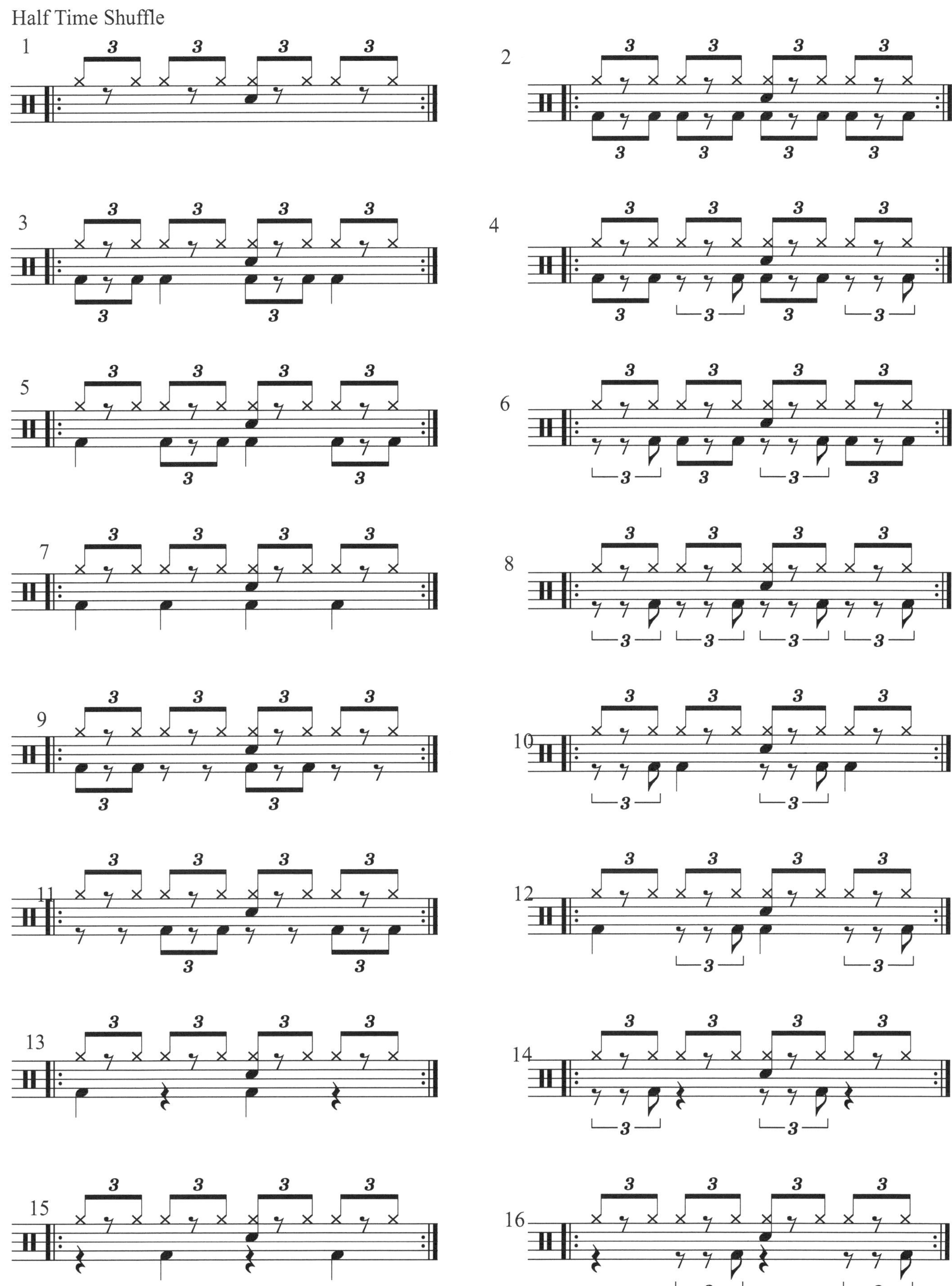

Play the triplet rhythms on the bass drum.

1Shuffle Ostinato

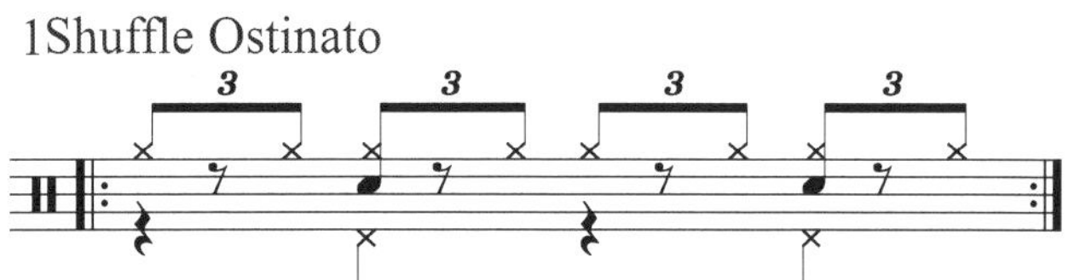

2

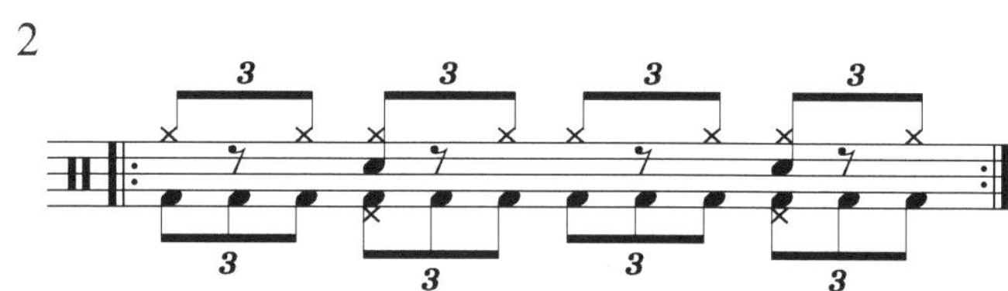

3

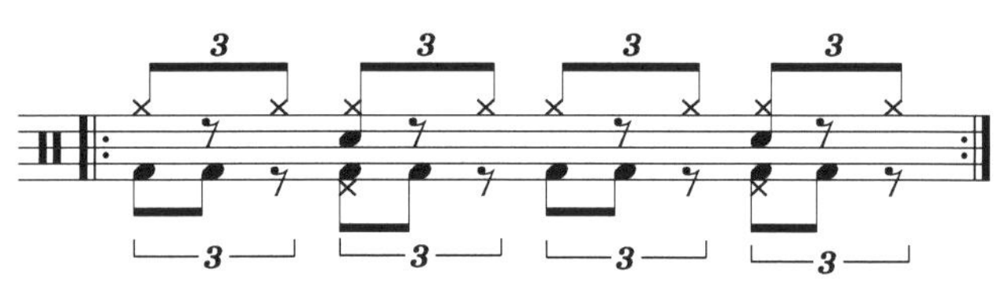

4

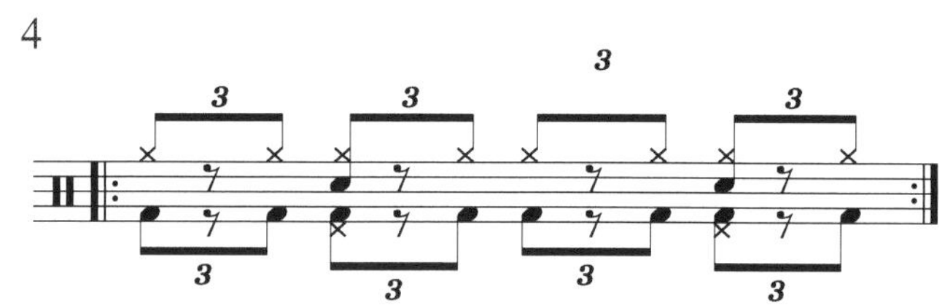

5

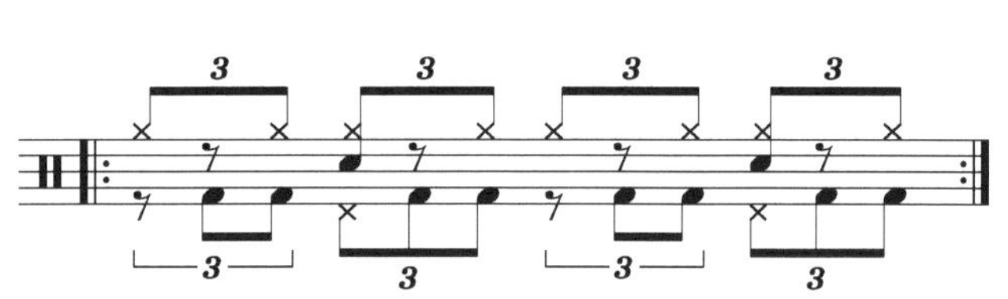

6

7

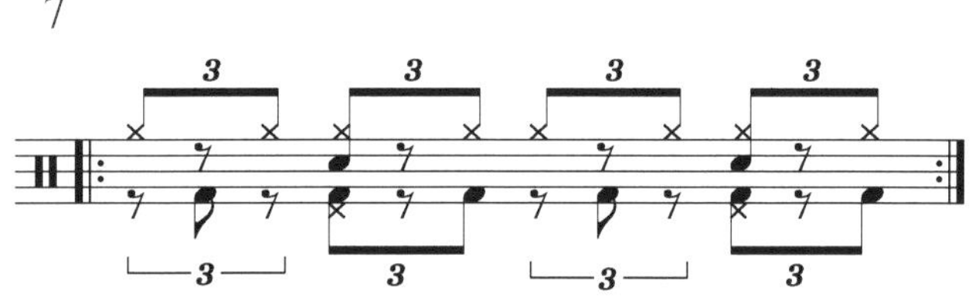

8

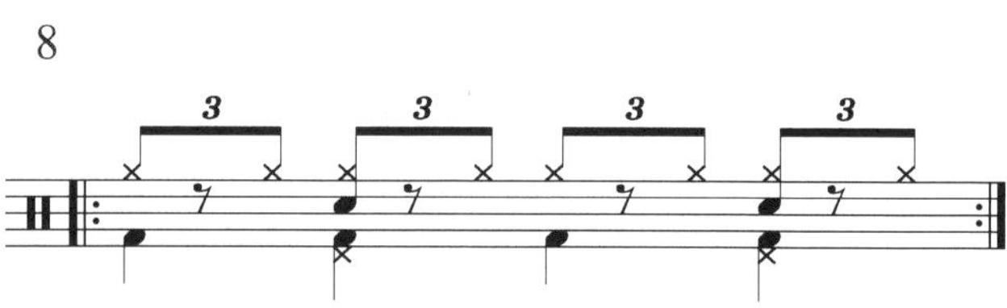

9

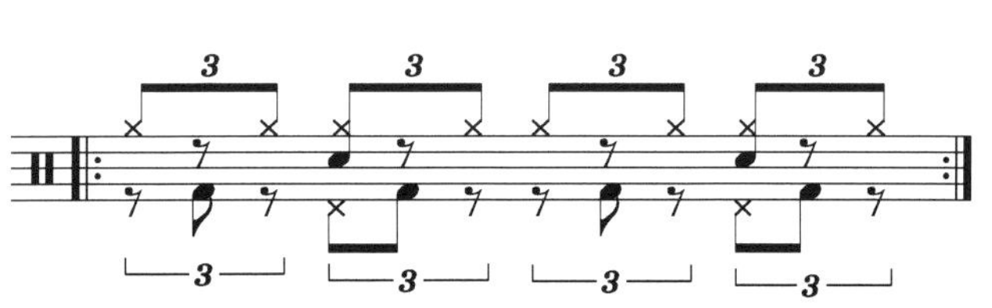

10

Play the triplet rhythms on the snare drum.

Swing Ostinato

1

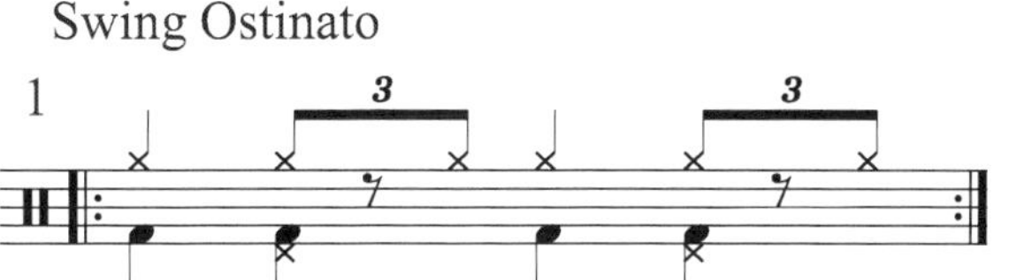

2

3

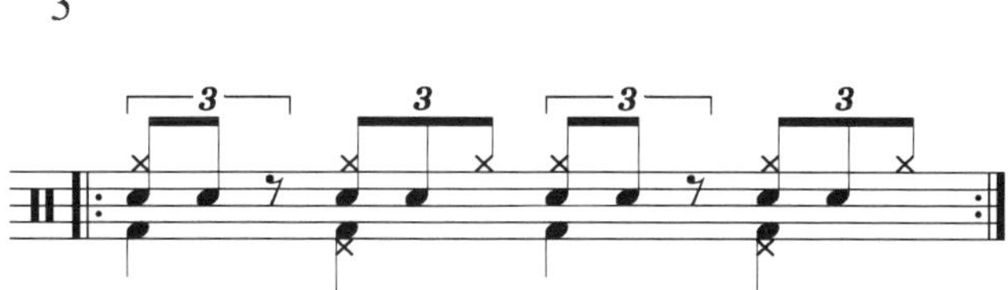

4

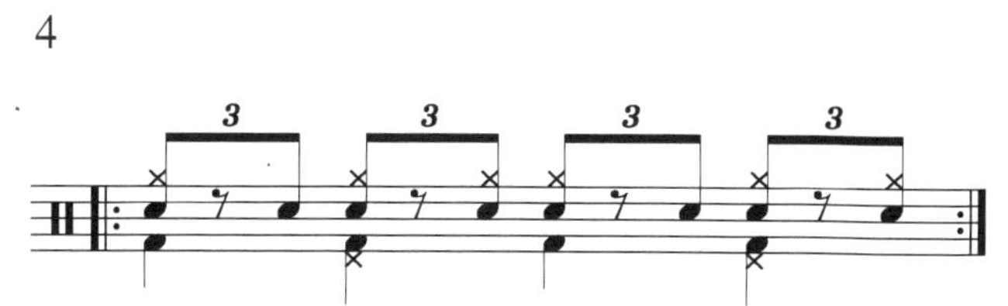

5

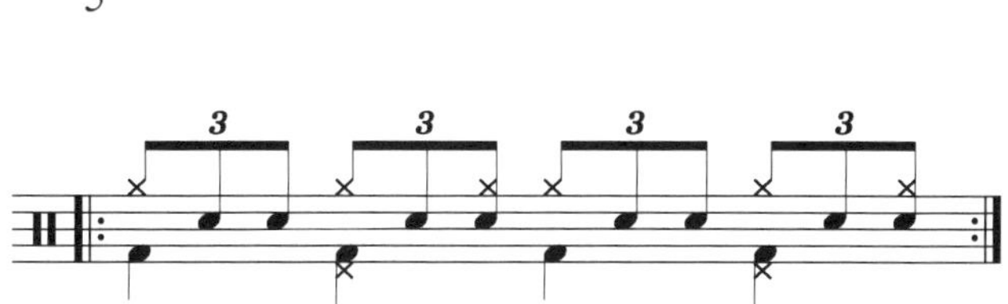

6

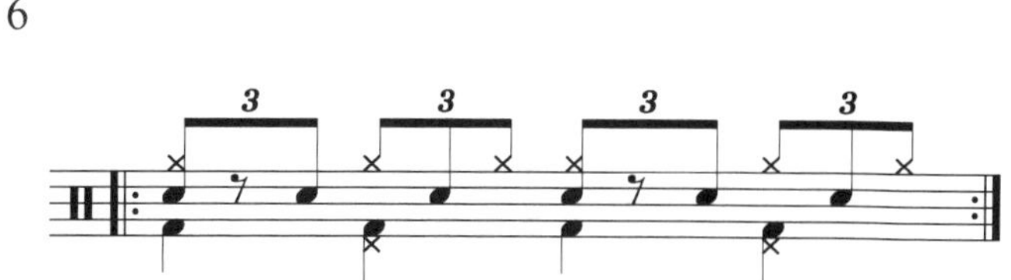

7

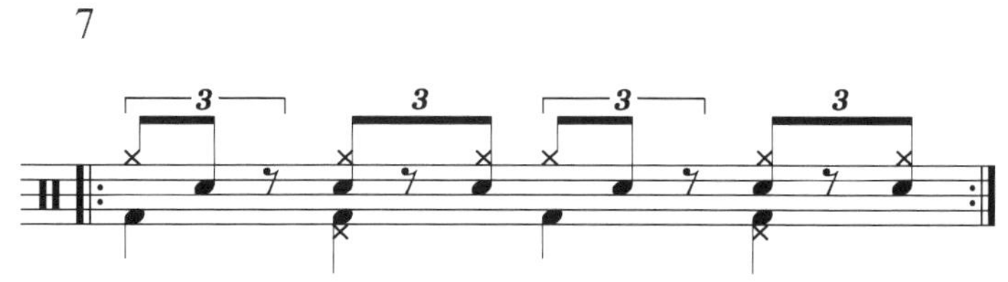

8

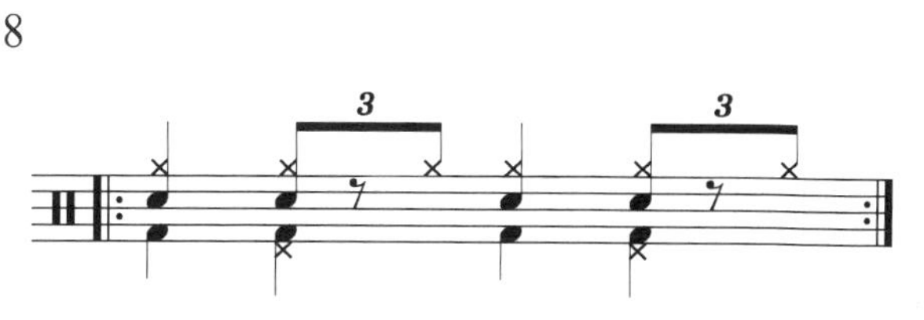

9

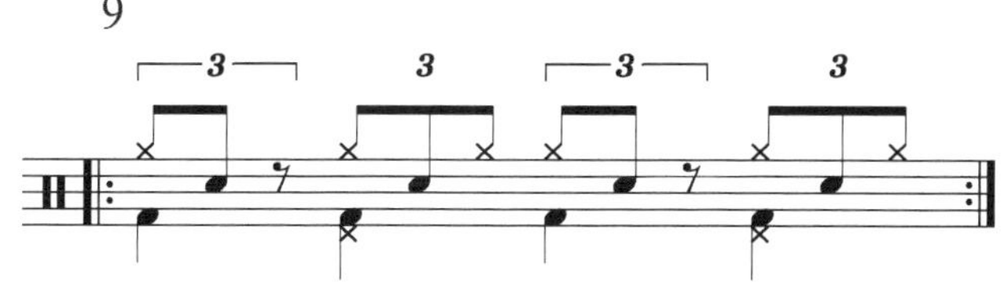

10

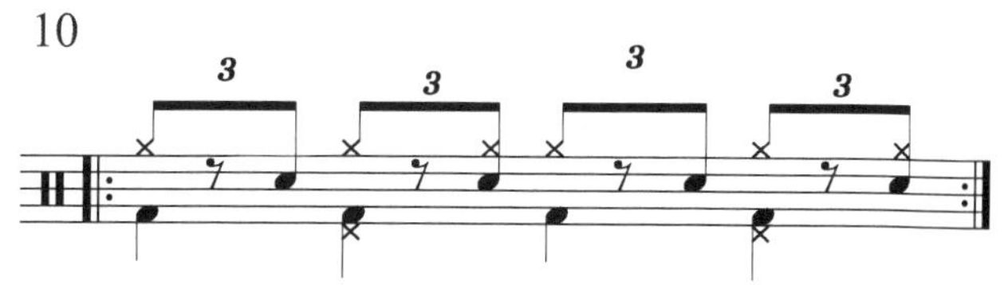

Hand Drumming - Bass Tone Slap

Play the accents as a slap and the non-accented notes as tone, or bass.

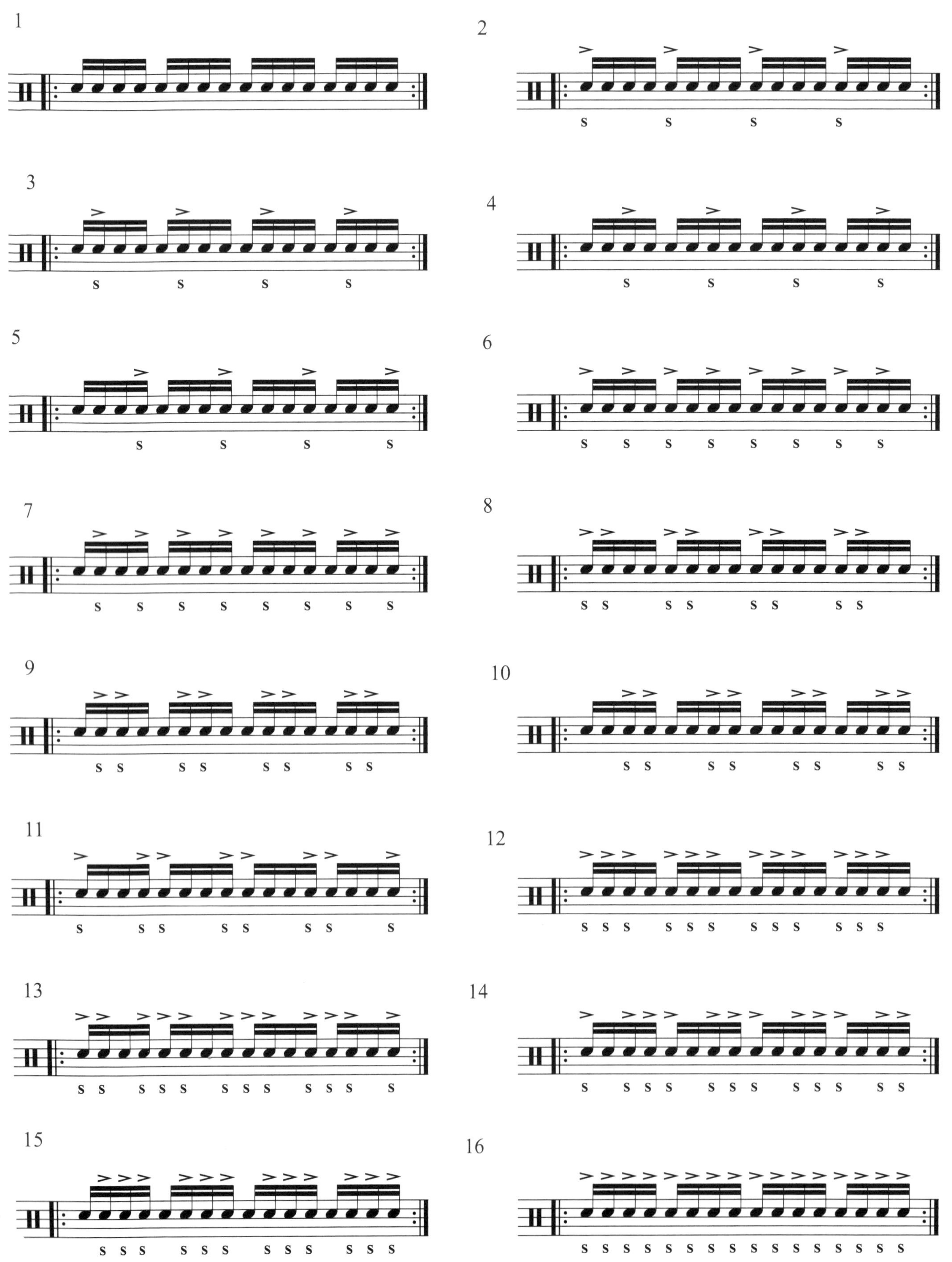

Hand Drumming - Bass Tone Slap

Play the accents as bass in the first half of the measure, as a Slap in the second half and the non-accented notes as tone.

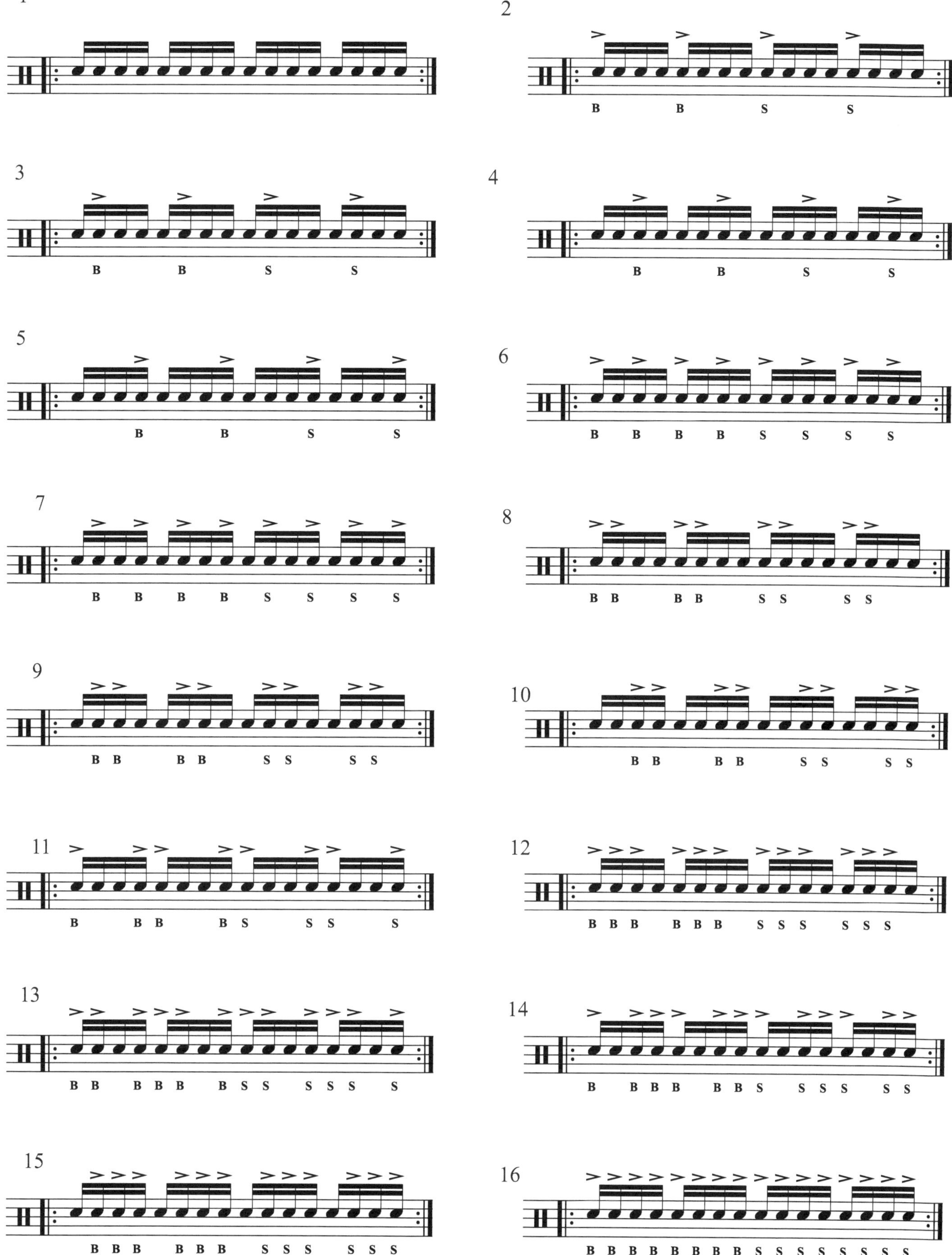

Hand Drumming - Bass Tone Slap

Alternate playing accents as bass in beats 1 and 3, as a slap in beats 2 and 4, tones for the non-accented notes.

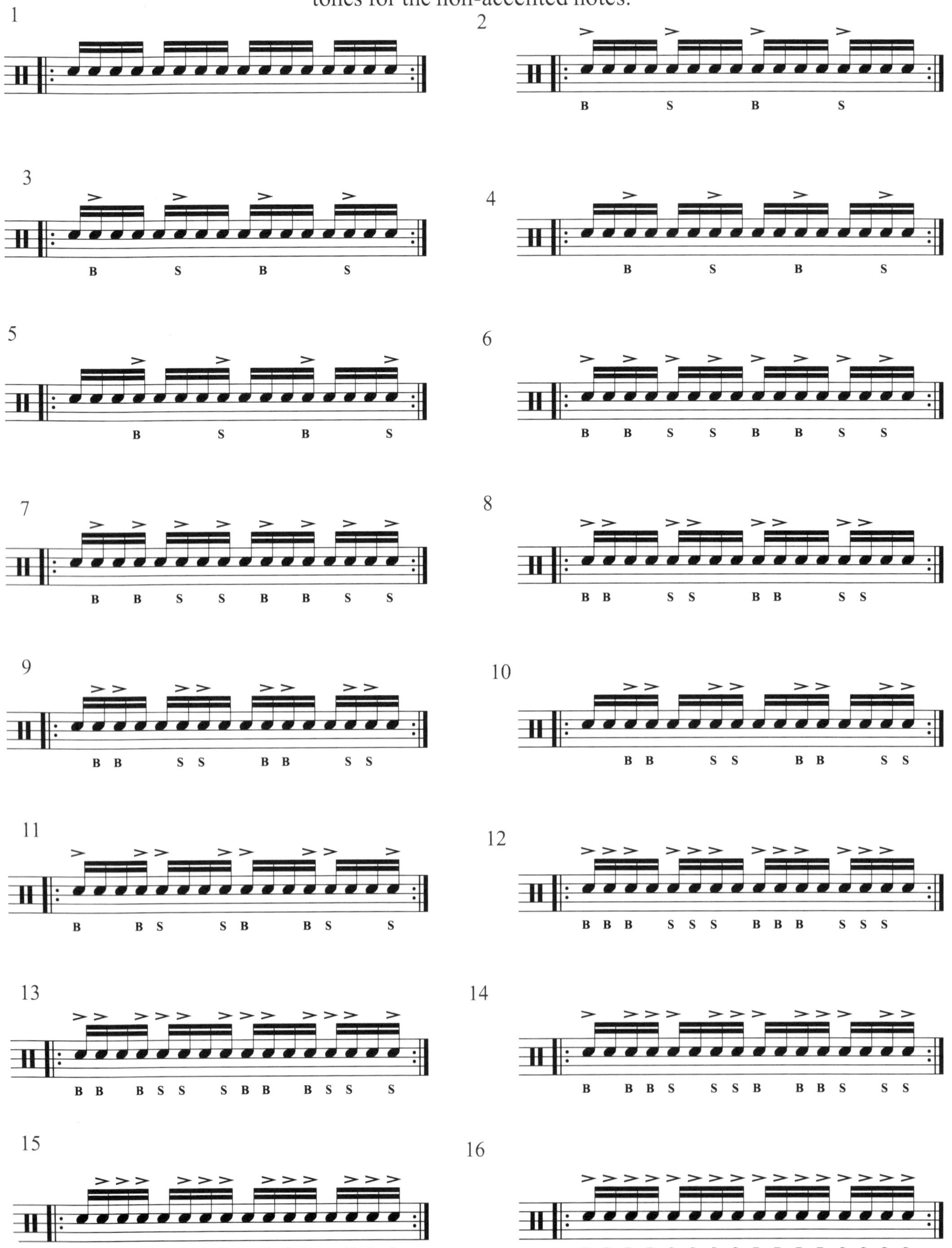

Mike's Multipurpose Polyrhythmic Utility Tooles

By Michael Tooles

Edition 1.0

14809750R00185

Made in the USA
Charleston, SC
02 October 2012